LENIN /
VOLUME ONE /
BUILDING THE PARTY

Tony Cliff

LENIN

Volume One

Building the Party

Pluto  Press

First published 1975 by
Pluto Press Limited
Unit 10, Spencer Court
7 Chalcot Road, London NW I 8LH

Copyright © Pluto Press 1975

ISBN 0 902818 57 0 paperback
ISBN 0 902818 58 9 hardback

Printed by
Compton Press Limited
Compton Chamberlayne,
Salisbury, Wiltshire

Designed by Richard Hollis GrR

Contents

The dates given in this volume refer to the Julian calendar, which was thirteen days behind the Western Gregorian calendar in the period covered.

1

Lenin Becomes a Marxist

In all religions not only the holy man, but also his ancestors, are endowed with extraordinary piety. In just the same way, the Stalinist legend-makers attributed revolutionary convictions not only to Lenin from his early childhood, but also to his parents. A 602-page official biography of Lenin issued under the auspices of the Institute of Marxism-Leninism and published in Moscow in 1960 (*Vladimir Ilyich Lenin, Biografiia*) described Lenin's father as a progressive, radical educationalist, and his home in Simbirsk as a sort of revolutionary club. 'The tone was set by Alexander' (Lenin's elder brother), while Vladimir also 'participated frequently in the discussion and with great success'.

All this is nonsense. Lenin's father, Ilya Nikolaevich Ulyanov, was not a progressive educationalist. In 1869 he was appointed to the post of Inspector of Schools in the small Volga town of Simbirsk. In 1874 he was promoted to the position of Director of Schools for the entire province. He was now an Actual State Councillor, decorated with the Order of Stanislav, first class, and referred to as His Excellence. This made him a high-ranking nobleman, fourth in a table of fourteen ranks, with hereditary status.

These two dates in his father's rise – 1869 and 1874 – are significant. Lenin singles them out in an article written in 1901, tracing the history of the Tsarist struggle against local government (the *Zemstvo*), entitled 'The Persecutors of the Zemstvo and the Hannibals of Liberalism'[1] as being precisely the years in which the Tsarist bureaucracy acted against these local organs of self-government and itself took over the supervision of public education. Ilya Nikolaevich's standing in the Ministry of Education, and his steady rise up the hierarchical ladder, somehow do not fit the image of a revolutionary, or even of a radical.

Lenin once recalled how, when Alexander II was assassinated in 1881, his father sadly buttoned on his official's uniform and went to Simbirsk cathedral to mourn the autocrat. He was a devout and practising Greek Orthodox Christian to the end of his life, and an unquestioning supporter of the Tsarist autocracy. There is, of course, no reason to expect the father of a revolutionary to be a revolutionary himself.

The cult-builders went even further, and endowed Lenin himself with superhuman attributes. He comes to life fully equipped, a marxist and revolutionary practically from childhood. And from his bald head springs fully fledged the party that is destined to lead and shape the working class in revolution! The reality was very different. It took months, in fact years, of studying and thinking for the young Lenin to become a marxist; first he had to break with the conservative views of his father, and then with the Narodnik stand of his elder brother.

On May 8 1887, Alexander Ilyich Ulyanov, Lenin's elder brother, was hanged for plotting the assassination of the Tsar. This was a terrible shock for the young Vladimir, who was seventeen years old at the time. He had not suspected that his brother was interested in politics. Alexander was reticent, introspective, 'always meditating and sad'. He concealed his political ideas from everyone in the family, so that even his sister Anna, two years his senior, who was with him in Petersburg while he was involved in the assassination plot, knew nothing at all about his politics. Some years after the event, in 1893, the Social Democrat Lalayants questioned Lenin about the plot. Lenin answered: 'For me as well as for the whole family the participation of my brother in the 1st of March affair came as a complete surprise.'[2]

The Ulyanov family was close and their personal relations very warm. It was in order to spare them that Alexander kept secret his political involvement. He was an extremely fine person, very much like his mother, 'The same rare combination', writes Anna, 'of extraordinary firmness and serenity with wonderful sensitivity, tenderness and fairness: but he was more austere and single-minded, and even more courageous.'

Vladimir, four years younger than Alexander, had always tried to emulate his brother. When asked whether cereal should be eaten with butter or with milk, he replied 'Like Sasha.' He wanted to do everything 'like Sasha' – except follow his politics. When in the summer of 1886 Alexander Ulyanov returned from St Petersburg to spend the university vacation with his family, he brought with him several books on economics, including Marx's *Capital*. According to Anna's memoirs, Vladimir did not even look at, let alone read, these books belonging to his brother, with whom he was sharing a room. At that time, she reports, he showed no interest at all in politics.[3]

The execution of Alexander must not only have had a deep, permanent effect on Vladimir, but also probably presented him with two alternatives for himself: either to follow in the footsteps of his martyred brother, become a Narodnik and a terrorist; or to flinch from revolutionary activity. For Stalinist legend-makers all is simple – the dilemma does not even exist. The story goes that, on receiving the news of his brother's execution, Vladimir cried out: 'No, we will not follow that road. That is not the road to take.'[4]

This is supposed to be the reaction of a young man of seventeen, who had broken with religion only a few months earlier, who did not yet know the name of Marx, who had not read a single illegal book, and knew nothing of the history of the Russian revolutionary movement!

His biographer Trotsky ironically asks to whom Vladimir addressed these wise words. Obviously not to his father, who had died a year before. Nor to Alexander, who had just perished on the scaffold. Nor to his sister Anna, who was in prison. Nor to his mother, who had gone to St Petersburg, to beg one minister after another to save her son. 'Evidently,' writes Trotsky, 'Vladimir confided his revelations as a tactician to Dimitri who was thirteen, and Maria who was nine!'

If Lenin had made up his mind in March 1887, to follow

in Sasha's footsteps, or to take another path of revolutionary struggle, or to avoid revolutionary politics altogether, his behaviour in the next six years would be incomprehensible. He did not involve himself in any political activities; instead, he studied.

At the end of June 1887, the Ulyanov family moved to Kazan, where Lenin started his law studies at the university. However, this undertaking was cut short, as on 4 December he took part in a student demonstration, and although he did not play an important role, after a night in the police station he was expelled from the university and from the city of Kazan. The reason was simply that he was the brother of the other Ulyanov. Vladimir and the rest of the family moved to Kokushkino, some thirty miles from Kazan, where his mother had an estate.

In the autumn of 1888 the entire Ulyanov family, except Anna, who had been arrested in March 1887 when visiting Alexander's room, was allowed to take up residence once again in Kazan. Now Vladimir entered a socialist circle of which very little is known. It was made up of a few students who read good books together and exchanged ideas about what they read. The most important circle in Kazan was the one led by N.E.Fedoseev, who even at that time was a marxist. According to Maxim Gorky, who lived on the Volga in those years, and moved in radical circles, Fedoseev proclaimed his support for Plekhanov's first important marxist tract, *Our Differences*, as early as 1887. The Fedoseev group possessed a small illegal library and even an underground press. Vladimir, while in Kazan, came into contact with some of its less important members.

In July 1889 widespread arrests took place in Kazan. Not only were Fedoseev and his circle seized, but also members of the circle to which Vladimir belonged. However, he was fortunately not arrested himself, the Ulyanov family having moved out of town on 3 May to the village of Alakayevka, near Samara. On 11 October they moved again, to the town of Samara itself. Here Vladimir stayed until the end of August 1893, when he moved to Petersburg. The fact that

Lenin was willing to spend four years in the dead-end town of Samara is proof enough that he was not yet ready to commit himself to active politics, that he was still studying and trying to decide which direction to take. Samara had almost no industry, and therefore virtually no industrial working class. Nor, unlike Kazan, did it have a university, and consequently there were no students. Thus there was neither worker nor student unrest in the town.

Lenin needed these years in order to make up his mind whether to follow in Sasha's footsteps, and, if not, what path to take. No doubt the young man was attracted to Narodism, whatever the Stalinist legend-makers say. One of his fellow students, arrested with Vladimir in Kazan in December 1887, describes how most of the arrested students exchanged light-hearted banter. At one point someone turned to Ulyanov, who was sitting apart lost in thought, and asked what he intended to do after his release. Ulyanov replied: 'What is there for me to think about? . . . My road has been paved by my elder brother.'[5]

In Samara Lenin sought out veterans of the terrorist underground, and questioned them closely on their conspiratorial techniques. In this way he acquired knowledge which he later put to use in organizing the Bolshevik Party. Before the Stalinist myth machine started working, quite a lot of evidence was produced to show that in his youth Lenin was under Narodnik influence. One witness to this effect was V. V. Adoratsky, the future director of the Marx-Engels-Lenin Institute. According to him, in 1905 Lenin told him that he was very much influenced by Narodnik ideas. He admitted that in 1888 he had thought very highly of the Narodnik terrorist movement, and that it took quite a time for him to free himself from these ideas. 'During his last years in Samara, 1892-93, Lenin was already a marxist, although he still retained traits associated with *Narodnaya Volya* (e.g. a special attitude towards terrorism).'[6]

Many years later, in *What is to be Done?* (1902), Lenin wrote:

Many of them [Russian Social Democrats] had begun their

revolutionary thinking as adherents of *Narodnaya Volya*. Nearly all had in their early youth enthusiastically worshipped the terrorist heroes. It required a struggle to abandon the captivating impressions of those heroic traditions, and the struggle was accompanied by the breaking off of personal relations with people who were determined to remain loyal to the *Narodnaya Volya* and for whom the young Social Democrats had profound respect.[7]

When Krupskaya cited this passage in her memoirs, she added that it represented a piece of Lenin's autobiography.

Lalayants, quoted above, who knew Lenin well in Samara, detected in him in March 1893 'certain sympathies for *Narodnaya Volya* terror', and notes that this propensity caused conflict between the two of them. When in the autumn of 1893 Lenin sought entry into a circle of St Petersburg Social Democrats, he was examined thoroughly on the question of terrorism and found too favourably disposed towards it.[8]

Vladimir needed to make a long, thorough study, not only because Narodism had very deep roots, but also because, as we shall see later, the demarcation lines between Narodism and marxism were not clearly defined for radical youth at the time. Another reason was that the ideas of Russian marxism had not yet taken on flesh and blood in an active industrial working-class movement. They were still the prerogative of a few isolated intellectuals.

Vladimir's main textbooks were the first and second volumes of Marx's *Capital*. (The third volume had not yet been published.) He studied these with utmost intensity throughout his later life, finding in them guidance for his thinking, and an ever new source of ideas. He learnt, as he himself said later, to 'confer' with Marx. During the same period he studied Russian radical journalism of the 1860s and 1870s, so that his knowledge of Narodism was very extensive. He made good use of this in later years, in his debates with the Narodniks and in his first efforts as a writer over the years 1893-99. As he later recalled, he never again in his life read as much as during the years 1888-93.[9]

He also made a serious study of statistical material on

the Russian national economy, and wrote his first independent monographs aimed at throwing light on the Russian
economic and social scene. From the records of the Samara
library for 1893, a single year for which they have accident-
ally been preserved, it may be seen that Vladimir did not
miss any relevant publications, whether official statistical
compilations or economic studies by the Narodniks.[10]

Lenin needed years of study in order to make up his
mind in relation to Narodism and marxism. The tragedy of
his brother struck him too deeply to allow for a quick decision. He started studying Marx's *Capital* some time in 1889.
This in itself does not mean that he decided to turn his back
on Narodism. As we shall see, the Narodniks studied Marx.
It seems that it was only in 1891 that he became acquainted
with Plekhanov's works, 'without which one could not have
arrived at Social Democratic positions', as Trotsky rightly
says.[11] In answering a questionnaire in 1919, Lenin made it
clear that he became a Social Democrat (a synonym at that
time for a marxist) in 1893.[12] In 1920, answering another
questionnaire, on when he had started to take part in the
revolutionary movement, he wrote: '1892-93'.[13]

The Stalinist legend, describing how young Vladimir
decided on the correct path immediately after hearing the
news of his brother's fate, is not only psychologically stupid,
but is also an insult to Lenin's intellectual and emotional integrity. In this legend he appears as a freak – rigid, dry, dead,
incapable of change.

His long investigation of Narodism was necessary for
him to be able to avoid the tragedy of his brother, who on
the eve of the plot was still in doubt whether he had taken
the right path.

In the last week of the year [1886] he [Sasha] still argued
against the plot, saying that it was absurd, and even suicidal,
to engage in any political activity before one had clarified
the principles on which it should be based. He felt the need
for more theoretical work and for a more precise definition
of aims and means ... But they answered his scruples with a
telling reproach: are we going to sit back, arms folded,
while our colleagues and friends are victimized and while

the nation at large is being oppressed and stultified? To engage now, they said, in the elaboration of theoretical principles would amount to surrender. Any philistine can theorize – the revolutionary has to fight. This was, of course, the voice of inexperience and impatience, the voice of youth. Alexander's sense of revolutionary honour was sensitive to it, and against his better knowledge he yielded: no, he would not sit back, his arms folded.[14]

The ideas of every age are closely connected with those of the preceding one. Lenin's state of mind in 1887 cannot be understood without taking account of the ideas of his elder brother. His intellectual development must be seen as flowing from and related to the Narodnik heritage. In order to come to grips with Narodism and to decide his attitude to it, Lenin, like any serious scientist, could not rely on the opinions of others, but had to study the subject at first hand.

In fact, he needed a much longer period of study than the next generation of Russian marxists, such as Trotsky. First of all, of course, Trotsky had not had the traumatic experience of having a brother hanged for Narodnik terrorism. Secondly, being nine years younger than Lenin, he came into contact with revolutionary politics much later, in 1896, when the marxists were already practically involved in strikes, even mass strikes, of workers. This was not the case in 1887, when the marxist movement consisted almost entirely of four or five émigrés, with a handful of students supporting them here and there. But even Trotsky had to contend with Narodnik ideas. The first group he joined in Nikolayev was made up of people who considered themselves Narodniks. They had a hazy notion of marxism. Only one member of the circle, a young woman named Alexandra Sokolovskaya, herself the daughter of a Narodnik, claimed to be a marxist. It took a few months of controversy in the circle for Trotsky, who in the beginning sided with the Narodniks, to be converted by Alexandra Sokolovskaya to marxism. (He later married her and they had two children; the fate of all three was tragically bound up with Trotsky's.)

It is hard to understand why Vladimir Ilyich Ulyanov, this serious and – as the future was to show – active man, avoided any political commitment for five or six years. To explain why Lenin waited we need to grasp the nature of Narodism, the interrelation of its ideas and those of marxism, and the deep passions that the heroism of the Narodniks raised in the hearts of the young radicals of the time. One has also to understand the ideological alternative to Narodism that was developed at the time by Plekhanov, the father of Russian marxism. Finally, the commitment of individuals – in our case that of Vladimir – is affected not only by pure reason, but also by the interrelation of ideas and actions. Hence we need to grasp the actual state of the working-class movement at the time – how many strikes took place, and whether the marxists or the Narodniks had any influence in them, and so on. To deal adequately with all this would demand far more space than we have at our disposal. However, without an understanding of the intellectual and political struggles of the period, Lenin's development is not comprehensible. His roots were deep in the Russian revolutionary tradition of the preceding two generations of Narodism, a tradition culminating for him in the martyrdom of Alexander. An excursion into Narodism and Russian marxism is therefore unavoidable. The personal evolution of Vladimir was closely linked with the evolution of the Russian revolutionary intelligentsia and the thin layer of revolutionary workers. His political biography is merged with the history of the movement.

The Narodniks

Narodism was a radical movement which began in the middle of the nineteenth century. It was born at the time of the Crimean War and the abolition of serfdom (1861), gained influence and renown during the sixties and seventies, and reached its zenith with the assassination of Tsar Alexander II (1881), after which it rapidly declined. However, it rose again out of its ashes on more than one occasion.

The foundations of the movement had been laid in the fifties and sixties by Herzen. He believed above all that the peasantry in Russia would be the foundation for socialism.

'The future in Russia belongs to the *peasant*, just as in France it belongs to the workmen', Herzen wrote to the French historian Michelet in 1851.

He believed that the collectively owned commune – the *obshchina* – which had survived in Russia, would form the foundation of socialism, rather than the publicly owned factory. Capitalist development could be avoided in Russia, Herzen argued. He wrote to Mazzini, 'I believe that there can be no revolution in Russia except for a peasant war', and he referred to Emelian Pugachev, the leader of the peasant war of 1773-75. This revolution was to strike at 'the glacial despotism of Petersburg'. It would destroy the state. It would retain the periodical redistribution of the land traditional in village Russia, thus insuring against the formation of a proletariat and hunger. It would develop internal self-administration. 'Why should Russia now lose her rural commune, since it has been preserved throughout the period of her political development, since it has been held intact under the weighty yoke of Muscovite Tsarism as well as under the European style autocracy of the emperors?'

But was Russia capable of achieving such a revolution? Two factors encouraged an affirmative answer to his question: the strength of the Russian peasant, who despite a succession of despotisms had retained his humanity, together with a feeling of independence and remoteness from authority; and above all the spiritual and intellectual life of modern Russia.[15] What was needed, Herzen argued, were revolutionaries who would dedicate themselves to the people. In an appeal written to students in 1861 he said: 'To the people! ... That is your place ... Prove that out of you will come not clerks, but soldiers of the Russian people.'

N.G.Chernyshevsky came to more extreme conclusions than Herzen. The historian of Narodism, Franco Venturi, has described the relation between Herzen and Chernyshevsky in this way: 'Herzen created Populism; Chernyshevsky was its politician. He provided Populism with its most solid content, and not only gave it ideas but inspired its main course of action by his brilliant publicizing activities undertaken between 1853 and 1862.'[16]

In July 1848 Chernyshevsky wrote in his diary that he 'was more and more being convinced by the ideas of the socialists'. Already he felt the need to translate these convictions into Russian. What could the words 'revolution' and 'socialism' mean in his own country? He answered that the only hope lay in a peasant revolt. 'The only thing that is lacking is unity between the various local risings.'[17] A letter to Herzen, of anonymous authorship, but certainly expressing the views of Chernyshevsky and his friend, N.A.Dobrolyubov, clearly put forward the call for a peasant uprising.

> You are evidently mistaken about the situation in Russia. Liberal landowners, liberal professors, liberal writers, lull you with hopes in the progressive aims of our Government ... You must not forget even for a moment that Alexander II will show his teeth, as Nicholas I did. Don't be taken in by gossip about our progress. We are exactly where we were before ... Don't be taken in by hope, and don't take in others ... No, our position is horrible, unbearable, and only the peasants' axes can save us. Nothing apart from these axes is of any use. You have already been told this, it seems, and it is extraordinarily true. There is no other means of salvation. You did everything possible to help a peaceful solution of the problem, but now you are changing your tune. Let your 'bell' sound not for prayer but for the charge. Summon Russia to arms.[18]

Chernyshevsky, like Herzen, saw in the *obshchina* the foundation for socialism. But he did not idealize this institution, which had been inherited from patriarchal times. It needed to be revivified and transformed by western socialism. For Chernyshevsky the main enemy was not capitalism but Russian backwardness – 'Asiatic conditions of life, Asiatic social structure, Asiatic order', and his primary aim was the overthrow of the Tsarist political regime.

In 1860 in Petersburg, a small underground organization known as 'Young Russia' was formed. Its immediate aim was 'A bloody and implacable revolution, which shall radically change the whole foundation of contemporary society', and its inspiration was Chernyshevsky. In 1862 Chernyshevsky was arrested and spent more that eighteen months in the Peter and Paul fortress. Then he was sent to do hard labour in Siberia, where he remained till 1883. He was then allowed to live in Astrakhan, and eventually, a few months before his death in 1889, to return to his native town of Saratov.

In 1862-63 *Zemlya i Volya* (Land and Freedom) was established. This was a loose collection of groups made up mainly of students. The guiding spirit of the movement, even after his arrest, remained Chernyshevsky. One result of the formation of *Zemlya i Volya* was a rise in terrorist acts against the autocracy. On 4 April 1866 an attempt was made on the life of the Tsar by the student Dimitri Karakozov. He failed and was executed, but his was the first act in a revolutionary drama that ended with the overthrow of Tsarism half a century later.

The decade of the 1860s, which opened on 19 February 1861 with the liberation of the serfs, closed with the solitary confinement in Peter and Paul fortress of Nechaev, one of the great figures in the heroic gallery of Narodism. He had attempted to create a tightly conspiratorial society called 'The People's Revenge', which aimed to lead a peasant uprising. It failed and no insurrection took place, but Nechaev's efforts were rewarded by solitary confinement in prison.

A second wave of the revolutionary movement opened at the beginning of the seventies, with a complete swing of the pendulum away from Nechaev's conspiratorial methods (aided by revulsion against Nechaev's organization of the murder of one of his own collaborators). Instead there was a mass pilgrimage of intellectuals to the countryside to convert the peasantry. How widespread the movement was one can gauge from the fact that in 1874 four thousand people were imprisoned, questioned or at least harassed by the police.[19]

In that period in 1874, called 'the mad summer', hundreds of thousands of young men and women

> gave up their homes, their riches, honours and families. They threw themselves into the movement with a joy, an enthusiasm, a faith which one can feel only once in one's life and

which, once lost, can never be found again. It was not yet a political movement. Rather it was like a religious movement, with all the infectious nature of such movements. Men were trying not just to reach a certain practical end, but also to satisfy a deeply felt duty, an aspiration for moral perfection.[20]

The Russian peasant turned out to be less receptive to socialist ideas than the revolutionary intellectuals had been led to believe. They found it very difficult to communicate with the peasants, and the peasants were very suspicious of them. They were even frequently turned over to the police by the very people they had come to serve.

The Narodnik movement now acquired practical experience, and as a result new policies had to be drawn up. If the peasants were not ready to act, the revolutionaries had to act on their own. One of the new leaders, P.M.Tkachev, writing a few years later in 1879, spoke of 'the complete fiasco' of going among the people, and added proudly :

We were the *first* to point out the inevitability of this fiasco; we were the *first* ... to implore youth to abandon that fatal anti-revolutionary path and to return once more to the traditions of direct revolutionary work and a fighting, centralized revolutionary organization [i.e. to the traditions of the Nechaev trend]. And ours was not a voice crying in the wilderness ... The fighting organization of the revolutionary forces, the disorganization and terrorization of the government authorities, these have been from the very beginning the basic demands of our programme. And at present these demands have at last begun to be put into practice ... *at the present our only task* is to terrorize and disorganize government authority.[21]

So, after going to the people, the pendulum swung back to terrorism. On 24 January 1878, a solitary young girl, Vera Zasulich, shot at the head of the Petersburg police, General Trepov, who had recently subjected a prisoner, Bogolyubov, to corporal punishment. In May the head of the gendarmerie in Kiev was assassinated. In August 1879 Kravchinsky killed the chief of the Russian gendarmerie. Unlike Vera Zasulich, Kravchinsky was not alone. He was a member of *Zemlya i*

Volya, which was by now a very well organized and disciplined group.

On 2 April 1879, Alexander Solovev, having personally informed *Zemlya i Volya* of his intention to assassinate Tsar Alexander II, but without the support of the organization, made the attempt and failed. A few weeks later an active terrorist organization 'Death or Liberty' constituted itself within *Zemlya i Volya*. On 1 March 1881 it succeeded in assassinating the Tsar.

But the hopes of the revolutionaries were bitterly disappointed. Their act did not lead to a popular uprising, but instead to a strengthening of the autocracy and to the suppression of all revolutionary activities for many years. The superhuman courage and moral fortitude of the terrorists were not enough to overthrow Tsarism.

The Narodniks 'Adapt' Marxism

To understand the development of Russian marxism, one must grasp the attitude of the Narodniks towards it. In 1848, and for years afterwards, the works of Marx and Engels could be imported into Russia legally, because, according to the censor, they constituted 'an abstract speculation' with no relevance to Russia.[22] In 1872 Marx's *Capital* (Vol. I) was published in Russian (many years before it was published in French and English). It had an immediate sale of 3000 copies. The Executive Committee of *Narodnaya Volya* wrote to Marx in 1880: 'Citizen! The intellectual and progressive class in Russia . . . has reacted with enthusiasm to the publication of your scholarly works. They scientifically recognize the best principles of Russian life.'

Marx's description of the atrocities of the primitive accumulation of capital and the industrial revolution in England, of the theory of surplus value, his attack on the capitalist division of labour and alienation, his criticism of 'formal' bourgeois parliamentary democracy, were interpreted by the Narodniks as proving that every effort should be made to prevent the development of capitalism in Russia. 'Having learned from Marx about the high price of capitalist development he [the Narodnik, T.C.] refused to pay this price, and set his hopes on the alleged possibility of restoring the archaic forms of social life and adapting them to fit the new conditions.'[23]

The fact that for Marx capitalism was progressive compared with feudalism, that parliamentary democracy, however formal and limited, was a step forward in comparison with autocracy – this the Narodniks failed to see. Using their knowledge of Marx's *Capital*, Narodnik economists wrote books proving the possibility and necessity of non-capitalist development in Russia. The most original of these economists was V.P.Vorontsov, who used the pseudonym V.V. In his book *The Fate of Capitalism in Russia* (1882), he argued that Russian capitalism, being a latecomer, could not find external markets for its products. At the same time its internal markets were not expanding, but on the contrary contracting, because capitalism ruined the peasants and artisans and reduced their purchasing power. Capitalism could not go beyond the creation of the small islands of modern industry needed to satisfy the wants of the upper classes. It could not become the dominant form of production. It could ruin millions of peasants and artisans, but could not give them employment or bring them into 'socializing production'. It could develop *intensively* by the exploitation of labour, but not *extensively* by increasing employment. In the backward countries generally, it could only be destructive – a 'parody of capitalism', an 'illegitimate child of history'. To the extent that islands of capitalism did exist in Russia they were the artificial product of the state's efforts.

While adapting marxism, the Narodniks were basically utopian socialists. Seeing the Russian masses inert while they themselves held socialism to be a desirable ideal, they made no real causal connection between the masses of the present and the future. N.K.Mikhailovsky, one of the theoreticians of Narodism, expressed this dualism by speaking of two kinds of truths – 'the truth of verity', i.e. what actually is, and 'the truth of justice', i.e. what ought to be. The 'world of what ought to be, the world of the true and just', had no connection with the objective course of historical development. Marx's description of the main characteristics of the outlook of the utopian socialists of his time fits the Narodniks well. Their main defect, the *Communist Manifesto* argues, was due to the fact that 'the proletariat . . . offers to them the spectacle of a class without any historical initiative or any independent political movement', that they had not yet adopted the standpoint of the class struggle and that the proletariat existed for them only in view of its being the 'most suffering class'.[24] One has only to substitute the word 'peasantry' for 'proletariat' for this description to fit the Russian populists perfectly. From their utopian position arose their élitist concept of the role of the intelligentsia – the maker of history, whose task is to shape the inert, ignorant masses.

In the same way that one and the same religion can be professed by people of different levels of economic development, each giving it a different content, so the 'marxism' used by the Narodnik intelligentsia was different from the marxism of a working-class movement. The grotesque combination of 'marxism' and Narodism was explained by the ageing Engels in a letter of 26 February 1895:

> in a country like yours, where modern large-scale industry has been grafted on to the primitive peasant commune and where, at the same time, all the intermediate stages of civilization co-exist with each other, in a country which, in addition to this, has been enclosed by despotism with an intellectual Chinese wall, in the case of such a country one should not wonder at the emergence of the most incredible and bizarre combinations of ideas.[25]

One cannot but agree with A.Walicki, author of an important study of the social philosophy of the populists, when he writes that populism

> was a Russian reaction to Western capitalism and, also, a Russian response to Western socialism – a reaction to Western capitalism and Western socialism by democratic intelligentsia in a backward peasant country at an early stage of capitalist development. And it is quite understand-

able that the classical Russian Populism was, first of all, a reaction to Marxism – after all, Marx was by then the leading figure of European socialism and, at the same time, the author of the most authoritative book on the development of capitalism. It is by no means an accident that the beginning of the full-fledged, classical Populism coincided in time with the first wave of the diffusion of Marxist ideas in Russia . . . It is not an exaggeration to say that the encounter with Marx was of paramount importance for the formation of the Populist ideology, that without Marx it would have been different from what it was.[26]

Without understanding the intimate relations between Narodism and marxism, one cannot grasp the great difficulties faced by Russian marxists on their way forward from Narodism, obstacles that took years for Plekhanov, the father of Russian marxism, to overcome, which reappeared in the pathway of his follower, Vladimir Ilyich Ulyanov.

The Heroism of the Narodniks

Our sketchy survey of the ideas of the Narodniks in the 60s and 80s of the last century is far from giving an accurate picture of the nature of Narodism. Their ideas were held with an extraordinary passion, which gave them the moral courage and determination to face many kinds of dangers and suffering. They went by the hundreds to solitary confinement in the Peter and Paul fortress, to Siberia, even to the gallows.

One can find no better witness to the heroism of the Narodniks than the American writer George Kennan, who started out as their opponent. Since Kennan had publicly condemned the terrorists in 1882, the Russian authorities willingly allowed him to enter Russia and visit prisons and forced labour camps, in the hope that his negative attitude towards the Russian revolutionaries would help attract world opinion to the side of the Russian government. However, after spending the years 1884-86 in Siberia, Kennan had this to say (in a letter quoted by Mrs Dawes in the August 1888 issue of the American magazine *The Century*): 'What I saw and learned in Siberia stirred me to the very depth of my soul – opened to me a new world of human experiences, and raised, in some respects, all my moral standards.'

> I made the acquaintance of characters as truly heroic in mould – characters of as high a type as any outlined in history, and saw them showing courage, fortitude, self-sacrifice and devotion to an ideal beyond anything of which I could believe myself capable . . . I went to Siberia, regarding the political exiles as a lot of mentally unbalanced fanatics, bomb-throwers and assassins. When I came away from Siberia I kissed those same men good-bye with my arms round them and my eyes full of tears.[27]

The 1880s were years of terrible reaction. After the assassination of Alexander II the country was like a graveyard. There was hardly any further resistance. In 1883 Vera Figner, one of the most admirable figures on the executive committee of *Narodnaya Volya*, was arrested. The year after, G.A. Lopatin, who had been in close touch with Marx and Engels while abroad, returned to Petersburg to renew terrorist activities, but was soon arrested. With his arrest numerous addresses fell into the hands of the police, leading to the liquidation of the remnants of *Narodnaya Volya*.

The last issue of the journal *Narodnaya Volya*, which came out on 1 October 1885, when the party itself no longer existed, painted in bleak colours the morale of the intellectuals:

> Complete intellectual disintegration, a chaos of the most contradictory opinions on the most elementary questions of social life . . . on the one hand, pessimism both personal and social, on the other hand, socio-religious mysticism . . . There was a flood of renegades of every kind. The more established strata of the intelligentsia frankly announced that they were sick and tired of peasants. Time to live for ourselves! The fading radical and liberal journals revealed the decline of social interest.[28]

Another description of the period comes from the pen of Rosa Luxemburg, writing while in prison during the First World War:

> After the murder of Alexander II a period of rigid hopelessness overcame the whole of Russia . . . The lead roofs

[prisons] of Alexander III's government contained the silence of the grave. Russian society fell into the grip of hopeless resignation, faced as it was by the end of all hopes for peaceful reform, and the apparent failure of all revolutionary movements.[29]

Characteristic of the time was the defection of one of the Narodniks' most important leaders, Lev Tikhomirov, who published in Western Europe a confession called *Why I Ceased to be a Revolutionary*. (Soon afterwards he became one of the strongest supporters of Tsarism.) Large numbers of other ex-revolutionaries found their prophet in Leo Tolstoy, who, while rejecting the abomination of Tsarism, preached the doctrine of non-violence. Tolstoy's teaching seemed to provide moral support for the disillusioned and passive intelligentsia.

However, within the general tide of reaction there were small eddies. The most important was the plot of March 1887 in which Alexander Ulyanov was a central figure. Six people took part. Three of them, including Ulyanov, considered themselves adherents of *Narodnaya Volya*, three others called themselves Social Democrats. The distinction between the former and latter, however, was not at all clear.

Alexander himself had read Marx diligently, but he was still a Narodnik, as is clear from the programme he wrote for the group : *Programme of the Terrorist Faction of the Party Narodnaya Volya*. He saw the main revolutionary force not in the peasantry but in the industrial working class. Socialism was 'a necessary result of capitalist production and the capitalist class structure'.[30] This, however, the *Programme* argued, did not rule out 'the possibility of another, more direct transition to socialism, provided that there are special, favourable conditions in the habits of the people and in the character of the intelligentsia and of the government'.

Capitalism was not a necessary stage before socialism. Capitalism was necessary only where 'the process of transition is left to develop spontaneously, if there is no conscious intervention on the part of a social group'. The *Programme* recognized the necessity of 'organizing and educating the working class', but this task had to be deferred, as revolutionary activity among the masses 'under the existing political regime is almost impossible'. The autocracy had to be overthrown by means of terror, so that the working class could enter the political arena.

This peculiar eclecticism was an attempt to combine Narodism and marxism. As we mentioned above, Alexander needed time to sort out his ideas. This he was not given. Lenin told Lalayants in 1893 that Alexander 'considered himself a marxist'. This was of course an exaggeration. Alexander's tragedy was that he was a man of the transition in the period of transition. In his work on Russian social thought, Ivanov-Razumnik, describing the transitional character of the 1880s, says: 'Before them stood *Narodnichestvo*, after them stood marxism, themselves they represented an ideological void.'[31]

Plekhanov Breaks with 'Zemlya i Volya'

As a result of the zigzags in its fortunes, there was a tug of war within *Zemlya i Volya* in the years 1878-79 between the supporters of mass agitation – going to the people – and the supporters of terrorism. The main proponent of the first tendency was Georgii Valentinovich Plekhanov.

By October 1879 *Zemlya i Volya* had ceased to exist. The agitators created a separate organization called *Chernyi Peredel* (Black Redistribution). The name meant literally an equal distribution of the land among the 'black' people, i.e. among the peasants. The terrorists adopted the name *Narodnaya Volya*, which, owing to the double meaning of the word *Volya*, meant at one and the same time 'People's Will' and 'People's Freedom'.

Chernyi Peredel was practically stillborn. 'The organization had no luck from the first day of its creation', complained Deutsch, one of its founders, in his memoirs. 'O.V. Aptekman, the chronicler of *Chernyi Peredel* and one of its leading members, begins his account of it with these doleful words: "Not in fortunate times was the organization *Chern-*

yi Peredel born. God did not give it life, and three months later, it expired".'[32]

As a result of the activities of a traitor within the organization, its leaders, Plekhanov, Axelrod, Zasulich and Deutsch, were compelled to emigrate from Russia one after another. After a series of police raids, resulting in the seizure of the group's printing press and the arrest of nearly all its members who were not out of the country, the group practically ceased to exist. Nevertheless *Chernyi Peredel* was destined to play an important historical role. It became a bridge from populism to marxism.

Turning to the Working Class

Empirically, and without a clear theoretical understanding of their problem, individuals amongst the Narodniks turned again and again towards the industrial working class. Without a consideration of these small shoots the growth of Russian marxism cannot be understood.

In the year 1870, for the first time in Russian history, a group of students, led by N.V.Chaikovsky, planted the seed of a working-class organization.* They did this not because they regarded the proletariat as the agent of socialism, but because they saw in the factory workers agents for spreading the Narodnik message among the peasants.

> They therefore made contact with those who were least skilled and who were most directly bound to the life and spirit of the countryside. On principle they always chose textile rather than metal workers, for they recognized in them the representatives of what they considered to be the real people. A.V.Nizovkin, one of their most active propagandists, said that the metal workers had already been marked by urban civilization. They dressed better; they no longer lived communally; and the traditions of the artel were dying out among them. The textile workers, on the other hand . . . still dressed in country fashion and retained the habits which were typical of the village – from a communal spirit to drunkenness.[33]

---

* Chaikovsky ended his life as head of the White Government of Archangel after the October Revolution, and then died as an émigré in France.

The Chaikovists were very few in number.

It is difficult to say exactly how many members there were in the St Petersburg group of the Chaikovists . . . In 1928, nearly half a century later, three of the survivors . . . tried to make up an exact list of their comrades between 1871 and 1874. They estimated a group of nineteen in Moscow, eleven in Odessa, eight in Kiev and some in Kharkov, Orel, Kazan and Tula.[34]

Each Chaikovist began his political work by contacting a small group of between three and five workers, whom he taught to read and write. He also gave them lessons in geography, history, physics and other subjects. Lectures were held on such topics as the history of rebellions in Russia, the International, the German working class movement and political economy (based on the works of Marx). A library had been set up for those workers who were ready to pay two per cent of their wages towards its upkeep. Unfortunately the Chaikovists did not survive police persecution. In 1873 they ceased to exist as an organized body.

While the Chaikovists were at work in St Petersburg, an even more important and far more proletarian group was established in Odessa. It was centred round the figure of E. Zaslavsky, who directed it for eight or nine months, and it was called the Union of Workers of South Russia. This can be regarded as the first organization of a truly working-class nature to come into being in the Russian empire.[35] The Union, which had fifty to sixty members in its central organization, was able to support two strikes, the first in January 1875, at the Bellino-Venderich factory and the second in August at Gullier-Blanchard's. A manifesto was drawn up and distributed on the second of these occasions. The Union's influence rapidly increased, not only in Odessa but also in other towns along the Black Sea coast. Its programme contained certain novel points. The tasks it set itself included '(a) the propaganda of the idea of the emancipation of the workers from the yoke of capital and of the privileged classes; and (b) the organization of the workers of the South of Russia for the coming struggle against the existing economic and political order'.[36] At the end of 1875 an informer enabled the authorities virtually to put an end to the Union by arresting all its leaders.

But the arrest of the Chaikovists at the beginning of 1874, which smashed the cadres of that organization, did not stop the slow and imperceptible spread of revolutionary ideas among the St Petersburg workers. One of the most dramatic expressions of this, the culmination of six long years of the dissemination of ideas, was a demonstration in the Square of Kazan Cathedral on 6 December 1876. This was the landmark in the history of the Russian revolutionary movement. Plekhanov, who played a central role in the demonstration, described the event years later. Inspired by a demonstration staged by intellectuals in the spring of 1875 at the funeral of a student who was murdered by his jailers, a group of workers proposed a demonstration of their own. They assured Plekhanov that something like 2,000 of their number would attend. On the day a crowd, composed mainly of students, but with some workers, gathered in front of the cathedral. Estimates of the number of the people in the crowd vary from 150 to 500. After delaying the proceedings for some time in the hope that more workers would turn up, and threatened with the danger that the whole effort would collapse, Plekhanov stood up and made a speech which ended with the words: 'Long live the social revolution. Long live *Zemlya i Volya*.' A red banner with the words 'Land and Liberty' was then unfurled. This small demonstration was the first workers' demonstration in the history of Russia.

A wave of strikes took place in Petersburg between 1877 and 1879. There were twenty-six in all, an unprecedented level of strike activity, which was not repeated until the 1890s. It was at this period that a new organization of workers arose in Petersburg, the Union of Workers of North Russia. It had about two hundred members, with groups in all the working-class districts of the city. Its founder was the joiner Stepan Khalturin, the son of a peasant from the province of Vyatka. However, after only a few months of active life, the Northern Union was in its turn smashed by the police, and in 1880 it ceased to exist.

In 1879 Plekhanov, leading *Chernyi Peredel*, turned his back on Narodnik terrorism, and putting the emphasis on propaganda, also argued on empirical grounds for turning towards the working class. But the umbilical cord connecting his thinking with the Narodnik evaluation of the peasantry as agents of socialism had still not been cut. In February 1879 he wrote: 'Agitation in the factories is increasing daily: that is the news of the day.' This agitation constituted one of those problems that 'life itself brings to the forefront, its rightful place, despite the *a priori* theoretical decisions of the revolutionaries . . . In the past, and not without reason, we put all our hopes and directed all our forces at the village masses. The urban worker held only second place in the revolutionaries' calculations. . . .'

Whereas the peasants in the village were under the influence of 'the more conservative and timorous members of the peasant family' the 'city workers . . . constitute the most mobile, the most susceptible to incitation, the most easily revolutionized stratum of the population'.

> Our large industrial centres group together tens and sometimes even hundreds of thousands of workers. In the great majority of cases these men are the same peasants as those in the villages . . . The agricultural problem, the question of the self-administration of the *obshchina*, land and liberty: all these are just as close to the heart of the workers as of the peasants. In a word, it is not a question of masses cut off from the countryside but of part of the countryside. Their cause is the same, their struggle can and must be the same. And besides, the towns collect the very flower of the village population, younger people, more enterprising . . . there they are kept far removed from the influence of the more conservative and timid elements of the peasant family . . . Thanks to all this they will constitute a precious ally for the peasants when the social revolution breaks out.[37]

The coming socialist revolution would be a peasant revolution, but the workers were destined to be invaluable allies of the peasantry, as they were still basically peasants themselves, and they could act as intermediaries between the intelligentsia in the towns and the peasantry in the countryside.

Narodnaya Volya, for years after Plekhanov's break, also called for more emphasis on propaganda activity among industrial workers. Thus a programmatic article entitled 'Preparatory Work of the Party' in *Kalendar Narodnoi Voli* (1883) states: 'The working population of the towns, which is of particularly great significance for the revolution both by its position and its great development, must be the object of the party's serious attention.'[38]

However, there is a basic difference between the Narodniks' attitude, including Plekhanov's in 1879, regarding propaganda work among industrial workers, and that of marxists. The latter are 'convinced that the workers are not necessary *for the revolution*, but the revolution *for the workers*'.[39] For the Narodniks, the workers are important for the revolution. A Narodnik can ask the question 'Why the working class?', while a marxist can only ask the question 'Why marxism?', as the working class is the subject of history for him, not the object.

Once more, in the attitude of the Narodniks to work amongst the proletariat, we have the case of a theory being outgrown by practice – a change in tactics without the understanding of theoretical consequences necessary for a consistent change of course. Narodism had outlived its time, and elements of marxism emerged *within* the ideological framework of Narodism.

Plekhanov, Marxist Pioneer

Between 1880 and 1882 Plekhanov went all the way from Narodism to marxism. In 1883 the Emancipation of Labour Group was established.

Also in 1883 Plekhanov wrote the first major Russian marxist work, *Socialism and the Political Struggle*. This itself was by no means a short pamphlet, and it was followed a year or so later by the thick book *Our Differences*. The Bolshevik historian Pokrovsky stated what was common knowledge when he said that this work contained 'practically all the basic ideas that formed the stock-in-trade of Russian marxism up to the end of the century'.[40]

The future, Plekhanov said, submitting the commune to a searching analysis, did not belong to the peasants and their 'commune'. He cited impressive data proving the increasing inequality and individualism amongst the communal peasantry. On the one hand many peasants had lost, or were losing, the capacity to till the land allotments, and surrendered their rights to other peasants, becoming wage earners themselves. At the same time others, the rich peasants or kulaks (*kulak* in Russian means 'fist'), were increasingly cultivating the allotments of other peasants in addition to their own, purchased or rented additional land, and employed hired labour.

Plekhanov also attacked the idealization of the commune's past: 'Our village community . . . in reality has been the main buttress of Russian absolutism' and 'is becoming more and more an instrument in the hands of the rural bourgeoisie for the exploitation of the majority of the agrarian population.'[41] He shattered the argument of the Narodnik economist, V.V., that capitalism could not develop in Russia because of the lack of markets. With great historical sweep, using examples from Colbert's France, Germany under the Zollverein and the United States, he showed that the state always intervened to protect young, growing industries against the overwhelming supremacy of Britain.

Further, contrary to V.V.'s arguments, home markets did not precede the development of capitalism as a precondition for it, but were created by capitalism itself. 'The bourgeoisie *created* the markets, they did not find them *ready made*.'[42] The ruin of artisans and the invasion of agriculture by money relationships creates the market. 'Any country's transition from natural to money economy is necessarily accompanied by an enormous expansion of the home market and there can be no doubt that in our country this market will go over in its entirety to our bourgeoisie.'[43]

Plekhanov argued that it was utopian to believe, as the Narodniks did, that capitalism could be prevented from transforming Russian economy and society. He concluded that socialists should turn to the industrial working class as the harbingers of the future : 'the rural population of today, living in backward social conditions, is not only less capable of conscious political *initiative* than the industrial workers, it is also less *responsive* to the movement which our revolutionary intelligentsia has begun'. 'And besides' Plekhanov continued, 'the peasantry is now going through a difficult, critical period. The previous "ancestral" foundations of its economy are crumbling, the ill-fated village community itself is being discredited in its eyes, as is admitted even by such "ancestral" organs of Narodism as *Nedelya*; and the new forms of labour and life are only in the process of formation, and this creative process is more intensive in the industrial centres.'[44]

Plekhanov was the first Russian to argue that the working class was to play the chief role in the impending Russian revolution against the Tsarist autocracy. Thus in a statement to the founding congress of the Socialist (Second) International (July 1889) he proclaimed : 'The revolutionary movement in Russia can triumph only as the revolutionary movement of the workers. There is not and cannot be any other way for us !'[45]

Still Inclined towards Narodism

Plekhanov was still, however, attracted by the Narodniks. Narodnik ideas abound in his writings, especially those of 1883 and 1884. At that time he did not contrast the future Social Democrats with *Narodnaya Volya*, but merely demanded that the latter should adopt marxism. In *Our Differences* he wrote :

> In presenting this first attempt at a programme for the Russian marxists to the comrades working in Russia, we are far from wishing to compete with *Narodnaya Volya*; on the contrary, there is nothing we desire more than full and final agreement with that party. We think that the *Narodnaya Volya* party *must* become a marxist party if it at all wishes to remain faithful to its revolutionary traditions and to get the Russian movement out of its present stagnation.[46]

Despite his criticisms of the role of the rural communes,

his concessions to Narodism were far-reaching even on this score. Thus he wrote:

> when the hour of the decisive victory of the workers' party over the upper sections of society strikes, once more that party, and only that party, will take the initiative in the socialist organization of national production . . . the village communities still existing will in fact begin the transition to a higher, communist form . . . communal land tenure will become not only *possible*, but *actual*, and the Narodist dreams of our peasantry's exceptionalist development will come true.[47]

He also compromised with individual Narodnik terrorism. 'And what about terror? . . . we by no means deny the important role of the terrorist struggle in the present emancipation movement. It has grown naturally from the social and political conditions under which we are placed, and it must just as naturally promote a change for the better.' The Narodnik Party should

> turn to the working class as to the most revolutionary of all classes in present-day society . . . we are pointing out a way of making the struggle broader, more varied, and therefore more successful . . . There are other sections of the population [i.e. other than the workers – T.C.] for whom it would be far more convenient to undertake the terrorist struggle against the government. Propaganda among the workers will not remove the necessity for terrorist struggle, but it will provide it with opportunities which have so far never existed.[48]*

Plekhanov also made allowances for the élitist attitude of the Narodniks towards the intelligentsia:

---

* In the 1905 edition of *Our Differences* Plekhanov gives the following lame explanation for the above statement on terrorism, made in 1884: 'On the basis of this passage it was subsequently said that the Emancipation of Labour Group sympathized with "terrorism". But as long as it has existed that group has held that terrorism is *inconvenient* for the workers; it was certainly useless at that time to pronounce against the terrorist activity of the intelligentsia who believed in it as in a god.'[49]

our socialist intelligentsia has been obliged to head the present-day emancipation movement, whose direct task must be to set up free political institutions in our country, the socialists on their side being under the obligation to provide the working class with the possibility to take an active and fruitful part in the future political life of Russia . . . That is why the socialist intelligentsia has the obligation to organize the workers and prepare them as far as possible for the struggle against the present-day system of government as well as against the future bourgeois parties.[50]

Plekhanov introduced authentic marxism into Russia and made it a weapon adapted to the needs of the revolution. He discovered the working class as the bearer of the future Russian revolution. To make such a stride forward required a broad historical outlook, which Plekhanov most certainly possessed. He was one of the most learned, discerning and cultured men of his time, with a powerful and original mind, critical and creative talents in many fields and a brilliant literary talent. He studied such diverse subjects as organic chemistry, geology and anthropology, zoology and comparative anatomy, his enquiries ranging into fields as varied as history and aesthetics, ethnography, literature, epistemology and art. He initiated marxist literary criticism and pioneered the extension of marxist research into a number of other fields.

It is difficult to grasp the importance of Plekhanov's contribution to the Russian revolutionary movement, unless one can project oneself in imagination into the milieu of the radical intelligentsia of the early 1880s, steeped in a Narodism made sacrosanct by decades of struggle and the blood of martyrs. Only then can one understand the real excitement of being the pioneer, the first man to translate marxism into Russian terms. Plekhanov's first marxian treatise, *Socialism and the Political Struggle*, Lenin testifies, had a significance for Russia comparable with that of the *Communist Manifesto* for the West. Plekhanov's book *On the Development of the Monist Concept of History* (1894), according to Lenin, 'reared a whole generation of Russian marxists'. Trotsky stated that 'the marxist generation of the 1890s stood on the foundations laid down by Plekhanov . . . next to Marx and Engels, Vladimir owed the most to Plekhanov'.[51]

The 'Strength' of the Emancipation of Labour Group

To understand why it took the young Vladimir Ulyanov so long to become converted to Plekhanov's ideas, one must see that they were indeed disembodied ideas with no movement – no mass strikes or demonstrations of numerous followers to support them. In fact, for ten years, 1883-93, the Emancipation of Labour Group existed only in exile. It *was* practically the whole of the marxist movement.

At the outset, the group consisted of just five people! Plekhanov, Axelrod, Deutsch, Vera Zasulich and V.I.Ignatov. Very soon it was reduced to three. Ignatov, who had provided a substantial amount of money to back the organization, died in 1895 of tuberculosis, which had from the start prevented him from taking a very active part in the work of the group. Deutsch was arrested in mid-1884 while trying to organize the dispatch of literature into Russia. Plekhanov and the other two faced a decade of practically complete isolation. It is true that throughout the 80s there existed circles in various Russian cities engaged in activities among the workers. But they were so feeble, the results of their work so imperceptible, the persecution of the police so effective, that they hardly managed to establish roots anywhere, and remained in complete isolation from one another. It took several decades of historical research to unearth even the existence of such groups, which, working under the most frightful conditions, were doing important groundwork in preparing for the extensive activity of the succeeding decade.

In 1884 a small group of intellectuals and workers, headed by the Bulgarian student Blagoev (later the founder of the Bulgarian Communist Party) wrote to the Emancipation of Labour Group: 'We have come to the conclusion that there is much in common between our views and those of the Emancipation of Labour Group.' Deferring to their 'foreign comrades, who have much more literary preparation and greater revolutionary experience,

> the Blagoevtsi requested the establishment of regular relations, the shipment of literature, and a discussion of points of the programme, and they promised to provide funds. No wonder that Plekhanov cried with relief to Axelrod, 'We are not suffering in vain.' Thus began a period of a year of collaboration that ended only in the winter of 1885-86, when the Blagoev group, like others before it, was raided out of existence.[52]

Shortly after the destruction of the Blagoevtsi, another group, called the Tochiisky circle, rose, but this also had a very short existence, confined to 1888. Hardly had the police succeeded in liquidating it, when in 1889 a new revolutionary group arose, known as the Brusnev group, after its leader, an engineer of that name. Among the members of this group were a number of prominent workers, such as Bogdanov, Norinsky, Shelgunov and Fedor Afanasiev. It ceased to exist after the police raids of 1892.

All in all the 1880s were years of very small marxist propaganda circles among Russian workers. Generally they were remembered as a time of darkness. 'A man of the 80s' is a disappointed man, despondent and idle. In literature this mood found expression in the plays of Chekhov – Uncle Vanya, Ivanov, and other characters – all manifestations of despair and small deeds.

There were very few workers' strikes in the 1880s. In the six years 1881-86 there were only forty-eight strikes,[53] and the marxists hardly influenced any of them. One Russian labour historian could write, quite justifiably, in 1893, that until that year labour unrest in Russia 'had no connection whatsoever with any of the Social Democratic units'.[54]

The Same, Yet Different

In order to clarify his own ideas, to investigate his own relationship with Narodism, the young Vladimir Ulyanov started writing polemics against the Narodniks. 'One cannot develop new views other than through polemics', he wrote two decades later.[55] The history of ideas is the history of the conflict of ideas. These early polemical writings are not empty studies, but delve deeply into the facts of Russia's economic and social development. Above all Lenin wanted to grasp the reality of the society in which he lived, and which he was destined to participate in radically changing.

At the end of the Samara period a manuscript by Ulyanov was circulating among the comrades. It was called *A Dispute between a Social Democrat and a Populist*, and most probably was a summary of Samara disputes presented in dialogue form. Unfortunately the paper has been lost. Then he wrote a review of book-length study of the agrarian question called *New Economic Developments in Peasant Life (On V.Y.Postnikov's Peasant Farming in South Russia)*. The review, filled with statistics, and written for a legal magazine, was rejected – perhaps because of its length, perhaps because of its sharp critique of the prevailing Narodnik viewpoint. Ulyanov read his manuscript in the Samara study circle, where it instantly established his authority. One of the two handwritten copies of the review has come down to us, thanks to those indefatigable collectors of revolutionary manuscripts, the Tsarist secret police. It is a very mature, unusually penetrating analysis of the economic and social scene in the countryside, although Ulyanov was still only twenty-three years old. The bulk of it was incorporated into his book, *The Development of Capitalism in Russia*, written half a decade later.

Ulyanov's third piece of writing was another polemic against the Narodniks. It was called *On the So-called Market Question*, and was written in Petersburg in the autumn of 1893. Its main points were first outlined by Lenin at a meeting of a marxist circle, at which a lecture called *The Market Question* by another young marxist, G.B.Krasin, was discussed. According to participants in the meeting, Lenin's paper made a great impression on all present.[56] The paper shows a very clear grasp of the second volume of Marx's *Capital*. It is a fine, hard-hitting criticism of V.V.'s theory of the impossibility of 'extensive' development of industry in

Russia because of lack of markets. (The single copy of the manuscript was long considered lost, but was in fact found in 1937.) Ulyanov's chief writing in 1894 was a work entitled *What the 'Friends of the People' are and How They Fight the Social-Democrats* (*A Reply to Articles in Russkoye Bogatstvo* opposing the Marxists*). It circulated in three stout, carefully written notebooks. The notebooks created a remarkable stir among the few marxists in Petersburg, and were soon hectographed and passed from hand to hand. Only the first and third parts of the work have survived, and they occupy 199 pages in Lenin's *Collected Works* (fourth Russian edition). One can imagine the amount of sheer labour involved in writing all this out, neatly in the manuscript notebooks, and then all over again, letter by letter, on the hectographed sheets.

His next main work, written at the end of 1894 and the beginning of 1895, was yet another criticism of the Narodniks, *The Economic Content of Narodism and the Criticism of it in Mr Struve's Book* (*The Reflection of Marxism in Bourgeois Literature*). *P.Struve, Critical Remarks on the Subject of Russia's Economic Development, St.Petersburg, 1894*. This again is quite a lengthy work – occupying 166 pages in the *Collected Works*. It was the first of his writings to be printed. But the police seized it, and only a few copies were saved.

For the rest of 1895 and 1896 Ulyanov wrote nothing more against the Narodniks. But in 1897 he wrote a further major attack on them, of 118 pages, entitled *A Characterization of Economic Romanticism* (*Sismondi and our Native Sismondists*). Lastly came his major theoretical work, *The Development of Capitalism in Russia*, which fills practically the whole of Volume 3 of the *Works* (535 pages). This was a marxist analysis of Russia's economic development, polemically written against the Narodniks. All the research for and the writing of this book took place while Ulyanov was a

---

* *Russkoye Bogatstvo* was a leading journal of economics, sociology, philosophy and literature, edited by the most prominent veteran Narodnik theoretician, N.K.Mikhailovsky.

police ward : first in prison, then in Siberia. He made use of 299 works in Russian, and 38 foreign studies in German, French and English (or in Russian translation). These he purchased or borrowed by mail from distant libraries while he was living in prison or in Siberia. The book appeared during the last year of his exile in Siberia (1899) under the authorship of V.Ilyin.

In many ways these works follow the path already opened up by Plekhanov, and Lenin never failed to note with gratitude his intellectual debt to Plekhanov. The last thing in his mind was a search for originality. He probably remembered the words of his great teacher and inspirer, Chernyshevsky :

> A preoccupation with originality destroys originality itself, and true independence is given only to those who do not stop to think of the possibility of not being independent. Only the feeble talk of their strength of character. And only the man who is afraid of being easily discomfited is afraid of exposing himself to the influence of others. Current preoccupation with originality is a preoccupation with form. A man who has any real content will not worry unduly about originality. Preoccupation with form leads to baseless fabrications and emptiness.[57]

However, in a number of ways Lenin's writings against the Narodniks are indeed original, being radically different from those of Plekhanov. On the one hand the young pupil had not the historical sweep of the old master. Where Plekhanov used historical examples from different countries, anthropological research into the fate of primitive communes, and so on, none of this appeared in Lenin's writings. Nor is there the same wealth of literary and cultural allusions and brilliance of style. On the other hand, Lenin's grasp of economic and social reality is far superior. His use of statistical data in detailed analysis of the actual situation is better than anything Plekhanov wrote. His penetration into the very complicated forms of feudal enslavement following the new capitalist relations in the countryside is nowhere to be matched. While still a disciple, Ulyanov branched out with his own distinct ideas, deviating from his master on two inter-related and, as the future was to show, decisive points: (1) his attitude to capitalist development as such, and (2) his attitude to the Narodniks.

The differences on the first point appear most clearly in *The Economic Content and the Criticism of it in Mr Struve's Book*. In order to appreciate them we must understand the background against which it appeared. For a long time the Tsarist authorities were unconcerned about marxism. During the seventies and eighties both Volumes I and II of Marx's *Capital* were passed by the Tsarist censor.

'One can with certainty say', declared the Censor Skuratov in 1872 in the report on the first volume of *Capital*, 'that in Russia only a few will read the book and still fewer understand [it].' The authorities of Alexander III also passed without hesitation the second volume, which existed in a Russian edition in 1885, as it was 'in content and presentation a serious economic study comprehensible only to the specialist'.[58]

To encourage the fight against the Narodniks, in whom the Tsar saw the main enemy, 'legal marxism' was permitted in the middle nineties. As early as the 1880s a secret police agent advised his superiors to allow the build-up of marxist forces as a counter to the more dangerous Narodniks. Since most marxist writing in some way discredited Narodism, the officials supposed it would help to kill off the major oppositional ideology. From the marxists themselves the government anticipated no trouble. Typically, a Nizhni-Novgorod police colonel expressed the opinion that they 'are not dangerous at present'; and a Petersburg procurator considered them to be 'as yet only theoreticians'.[59]

In 1894 Peter Struve submitted for publication a work clearly marxist in orientation, called *Critical Notes Concerning the Economic Development of Russia*, and the censor allowed it. Its publication in September 1894 marked the beginning of the period of 'legal marxism', which continued for the next five years.

Although Lenin took advantage of the legal opening for publishing marxist literature, as, for instance, with his own book *The Development of Capitalism in Russia*, from the beginning he drew a clear distinction between himself and the leading legal marxist, Struve. Struve's book was a sharp attack on Narodism, but at the same time it was an apologia for capitalism.

Plekhanov, however, had nothing but praise for it. Like Struve, he largely overlooked the contradictory, painful and tragic aspects of capitalist development in Russia. Quite often he wrote almost as an apologist for capitalist industrialization. Against Narodnik 'subjectivism' he put forward rigid 'objectivism'. The scientific socialists, he believed, were struggling for socialism not because it *should be*, but because it was the next stage in the magnificent and irresistible march of history.[60] 'The Social Democrat swims with the stream of history,'[61] and the causes of historical development 'have nothing to do with human will and consciousness'.[62] Gramsci quite rightly accused Plekhanov of 'relapses into vulgar materialism'.[63] Because of his basic attitude, Plekhanov could approvingly quote Struve's words: 'We must conclude that we lack culture, and go to the school of capitalism.'[64]

Although Lenin is no less critical of the Narodniks than Struve or Plekhanov, his attitude to them is radically different. At the very beginning of his essay on the economic content of Narodism, and the criticism of it in Struve's book, Lenin makes it clear that marxism has nothing in common with 'faith in the necessity of each country to pass through the phase of capitalism' or any other such mistaken ideas.[65]

> Marxism does not base itself on anything else than the facts of Russian history and reality; it is also [like Narodism – T.C.] the ideology of the labouring class; only it gives a totally different explanation of the generally known facts of the growth and achievements of Russian capitalism, has quite a different understanding of the tasks that reality in this country places before the ideologists of the direct producers.[66]

Lenin sharply attacked Struve's 'narrow objectivism',

> which is confined to proving the inevitability and necessity of the process and makes no effort to reveal at each specific stage of this process the form of class contradiction inherent

in it – an objectivism that describes the process in general, and not each of the antagonistic classes whose conflict makes up the process.[67]

When demonstrating the necessity for a given series of facts, the objectivist always runs the risk of becoming an apologist for these facts.[68]

Against this Lenin counterposes the method of the materialist, 'who discloses the class contradictions and in so doing defines his standpoint'.[69]

For Lenin capitalism was progressive compared with feudalism, because capitalism creates its own gravedigger. Capitalism awakens millions from feudal torpor and organizes them, and in this lies its progressiveness. To sharpen the class struggle of the proletariat against the capitalists – in this lies the main task of marxists.

Plekhanov and Axelrod in their turn criticized Lenin's article on Struve. He was in their eyes too sharp towards the liberal bourgeoisie. Thus Axelrod in his memoirs describes his discussion with Lenin.

> 'You show,' I said, 'exactly the opposite tendency to the one expressed in the article I had prepared . . . I . . . wanted to show that in the given historic moment the immediate interests of the Russian proletariat coincide with the vital interests of the other progressive elements of society . . . Both face the same urgent problem . . . the overthrow of absolutism . . .'

> Ulyanov smiled and observed: 'You know, Plekhanov made exactly the same remarks about my articles. He expressed his thoughts in picturesque fashion: "You", he said, "turn your behind to the liberals, but we our face." '[70]

This disagreement anticipated the future antagonism between Lenin on the one hand and Plekhanov and Axelrod on the other over their attitude to the liberals. From a careful reading of Plekhanov's *Socialism and the Political Struggle*, one can predict Plekhanov's eventual relationship with the liberals. He argues in this pamphlet that one should limit the aims of the anti-Tsarist revolution to the 'demand for a democratic constitution'.

Without trying to scare anybody with the yet remote 'red spectre', such a political programme would arouse sympathy for our revolutionary party among all those who are not systematic enemies of democracy; it could be subscribed to by very many representatives of our liberalism as well as by the socialists . . . Then the interests of the liberals would indeed 'force' them to act 'jointly with the socialists against the government', because they would cease to meet in revolutionary publications the assurance that the overthrow of absolutism would be the signal for a social revolution in Russia. At the same time another, less timid and more sober section of liberal society would no longer see revolutionaries as unpractical youths who set themselves unrealizable and fantastic plans. This view, which is disadvantageous for revolutionaries, would give place to the respect of society not only for their heroism but also for their political maturity. This sympathy would gradually grow into active support, or more probably into an independent social movement, and then the hour of absolutism's fall would strike at last.[71]

Lenin also differed from Plekhanov in his attitude to the Narodniks. While the Lenin of 1893-95 drew clear lines of demarcation between himself and the Narodniks (much sharper than Plekhanov did in 1883-84), he never forgot that Narodism had a progressive, democratic – revolutionary aspect – unlike Plekhanov, who, once he had broken completely with Narodism, ceased to find anything progressive in it.

It is clear [Lenin argues] . . . that it would be absolutely wrong to reject the whole of the Narodnik programme indiscriminately and in its entirety. One must clearly distinguish its reactionary and progressive sides. Narodism is reactionary insofar as it proposes measures that tie the peasant to the soil and to the old modes of production, such as the inalienability of allotments etc., insofar as it wants to retard the development of money economy . . . But there are also other points, relating to self-government, to the 'people's' (that is to say, small) economy by means of cheap credits, technical improvements, better regulation of marketing, etc., etc . . . such general democratic measures are progressive . . . the Narodnik, in matters of theory, is just as much a Janus, looking with one face to the past and the other to the future, as in real life the small producer is, who looks with one face to the past, wishing to strengthen his small farm without knowing or wishing to know anything about the general economic system and about the need to reckon with the class that controls it – and with the other face to the future, adopting a hostile attitude to the capitalism that is ruining him.[72]

For many years, as we shall see, Lenin fought for an alliance, not with the liberals, the Cadet Party, as proposed by Plekhanov, but with the Trudoviks, the petty bourgeois heirs of Narodism. In 1912 Lenin pointed out the connection between Bolshevism and the attempt to extract from Narodism its 'valuable democratic kernel'.

> Clearly the marxists must carefully extract the sound and valuable kernel of the sincere, resolute, militant democracy of the peasant masses from the husk of Narodnik utopias. In the old marxist literature of the eighties one can discover systematic effort to extract this valuable democratic kernel. Some day historians will study this effort systematically and trace its connection with what in the first decade of the twentieth century came to be called 'Bolshevism'.[73]

> While fighting Narodism as a wrong doctrine of *socialism*, the Mensheviks, in a doctrinaire fashion, overlooked the historically real and progressive historical *content* of Narodism as a theory of the mass *petty-bourgeois* struggle of democratic capitalism against liberal-landlord capitalism . . . Hence their monstrous, idiotic, renegade idea . . . that the peasant *movement* is reactionary, that a Cadet is more progressive than a Trudovik.[74]

Again and again Lenin repeated: 'The Russian Social Democrats have always recognized the necessity to extract and absorb the revolutionary side of the Narodnik doctrine and trend.'[75]

In *What is to be Done?* (1902), Lenin argued that the revolutionary marxists must also not overlook the positive achievements of the Narodniks in terms of organizational structure:

> the magnificent organization that the revolutionaries had in the seventies . . . should serve us as a model . . . no militant centralized organization which declares determined war

upon Tsarism . . . can dispense with such an organization . . .
Only a gross failure to understand marxism (or an 'understanding' of it in the spirit of 'Struveism') could prompt the
opinion that the rise of a mass, spontaneous working-class
movement *relieves* us of the duty of creating as good an
organization of revolutionaries as the *Zemlya i Volya* had,
or indeed, an incomparably better one.[76]

We shall encounter Plekhanov again, first as Lenin's
teacher, then as his elder colleague, and finally as his implacable opponent. However, right from the beginning, the pupil
showed his independence of his teacher, even when repeating
and re-arguing the case for Russian marxism against Narodism.

In Anticipation

There is little interest in hunting for the influence of
Plekhanov or anyone else on the young Ulyanov, since what
matters is not what was borrowed, but what was made of the
borrowings, and this depends on the experiences and the history of the individual who borrows, and on his actions in the
struggle.

Vladimir Ulyanov's break with Narodism, his original
position with relation to the liberalism of Struve, and his dialectical attitude, i.e. his critical support of Narodism to the
extent that the latter was a revolutionary democratic movement, are basic to his whole future development. Throughout his political career Lenin regarded as fundamental the
relation of revolutionary socialists to three social classes:
the proletariat, the peasantry, and the bourgeoisie.

Lenin's statements of this period already contain in embryo the central themes of his further theoretical development: the relentless opposition to the liberal bourgeoisie, the
hegemony of the proletariat over the peasantry, and the alliance of the proletariat of the industrial countries with the
national liberation movement in the colonies, which is largely a peasant movement. Being petty bourgeois, the peasantry
vacillates between the proletariat and the bourgeoisie; it is
revolutionary to the extent that it fights feudalism and imper-

ialism, and reactionary to the extent that it clings to petty private property. The proletariat must both ally itself with the peasantry, and remain separate from it. It must lead it without merging with it, without following its vacillations. In Lenin's attitude the marxism brought from the West is merged with the Russian national traditions of revolutionary struggle carried on by the Narodniks.

Marx wrote, 'The philosophers hitherto interpreted the world, the task is to change it.' Lenin brought to this task not only his own personal passion and activism, but also the heroic traditions of the Narodniks. When one of the great heroes of Narodism, Zhelyabov (who organized the assassination of Alexander II) stated: 'History moves too slowly, it needs a push', Lenin was ready to do just that. Lenin represented the Russian proletariat, a youthful class very close to the peasantry, not hindered by shackles of routine and conservatism, bold and daring because outside it there were millions of other people – peasants – also oppressed, starved, lacking rights, humiliated. When the proletariat fights for democracy it fights not only in its own class interests, but also as the representative of the whole mass of the people, above all the peasantry. Instead of the solitary Narodnik 'going among the people', one has the proletariat as the leader of the countryside. But we are running ahead of the story of the present book.

2

From the Marxist Study Circle to Industrial Action

On 31 August 1893 Vladimir Ulyanov arrived in St Petersburg. In the autumn of the same year he joined a marxist circle of Technological Institute students (G.M.Krzhizhanovsky, S.I.Radchenko, V.V.Starkov, G.B.Krasin and others). As we have seen, in the spring of 1892 the police had arrested many of the members of the Brusnev group in St Petersburg. However, a number of worker members of the group remained free, and a rather loose and informal workers' organization continued to exist. It was mainly, if not entirely, made up of workers whose chief interest was study. Workers joining the circles (*kruzhki*) showed an insatiable thirst for knowledge.

Plekhanov described the kind of worker who joined these study groups:

> After working at the factory 10-11 hours a day, and returning home only in the evening, he would sit at his books until 1 o'clock at night . . . I was struck by the variety and abundance of the theoretical questions which concerned him . . . Political economy, chemistry, social questions, and the theory of Darwin all occupied his attention . . . It would have taken decades for him to assuage his intellectual thirst.[1]

> When I asked the workers themselves what exactly they wanted from revolutionary writings, I met with the most varied answers. In most cases, each of them wanted a solution to those problems which for some reason were of special interest to my individual hearer at that particular moment. In the mind of the workers such problems were increasing enormously, and each had his favourite questions according to his own tendencies and character. One was particularly interested in the problem of God and claimed

that revolutionary literature ought to use its energies mainly for destroying the religious beliefs of the people. Others
were interested in historical or political problems, or in the
natural sciences. Among my acquaintances in the factories
there was also one who was specially interested in the
question of women.[2]

The leaders of a Jewish workers' socialist study group
tried to enlighten the workers on a very wide range of subjects. Thus Leon Bernshtein in Vilna taught his pupils 'how
the world was created, the sun and the earth, the seas and the
volcanoes', as well as lecturing on 'the life of the people beginning with wild tribes and ending with the English with
their Parliament and their trade unions'. In another circle,
'among the topics discussed were the emergence of social
classes, slavery, serfdom and capitalism. Circle members
studied Darwin and Mill, and read the masterpieces of Russian literature.'[3]

A historian of the Russian labour movement of that period wrote as follows :

These workers discerned in literacy and enlightenment a
way out of their hopeless social situation, and therefore
eagerly took advantage of the opportunities afforded by the
kruzhki. A number of the more perceptive workers not only
mastered the basic elements of learning, but displayed a
keen interest in 'science' and in a scientific understanding of
their surrounding world.[4]

A worker addressing his comrades at a secret May Day
celebration in 1891 vividly summarized the prevalent approach among members of a study circle :

At this time the only thing we can do is devote ourselves to
the education and organization of workers – a task that, I
hope, we shall carry through regardless of the threats and
obstacles raised by our government. In order to make our
efforts bear fruit, we must do our best to educate ourselves
and others intellectually and morally; we must work at this
as energetically as possible, so that the people around us will
regard us as intelligent, honest and courageous men, have
greater trust in us, and take us as an example for themselves
and others.[5]

In practice the kruzhki relied on the peaceful dissemination of marxist ideas to further the progress of the revolution.

> The circles were intended to be schools of socialism, but the workers sometimes regarded them only as schools, placing all their hopes in the power of learning and paying little attention to revolutionary doctrines. This attitude was well expressed by a Vilna worker, who stated in 1892 that 'Like a faithful mother knowledge will guide us peacefully over the sea of fears and pain to the land of life.'[6]

Their perspectives were vague, the outlook of P.N. Skvortsov being typical. He was one of the earliest Russian marxists, and the founder of the first marxist circle in Nizhni Novgorod. His pupil, Mitskevich, describes his attitude thus:

> We had long conversations on the future of the workers' movement. How abstractly we still conceived the future forms of the workers' movement is indicated by the perspectives outlined by Skvortsov: gradually the number of workers studying Marx will increase; they will draw still more numbers into the circles studying Marx; with time all Russia will be covered with such *kruzhki* and then we will form a workers' socialist party. What tasks this party was to perform and how it should conduct its struggle remained unclear.[7]

The official rules of the Social Democratic 'Workers' Union' in Ivanovo-Voznesensk defined its membership as 'critically thinking individuals seeking to realize progress in mankind' and declared its chief aim to be 'propaganda among the more cultured workers of both sexes'.[8]

Worse than this, many circle members became alienated from their fellow workers. 'As a result of protracted exposure to the intellectual diet of the socialist world, many workers became almost indistinguishable from the intelligentsia in outlook and in the range and depth of their learning.'[9]

> The 'advanced' workers, coming for the most part from the skilled trades, were almost as alienated from average workers as the intelligentsia. They spoke a more cultivated language than their fellows, prided themselves on book knowledge, and dressed more fastidiously even than the democratically minded *intelligenty*. Since many of them

abstained from smoking, drinking and cursing, they were occasionally mistaken for Pashkovites [members of a Bible tract sect] and made the butts of ridicule from their fellow workers. More alarming, they tended to stand aloof from strikes and other forms of elemental protest, which were becoming increasingly frequent.[10]

The workers in the circles, as described by Martov,

saw themselves as individuals emerging from a backward multitude and creating a new cultural environment. But this was only half the trouble. The [main] trouble was that, given this outlook, they viewed the entire process of the future rise of their class in oversimplified rationalistic manner: they thought it would occur from the spread of that knowledge and those new moral concepts which they themselves had acquired in the circles and from reading. Arguments with them led us to the astounding discovery that their whole manner of social thinking was idealistic, that their socialism was still thoroughly abstract and utopian, and that the idea of employing the class struggle to transform the uncultured environment itself, in protest against which their own social awakening had occurred was still entirely alien to them.[11]

Some workers even acquired 'a sort of condescending, contemptuous attitude towards the masses, who one might say were not considered worthy of socialism's teachings'. The circles were for many only 'a means of acquiring knowledge and a personal escape from the gloom in which the working masses lived'.[12]

Towards Agitation

The famine of 1891 led Plekhanov to try, however unsuccessfully, to begin a new chapter in the marxist movement: to move from circle work to mass agitation. In his pamphlet, *On the Tasks of Socialists during the Famine in Russia*, he argued that the marxists should conduct their educational work among the proletariat on two levels – 'propaganda' and 'agitation'. 'A sect', he explained, 'can be satisfied with propaganda in the narrow sense of the word: a political party never ... A propagandist gives *many* ideas to one or a few people, while an agitator gives only one or only a few ideas but to masses of people . . . Yet history is made by the masses.'[13]

In short, instead of restricting themselves to 'the organization of workers' socialist circles', the revolutionaries should try to move outwards and arouse mass discontent on the basis of political or 'economic' slogans, such as the demand for the eight-hour working day. Demands of this kind would attract all the workers towards the socialist movement. 'Thus all – even the most backward – workers will be clearly convinced that the carrying out of at least some socialist measures is of value to the working class . . . Such economic reforms as the shortening of the working day are good if only because they bring direct benefits to the workers.' It was the duty of the party 'to formulate economic demands suitable for the present moment'.[14]

Plekhanov's call found no echo among the Russian workers. However, there was a response from Jewish workers living in the western part of the Russian empire, in Poland. In general the socialist movement in Poland was far in advance of that in Russia. As the Soviet historian, S.N.Valk, put it: 'The socialist movement in Poland, from its inception, was a workers' movement as well as a mass movement, in sharp contrast to the Russian revolutionary socialist movement, in which the tone was set by the intelligentsia and by the circles.'[15] In May 1891 there was a wave of strikes in many Polish towns, which came to a climax the following year with a general strike in Lodz.

Even more successful in organizing agitation were Jewish socialists. In the regions of heavy Jewish population, strikes became very frequent, and reached a high point in 1895 in a textile industry strike in Bialystok, which involved as many as 15,000 workers. In fact Jewish workers were far ahead of Russian workers in terms of trade union organization. While as late as 1907 only seven per cent of the St Petersburg workers were organized in trade unions,[16] in 1900, 20 per cent of Jewish workers in Bialystok were organized in trade unions, 24 per cent in Vilna, 40 per cent in Gomel and 25-40 per cent in Minsk.[17]

It is therefore not surprising that Plekhanov's call for agitation among the workers was taken up first of all by the Jewish socialists who later organized themselves into the Jewish Bund. In 1894 A.Kremer, a leading member of the Jewish socialist organization, wrote a pamphlet, *Ob Agitatsii* (On Agitation) in collaboration with Martov. *Ob Agitatsii* sharply condemned the preoccupation of the members of marxist circles with their own 'self-perfection'. 'Precisely the worker Social Democrats for the most part support that very preoccupation (circle propaganda) which we condemn as useless.' Reviewing the accomplishments of *kruzhkovshchina*, the pamphlet argued that 'only the superior, more capable workers have thus obtained theoretical knowledge, which they associate in a very superficial way with real life and surrounding conditions . . . the workers' striving for knowledge, for escape from darkness, was exploited for the purpose of foisting on them the generalizations and tenets of scientific socialism.'[18]

The task was not to create worker intellectuals alienated from the working class, but to train agitators. The mass of the workers could not be educated to socialism through abstract intellectual activity. 'The broad masses are drawn into the struggle not by intellectual considerations but by the objective course of events.'[19]

> The [economic] struggle . . . teaches the worker to stand up for his own interests, it elevates his courage, it gives him confidence in his own strength and consciousness of the necessity for unity, it places before him more important tasks demanding solution. Prepared thus for a more serious struggle, the working class proceeds to come to grips with these vital questions. The class struggle in this more conscious form creates the soil for political agitation, the goal of which is to change the existing political conditions to the advantage of the working class. The further programme of Social Democracy becomes self-evident.[20]

> In order to get hold of that trifling issue capable of rallying the workers to the struggle, it is necessary to understand which abuses most easily excite the workers' interests, to choose the most auspicious moment to begin, to know what methods of struggle under the given conditions of time and

place are the most effective. Such knowledge demands that the agitator be in constant touch with the working masses, that he continually follow developments in a given branch of industry. In every factory there are countless abuses and the worker may be interested in the most trivial details; to discern just when to advance a given demand, to know ahead of time about possible complications – such is the real task of the agitator . . . knowledge of the conditions of life, knowledge of the feelings of the masses . . . will make him their natural leader.[21]

The role of socialists as leaders of the masses was defined thus:

The task of Social Democrats is one of constant agitation among factory workers on the basis of their everyday needs and demands . . . It is understood that the Social Democratic views of the agitator will determine the path along which he will lead the crowd. He must always be one step ahead of the masses, he must illuminate their struggle for them, explaining from a more general point of view the irreconcilability of their interests [with those of the employers] and thus he must expand the horizons of the masses.[22]

Ob Agitatsii had a mechanical theory of the relation between the industrial struggle, the struggle against the employers, and the political struggle against Tsarism, based on the concept of 'stages'. In later years this became the theoretical foundation for the development of 'economism', so harshly condemned by Lenin. Thus the pamphlet stated:

Abstaining for the time being from presenting the masses with wider tasks, Social Democracy was to leave it to the experience of the struggle itself to confront the workers no longer with individual employers but with the entire bourgeois class and the government power which stood behind it, and on the basis of this experience to widen and deepen its agitation.[23]

The initial reaction of the members of the circles to *Ob Agitatsii* was in many cases very hostile. Martov records that representatives of Social Democratic circles from Kiev and Kharkov visiting Vilna argued against adopting agitation. One of them argued that it would constitute an 'infraction of the system of strict conspiracy which it had taken years to build up, and upon which the whole edifice of circle propaganda depended'. Another objected that agitation 'only touched the surface of proletarian consciousness, whereas the real task of Social Democracy was to train a "class-conscious workers' vanguard", by which they understood "well-rounded, educated, worker-marxists".'[24] Akimov, an early chronicler of the movement, quoted a worker, a member of one of the marxist circles, as saying: 'Leaflets are a waste of time. What can you explain in a single leaflet? The worker should be given a book, not a leaflet. He must be taught. He must be drawn into a circle!'[25]

A comrade from Kiev related:

I went to see a woman worker and found her in tears. I asked what troubled her, and she said that some of her friends, former members of a workers' circle, had visited her and ridiculed her for presuming to preach without undergoing circle training herself: 'They seem to have turned you into a half-baked Social Democratic agitator, haven't they? You ought to do some studying yourself before you teach!'[26]

One worker, Abram Gordon, in a pamphlet called *Letter to the Intellectuals*, reminded the Social Democratic intellectuals of their duty to serve the workers rather than to use them as 'the cannon fodder of the revolution'. He denounced agitation as another attempt to keep the workers in semi-ignorance and to perpetuate their dependence on intellectual leaders of bourgeois origin.[27]

Criticizing this attitude, Akimov said that such workers

failed to understand the profound significance of this change of tactics. It seemed to them that by abandoning propaganda activity in workers' circles the *intelligenty* were giving up their cultural role, that they were seeking to exploit the unconscious elemental movement of the masses and regarded the workers as mere 'cannon fodder'. Indeed, the workers who belonged to the circles proved to be less democratic than the revolutionaries who were drawn from the intelligentsia. They felt superior to the masses and were irritated by the appearance of ignorant workers at the meetings. As a result entire trades, including the typesetters, who until now had set the pace, withdrew from the movement.[28]

Many worker members of the circles 'considered self-education, in the noblest sense of the word, the alpha and omega of the socialist movement, and they found unbearable the idea that, instead of devoting all the time to making themselves into "critically thinking personalities" they ought to pick persons with agitational talents and equip them with that minimum of knowledge necessary to influence the masses."[29]

Despite this strong opposition from inside the circles, agitation did take root and pushed aside the *kruzhkovshchina*. In April 1894, a copy of *Ob Agitatsii* reached Moscow, where it was hectographed and sent to other Social Democratic groups all over Russia. In 1896 it was printed abroad in Geneva by the Emancipation of Labour Group with a preface by Axelrod, and achieved a wide distribution.

Plekhanov Fails the Test

The transition to agitation failed to be made by a large proportion, possibly a majority, of worker members of the circles. But although it was Plekhanov who in 1891 first argued the need to move towards agitation, when it came to practice, he and his Emancipation of Labour Group were themselves found wanting.

As early as 1892, A.Voden, a literate young marxist from St Petersburg, visited Plekhanov to pass on a request from the Brusnev group for popular literature for workers. Plekhanov remarked caustically that obviously these young *praktiki* 'lacked the desire to learn to think like marxists', and it seemed to Voden that he spoke 'with vexation accumulated over a long period of time'.[30] There were no less than six such missions before 1895, all resulting in insoluble conflicts. Plekhanov's wife, Rosaliya Markovna, described his irritation with the 'uncouthness, crudeness, and presumptuousness . . . of these various provincial Lassalles' who in his words 'came to measure shoulders with us'.[31]

In 1897 Tuchapsky, a marxist from Kiev, was sent to Switzerland to ask Plekhanov and Axelrod to publish a series of popular propaganda pamphlets for Russian workers. The request was immediately rejected on the ground that they had no time for such tasks.[32]

It is true that a year earlier Plekhanov's group had agreed to publish a journal, *Listok Rabotnika* (The Workers' Supplement) to be devoted primarily to news of the labour movement and industrial unrest in Russia. Plekhanov himself, though, refused to be involved with it, and Vera Zasulich and Axelrod were clearly resentful at having to undertake the task. In a letter written late in 1896, Vera Zasulich complained that she 'began to revolt' when she set eyes on 'the hopeless incredible phrases' of the articles presented for *Listok Rabotnika*.[33] Axelrod wrote: 'Of course it is possible to publish such literary caricatures without me'.[34] Two years later he wrote to Plekhanov that he and Vera Zasulich were 'eager to escape having to edit illiterate and semi-literate publications'.[35]

The lack of enthusiasm for the publication of workers' popular literature ensured that well over half a year went by between the decision to publish and the first appearance of *Listok Rabotnika*, and that only one issue of the journal appeared between November 1896 and November 1897!

The gulf between the Emancipation of Labour Group's theoretical support for a turn to mass agitation and its unwillingness to carry this out in practice may be explained by the lack of immediate revolutionary prospects in the 80s and early 90s, the period during which the group was formed. Vera Zasulich frankly pointed out the gulf between the group and the newly rising agitators in Russia. She wrote to Plekhanov: 'Is it not clear to you that we cannot work with this kind of person in one organization? And not because he is bad! It is simply a difference in years, understanding, and mood.'[36] A few weeks later she wrote again:

Against us is practically the entire younger emigration in union with those elements of the students who have already acted or are getting ready to act seriously. They are full of energy, feel that Russia is behind them ... We cannot carry out the function of the Union, to create a worker literature ... We cannot publish a literature for the workers that would satisfy the demands of the Russians. And it seems to everyone that we are hampering those who can . . . They will not attain their ideal either, but they possess such an ideal and we do not. They are thirsting for activity of that kind but not under our direction.

I am for a simple avowal that we ourselves have not found the results of our editing of worker literature brilliant and that we give to our critics the opportunity to try their hand.[37]

Lenin as Factory Agitator

Lenin adapted himself perfectly to the needs of industrial agitation. Furthermore, whatever the official biographers may say, the truth is that in the years 1894-96 he did not denounce *Ob Agitatsii* as one-sided, mechanical and 'economist'. His writings of the period coincide exactly with the line which it put forward.

While in prison in 1895 he wrote a draft programme for the Social Democrats. This document was smuggled out of gaol, then lost and rediscovered only after the revolution. It is an interesting work, summing up very clearly Lenin's views on *Ob Agitatsii*. He wrote:

This transition of the workers to the steadfast struggle for their vital needs, the fight for concessions, for improved living conditions, wages and working hours, now begun all over Russia, means that Russian workers are making tremendous progress, and that is why the attention of the Social Democratic Party and all class-conscious workers should be concentrated *mainly* [my emphasis – T.C.] on this struggle, on its promotion.[38]

This economic struggle, Lenin argued, in the first place demonstrated to the worker the nature of economic exploitation; secondly, imbued him with a fighting spirit, and thirdly, developed his political consciousness. Class consciousness, including political consciousness, develops automatically from the economic struggle.

The workers' class consciousness means the workers understanding that the only way to improve their conditions and to achieve their emancipation is to conduct a struggle against the capitalist and factory-owner class created by the big factories. Further, the workers' class consciousness means their understanding that the interests of all the workers of any particular country are identical, that they all constitute one class, separate from all the other classes in society. Finally, it means the workers' understanding that to achieve their aims they have to work to influence the affairs of state, just as the landlords and the capitalists have done and continue to do.

> By what means do the workers reach an understanding of all this? They do so by constantly gaining experience from the very struggle that they begin to wage against the employers and that increasingly develops, becomes sharper, and involves larger numbers of workers as big factories grow.
> The living conditions of the mass of working folk place them in such a position that they do not (cannot) possess either the leisure or the opportunity to ponder over problems of state. On the other hand, the workers' struggle against the factory owners for their daily needs automatically and inevitably spurs the workers on to think of state, political questions, questions of how the Russian state is governed, how laws and regulations are issued, and whose interests they serve. Each clash in the factory necessarily brings the workers into conflict with the laws and representatives of state authority.[39]

Lenin pursued this line of thought consistently in the agitational leaflets and pamphlets which he wrote during 1894-96. Step by step the reader was led to political conclusions which were not, however, explicitly stated. Thus, for instance, the conclusion of the pamphlet *Explanation of the Law on Fines imposed on Factory Workers*, written in prison in 1895, stated that the workers

> will understand that the government and its officials are on the side of the factory owners, and that the laws are drawn up in such a way as to make it easier for the employer to oppress the worker . . . Once they have understood this, the workers will see that only one means remains for defending themselves, namely, to join forces for the struggle against the factory owners and the unjust practices established by the law.[40]

At that time the tone of his demands was in quite a low

key. Thus, for instance, his leaflet *The Working Man and Woman of the Thornton Factory* concentrated exclusively on economic issues, and made no allusion to politics. It ended with very moderate language: 'In defending these demands, comrades, we are not rebelling at all; we are merely demanding that we be given what all the workers of other factories now enjoy by law, the return of what has been taken from us by those who placed all their hopes on our inability to uphold our own right.'[41]

In November 1895, in an article called 'What are our Ministers Thinking About?' Lenin urged the expediency of leaving the Tsar out of the argument, and talking instead about the new laws that favoured employers and of cabinet ministers who were anti-working class. The monarch was still 'The Little Father' to the workers and peasants, and Lenin's sister Anna quotes him as saying: 'Of course, if you start right away talking against the Tsar and the existing social system you only antagonize the workers.'[42]

Late in 1894 Lenin and G.M.Krzhizhanovsky met Greshin-Kopelzon, Nikitin-Sponti, and Liakhovsky, who were then working in the marxist groups of Vilna, Moscow and Kiev respectively, but who all had first-hand experience of the Vilna strike movement. The meeting accepted the basic thesis of *Ob Agitatsii*. Following this meeting, in 1895, Lenin, Martov, Krzhizhanovsky and others founded the St Petersburg League of Struggle for the Emancipation of the Working Class. The League was made up of about two dozen intellectuals and workers and played a crucial role in getting Social Democratic agitation started among the working class of St Petersburg. From its foundation marxism never ceased to be associated with the workers of St Petersburg. Martov and Lenin were the acknowledged leaders of the League, and its main activity was the issuing of factory leaflets. In preparing these, Lenin was greatly aided by Nadezhda Konstantinovna Krupskaya, the young woman he met in 1894 and married a few years later.

In 1890 Krupskaya had joined the marxist circle of Brunev and for five years (1891-96) taught at what was called 'Evening Sunday-School' in the industrial suburbs of St Petersburg. On Sundays and two nights a week, she taught workers arithmetic, history and Russian literature, from a level of illiteracy to quite an advanced stage. The school provided contact with serious workers, which was the attraction for the young Krupskaya and the other marxist teachers in the same school. There were Alexandra Kalmykova, a well-to-do woman publisher and owner of a popular bookshop that in later years financed Lenin's first émigré newspaper *Iskra*, Lydia Knipovich, who was destined to serve as one of the underground agents of the same paper, and also Elena Stasova, who in 1917 was to replace Krupskaya as party secretary. The marxist teachers in the school founded an underground circle to coordinate their activities.

> The workers displayed unlimited confidence in the 'school mistresses'. Thus the gloomy watchman from the Gromov timberyards, with face beaming, told the teacher that he had been presented with a son; a consumptive textile-worker wanted her to teach her enterprising suitor to read and write; a Methodist workman who had spent his whole life seeking God wrote with satisfaction that only on Passion Sunday had he learned from Rudakov (another pupil) that there was no God at all.[43]

The school served as a source of recruitment for revolutionary workers.

> Workers belonging to our organization went to the school in order to observe the people and note who could be brought into the circles or drawn into the movement. These workers did not regard all the women teachers in the same light. They distinguished to what extent the teachers were versed in the work of our circles. If they recognized a schoolmistress to be 'one of us', they would make themselves known to her by some phrase or other.[44]

Krupskaya talked easily to worker-students at the school and played a central role both in gathering information about factory conditions for use in the League's leaflets and in organizing the distribution of the leaflets in the factories.

To elicit the necessary information for their leaflets, the

League began to distribute questionnaires to individual workers, with whom contact had been made through the teachers. Fitter Ivan Babushkin reported, 'We received lists with prepared questions, which demanded from us a careful observation of factory life . . . My tool box was constantly packed tight with the most varied notices, and I exerted myself to write down unobserved the amount of the daily wages in our workshop.'[45]

And Lenin writes:

> I vividly recall my 'first experiment' which I would never like to repeat. I spent many weeks 'examining' a worker, who would often visit me, regarding every aspect of the conditions prevailing in the enormous factory at which he was employed. True, after great effort, I managed to obtain material for a description (of the one single factory!), but at the end of the interview the worker would wipe the sweat from his brow, and say to me smilingly: 'I find it easier to work overtime than to answer your questions.'[46]

The information obtained in this way was edited and written up in the form of leaflets for the workers of the individual plants. The leaflets dealt with concrete issues that all the workers understood.

Lenin spent months studying labour legislation, so that he could explain clearly the relevant laws and practices prevailing in the factories, and formulate the demands about which workers should complain to management. Krupskaya wrote:

> Vladimir Ilyich was interested in the minutest detail describing the conditions and life of the workers. Taking the features separately he endeavoured to grasp the life of the worker as a whole – he tried to find what one could seize upon in order better to approach the worker with revolutionary propaganda. Most of the intellectuals of those days badly understood the workers. An intellectual would come to a circle and read the workers a kind of lecture.[47]
> I remember for example, how the material about the Thornton factory was collected. It was decided that I should send for a pupil of mine named Krolikov, a sorter in that factory, who had previously been deported from Petersburg. I was to collect from him all information according to a plan drawn

up by Vladimir Ilyich. Krolikov arrived in a fine fur coat he had borrowed from someone and brought a whole exercise-book full of information, which he further supplemented verbally. This data was very valuable. In fact Vladimir Ilyich fairly pounced on it. Afterwards I and Apollinaria Alexandrovna Yakubova put kerchiefs on our heads and made ourselves look like women factory-workers, and went personally to the Thornton factory-barracks, visiting both the single and married quarter. Conditions were most appalling. It was solely on the basis of material gathered in this manner that Vladimir Ilyich wrote his letters and leaflets. Examine his leaflets addressed to the working men and women of the Thornton factory. The detailed knowledge of the subject they deal with is at once apparent. And what a schooling this was for all the comrades working then! It was just then that we were learning attention to details. And how profoundly these details were engraved in our minds.[48]

What agitation looked like in practice at that time may be gathered from recollections of Krupskaya concerning the fate of one of the leaflets Lenin wrote: 'I remember that Vladimir Ilyich drew up the first leaflet for the workers of the Semyannikov works. We had no technical facilities at all then. The leaflet was copied out by hand in printed letters and distributed by Babushkin. Out of the four copies two were picked up by the watchman, while two went round from hand to hand.'[49]

The immediate effect of the industrial agitation carried out by the St Petersburg League – Lenin, Martov and their friends – was quite small. One historian described it thus:

Lenin's proclamation [to Thornton workers] was issued on the group's mimeograph on November 10, 1895, but on the same day the weavers went back to work without having gained concessions from the management. The *stariki* [veterans – Lenin, Martov, etc. – T.C.] thus failed in their first effort to fan the flames of industrial discontent.

While the Thornton strike was still in progress, a spontaneous strike also broke out at the Leferm tobacco factory (November 9), and four days later another occurred at the shoe factory Skorokhod. In both cases, on the basis of materials supplied by workers from the striking factories through the Central Worker Group, the *stariki* prepared proclamations defining the demands of the strikers. In neither case did they exert any influence on the course of events, for both strikes were short-lived and ended without any concessions being made to the workers. But the efforts did help to spread word of the illegal organization.

The only strike which the *stariki* succeeded in stimulating before the police closed in on them took place in one section of the Putilov Works. Zinoviev, a worker at Putilov and one of its representatives in the Central Group, wrote a proclamation to workers in the steam-engine division, urging them to strike. His proclamation was mimeographed by Martov and led to a one-day work stoppage on December 5. An appeal by Martov to the spinners of the Kenig factory issued at the same time seems to have produced no result.

In terms of actual achievement, the result of the appeals and proclamations issued by the *stariki* in November and early December was virtually nil.[50]

Lenin and five other members of the League were arrested in December 1895, and several more, including Martov, early in the new year. But the struggle did not prove fruitless. A few months later the first mass strike in Russia proper took place under the banner of Social Democracy. This was a strike of textile workers in May 1896 in St Petersburg. The members of the League, or rather those of its members who survived arrest, played a central role in the massive strike. It began as a protest against the non-payment of wages for the three-day holiday celebrating the coronation of Nikolai II. But it soon developed into a struggle for shorter hours and higher wages and spread to twenty of the biggest factories in Russia, employing 30,000 workers. The workers carried on the fight for the 10½-hour working day for three weeks, and when they finally decided to return to work, they did so as one man in all factories at the same time. This was not only the biggest strike in Russia. It was also the first to go beyond the bounds of a single industrial plant. And the St Petersburg League played a central part in it. For the first time in the long history of the revolutionary movement in Russia, the revolutionaries had drawn the masses into action. Social Democracy became a significant movement.

How far Russia had moved since the end of 1895 may

be gauged by reading a confidential circular from the Minister of Finance to the Factory Inspectorate of that time : 'Fortunately Russia does not possess a working class in the same sense as the West does; consequently we have no labour problem; nor will either of these find in Russia a soil to produce them'![51]

Defeat in Victory

The success of the movement, however, led to a grave internal crisis. The Social Democratic movement began to divide into 'economist' and 'political' currents. The correction of the one-sidedness of the *kruzhkovshchina* – an excess of emphasis on theory – led to its equally one-sided opposite, 'economism'. This danger was already inherent in Ob Agitatsii, as Lenin and others noted with hindsight in 1898. One must bear in mind the conclusion reached by Ob Agitatsii :

> That the task of the Social-Democrats consists of constant agitation among the factory workers on the basis of existing petty needs and demands. The struggle provoked by this agitation will train the workers to defend their own interests, heighten their courage, give them confidence in their own powers and an awareness of the necessity for union, and in the final analysis ultimately confront them with more important questions demanding a solution. Prepared in this way for a more serious struggle, the working class will move on to the solution of its most basic questions.

This formula opened the door to the theory of stages characteristic of the future 'economists'. Socialists should limit their agitation to purely economic issues, first to the industrial plant, then to inter-plant demands, and so on. Secondly, from the narrow economic agitation the workers would learn, through experience of the struggle itself, the need for politics, without the need for socialists to carry out agitation on the general political and social issues facing the Russian people as a whole. The arrest of Lenin, Martov and others accelerated the move towards 'economism' in the St Petersburg League. The new comrades who joined the group had less theoretical training.

'Everything went in agitation', Krupskaya wrote. 'There

was not time even to think of propaganda . . . The weavers'
strike of 1896 took place under Social Democratic influence.
This turned the heads of many comrades. The basis arose for
the growth of "economism".[52]

In the political testament of F.I.Dan, the veteran Menshevik leader, written some fifty years later, the rise of the
'economist' trend in Social Democracy was explained thus:

> In responding sympathetically to the political notes that
> rang out in the economic agitation of the League, tens of
> thousands of workers, drawn into an active organizational
> struggle for the first time, nevertheless accepted political
> emancipation merely as a remote 'ultimate' goal of their
> movement. For them the 'immediate' practical objective
> was those economic demands in whose name they were
> ready to risk striking and a possible loss of wages. In this
> respect the temper of the new layer of advanced workers,
> the new 'workers' intelligentsia' that was beginning to take
> shape in the fire of the mass struggle, fundamentally
> diverged from the temper not only of the marxist intelli-
> gentsia but also of the first generation of Social Democratic
> workers, which had come to Social Democracy not by the
> 'practical' way of economic struggle but by the 'ideological'
> way of propaganda in small groups.[53]

A historian of this period of Russian Social Democracy
put the 'economists' into correct perspective when he said:

> The roots of Economism are best sought in the agitational
> method of Social Democratic work. The socialists who had
> devised this method acknowledged the indifference of labour
> to politics and proposed to overcome it by demonstrating
> the allegedly indissoluble link between economic interests
> and the country's political order. Whereas in theory agita-
> tion was political, in practice it remained confined to eco-
> nomics. From agitation, which pushed politics into the
> background as a matter of tactical expedience, it was only
> one step to Economism proper, which subordinated politics
> to economics as a matter of principle. Economism thus
> came into being in Russia in 1896-97, in the wake of the
> emerging mass labour movement.[54]

To add to the impact of 'economism' and the threat to
socialism involved in it, there are two other factors affecting

the Russian labour movement at that time. One was the labour policy of the Tsarist secret police. The other was the rise of the powerful current of revisionism, led by Eduard Bernstein, in the German Social Democratic Party, which was by far the most important socialist party in the world.

The secret police fancied the idea of 'economism' as a reaction to the rising industrial struggle in Russia. General Trepov, head of the secret police, wrote in 1898 :

> If the minor needs and demands of the workers are exploited by the revolutionaries for such profound anti-governmental aims, then is it not up to the government as soon as possible to seize this weapon, that is so rewarding for the revolutionaries, from their hands and itself to assure the fulfilment of the task . . . the police are obliged to be interested in the same thing as the revolutionary.

Following this logic, as we shall see later, Colonel Zubatov, head of the Moscow Security Police, organized police-controlled trade unions, first among Jewish workers, where 'economist' agitation was most successful, and then among the Russians, an enterprise culminating in Father Gapon's organization of trade unions in St Petersburg, which led to 'Bloody Sunday' and the beginning of the 1905 revolution.

The second factor bolstering 'economism' – German revisionism – was heralded by the publication in January 1899 of Eduard Bernstein's *The Premises of Socialism and the Tasks of Social Democracy*. The central idea of this book was that of gradualism, of stages in reforming capitalism, culminating in its transformation into socialism. The party's influence, he wrote, 'would be far greater than it is today, if Social Democracy could find the courage to free itself from outmoded phraseology and strive to appear as what in fact it now is, a Democratic Socialist party of reform.' 'What is generally referred to as the ultimate aim of socialism means nothing to me; it is the movement itself which means everything.' This coincided perfectly with the ideas of the Russian 'economists'. For them too 'the movement', in the sense of securing small concrete improvements in the economic conditions of workers, was all-important. Thus the whole political aim of the movement – above all the overthrow of Tsarism – dropped out of sight.

The link between 'economism' and Bernstein's revisionism was given concrete expression in a document called the *Credo* (1899). Its author was Y.D.Kuskova, at the time a member of the Union of Russian Social Democrats Abroad. It declared forthrightly that Bernstein's revisionism was its theoretical base. The general law of working-class activity, it declared, should be to follow 'the line of least resistance'. 'In Russia the line of least resistance will never tend towards political activity. The incredible oppression will prompt much talk about it, and cause attention to be concentrated precisely on this question, but will never prompt political action.' The 'line of least resistance in Russia' was economic action against the employers and an attempt to organize trade unions.

> The economic struggle too is hard, infinitely hard, but it is possible to wage it, and it is in fact being waged by the masses themselves. By learning in this struggle to organize, and coming into constant conflict with the political regime in the course of it, the Russian worker will at last create what may be called a form of labour movement, the organization or organizations best conforming to Russian conditions. At the present, it can be said with certainty that the Russian working-class movement is still in the amoeba state and has not yet acquired any form. The strike movement, which goes on with any form of organization, cannot yet be described as the crystallized form of the Russian movement, while the illegal organizations are not worth consideration even from the mere quantitative point of view (quite apart from the question of their usefulness under present conditions).
>
> . . . well, what is there for the Russian marxist to do? The talk about an independent workers' political party merely results from the transplantation of alien aims and alien achievements to our soil . . .
>
> For the Russian marxist there is only one course : participation in, i.e. assistance to, the economic struggle of the proletariat, and participation in liberal opposition activity.[55]

Thus, the duty of socialists was to support the workers

in the effort to build trade unions, and the liberal bourgeoisie in the political struggle.

When Lenin, in exile in Siberia, received a copy of the *Credo*, he hastened to write a reply, *A Protest by Russian Social Democrats* (August 1899). The draft was discussed at a meeting of seventeen marxists in exile in Minusinsk region, and adopted by them. It made Lenin quite widely known in Social Democratic circles and accomplished its purpose well. As Martov said years later, it rallied the hundreds of exiles scattered all over Siberia to revolutionary marxism.[56]

The years 1883-99 had witnessed the erratic development of the Russian marxists from a propaganda sect isolated from the working class, to an agitational organization restricting itself to the immediate day-to-day struggle of the workers, from pure theory to narrow practice. Lenin's sharp rebuke to the *Credo* made it clear that a synthesis of theory and practice was necessary.

> The notorious Bernsteinism – in the sense in which it is commonly understood by the general public, and by the authors of the *Credo* in particular – is an attempt to narrow the theory of marxism, to convert the revolutionary workers' party into a reformist party.
> On the one hand, the working-class movement is being sundered from socialism, the workers are being helped to carry on the economic struggle, but nothing, or next to nothing, is done to explain to them the socialist aims and the political tasks of the movement as a whole. On the other hand, socialism is being sundered from the labour movement; Russian socialists are again beginning to talk more and more about the struggle against the government having to be carried on entirely by the intelligentsia because the workers confine themselves to the economic struggle.[57]

Against this, Lenin posed the synthesis of the economic and political struggles of the working class as seen by marxists.

> For the socialist, the economic struggle serves as a basis for the organization of the workers into a revolutionary party, for the strengthening and development of their class struggle against the whole capitalist system. If the economic struggle is taken as something complete in itself there will be nothing

socialist in it . . . It is the task of the bourgeois politician 'to assist the economic struggle of the proletariat'; the task of the socialist is to bring the economic struggle to further the socialist movement and the successes of the revolutionary working-class party. The task of the socialist is to further the indissoluble fusion of the economic and political struggle into the single class struggle of the socialist working-class masses.

Agitational activity among the masses must be of the broadest nature, both economic and political, on all possible issues and in regard to all manifestations of oppression whatever their form. We must utilize this agitation to attract growing numbers of workers into the ranks of the revolutionary Social Democratic party, to encourage the political struggle in all conceivable manifestations, to organize this struggle and transform it from its spontaneous forms into the struggle of a single political party. Agitation, therefore, must serve as *a means* of widely expanding the political protest and the more organized forms of political struggle. Today our agitation is too hemmed in; the range of questions it touches upon is too limited. It is our duty therefore not to legitimize this narrowness but to try to liberate ourselves from it, to deepen and expand our agitational work.[58]

Lenin points out that the historical roots of reformism lie in the one-sidedness both of the *kruzhkovshchina* and of the reaction to it. 'In their early activity, Russian Social Democrats restricted themselves merely to work in propaganda circles. When we took up agitation among the masses we were not always able to restrain ourselves from going to the other extreme.'[59] He goes on to point out that a certain organizational narrowness, which characterized both the *kruzhkovshchina* stage and the industrial agitation stage, also fostered 'economism':

working in the isolation of small local workers' circles, the Social Democrats did not devote sufficient attention to the necessity of organizing a revolutionary party which would combine all the activities of the local groups and make it possible to organize the revolutionary work on correct lines. The predominance of isolated work is naturally connected with the predominance of the economic struggle.[60]

The conflict between the orthodox marxists, like Lenin

and Martov, and the 'economists' also took on an organizational form, which anticipated the debate on organization between Bolsheviks and Mensheviks. At this point, however, the protagonists of the two future tendencies, Lenin and Martov, were on the same side in the argument.

After the successful strike in St Petersburg in 1896, many newly recruited members of the movement, workers and intellectuals alike, demanded to shift the organization from being in its core of professional revolutionaries. The 'economists' explained that the political and highly conspiratorial character of the League resulted from the priority given by the intellectuals to political activity and their lack of understanding of the real needs of the mass of the workers. In mainly agitational economic activity the need for conspiracy and centralism would be much less. An 'economist' organization would be local in character, concerned with problems facing workers in a single factory, or at most a number of factories in one locality, and the loose local factory and area workers' organization would suffice. Centralism versus parochialism was the organizational reflection of the split between the political revolutionaries and the 'economists'. The professional revolutionary, in the 'economists'' scheme, would be relegated and replaced by workers who did not have to leave their place of work and their normal local habitat.

Many of the members of the circles, as we have seen, did not make the transition to industrial agitation. But of those who did, very few fell into 'economism'. It was the new activists who emerged in the industrial struggle itself, culminating in the textile strike of 1896, who were the main ones to succumb. The testimony of the Menshevik leader Dan, writing some fifty years after the events, relates this to the later development of Bolshevism and Menshevism:

> It is worth noting that later on almost all the most eminent of the working-class Social Democrats of this 'first call-up' who lived to see the 1905 and 1917 revolutions (Babushkin, Shelgunov, Shapoval, Poletayev and others) turned up in the ranks of the Bolsheviks, while out of the ranks of the 'worker

intelligentsia', baptized in the strike movement of the second half of the 90s, there emerged those future cadres of the legal and semi-legal trade unions, co-operative, cultural enlightenment, etc., workers' movement that for a long time were the chief support of Menshevism.[61]

Bending the Stick

The years 1894-96 were important for Lenin's development into a workers' leader. To quote Krupskaya:

This Petersburg period of Vladimir Ilyich's work was one of extreme importance, although the work was unobserved and not apparent in substance. He himself so described it. There were no external effects. We were not concerned with heroic moves, but with how to establish close contact with the masses, to become intimate with them, to learn to be the expression of their best aspirations, to learn how to make them understand us and follow our lead. But it was precisely during this period of work in St Petersburg that Vladimir Ilyich became moulded as leader of the working masses.[62]

Despite the one-sidedness of the factory agitation at the time, Lenin always valued this period as a very important and necessary stage in the development of Russian Social Democracy. He was ready to admit both its progressive role and the dangers inherent in it. Thus in a letter he wrote on 9 November 1900 to Plekhanov, he said:

The economic *trend*, of course, was always a mistake, but then it is very young; while there has been *overemphasis* of 'economic' agitation (*and there still is here and there*) even without the trend, and it was the legitimate and inevitable companion of *any step forward* in the conditions of our movement which *existed in Russia* at the end of the 1880s or the beginning of the 1890s. The situation then was so murderous that you cannot probably even imagine it, and one should not censure people who stumbled as they clambered up out of that situation. For the purposes of this clambering out, some narrowness was essential and legitimate: *was*, I say, for with this tendency to blow it up into a theory and tie it in with Bernsteinism, the whole thing of course changed radically . . . the overemphasis of 'economic' agitation and catering to the 'mass' movement were natural.[63]

This readiness to bend the stick too far in one direction,

and then to go into reverse and bend it too far in the opposite direction was a characteristic that he retained throughout his life. It was already clearly apparent at this early stage of his development as a revolutionary leader.

At every stage of the struggle Lenin would look for what he regarded as the key link in the chain of development. He would then repeatedly emphasize the importance of this link, to which all others must be subordinated. After the event, he would say: 'We overdid it. We bent the stick too far', by which he did not mean that he had been wrong to do so. To win the main battle of the day, the concentration of all energies on the task was necessary.

The uneven development of different aspects of the struggle made it necessary always to look for the key link in every concrete situation. When this was the need for study, for laying the foundations of the first marxist circles, Lenin stressed the central role of study. In the next stage, when the need was to overcome circle mentality, he would repeat again and again the importance of industrial agitation. At the next turn of the struggle, when 'economism' needed to be smashed, Lenin did this with a vengeance. He always made the task of the day quite clear, repeating what was necessary *ad infinitum* in the plainest, heaviest, most single-minded hammer-blow pronouncements. Afterwards he would regain his balance, straighten the stick, then bend it again in another direction. If this method has advantages in overcoming current obstacles, it also contains hazards for anyone wanting to use Lenin's writing on tactical and organizational questions as a source for quotation. Authority by quotation is nowhere less justified than in the case of Lenin. If he is cited on any tactical or organizational question, the concrete issues which the movement was facing at the time must be made absolutely clear.

Another of Lenin's characteristics already apparent at this early stage of his development is an attitude to organizational forms as always historically determined. He never adopted abstract, dogmatic schemes of organization, and was ready to change the organizational structure of the party at every new development of the class struggle. Organization, he was convinced, should be subordinated to politics. This, however, did not mean that it had no *independent* influence on politics. There was a reciprocal relation between them. In certain situations, organization might even be granted priority.

3
Towards the Building of the Party

'Give us an organization of revolutionaries, and we will overturn Russia.'[1]

In March 1898 a 'Congress' of the Social Democrats took place at Minsk. It was a tiny affair, with only nine delegates, from Petersburg, Moscow, Kiev, the journal *Rabochaya Gazeta* and the Jewish socialist organization, the Bund. It failed to adopt a programme or a paper. Its only achievements were the issue of a manifesto, drafted by Peter Struve (an 'economist' who later became a liberal leader and then a monarchist), the promulgation of the idea of a nationwide party, and the election of a Central Committee of three. Eight of the nine delegates and two of the three Central Committee members were arrested a few days after the end of the conference.*

---

* The organizational concept of this first Congress was federalist and loose. One article stipulated that the Central Committee should not decide any questions that could be deferred to the next Congress, and that only the most urgent questions were to be resolved by the Central Committee on its own authority. Even in this case, the decision of the CC had to be unanimous.[2]

At that time Lenin was in Siberia. The failure of the 1898 Congress convinced him that the building of a national party to lead Russian Social Democracy out of its crisis demanded serious and systematic preparation. Months of thought during his last period of Siberian exile produced a plan in his mind for a national newspaper, and a chain of agents to smuggle it across the border and distribute it in cities and factories. The paper would act as a means of fusing the local circles into a national organization. It would clarify and unify in the fields of both theory and practical activity.

Krupskaya recalled this period: 'Vladimir Ilyich began to spend sleepless nights. He became terribly thin. It was these nights that he thought out his plan in every detail, discussed it with Krzhizhanovsky, with me, corresponded about it with Martov and Potresov, conferred with them about the journey abroad.'[3]

The Need to Generalize the Struggle

It was fear of the danger to the movement occasioned by the rise of Russian 'economism' and German revisionism in the second half of 1899 that motivated Lenin to bend the stick right over again, away from the spontaneous, day-to-day fragmented economic struggle and towards the organization of a national political party. In an article entitled 'Our Immediate Tasks', written towards the end of 1899, he wrote:

> When the workers of a single factory or of a single branch of industry engage in struggle against their employer or employers, is this class struggle? No, this is only a weak embryo of it. The struggle of the workers becomes a class struggle only when all the foremost representatives of the entire working class of the whole country are conscious of themselves as a single working class and launch a struggle that is directed, not against individual employers, but against the *entire class* of capitalists and against the government that supports that class ... It is the task of the Social Democrats, by organizing the workers, by conducting propaganda and agitation among them, to *turn* their spontaneous struggle against their oppressors into the struggle of the whole class,

into the struggle of a definite political *party* for definite political and socialist ideals. This is something that cannot be achieved by local activity alone.[4]

The narrow, economistic concept of organization had therefore to be overcome.

Our chief drawback, to the overcoming of which we must devote all our energy, is the narrow 'amateurish' character of local work. Because of this amateurish character many manifestations of the working-class movement in Russia remain purely local events and lose a great deal of their significance as examples for the whole of Russian Social Democracy, as a stage of the whole Russian working-class movement.[5]

The conclusions are clear:

The seeds of Social Democratic ideas have been broadcast throughout Russia; workers' leaflets – the earliest form of Social Democratic literature – are known to all Russian workers from St Petersburg to Kranoyarsk, from the Caucasus to the Urals. All that is now lacking is the unification of all this local work into the work of a single *party* . . . Enough of our amateurishness! We have attained sufficient maturity to go over to *common action*, to the elaboration of a common party programme, to the joint discussion of our party tactics and organization.[6]

In order to achieve the unification of the socialists, the *central* task was to establish a journal for the whole of Russia.

we must have as our immediate aim, *the founding of a party organ that will appear regularly and be closely connected with all the local groups.*
We believe that *all* the activity of the Social Democrats should be directed to this end throughout the whole of the forthcoming period. Without such an organ, local work will remain narrowly 'amateurish'. The formation of the party – if the correct representation of that party in a certain newspaper is not organized – will to a considerable extent remain bare words. An economic struggle that is not united by a central organ cannot become the *class* struggle of the entire Russian proletariat. It is impossible to conduct a political struggle if the party as a whole fails to make statements on all questions of policy and to give direction to the various manifestations of the struggle. The organization and disci-

plining of the revolutionary forces and the development of revolutionary technique are impossible without the discussion of all these questions in a central organ, without the collective elaboration of certain *forms and rules for the conduct of affairs*, without the establishment – through the central organ – of every party member's *responsibility* to the entire party.[7]

In another article, written at the same time and called 'An Urgent Question', Lenin argued that the unification of the marxists into a national party would make it possible to develop a division of labour in the movement and thus raise efficiency.

It is essential for individual party members or separate groups of members to specialize in the different aspects of party work – some in the duplication of literature, others in its transport across the frontier, a third category in its distribution inside Russia, a fourth in its distribution in the cities, a fifth in the arrangement of secret meeting places, a sixth in the collection of funds, a seventh in the delivery of correspondence and all information about the movement, an eighth in maintaining relations etc. etc. We know that this sort of specialization requires much greater self-restraint, much greater ability to concentrate on modest, unseen, everyday work, much greater real heroism than the usual work in study circles.[8]

Lenin's plan envisaged the creation of two papers: a bi-monthly theoretical journal (the future *Zarya*) and a more widely distributed fortnightly (*Iskra*), which would undertake the organizational and ideological consolidation of the movement.

How 'Iskra' Was Nearly Extinguished

While he was in Siberia Lenin corresponded with two other exiles, Martov and Potresov, who basically agreed with him about the plan for a national paper and organization. They carried on a lengthy correspondence about the future paper: who should write for it; when it should be printed; how it would be smuggled into the cities; what its position would be on a number of questions. The three were very close, being of much the same age (Potresov a year older, Martov three years younger than Lenin), their terms of exile ending at more or less the same time, and all of them going abroad in pursuance of the plan to launch the paper – they were so close, in fact, that Lenin called them 'the triple alliance'.

All three also looked up to Plekhanov as their master. However, Lenin's meeting in August 1900 with the 'Father of Russian marxism' was a disastrous shock. The incident is well worth relating, as it throws quite an interesting light on his emotional nature, which he was to suppress for decades to come. It is also important as a forewarning of the future break between Lenin and the old masters, that generation of pioneers of Russian marxism, Plekhanov, Axelrod and Zasulich.

The meeting is described in a long confidential report (taking up some 18 pages in the *Collected Works*). It was intended for the eyes only of Krupskaya, Martov and a few close adherents and was called 'How the "Spark" was nearly Extinguished' (a pun on the title of the newspaper *Iskra*, which means 'Spark').

When they met, Plekhanov

> was suspicious, distrustful, and *rechthaberisch* to the *nec plus ultra* (holding himself to be right to the *n*th degree). I tried to observe caution and avoided all 'sore' points, but the constant restraint that I had to place on myself could not but greatly affect my mood ... There was also 'friction' over questions concerning the tactics of the magazine, Plekhanov throughout displaying complete intolerance, an inability or an unwillingness to understand other people's arguments, and, to employ the correct term, insincerity.[9]

Plekhanov had also acted in an insensitive and incorrect manner towards Struve during the emergence of his 'economism'. This he was not prepared to admit. Lenin says:

> We declared that we must make *every possible* allowance for Struve, that *we ourselves* bore some guilt for his development, since we, *including Plekhanov*, had failed to protest when protest was necessary (1895, 1897). Plekhanov abso-

lutely refused to admit even the slightest guilt, employing transparently worthless arguments by which he *dodged* the issue without clarifying it. This diplomacy in the course of comradely conversations between future co-editors was extremely unpleasant. Why the self-deception with the pretence that he, Plekhanov, had in 1895 been 'ordered (??) not to shoot' (at Struve) and that he was accustomed to doing as he was ordered (really!)? Why the self-deception with the assertion that in 1897 (when Struve wrote in *Novoye Slovo* that his object was to refute one of the fundamental theses of Marxism) he had not opposed it, because he never could (and never would) conceive of polemics between collaborators in one and the same magazine? This insincerity was extremely irritating.[10]

Lenin, on the other hand, while arguing that the proposed paper ought to be the unswerving champion of revolutionary marxism, was in favour of opening it up to polemics with liberals, 'economists' and revisionists. He prepared the draft of an editorial board declaration, in which he explained

> the aims and the programme of the publications. This was written in an 'opportunist' spirit (from Plekhanov's point of view) – polemics between members of the staff were to be permitted, the tone was modest, allowance was made for the possibility of a peaceful ending of the controversy with the 'economists', etc. The declaration laid stress on our belonging to the party and on our desire to work for its unification.[11]

He favoured inviting Struve and Tugan-Baranovsky to write for the journals. But Plekhanov, opposing the admission of contrary views altogether, displayed an animosity towards 'allies' which 'bordered on the indecent (suspecting them of espionage, accusing them of being swindlers and rogues, and asserting that he would not hesitate to "shoot" such "traitors", etc.)'.[12]

A few days later Plekhanov, Axelrod and Zasulich met Lenin and Potresov to try and negotiate an agreement between the two generations. The strained relations flared into open conflict. 'Plekhanov's desire to have unlimited power was obvious', but he started off 'diplomatically':

> he stated that it would be better if he were a contributor, an

ordinary contributor, for otherwise there would be continual friction, that evidently his views on things differed from ours, that he understood and respected our party, point of view, but he could not share it. Better therefore, that we be the editors and he a contributor. We were amazed to hear this, positively amazed, and began to argue against the idea.

When Lenin and his associates insisted that Plekhanov be on the editorial board, the latter asked pointedly how the voting would go with an even number of six editors (Plekhanov, Axelrod and Zasulich from among the veterans, and Lenin, Martov and Potresov from the younger generation). Vera Zasulich then moved that Plekhanov be given two votes, while all the others had one vote each.

Upon that Plekhanov took the reins of management in his hands and with the air of editor-in-chief began apportioning departments among those present and assigning articles to this one and that in a tone that brooked no objection. We sat there as if we had been ducked; mechanically we agreed to everything, unable as yet to comprehend what had taken place. We realized that we had been made fools of.[13]

My 'infatuation' with Plekhanov disappeared as if by magic, and I felt offended and embittered to an unbelievable degree. Never, never in my life, had I regarded any other man with such sincere respect and veneration, never had I stood before any man so 'humbly' and never before had I been so brutally 'kicked'. That's what it was, we had actually been kicked.[14]

It is with deep bitterness that Lenin describes his and Potresov's reaction to Plekhanov's authoritarian behaviour:

our indignation knew no bounds. Our ideal had been destroyed; gloatingly we trampled it underfoot like a dethroned god. There was no end to the charges we hurled against him. It cannot go on like this, we decided. We do not wish, we will not, we *cannot* work together with him under such conditions. Good-bye magazine! We will throw everything up and return to Russia, where we will start all over again, right from the very beginning, and confine ourselves to the newspaper. We refuse to be pawns in the hands of that man; he does not understand, and cannot maintain comradely relations. We did not dare undertake the editorship *ourselves*; besides, it would be positively repulsive to do so now, for it would appear as though we really coveted the editor's post, that we really were *Streber*, careerists, and that we too were inspired by motives of vanity, though in a smaller way ... It is difficult to describe adequately what our feelings were that night – such mixed, heavy, confused feelings.

And all because we had formerly been infatuated with Plekhanov. Had we not been so infatuated, had we regarded him more dispassionately, more level-headedly, had we studied him more objectively, our conduct towards him would have been different and we would not have suffered such disaster, in the literal sense of the word ... We had received the most bitter lesson of our lives, a painfully bitter, painfully brutal lesson. Young comrades 'court' an elder comrade out of the great love they bear for him – and suddenly he injects into this love an atmosphere of intrigue ... An enamoured youth receives from the object of his love a bitter lesson – to regard all persons 'without sentiment', to keep a stone in one's sling. Many more words of an equally bitter nature did we utter that night.[15]

The incident illustrates the contempt which Lenin was to retain throughout his life towards any pecking order in the movement, and overbearing attitude in its leaders, any dishonest covering-up of the leaders' own past mistakes. It shows him flexing his muscles for the first time, to become a leader in his own right. It taught him never to mix the personal and political aspects of his future alliances and quarrels – he learned to discipline the emotional side of his nature.

We had agreed among ourselves not to relate what had passed to anyone except our most intimate friends ... Outwardly it was as though nothing had happened . . . but within a chord had broken, and instead of splendid personal relations, dry, business-like relations prevailed, with a constant reckoning according to the principle: *si vis pacem, para bellum* [If you desire peace, prepare for war].[16]

This episode, to which Lenin never referred again in any of his writings, not only anticipated the future conflict between individuals – Lenin versus Plekhanov (and his close friends Axelrod and Zasulich) – but was also an expression of the real, fundamental weakness of the Father of Russian marxism, for which the main reason was probably his years of isolation from any real fighting movement. As Krupskaya describes it:

> The destiny of Plekhanov was tragic. In the theoretical sphere his services to the labour movement were very great. But the years of emigration were not without effect on him – they isolated him from the real life of Russia. The labour movement of the broad masses only developed after he had already gone abroad. He saw the representatives of the various parties, writers, students, and even individual working men, but he neither saw nor worked nor felt with the Russian labouring masses. When any correspondence happened to come from Russia that lifted the curtain over new forms of the movement, and made one grasp its perspectives, Vladimir Ilyich, Martov and even Vera Ivanovna, would read and re-read the letters: Vladimir Ilyich would afterwards pace up and down for a long while, and could not get off to sleep. When we moved to Geneva, I endeavoured to show Plekhanov correspondence of this kind, and the way he reacted astonished me: he seemed to lose the ground beneath his feet, and a look of mistrust appeared to come over his face. Afterwards he never talked about those letters ... At first I was somewhat offended at this; but afterwards I began to think out the reason for his attitude. He had long since left Russia, and he did not possess that gauge – fashioned by experience – which makes it possible to grasp the relative value of each letter, to read a great deal between the lines.
>
> Workers often came to the *Iskra*, and they all, of course, wanted to see Plekhanov. To get in to see Plekhanov was much more difficult than to see us or Martov, but even if a worker succeeded in seeing him he came away feeling confused. The worker would be enthralled with Plekhanov's brilliant intelligence, his knowledge, and his wit, but somehow it seemed that, on leaving him, he would feel only what a great gap there was between this brilliant theoretician and himself. Of the things he had wished to speak about, or seek his advice on, the worker would not say a word.
>
> And if the worker did not agree with Plekhanov and tried to expound his own opinion, Plekhanov began to be annoyed: 'Your fathers and mothers were still infants when I –'
>
> I dare say things were not like this in the first years of emigration, but by the beginning of the present century

Plekhanov had already lost all capacity for directly sensing Russia. In 1905 he did not go to Russia.[17]

Trotsky summarized Plekhanov's condition aptly.

Plekhanov was already beginning to enter upon a state of decline. His strength was being undermined by the very thing that was giving strength to Lenin – the approach of the revolution. All of Plekhanov's activity took place during the preparatory, theoretical days. He was marxian propagandist and polemicist-in-chief, but not a revolutionary politician of the proletariat. The nearer the shadow of the revolution crept, the more evident it became that Plekhanov was losing ground. He couldn't help seeing it himself, and that was the cause of his irritability toward the younger men.[18]

In contrast with Plekhanov, Lenin knew and understood the lives and the struggle of the Russian workers.

Exceptional Single-Mindedness

The sharp conflict with Plekhanov was a very early test of Lenin's willpower and single-mindedness.

There has probably never been a revolutionary more single-minded, purposeful and persistent than Lenin. It is significant that the most commonly recurring words in his writings are probably 'relentless' and 'irreconcilable'. Above all he had unbending willpower. As Lunacharsky wrote in his *Revolutionary Silhouettes*, 'the dominating trait of his character, the feature which constituted half his make-up, was his will : an extremely firm, extremely forceful will capable of concentrating itself on the most immediate task but which yet never strayed beyond the radius traced out by his powerful intellect and which assigned every individual problem its place as a link in a huge, world-wide political chain.'[19] The Russian language, significantly, has the same word for freedom and for will.

Lenin's life-style was a model of discipline, orderliness and patient self-restraint. Gorky described him as 'personally undemanding, a teetotaller, a non-smoker, busy from morning till night with complicated, difficult work, quite unable to take proper care of himself.'[20] In his letters Lenin never described his environment – whether he was in prison, or in Siberia, Geneva, Paris or London, he was completely engrossed in his work. At their most personal they were a brief summary of his everyday activity. When his family complained that he did not write from Siberia, Krupskaya wrote: 'Volodya is quite unable to write about the ordinary side of life.'[21]

In a hostile memoir written in 1927, Potresov admitted: 'And yet ... all of us who were closest to the work ... valued Lenin not only for his knowledge, brains and capacity for work, but also for his exceptional devotion to the cause, his unceasing readiness to give himself completely, to take upon himself the most unpleasant functions, and without fail to discharge them with the utmost conscientiousness.'[22]

Vera Zasulich, according to Trotsky, once said to Lenin: 'George [Plekhanov] is a hound – he will shake a thing for a while, and then drop it; whereas you are a bulldog – yours is the death-grip.' When she later reported the conversation to Trotsky, she added: 'This appealed to Lenin very much – "a death-grip", he repeated, with obvious delight.'[23]

The following interchange between Axelrod (one of the founders of Russian marxism, and later a Menshevik leader) and a member of the International Socialist Bureau is quite illuminating:

Member of the International Socialist Bureau: Do you mean to say that all these splits and quarrels and scandals are the work of one man? But how can one man be so effective and so dangerous?
Axelrod: Because there is not another man who for twenty-four hours of the day is taken up with the revolution, who has no other thoughts but thoughts of revolution, and who, even in his sleep, dreams of nothing but revolution. Just try and handle such a fellow.[24]

And this is what Lenin said to his close friend, the German revolutionary, Clara Zetkin:

The revolution demands concentration, increase of forces. From the masses, from individuals. It cannot tolerate orgiastic conditions, such as are normal for the decadent heroes and heroines of D'Annunzio. Dissoluteness in sexual life is bourgeois, is a phenomenon of decay. The proletariat is a rising class. It doesn't need intoxication as a narcotic or a stimulus. Intoxication as little by sexual exaggeration as by alcohol. It must not and shall not forget, forget the shame, the filth, the savagery of capitalism. It receives the strongest urge to fight from a class situation, from the Communist ideal. It needs clarity, clarity, and again clarity. And so I repeat, no weakening, no waste, no destruction of forces. Self-control, self-discipline is not slavery, not even in love.[25]

4

'What is to be Done?'

Several years of thought by Lenin on the organizational tasks facing Russian Social Democracy culminated in the writing of the very important book *What is to be Done?* in 1902. Its main theme was 'the three questions – the character and main content of the necessary political agitation; the organizational tasks; and the plan for building, simultaneously, and from various sides, a militant, all-Russian organization'.[1]

The Difference between Trade Union Consciousness and Socialist Consciousness

Lenin's views on 'the character and main content of the necessary political agitation' developed into an exposition of the difference between trade union politics and socialist politics. As he expressed it: 'The history of all countries shows that the working class, exclusively by its own effort, is able to develop only trade union consciousness, i.e. the conviction that it is necessary to combine in unions, fight the em-

ployers, and strive to compel the government to pass necessary labour legislation, etc.'[2]

Elsewhere he wrote :

> the *spontaneous* development of the working-class move-
> ment leads to its subordination to bourgeois ideology . . . for
> the spontaneous working-class movement is trade unionism,
> is *Nur-Gewerkschaftlerei*, and trade unionism means the
> ideological enslavement of the workers by the bourgeoisie.[3]

> But why, the reader will ask, does the spontaneous move-
> ment, the movement along the line of least resistance, lead
> to the domination of bourgeois ideology? For the simple
> reason that bourgeois ideology is far older in origin than
> socialist ideology, that it is more fully developed, and that it
> has at its disposal *immeasurably* more means of dissemina-
> tion.[4]

> Hence, our task, the task of Social Democracy, is *to combat
> spontaneity*, *to divert* the working-class movement from this
> spontaneous, trade unionist striving to come under the wing
> of the bourgeoisie, and to bring it under the wing of revolu-
> tionary Social Democracy.[5]

He went on to say :

> Class political consciousness can be brought to the workers
> *only from without*, that is, only from outside the economic
> struggle, from outside the sphere of relations between
> workers and employers. The sphere from which alone it is
> possible to obtain this knowledge is the sphere of relation-
> ships of *all* classes and strata to the state and the govern-
> ment, the sphere of the interrelations between *all* classes.[6]

There is no doubt that this formulation overemphasized
the difference between spontaneity and consciousness. For
in fact the complete separation of spontaneity from consciousness is mechanical and non-dialectical. Lenin, as we
shall see later, admitted this. Pure spontaneity does not exist
in life – 'every "spontaneous" movement contains rudimentary elements of conscious leadership, of discipline'.[7] The
smallest strike has at least a rudimentary leadership.

Lenin himself, in an article written at the end of 1899,
entitled 'On Strikes', sharply contradicted his later statements
in *What is to be Done?* on the relation between the spontane-

ous class struggle and socialist consciousness. Thus, for instance, he wrote:

> Every strike brings thoughts of socialism very forcibly to the worker's mind, thoughts of the struggle of the entire working class for emancipation from the oppression of capital.[8]

> A strike teaches workers to understand what the strength of the employers and what the strength of the workers consists in; it teaches them not to think of their own employer alone and not of their own immediate workmates alone but of all the employers, the whole class of capitalists and the whole class of workers.[9]

> A strike, moreover, opens the eyes of the workers to the nature, not only of the capitalists, but of the government and the laws as well.[10]

The logic of the mechanical juxtaposition of spontaneity and consciousness was the complete separation of the party from the *actual* elements of working-class leadership that had already risen in the struggle. It assumed that the party had answers to all the questions that spontaneous struggle might bring forth. The blindness of the embattled many is the obverse of the omniscience of the few.

In general the dichotomy between economic and political struggle is foreign to Marx. An economic demand, if it is sectional, is defined as 'economic' in Marx's terms. But if the same demand is made of the state it is 'political':

> the attempt in a particular factory or even in a particular trade to force a shorter working day out of individual capitalists by strikes, etc., is a purely economic movement. On the other hand the movement to force through an eight-hour, etc., *law*, is a *political* movement. And in this way, out of the separate economic movements of the workers there grows up everywhere a *political* movement, that is to say, a movement of the *class*, with the object of enforcing its interests in a general form, in a form possessing general, socially coercive force . . . every movement in which the working class comes out as a *class* against the ruling classes and tries to coerce them by pressure from without is a political movement.[11]

In many cases economic (sectional) struggles do not give rise to political (class-wide) struggles, but there is no Chinese wall between the two, and many economic struggles *do* spill over into political ones.

Lenin's 'bending of the stick' right over to mechanical over-emphasis on organization in *What is to be Done?* was, nevertheless, quite useful operationally, whereas, over a period of some four to five years, the marxists in Russia had aroused a desire in the working class for confrontation at factory level, the step now necessary was to arouse, at least in the politically conscious section of the masses, a passion for political action.

The Struggle for Democracy and Socialism

A theme that runs through all Lenin's writings on the 'organizational tasks of the movement' is the need for the revolutionary socialist to support every movement against oppression, not only economic, but also political and cultural, and not only of workers, but of any downtrodden section of society.

> The rural superintendents and the flogging of peasants, the corruption of the officials and the police treatment of the 'common people' in the cities, the fight against the famine-stricken and the suppression of the popular striving towards enlightenment and knowledge, the extortion of taxes and the persecution of the religious sects, the humiliating treatment of the students and liberal intellectuals – all these and a thousand other similar manifestations of tyranny, though not directly connected with the 'economic' struggle, represent, in general, *less* widely applicable means and occasions for political agitation and for drawing the masses into the political struggle.[12]

> Working-class consciousness cannot be genuine political consciousness unless the workers are trained to respond to *all* cases of tyranny, oppression, violence, and abuse, no matter *what class* is affected – unless they are trained, moreover, to respond from a Social Democratic point of view and no other.[13]

If these tyrannies are exposed,

the most backward worker will understand, *or will feel*, that the students and religious sects, the peasants and the authors are being abused and outraged by those same dark forces that are oppressing and crushing him at every step of his life. Feeling that, he himself will be filled with an irresistable desire to react, and he will know how to hoot the censors one day, on another day to demonstrate outside the house of a governor who has brutally suppressed a peasant uprising, on still another day to teach a lesson to the gendarmes in surplices who are doing the work of the Holy Inquisition, etc.[14]

It was in this spirit of support for all those oppressed that Lenin in 1903 suggested the publication of a special periodical for members of religious sects (who number over 10 million in Russia). This is the resolution which he moved at the second Congress:

DRAFT RESOLUTION ON THE PUBLICATION OF A PERIODICAL FOR MEMBERS OF RELIGIOUS SECTS

Bearing in mind that in many of its aspects the sectarian movement in Russia represents one of the democratic trends in Russia, the second Congress calls the attention of all party members to the necessity of working among members of sects so as to bring them under Social Democratic influence. By way of experiment, the Congress permits Comrade Bonch-Bruyevich* to publish, under the supervision of the editorial board of the Central Organ, a popular newspaper entitled *Among Sectarians*, and instructs the Central Committee and the editorial board of the Central Organ to take the measures necessary to ensure successful publication of this newspaper and to create all the conditions for its proper functioning.[15]

Accordingly a paper called *Rassvet* (Dawn) was launched, directed towards members of the religious sects. The first is-

---

* V.Bonch-Bruyevich was a leading authority on the sectarian movements in Russia and had published a number of volumes of his investigations. He was a close collaborator with Lenin, who supported him at the second Congress and remained in the Bolshevik camp throughout. During and after the 1905 revolution he was active in organizing the Bolshevik underground press.

sue appeared in January 1904 and it went on appearing—nine issues altogether – until September of the same year. Work among the religious sects had great socialist value. One has only to read Trotsky's autobiography to see how working-class areas teemed with religious sects opposed to the Greek Orthodox Church. On the whole, this opposition had directly political implications.[16]

Pursuing the theme of the need to react against *all* forms of oppression, Lenin describes the revolutionary Social Democrat, by comparison with the trade union secretary.

> For the secretary of any, say English, trade union always helps the workers to carry on the economic struggle, he helps them to expose factory abuses, explains the injustice of the laws and of measures that hamper the freedom to strike and to picket (i.e. to warn all and sundry that a strike is proceeding at a certain factory), explains the partiality of arbitration court judges who belong to the bourgeois classes, etc. etc. In a word every trade union secretary conducts and helps to conduct 'the economic struggle against the employers and the government' ... the Social Democrat's ideal should not be the trade union secretary, but *the tribune of the people*, who is able to react to every manifestation of tyranny and oppression, no matter where it appears, no matter what stratum or class of the people it affects; who is able to generalize all these manifestations and produce a single picture of police violence and capitalist exploitation; who is able to take advantage of every event, however small, in order to set forth *before all* his socialist convictions and his democratic demands, in order to clarify for *all* and everyone the world-historic significance of the struggle for the emancipation of the proletariat.[17]

The Need for a Highly Centralized Organization of Professional Revolutionaries

The organizational forms needed by Social Democracy were derived from the nature of the political tasks. These new tasks of the movement demanded, first of all, a fight to the death against what Lenin called *Kustarichestvo* – a primitive 'handicraft method of organization'. This is how Lenin described the typical marxist study circle existing during the period 1894-1901.

A students' circle establishes contacts with workers and sets to work, without any connection with the old members of the movement, without any connection with study circles in other districts, or even in other parts of the same city (or in other educational institutions), without any organization of the various divisions of revolutionary work, without any systematic plan of activity covering any length of time. The circle gradually expands its propaganda and agitation; by its activities it wins the sympathies of fairly large sections of workers and of a certain section of the educated strata, which provide it with money and from among whom the 'committee' recruits new groups of young people. The attractive power of the committee . . . grows, its sphere of activity becomes wider, and the committee expands this activity quite spontaneously.

[It will] now establish contacts with other groups of revolutionaries, procure literature, set to work to publish a local newspaper, begin to talk of organizing a demonstration, and finally turn to open warfare (which may, according to circumstances, take the form of issuing the first agitational leaflet or the first issue of a newspaper, or of organizing the first demonstration). Usually the initiation of such actions ends in an immediate and complete fiasco. Immediate and complete, because this open warfare was not the result of a systematic and carefully thought-out and gradually prepared plan for a prolonged and stubborn struggle, but simply the result of the spontaneous growth of traditional study circle work.[18]

One cannot help comparing this kind of warfare with that conducted by a mass of peasants, armed with clubs, against modern troops. And one can only wonder at the vitality of the movement which expanded, grew, and scored victories despite the total lack of training on the part of the fighter. True, from the historical point of view, the primitiveness of equipment was not only inevitable at first, but *even legitimate* as one of the conditions for the wide recruiting of fighters, but as soon as serious war operations began (and they began in fact with the strikes in the summer of 1896), the defects in our fighting organizations made themselves felt to an ever-increasing degree.[19]

The amateur nature of the movement made it vulnerable to disastrous police raids.

> The government . . . very soon adapted itself to the new conditions of the struggle and managed to deploy well its perfectly equipped detachments of *agents provocateurs*, spies, and gendarmes. Raids became so frequent, affected such a vast number of people, and cleared out the local study circles so thoroughly that the masses of the workers lost literally all their leaders, the movement assumed an amazingly sporadic character, and it became utterly impossible to establish continuity and coherence in the work. The terrible dispersion of the local leaders; the fortuitous character of the study circles' memberships; the lack of training in, and the narrow outlook on, theoretical, political, and organizational questions were all the inevitable result of the conditions described above. Things have reached such a pass that in several places the workers, because of our lack of self-restraint and the ability to maintain secrecy, begin to lose faith in the intellectuals and to avoid them; the intellectuals, they say, are much too careless and cause police raids![20]

Harsh criticism indeed. Lenin spares no one, least of all himself.

> Let no active worker take offence at these frank remarks for as far as insufficient training is concerned, I apply them first and foremost to myself. I used to work in a study circle that set itself very broad, all-embracing tasks; and all of us, members of that circle, suffered painfully and acutely from the realization that we were acting as amateurs at a moment in history when we might have been able to say, varying a well-known statement: 'Give us an organization of revolutionaries, and we will overturn Russia!' The more I recall the burning sense of shame I then experienced, the bitterer become my feelings towards those pseudo-Social Democrats whose preachings bring disgrace on the calling of a revolutionary, who fail to understand that our task is not to champion the degrading of the revolutionary to the level of an amateur, but *to raise* the amateurs to the level of revolutionaries.[21]

His positive conclusions are that 'a stable organization of leaders maintaining continuity' be established;

that such an organization must consist chiefly of people professionally engaged in revolutionary activity; that in an autocratic state, the more we *confine* the membership of such an organization to people who are professionally engaged in revolutionary activity and who have been professionally trained in the art of combating the political police, the more difficult will it be to unearth the organization.[22]

And the recruitment of professional revolutionaries for the movement should not be restricted to the circles of students and intelligentsia.

A worker-agitator who is at all gifted and 'promising' *must not be left* to work eleven hours a day in a factory. We must arrange that he be maintained by the party; that he may go underground in good time; that he change the place of his activity, if he is to enlarge his experience, widen his outlook, and be able to hold out for at least a few years in the struggle against the gendarmes.[23]

A number of his opponents in the Menshevik camp in later years accused Lenin of raising the intelligentsia above the workers in *What is to be Done?* But this is not so. In fact, he attacks the intelligentsia for being 'careless and sluggish in their habits'. Unlike the workers, who are accustomed to discipline by factory life, the intellectuals have to be disciplined with an iron rod by the party. Above all, their role in the party is transitory. 'The role of the intelligentsia is to make special leaders from among the intelligentsia unnecessary.'[24]

'Iskra' as a Tool of Organization

From the moment when publication of *Iskra* was started, Lenin made it clear that the paper must serve as a weapon for building a centralized all-Russian organization. In an article called 'Where to Begin' (*Iskra*, No. 4) he wrote that 'the role of a newspaper' should not be

limited solely to the dissemination of ideas, to political education, and to the enlistment of political allies. A newspaper is not only a collective propagandist and a collective agitator, it is also a collective organizer. In this last respect it may be likened to the scaffolding round a building under construction, which marks the contours of the structure and facilitates communication between the builders, enabling them to distribute the work and to view the common results achieved by their organized labour. With the aid of the newspaper, and through it, a permanent organization will naturally take shape that will engage, not only in local activities, but in regular general work, and will train its members to follow political events carefully, appraise their significance and their effect on the various strata of the population, and develop effective means for the revolutionary party to influence those events. The mere technical task of regularly supplying the newspaper with copy and of promoting regular distribution will necessitate a network of local agents of the united party, who will maintain constant contact with one another, know the general state of affairs, get accustomed to performing regularly their detailed functions in the all-Russian work, and test their strength in the organization of various revolutionary actions.

This network of agents will form the skeleton of precisely the kind of organization we need – one that is sufficiently broad and many-sided to effect a strict and detailed division of labour; sufficiently well tempered to be able to conduct steadily *its own work* under any circumstances, at all 'sudden turns', and in face of all contingencies; sufficiently flexible to be able, on the one hand, to avoid an open battle against an overwhelming enemy, when the enemy has concentrated all his forces at one spot, and yet, on the other, to take advantage of his unwieldiness and to attack him when and where he least expects it.[25]

The Newspaper as Organizer of Leaders for a Future Armed Uprising

Lenin's creative imagination did not stop at seeing the paper as an organizer of a party of agitators. In *What is to be Done?* he explained that the network of the paper's agents should become the basis for the organization of a future armed uprising against Tsarism.

The organization, which will form round this newspaper . . . will be ready *for everything* from upholding the honour, the prestige and the continuity of the party in periods of acute revolutionary 'depression' to preparing for, appointing the time for, and carrying out the *nation wide armed uprising* ... picture to yourselves a popular uprising. Probably everyone will now see that we must think of this and prepare for it. But *how*? ... a network of agents that would form in the course of establishing and distributing the common newspaper would not have to 'sit about and wait' for the call for an uprising, but could carry on the regular activity that would guarantee the highest probability of success in the event of an uprising. Such activity would strengthen our contacts with the broadest strata of the working masses and with all social strata that are discontented with the autocracy, which is of such importance for an uprising. Precisely such activity would serve to cultivate the ability to estimate correctly the general political situation and, consequently, the ability to select the proper moment for an uprising. Precisely such activity would train *all* local organizations to respond simultaneously to the same political questions, incidents, and events that agitate the whole of Russia and to react to such 'incidents' in the most vigorous, uniform, and expedient manner possible; for an uprising is in essence the most vigorous, most uniform, and most expedient 'answer' of the entire people to the government. Lastly, it is precisely such activity that would train all revolutionary organizations throughout Russia to maintain the most continuous, and at the same time the most secret, contacts with one another thus creating *real* party unity; for without such contacts it will be impossible collectively to discuss the plan for the uprising and to take the necessary preparatory measures on the eve, measures that must be kept in the strictest secrecy.[26]

'The thing we need', he said, 'is a military organization of agents.'[27] 1905 was not far off!

The Party Structure

The organizational plan advocated by Lenin in *What is to be Done?* was further elaborated with great clarity in a document he wrote a few months later, called *Letter to a Comrade on our Organizational Tasks*, which was widely circulated and then printed as a pamphlet in 1904.

The party should have two leading centres: a CO (Central Organ) and a CC (Central Committee). The former should be responsible for ideological leadership, and the latter for direct and practical leadership. The former should be placed beyond the reach of the Russian gendarmes, and assured of consistency and stability, and hence would have to be abroad.

Below the level of the Central Committee the apparatus should consist of two kinds of groups: local and functional (industrial). The local committee 'should consist of fully convinced Social Democrats who devote themselves entirely to Social Democratic activities'. It should not be large.

> As far as possible the committees should not have very many members ... but at the same time they should include a sufficient number to take charge of *all* aspects of the work, and to ensure full representation and binding decisions. Should it happen that the number of members is fairly large and that it is hazardous for them to meet frequently, it might then be necessary to select from the committee a special and very small *executive* group (consisting of, say, five, or even fewer persons), which should without fail include the secretary and those most capable of giving practical guidance to the work as a whole.[28]

The following institutions would be needed under the jurisdiction of the local committees:

> (1) discussion meetings (conferences) of the 'best' revolutionaries, (2) district circles with (3) a propagandists' circle attached to each of these, (4) factory circles, and (5) 'meetings of representatives' of delegates from the factory circles of a given district. I fully agree with you that *all* further institutions (and of these there should be very many and extremely diversified ones, besides those mentioned by you) should be subordinated to the committee, and that it is necessary to have district groups (for the very big cities) and factory groups (always and everywhere).[29]

In large cities there was a need for district groups, which should serve as 'intermediaries' between the local committee and factory committees.

Now about the factory circles. These are particularly important to us: the main strength of the movement lies in the organization of the workers at the *large* factories, for the large factories (and mills) contain not only the predominant part of the working class, as regards numbers, but even more as regards influence, development, and fighting capacity. Every factory must be our fortress.

As soon as the factory subcommittee has been formed it should proceed to organize a number of factory groups and circles with diverse tasks and varying degrees of secrecy and organizational form, as, for instance, circles for delivering and distributing literature (this is one of the most important functions, which must be organized so as to provide us with a real postal service of our own, so as to possess tried and tested methods, not only for distributing literature, but also for delivering to the homes, and so as to provide a definite knowledge of all workers' addresses and ways of reaching them): circles for reading illegal literature; groups for tracking down spies; circles for giving circles of agitators and propagandists who know how to initiate special guidance to the trade union movement and the economic struggle; and to carry on long talks in an *absolutely legal* way (on machinery, inspectors, etc.).

The factory organization was to have as its core a small group of revolutionaries under the control of the local committee. 'Every member of the factory committee should regard himself as an agent of the committee, obliged to submit to all its orders and to observe all the "laws and customs" of the "army in the field" which he has joined and from which in time of war he has no right to absent himself without official leave.'[30]

Lenin's party structure aimed at achieving the maximum division of labour, a real interventionist, centralist leadership, and the widest possible spread of responsibility and initiative amongst the membership as a whole. The central principle of party activity was described as follows:

> while *the greatest possible centralization* is necessary with regard to the ideological and practical *leadership* of the movement and the revolutionary struggle of the proletariat, *the greatest possible decentralization* is necessary with regard to keeping the party centre (and therefore the party as a whole) *informed* about the movement, and with regard to *responsibility* to the party. The leadership of the movement should be entrusted to the smallest possible number of the

most homogeneous possible groups of professional revolutionaries with great practical experience. Participation in the movement would extend to the greatest possible number of the most diverse and heterogeneous groups of the most varied sections of the proletariat (and other classes of the people) . . . We must centralize the leadership of the movement. We must also . . . as far as possible *decentralize responsibility to the party* on the part of its individual members, of every participant in its work, and of every circle belonging to or associated with the party. This decentralization is an essential prerequisite of revolutionary centralization and an *essential corrective to it.*[31]

Lenin's Distaste for Red Tape and Rule-Mongering

On rules, Lenin has this to say :

what is needed is not rules but the organization of party information, if I may put it in this way. Each of our local organizations now spends at least a few evenings on discussing rules. If instead, each member would devote this time to making a detailed and well-prepared report *to the entire party* on his particular function, the work would gain a hundred fold.

And it is not merely because revolutionary work does not always lend itself to definite organizational form that rules are useless. No, definite organizational form is necessary, and we must endeavour to *give such form* to all our work as far as possible. That is permissible to a much greater extent than is generally thought, and achievable not through rules but solely and exclusively (we must keep on reiterating this) through transmitting organizational form connected with real responsibility and inner-party publicity.[32]

It will, I hope, have become clear to the reader that in fact it would perhaps be possible to get along *without rules*, substituting for them regular reports about each circle and every aspect of the work.[33]

As a matter of fact, when Lenin in late June or early July 1903 did draw up draft rules for the RDSLP they were extremely simple and few in number. And they were fully in the spirit of *What is to be Done?* and *Letter to a Comrade.*[34]

Lenin refers with amusement to Martov's rules :

drowned in a 'flood of verbiage and bureaucratic formulas (that is, formulas useless for the work and supposed to be useful for display)'.[35] This list of rules – 48 paragraphs as against Lenin's 12 – 'indeed, is hypertrophy of verbiage, or real bureaucratic formalism, which frames superfluous, patently useless or red-tapist, points and paragraphs.'[36]

In practice Lenin's faction was for a long time very informal indeed. He started to build his organization through *Iskra* agents. When, after the second Congress, as we shall see, he lost the support of his own Central Committee, he reorganized his supporters around a newly convened conference that elected a Russian Bureau. When in 1909 he split with Bogdanov, he removed him at a meeting of an enlarged editorial board of the journal *Proletary*, although Bogdanov had been elected to the Bolshevik Centre by the Congress of 1907.

An overformal party structure inevitably clashes with two basic features of the revolutionary movement: (1) the unevenness in consciousness, militancy and dedication of different parts of the revolutionary organization; and (2) the fact that members who play a positive, vanguard role at a certain stage of the struggle fall behind at another.

'Hero' and 'Crowd'

One of the main interpretations given to *What is to be Done?* both by later Menshevik opponents of Lenin and by his epigones, the Stalinists, was that it put the emphasis on 'heroes' to the detriment of the crowd.

This interpretation is completely unjustified. Indeed, throughout his life nothing was more alien to Lenin's way of thinking than to draw a distinction between the 'hero' and the 'crowd'. Even if the hero loves the crowd he cannot but look down on it. The shaping of an inert mass depends entirely on him. Lenin never looked at himself in the mirror of history. Lunacharsky contrasted Trotsky with Lenin, writing: 'Trotsky is undoubtedly often prone to step back and watch himself. Trotsky treasures his historical role and would probably be ready to make any personal sacrifice, not excluding the greatest sacrifice of all – that of his life – in order to go down in human memory surrounded by the aureole of a genuine revolutionary leader. His ambition has the same characteristic.'[37] As against this, 'Lenin is not in the least ambitious . . . I do not believe that Lenin ever steps back and looks at himself, never even thinks what posterity will say about him – he simply gets on with his job.'

Those who knew Lenin noted with surprise his complete lack of self-importance. Angelica Balabanova said that she could not remember when she first met him in exile, that 'externally he seemed the most colourless of all the revolutionary leaders'. Bruce Lockhart, British Consul in Moscow in 1917, when he first saw Lenin after the October revolution, thought 'at a first glance [that he] looked more like a provincial grocer than a leader of men.'[38] And Clara Zetkin tells the story of his reception of a delegation of German communists. Accustomed to the marxists of the Reichstag with their frock coats and their official self-importance, these Germans had expected something else. Lenin kept his appointment so punctually, entered the room so unobtrusively, and talked to them so naturally and simply, that it never occurred to them that they were meeting Lenin.

One old Bolshevik recorded in his memoirs, published in 1924: 'The impression he made on me, and probably not on me alone, was at first quite ambiguous. His homely, at first sight common, appearance, did not impress us very much.'[39]

Maxim Gorky described his first impression of Lenin thus: 'I had not expected Lenin to be like that. For me, there was something lacking. He rolled his "r"s and stood with arms akimbo, somehow poking his fists under his armpits. In a way he was too ordinary. He did not give the impression of a "leader".'[40]

He was personally very unassuming. One finds him filling in a party questionnaire, dated 13 February 1922, as follows: 'Spoken language: Russian. What other languages can you freely speak: I can freely speak in none.'[41] Actually Lenin read and spoke German, French and English fluently, and could read Italian as well. If there were any doubt of this, his participation in sessions and committees of the Comintern would be proof enough.

Above all, he never tried to bask in the reflected glory of his brother Alexander's martyrdom, following his execution by the Tsarist autocracy in 1887. In all the fifty-five volumes of the fifth, last, and most complete edition of Lenin's *Works*, Alexander's name is mentioned only incidentally, and only three times: in a purely factual statement in which Lenin was answering a questionnaire; in a letter written in 1921, in which he recommended a certain Chebotarev, 'I have known Chebotarev from the 1880s in connection with the case of my elder brother, Alexander Ilyich Ulyanov, hanged in 1887. Chebotarev is undoubtedly an honest man'; and in an article in which the name of Alexander Ulyanov was mentioned among others executed for the same plot.

The Rising Revolutionary Movement

The 'economism' that Lenin attacked so sharply in *What is to be Done?* was already on the decline and practically finished by the time the pamphlet saw the light of day. A few years later Lenin could state that from 1898 to 1900 the 'economist' *Rabocheye Dyelo*-ists were stronger than the *Iskrists* both abroad and in Russia.[42] But after that 'economism' declined rapidly. The period of industrial prosperity in Russia came to an end in 1898-99 and the strike movement began to weaken; the number of workers involved in strikes in 1901 was only one third of that in 1899. The character of the strikes also changed: they became much more desperate. Unemployment increased and there were several riots which were dealt with by police and troops. Revolutionary agitation increased and a series of organized street demonstrations took place.

The years 1900-03, during which Lenin was very busy building up *Iskra*, creating a national network of agents, of professional revolutionaries, as the backbone of a future party, were also years of a massive rise in revolutionary feeling in Russia.

As has happened before and since, the student movement preceded the mass working-class movement. When the crisis in society is deep, but the working class is not yet ready to take on the task of overcoming it, it is often the case that the students come forward. In 1899 a stormy student movement emerged. Different student organizations were formed and conflicts became more and more frequent. The students' protests against police oppression took on a mass character.

In February 1899 the brutal methods used by the Petersburg police against the students brought about a general strike of university students throughout the country. About five thousand students took part. A few months later a small student demonstration took place in Kiev, caused by the exile of some colleagues who had spoken at a student meeting. As a result, 183 students were arrested and drafted into the army. The procedure in Petersburg was similar, and 30 students were sent on military service as a punishment.

The entire student body became very agitated. Meetings were held in every university, and leaflets were distributed calling for a united protest. On 4 March, when a procession of students in the streets of Kharkov was broken up by the police, a mass of workers joined the students, and throughout the day there were clashes with the police in the streets; revolutionary songs were sung and calls against the government became louder. A few days later, when hundreds of Moscow students were arrested and imprisoned in Marstall, huge groups of workers and petty bourgeoisie gathered in front of the building, expressing their sympathy with the students.[43]

Such large-scale activity meant that the social crisis was deepening, but the working masses were still slow to move. The year 1900 passed comparatively peacefully for the working class. But there was a general strike in Kharkov on 1 May, brought about by the intensive agitation of the Social Democratic local committees. In this strike political demands were raised which, in a sense, made the strike a turning point in the development of the Russian working-class movement."

The movement grew rapidly after that. From 1901 onwards workers in Kharkov, Moscow, Tomsk and other cities also began to participate in student demonstrations, giving them a much more combative, forceful character. Bloody clashes with police and troops became more and more common. An attempt to crush the 1 May 1901 strike at the Obukhov munitions factory in the Vyborg district of St Petersburg turned into a military siege of the factory, as a result of which as many as 800 workers were arrested. (Many of them were sentenced to hard labour by a military court.)

In the winter of 1901-02 a general strike of more than 30,000 students took place. On 19 February 1901, on the fortieth anniversary of the emancipation of the peasants, a mass demonstration organized by students was joined by a large number of workers. Even more impressive were the demonstrations in Moscow on 23-26 February. There workers came out in tens of thousands, and several times drove back the Cossacks, who attacked them with whips. Moscow for the first time saw barricades in the streets. Following this, in March, and then in May, mass demonstrations took place in Petersburg, culminating in a battle between the workers of the Obukhov works and the police: six workers were killed and 80 wounded. Similar workers' riots took place in Tiflis in April and in Ekaterinoslav in December.

In November 1902 a railway strike took place in Rostov-on-Don. This turned into a general solidarity strike of all the city's factories. During the strikes, mass meetings of tens of thousands of workers took place, many addressed by Social Democratic speakers. In July 1903 a new wave of strikes broke out, this time not confined to single cities. They spread over the whole of Ukraine and Transcaucasia. Political strikes broke out in Baku, Tiflis, Odessa, Nikolayev, Kiev, Elizavetgrad, Ekaterinoslav and Kerch. About 250,000 workers took part in all. These strikes were accompanied by revolutionary demonstrations which were brutally suppressed by the police and the army.

During the years 1901-03, *workers* became the main

active political opponents of Tsarism. This is shown clearly from the data available for the occupations of the people in the liberation movement who were charged with state crimes.[45] For every 100 such persons there were:

	Nobles	Peasants	Workers	Intellectuals
1827-46	76	?	?	?
1884-90	30.6	7.1	15.1	73.2
1901-03	10.7	9.0	46.1	36.7
1905-08	9.1	24.2	47.4	28.4

Although urban workers were a minority of the population, they provided *almost half* of the participants. The intelligentsia and the students were already in second place.[46] Thus the course of events – as well as the activities of the *Iskrists* – cut the ground from beneath the feet of 'economism'. As Lenin said later: 'the fight against "economism" subsided and came to an end altogether as far back as 1902'.[47]

5

The 1903 Congress: Bolshevism is Born

Preparing the Congress

Lenin was ready and willing to deal not only with general problems of theory and politics, but also with the details of organizational work. This was one of his strengths and that of his faction or party, and was a characteristic which became evident during the *Iskra* period and the preparation for the second Congress – the years 1900-03.

Lenin was always anxious to meet active underground party workers. He invited released Siberian exiles and escaped prisoners to come and stay abroad for a time, and discussed with them the political, tactical and organizational problems they faced. He drew promising comrades into the central work of the organization, transferring them from one locality to another and using them as *Iskra* agents. There were at most twenty or thirty of these with whom Lenin maintained regular contacts. A key role in keeping in touch with Russia was played by Krupskaya.

> When I arrived, Vladimir Ilyich told me that he had succeeded in arranging that I should be made secretary of *Iskra* on my arrival. This, of course, meant that contact with Russia would be carried on under the closest control of Vladimir Ilyich. Martov and Potresov had nothing against this then, and the Emancipation of Labour Group did not put up their own candidate; indeed, they attached little importance to *Iskra* at that time. Vladimir Ilyich told me it had been rather awkward for him to have to arrange this, but that he considered it necessary for the good of the cause. I was immediately snowed under with work.[1]

There were a number of difficulties involved in corresponding with Russian activists – above all the intervention of the police.

> In reading now the correspondence with Russia, carried on in those days, one marvels at the naive forms of our conspiratorial work. All those letters about handkerchiefs (passports), brewing beer, warm fur (illegal literature), all those code-names for towns – beginning with the same letter as the name of the town ('Ossip' for Odessa, 'Terenty' for Tver, 'Petya' for Poltava, 'Pasha' for Pskov, etc.) all this substituting of women's names for men's and vice versa – all this was transparent in the extreme.[2]

Trotsky reports:

> Krupskaya ... was at the very centre of all the organization work; she received comrades when they arrived, instructed them when they left, established connections, supplied secret addresses, wrote letters, and coded and decoded correspondence. In her room there was always a smell of burned paper from the secret letters she heated over the fire to read. She often complained, in her gently insistent way, that people did not write enough, or that they got the code all mixed up or wrote in chemical ink in such a way that one line covered another, and so forth.[3]

Krupskaya succeeded in coordinating the underground *Iskra* organization to a degree never before achieved by any Russian revolutionary organization – and all this was done without a single assistant in the one-roomed 'head office', smelling 'of burned paper'.

Lenin's nerves suffered.

> Everything lay on Vladimir Ilyich. The correspondence with Russia had a very bad effect on his nerves. To wait weeks, or even months, for answers to letters, to be continually expecting the whole business to fall through, to be in a constant state of ignorance as to how things were progressing – all this was extremely incompatible with Vladimir Ilyich's character. His letters to Russia were overflowing with requests to write accurately: 'Once more we earnestly and categorically beseech and demand that you write us more often and in greater detail – in particular, do it *at once*, without fail, the very same day you receive this letter. Let us know you have received it, even if only a couple of lines.' His letters overflowed with requests to act more speedily. Ilyich would spend sleepless nights after receiving letters with such news as : ' "Sonia" is as silent as a grave', or 'Zarin did not come to the Committee in time', or 'no contact with "the old woman" ' . . . These sleepless nights remain engraved on my memory.[4]

Iskra played a central role in preparing for the Congress. This journal had a unique place in the history of journalism. It was the organizing centre of an underground party in Russia. The agents of the editorial board – nine in number by the end of 1901,[5] travelling secretly all over the country, got in touch with local groups, or set up groups where none existed, and coordinated their work. Previous attempts had encouraged pessimism. When in 1900 Lenin, Martov and Potresov

> went abroad to found a newspaper and by means of it a Russian organization, they risked suffering the fate of successive waves of Russian revolutionaries before them. These had gone abroad with the same hope that from Western Europe they would create a revolutionary movement in Russia; at best they had, one after another, founded organizations of *émigrés* if they succeeded in founding anything at

all. But this time, 'where these others failed, the triumvirate succeeded; their congress began truly as a congress of victors'.[6]

In preparing for the Congress which, after the abortion of the 1898 Congress, was to be the real founding Congress of the party and to establish unity among the revolutionary groups, Lenin left nothing to chance.

The following is part of a letter from him to one of the *Iskra* agent, F.V.Lengnick, written on 23 May 1902:

> your task now is to turn *yourself* into a committee for preparing the Congress . . . and to push your own people through into the largest number of committees possible, safeguarding yourself and your people more than the apple of your eye, until the Congress. Remember: all this is of the utmost importance! Be bolder, more pushy and more inventive in this respect, and in all others, as discreet and as careful as possible. Wise as serpents – and (with the committees: the Bund and St Petersburg) harmless as doves.[7]

Another agent, I.I.Radchenko, was told to be very cautious towards the Jewish socialist organization, the Bund.

> Behave *as impressively as you can* and act with *caution.* Take on yourself the greatest possible number of districts in which you undertake to prepare for the Congress, refer to the Bureau (giving it some other name), in a word, make sure that the whole thing is *entirely in your hands*, leaving the Bund, for the time being, confined to the Bund . . . And so, for the time being, *have in mind* the composition of a Russian Committee for Preparing the Congress which is most advantageous for us (you may find it convenient to say that you have already formed this committee, and are very glad to have the Bund *participate* or something like this). Take on yourself, *without fail*, to be secretary in this committee. These are the first steps, and then we shall see. I say have the composition 'in mind' to have as free a hand as possible: don't commit yourself to the Bund right away (you can say, for example, that connections have been established with the Volga, the Caucasus, the centre – we have a man from over there – and the South – we're sending two down there), and make yourself master of the undertaking. But do all this most carefully, without rousing objections.[8]

The loyalty declarations which appeared in the pages of

Iskra in the winter of 1902-03 clearly show that Lenin's agents were successful in carrying out their mission. *Iskra* won over one committee after another : in December, 1902 the Nizhni-Novgorod Committee; in January, 1903, the Saratov Committee; in February, the Northern Workers' Union, in March, the Don Committee (Rostov), the Siberian Workers' Union, the Kazan and Ufa Committees; in April, the Tula, Odessa, and Irkutsk Committees; and in May, the Mineworkers' Union of South Russia and the Ekaterinoslav Committee.[9]

The work of the *Iskra* agents was well described by the general of the gendarmerie Spiridovich :

> Welded into a compact conspiratorial group of professional revolutionaries, they travelled from place to place wherever there were party committees, established contacts with their members, delivered illegal literature to them, helped to establish printshops and garnered the information needed by the *Iskra*. They penetrated into local committees, carried on their propaganda against 'economism', eliminated their ideological opponents and in this way subjected the committees to their influence.[10]

After months of persistent effort, the correspondence with *Iskra* agents and others in Russia became regular and increased considerably in volume. It gave Lenin a real insight into the thinking and feeling of militant workers. As Krupskaya put it :

> The revolutionary movement in Russia continued to grow and at the same time correspondence with Russia also increased. It soon grew to three hundred letters a month, which was an enormous figure for those days. And it provided Ilyich with a spate of material! He really knew how to read workers' letters. I remember one letter, written by workers of the Odessa stone-quarries. It was a collective essay, written in several primitive -looking hands, devoid of subjects and predicates, and innocent of stops and commas. But it radiated an inexhaustible energy and readiness to fight to the finish, to fight until victorious. It was a letter in which every word, however naive, was eloquent of unshakable conviction. I do not remember now what the letter referred to, but I remember what it looked like – the paper and the

red ink. Lenin read that letter over many times, and paced up and down the room deep in thought. It had not been a vain endeavour when the Odessa quarrymen wrote Ilyich their letter: they had written to the right person, to someone who understood them best of all.[11]

Krupskaya was also treasurer of the Bolshevik Party, with sole access to its accounts. In addition, she organized the transportation of *Iskra* to Russia. This was an extremely onerous task. One of the people mainly concerned in carrying out the actual transportation of *Iskra* to Russia – Ossip A. Piatnitsky – gave a vivid description of the methods used:

To expedite the conveyance of literature into Russia in smaller quantities we used suit-cases with double bottoms. Even before my arrival in Berlin a small factory manufactured such suit-cases for us in large quantities. But the customs officials on the frontier soon smelled a rat, and several expeditions ended in failure. Apparently they recognized the suit-cases, which were all of the same style. Then we ourselves began to put double bottoms of strong cardboard into ordinary suit-cases, in which we could pack away 100 to 150 new numbers of the *Iskra*. These false bottoms were pasted over so skilfully that no one could tell that the suit-case contained any literature. Nor did the suit-case weigh much heavier as a result. We performed this operation on all the suit-cases of outgoing men and women students who were sympathetic to the *Iskra* group; and also on the suit-cases of all comrades who went to Russia, legally or illegally. But even that did not suffice. The demand for new literature was tremendous. We now invented 'breast plates': for the men we manufactured a kind of waistcoat into which we could stuff two or three hundred copies of the *Iskra* and thin pamphlets; for women we constructed special bodices and sowed literature into their skirts. With our equipment women could carry about three or four hundred copies of the *Iskra*.
This was called 'express transport' in our parlance. Everybody we could lay our hands on had to don these 'breast plates' – responsible comrades and ordinary mortals alike.[12]

This way of transporting *Iskra* into Russia was very cumbersome and very costly. As Krupskaya recalled many years later: 'Although a heap of money, energy, and time was put into all this transportation work, and tremendous risks were entailed, probably not more than one-tenth of the literature dispatched arrived at its destination.'[13] Rumour had it that the paper had a circulation of 100,000 in Kiev, but in fact the total number of copies printed of the first number was 8,000.[14]

Lenin was unique among revolutionary leaders at this time in his attitude towards the details of party organization. This may best be understood by contrasting his point of view with that, say, of Rosa Luxemburg and her friends in the leadership of the Polish Social Democratic Party, which has been described as follows:

> To a large extent each member of the élite acted on his own initiative and in accordance with his own predilections and habits. Orders were rare indeed; apart from exceptional cases . . . communication was a matter of dispensing rabbinical shades of opinion. Dzierzynski was horrified at this laxity and saw it as evidence of deterioration. 'No policy, no direction, no mutual assistance . . . everybody has to cope on his own' . . . Far from being an accidental lacuna in the party's administration, this haphazard informality was deliberate and jealously guarded. Some of the leaders very much disliked having to deal with money and organizational routine at all; it kept them from their writing. 'I have no wish to concern myself with money matters . . . You must approach Wladek [Olszewski], the cashier, in such matters', Marchlewski wrote indignantly to Cezaryna Wojnarowska in 1902. The same applied even more strongly to Rosa Luxemburg. At some stage a formal party decision was reached that she could not concern herself with organizational matters at all, that she should not participate in any of the official conferences or congresses.*

Like Rosa Luxemburg, Trotsky was also not involved in party administration. But this was because he did not, in fact, belong to any real party. Between 1904, when he broke with the Mensheviks, and 1917, when he joined the Bolsheviks, he

---

* Things changed in later years. By 1908 the informal consensus was disappearing, to be replaced by Jogiches' attempt to exercise a Leninist supremacy – without the loyalty of a cohesive group like the inner Bolsheviks.[15]

was associated only with a small loose group of writers.

The whole preparation of the 1903 Congress was in the hands of Lenin. 'How Vladimir Ilyich longed for the Congress!' Krupskaya reminisced.[16] But despite all his persistence, and all the hard work, the Congress took on a completely unexpected shape. Instead of being a unity congress, it was a congress in which the Russian marxists split radically into two separate trends and organizations – the Bolsheviks and the Mensheviks.

The 1903 Congress

At the beginning of the Congress things went well for the united leadership of Plekhanov, Lenin, Martov, Axelrod, Zasulich and Potresov. Of the 51 votes, 33, or a clear majority, belonged to adherents of the *Iskra* position. Lenin's careful preparation had helped to make this a certainty. *Iskra's* chief rival, *Rabocheye Dyelo*, the 'economist' paper, had only 3 votes, the Jewish Bund had 5, and 6 of the remaining delegates were unaligned. Plekhanov and Lenin called these last 'the swamp', as they sometimes voted with the *Iskrists*, sometimes against them. If the 33 *Iskrists* stuck together, they could certainly carry the day on every issue.

The first three sessions of the Congress (out of a total of 37) were devoted largely to trivial matters of procedure. After that came the discussion of the party programme, which was the most important item on the agenda. This was introduced by Plekhanov. The main question, about the dictatorship of the proletariat, drew practically solid support from all except the 'economists' Martynov and Akimov. When the programme was finally adopted, everyone present voted for it except Akimov, who abstained.

Akimov attacked the programme for its spirit of party tutelage over the proletariat.

> The concepts 'party' and 'proletariat' are set in opposition to each other, the first as an active, causative, collective being, the second as a passive medium on which the party operates. The name of the party is used throughout as subject, in the nominative case, the name of the proletariat as object, in

the accusative case . . . The essential condition for the social revolution is the dictatorship of the proletariat, i.e. the conquest of such power by the proletariat as will allow it to suppress all attempts at resistance on the part of the exploiters.

How could the endorsement of this dictatorship be reconciled with the demand for a democratic republic? One of the delegates, Posadovsky, asked the Congress whether the party ought to subordinate its future policy to this or that basic democratic principle, as having an absolute value, or 'must all democratic principles be subordinated exclusively to the interests of the party?' Plekhanov gave a clear and decisive answer:

> Every democratic principle must be considered not by itself, abstractly, but in relation to that which may be called the fundamental principle of democracy, namely *salus populi suprema lex*. Translated into the language of the revolutionist, this means that the success of the revolution is the highest law. And if the success of the revolution demanded a temporary limitation on the working of this or that democratic principle, then it would be criminal to refrain from such a limitation. As my own personal opinion, I will say that even the principle of universal suffrage must be considered from the point of view of what I have designated the fundamental principle of democracy. It is hypothetically possible that we, the Social Democrats, might speak out against universal suffrage. The bourgeoisie of the Italian republics once deprived persons belonging to the nobility of political rights. The revolutionary proletariat might limit the political rights of the higher classes just as the higher classes once limited their political rights. One can judge of the suitability of such measures only on the basis of the rule: *salus revolutiae suprema lex*.
> And we must take the same position on the question of the duration of parliaments. If in a burst of revolutionary enthusiasm the people chose a very fine parliament – a kind of *chambre introuvable* – then we would be bound to try to make of it a *long parliament*; and if the elections turned out unsuccessfully, then we would have to try to disperse it not in two years but if possible in two weeks.[17]

Plekhanov's statement precisely described the actual policies

of the Bolsheviks, especially in 1917; he lived to bitterly re-
gret his own words.

Martov, who by the time the Congress ended had become Lenin's opponent, did not at this stage disagree with
Plekhanov's statement regarding the dictatorship of the proletariat. However his definition was much less extreme. A few
weeks later, in a report on the Congress to the League Congress of Russian Social Democrats Abroad Martov tried to 'defend' Plekhanov by toning down his statement: 'These words
[Plekhanov's] aroused the indignation of some of the delegates; this could easily have been avoided if Comrade Plekhanov had added that it was of course impossible to imagine
so tragic a situation as that the proletariat, in order to con-
solidate its victory, should have to trample on such political
rights as freedom of the press. (Plekhanov: "Merci".)'[18]

Trotsky, who at a later stage in the Congress would side
with Martov against Lenin, at this point, in defending the
concept of the dictatorship of the proletariat, missed the
harsh reality that the dictatorship has to be directed against
the conservative ideas spread among the masses by the old
system of society which is still fighting for survival. He rose
to the defence of the programme with a paraphrase from the
Communist Manifesto:

> The rule of the working class was inconceivable until the
> great mass of them were united in desiring it. Then they
> would be an overwhelming majority. This would not be the
> dictatorship of a little band of conspirators or a minority
> party, but of the immense majority in the interests of the
> immense majority, to prevent counter-revolution. In short,
> it would represent the victory of true democracy.[19]

This, of course, was not an answer to Akimov's argument,
especially for Russia, where the proletariat was a tiny movement.

Lenin took very little part in the great programme debate, except for his intervention on the agrarian aspects of
the programme (see Chapter 11). It is clear, however, as his
policy in 1917 proved, that he was in complete agreement
with Plekhanov.

The programme adopted by the Congress was practically the same as the draft submitted to it.[20] The only differences were the addition of a demand for elected judges; and a few modifications of detail in the demands relating to legislation for the improvement of working conditions. It is interesting to note that during the debate on the programme Martynov, one of the 'economist' delegates, delivered a sharp attack on Lenin's *What is to be Done?*, but got no support at all.

It is worth repeating, in the light of later events, that the programme was adopted unanimously, with only one delegate abstaining. The unity of the *Iskrists* appeared less complete by the time the 16th and 17th sessions of the Congress took place. Several very close votes revealed that a number of them were voting with the Bund or the 'economists' against Lenin and Plekhanov. But these votes were all on small points.

The bombshell of the Congress exploded in the 22nd session, devoted to the party rules. The occasion was the discussion of the first paragraph of the draft statutes, which defined membership. Lenin proposed that Article I should define a party member as one 'who recognizes the party's programme and supports it by material means *and by personal participation in one of the party organizations*'. Martov proposed an alternative starting off in exactly the same way, but with the final italicized phrase reading: '*and by regular personal association under the direction of one of the party organizations*'.

Lenin, taking the floor again and again, explained his formulation: He wanted a tightly organized party of revolutionaries.

> the party must be only the vanguard, the leader of the vast masses of the working class, the whole (or nearly the whole) of which works 'under the control and direction' of the party organizations, but the whole of which does not and should not belong to a 'party' ... when most of our activities have to be confined to limited, secret circles and even to private meetings, it is extremely difficult, almost impossible in fact, for us to distinguish those who only talk from those

who do the work. There is hardly another country in the world where the jumbling of these two categories is as common and as productive of such boundless confusion and harm as in Russia. We are suffering sorely . . . It would be better if ten who do work should not call themselves party members (real workers don't hunt after titles!) than that one who only talks should have the right and opportunity to be a party member. That is a principle which seems to me irrefutable, and which compels me to fight against Martov . . . we must not forget that every party member is responsible for the party, and that *the party is responsible for every one of its members.*[21]

Martov, too, spoke repeatedly. He was for a broad party. Trotsky sided with Martov, which was surprising, as in a previous session he seemed to be an even more extreme centralist than Lenin. Thus he had stated :

The rules, he (Comrade Akimov) said, do not define the jurisdiction of the Central Committee with enough precision. I cannot agree with him. On the contrary, this definition is precise and means that inasmuch as the party is one whole, it must be ensured control over the local committees. Comrade Lieber said, borrowing my expression, that the rules were 'organized distrust'. That is true. But I used this expression in reference to the rules proposed by the Bund spokesmen, which represented organized distrust on the part of a section of the party towards the whole party. Our rules, on the other hand, represent the organized distrust of the party towards all its sections, that is, control over all local, district, national, and other organizations.[22]

Now Trotsky suddenly said : 'I do not believe that you can put statutory exorcism on opportunism. I do not give the statutes any sort of mystical interpretation . . . Opportunism is produced by many more complex causes than one or another clause in the rules; it is brought about by the relative level of development of bourgeois democracy and the proletariat.'

Axelrod also came out against Lenin. Plekhanov however rallied to his side : 'I have one preconceived idea, but the more I reflect on what has been said, the stronger is my conviction that the truth lies with Lenin . . . Intellectuals may hesitate for individualistic reasons to join the party, so much the better, for they are generally opportunists . . . For this reason if for no other, the opponents of opportunism should vote for his draft.'

The *Iskrists* were split and Lenin's proposal was outvoted 28 to 23. Martov's majority included the five Bund delegates and the two 'economists'. These seven gave Martov and his supporters a majority against Lenin sufficient to dominate the Congress thereafter.

How could Martov and Trotsky who wholeheartedly supported Lenin's *What is to be Done?*, which proposed that absolute authority should be given to the Central Committee of the party, reject Lenin's definition of party membership? To combine a strong centralist leadership with loose membership was eclecticism taken to an extreme.

The harsh necessity for democratic centralism within the revolutionary working-class party is derived from the harsh imperatives of the dictatorship of the proletariat. Martov and Trotsky baulked at this. Moreover, the leadership of a revolutionary party must provide the highest example of devotion and complete identification with the party in its daily life. This gives it the moral authority to demand the maximum sacrifice from the rank and file.

Years earlier, Engels, in arguing against the anarchists, had said that the proletarian revolution demanded a very strong discipline, a strong authority.

> Have these gentlemen ever seen a revolution? A revolution is certainly the most authoritarian thing there is; it is an act whereby one part of the population imposes its will upon the other part by means of rifles, bayonets and cannon, all of which are highly authoritarian means. And the victorious party must maintain its rule by means of the terror which its arms inspire in the reactionaries.[23]

Thus the revolutionary party cannot avoid making strong demands for sacrifice and discipline from its own members. Martov's definition of party membership fitted the weakness of his conception of the dictatorship of the proletariat.

After this decision regarding Article I of the party's

statutes, Lenin repeatedly found himself in a minority. In the 23rd to 26th sessions Martov – now constantly opposing Lenin – successfully carried the day on one issue after another. The issues, however, were of quite small significance.

Lenin gained a majority again in the 27th session, in which the Jewish Bund's desire to be the sole organization of Jewish workers, and to preserve its autonomy in the party, was defeated (by 41 votes to 5, with 5 abstentions). Soon afterwards the five Bund delegates walked out of the Congress. Then the two 'economist' delegates also walked out, because the Congress decided that the *Iskrist* League of Russian Revolutionary Social Democrats Abroad should be the sole representative of the party abroad. Martov thus lost 7 votes at one blow, reducing his support to 20 votes, while Lenin kept his 24.

The Congress now had to elect the leading bodies of the party. It had already agreed on the central structure. The rules had designated a Central Committee of three to operate inside Russia and had appointed *Iskra* as the Central Organ of the party for ideological leadership. Standing over both of them was to be a Party Council, consisting of five members – two appointed by the Central Committee, two by the Central Organ, and the fifth elected by the Congress.

With his majority Lenin got through his list of candidates for the Central Committee of three. It was the editorial board of *Iskra*, now the Central Organ of the party, which presented the difficulty, since it was generally assumed that the original six would be elected. Four of these, Martov, Potresov, Axelrod and Zasulich, were now opponents of Lenin. Lenin moved an editorial board of only three – Plekhanov, Lenin and Martov. This question was the one upon which the party split into the Bolsheviks (majority) and Mensheviks (minority).

Plekhanov, Lenin and Martov were elected editors. Noskov, Krzhizhanovsky and Lengnik, 'Leninists all three,' were elected as the Central Committee. Plekhanov was elected chairman of the Party Council. The discussion of the membership of the editorial board – whether to re-elect the six existing members, as Martov wished, or the three whom Lenin suggested – went on and on, and on, for nine long sessions of the Congress. The debate was bitter and acrimonious.

After the long and exhausting wrangle on this issue, the rest of the Congress, one day in all, passed as if the delegates were half asleep and did not care at all. Of the 24 items on the agenda, they had up to the last day handled only 4. After 5 p.m. on the last day – after a month of deliberation – the Congress began a desultory discussion of some resolutions on tactical questions. These included statements on demonstrations; on the trade union movement, and work among the sects; on work among the student youth; on how to behave under interrogation; on shop stewards; on the 1904 International Congress in Amsterdam; on the liberals (Starover's resolution); on the liberals (Plekhanov's resolution); on the Socialist Revolutionaries; on party literature; on anti-Jewish pogroms.

The most unfortunate resolution to be passed in this session was the one moved by Potresov (Starover) and supported by Martov and Axelrod on socialist support for liberals on the following conditions: (1) that the 'liberal or liberal-democratic trends' should 'clearly and unambiguously declare that in their struggle against the autocratic government they will resolutely side with the Russian Social Democrats'! (2) that the liberals 'shall not include in the programmes any demands running counter to the interests of the working class or the democracy generally, or obscuring their political consciousness', and (3) that they should make universal, equal, secret and direct suffrage the slogan of their struggle. (These were to become a cause of widespread misconceptions regarding the revolutionary potential of the liberals.) The delegates were so tired that they passed this resolution very quickly, along with a contradictory one moved by Plekhanov and supported by Lenin. In Potresov's resolution, supported by Martov, Zasulich and Axelrod (and, astonishingly, Trotsky), we have a foretaste of the Menshevism of 1905 and after.[24] It is interesting that both at the time of Congress and afterwards Lenin paid very little attention to this resolution, and was much more concerned about the conflict over the size of the editorial board.

The issue of whether there should be three or six on the editorial board, over which the party split, seemed like a storm in a teacup, a question of personal wrangling, too insignificant to split a serious movement. Lenin saw the differences as a conflict between those who accepted the party spirit of appointment of officials on the one hand, and those accustomed to circle attitudes and 'the old boy network', a conflict which had a large personal element in it. He was not at all sure, at the time, whether this justified a split.

The supporters of the old editorial board of *Iskra* used such arguments as: 'The Congress has neither the moral nor the political right to refashion the editorial board' (Trotsky); 'it is too delicate [*sic*!] a question' (Trotsky again); '*how will the editors who are not re-elected feel about the fact that the Congress does not want to see them on the board any more?*' (Tsaryov).

Lenin's comment was:

Such arguments simply put the whole question on the plane of *pity and injured feelings*, and were a direct admission of bankruptcy as regards real arguments of principle, real political arguments . . . If we adopt this standpoint, which is a *philistine* and not a party standpoint, we shall at every election have to consider: will not Petrov be offended if Ivanov is elected and not he, will not some member of the Organizing Committee be offended if another member, and not he, is elected to the Central Committee? Where is this going to land us, comrades? If we have gathered here for the purpose of creating a party, and *not of indulging in mutual compliments and philistine sentimentality*, then we can never agree to such a view. We are about to *elect officials*, and there can be no talk of lack of confidence in any person not elected: *our only consideration should be the interests of the work and a person's suitability for the post to which he is being elected.*

He argued against 'the old snug little band who insist on their circle "continuity".'[25]

These people are so accustomed to the bell-jar seclusion of

an intimate and snug little circle that they almost fainted as soon as a person spoke up in a free and open arena on his own responsibility . . . Intellectualist individualism and the circle mentality had come into conflict with the requirement of open speaking before the party.[26]

When Martov, refusing to abide by the Congress's decision regarding the editorial board, announced 'We are not serfs!', Lenin argued against this 'aristocratic anarchism' and said that they 'must learn to *insist* that the duties of a party member be fulfilled not only by the rank and file, but by the "people at the top" as well'.[27] Why did Martov and his friends try to deny the actual inefficiency of the members of the old editorial board now removed by the Congress?

> The old board of six was so ineffectual that *never once in all its three years* did it meet in full force. That may seem incredible, but it is a fact. *Not one* of the forty-five issues of *Iskra* was made up (in the editorial and technical sense) by anyone but Martov or Lenin. And *never once* was any *major* theoretical issue raised by anyone but Plekhanov. Axelrod did no work at all (he contributed literally nothing to *Zarya* and only three or four articles to all the forty-five issues of *Iskra*). Zasulich and Starover only contributed and advised, they *never* did any actual editorial work.[28]

Explaining his own motives, Lenin stated that, in the 45 issues of the old *Iskra*, Martov had contributed 39 articles, Lenin 32 and Plekhanov 24. Zasulich had written only 6 articles, Axelrod 4 and Potresov 8.[29]

The desire to express well-mannered support for the veterans instead of subordinating everything to the needs of the revolution was completely foreign to Lenin. It was not that he was cold towards the pioneers of Russian marxism. He was particularly attached to Vera Zasulich, and so was Krupskaya. ' "Wait till you see Vera Ivanovna", Vladimir Ilyich said, the first evening I arrived in Munich – "there's a person as clear as crystal." And it was the truth.'[30]

Her heroic past touched a deep chord in Lenin's heart. In January 1878, as a young woman of 29, she had shot General Trepov, head of the gendarmerie in Petersburg, in protest against the maltreatment and humiliation of a political prisoner. At her trial horrible police abuses were exposed. The jury was so shocked by the revelations and so impressed by the defendant that they acquitted her. When the police attempted to seize her outside the court, a sympathetic crowd rescued her and helped her escape. Abroad she kept in close touch with Karl Marx. She was deeply loved and admired by Lenin, and he knew well that to remove her from the editorial board of *Iskra* would be a very hard blow for her. As Krupskaya put it:

> Vera Ivanovna yearned very much for Russia. I think it was in 1899 she went to Russia illegally, not to work, but simply because 'I must take a look at the *mujik* and see what his nose has grown like.' And when the *Iskra* began to appear she felt that this was a real piece of Russian work and clung on to it grimly. To her, leaving *Iskra* would have meant once more becoming isolated from Russia, once more beginning to sink into the dead sea of *émigré* life, that drags one to the bottom.
>
> It was for that reason that, when the question of the editorship of *Iskra* was brought up at the second Congress, she revolted. For her it was not a question of self-love, but a question of life or death.[31]

However, Lenin was far too honest intellectually, too devoted to the cause, to sacrifice the needs of the organization to his own sentiments. And so Vera Zasulich had to go. Those who were ready to subordinate the needs of the movement to secondary considerations were later to show themselves to be conciliators, not revolutionaries. But this fact was as yet hidden even from the eagle eyes of Lenin.

Lenin's Attitude to the Comrades

From the incident described above one might draw the conclusion that Lenin was heartless, cold and inconsiderate towards his comrades. Nothing was further from the truth. In fact he was very warm and generous towards them, showing kindness and attention to all their needs. Even when he broke with people politically, he often did not lose his affection for them. A case in point was his attitude to Martov.

It was exceedingly difficult for him to break with Martov. Work together in Petersburg, the period of work on the old *Iskra*, had bound them closely together. In those days Martov, who was extremely impressionable, had shown a keen sense for grasping Ilyich's ideas and developing them in a talented manner. Afterwards, Vladimir Ilyich vehemently fought the Mensheviks, but every time that Martov, even in the slightest degree, took the correct line, his old attitude towards him revived. Such was the case, for example, in Paris in 1910, when Martov and Vladimir Ilyich worked together on the editorial of the *Social Democrat*. Coming home from the office, Vladimir Ilyich often used to relate in joyful tones that Martov was taking a correct line, or was even opposing Dan. Later, back in Russia, how pleased Vladimir Ilyich was with Martov's position in the July (1917) days; not because it was of any advantage to the Bolsheviks, but because Martov was acting worthily – as behoved a revolutionary.[32]

During the winter of 1919-20 Lenin heard that Martov was very ill and sent him the best doctors available in Moscow.

No *personal* element affected Lenin's political appreciation of individuals and vice versa. Krupskaya wrote:

One of Ilyich's characteristic traits was his ability to distinguish disputes on principles from personal disputes and his ability to place the interests of the cause above everything else. When an opponent attacked him, Ilyich was roused, he hit back, pressed his own point of view; but when new tasks arose and it was found possible to cooperate with the opponent, Ilyich was able to approach the opponent of yesterday as a comrade. He did not have to force himself to do this, it came naturally. Herein lay Ilyich's tremendous power. For all his jealousy touching questions of principle, he was a great optimist as far as persons were concerned. He would sometimes err, but on the whole this optimism was very beneficial for the cause.[33]

He could at one and the same time attack a person very strongly for his current political stance, but pay homage to his contributions in other fields.

In a letter commenting on Plekhanov's political bankruptcy in 1905, he wrote, 'I am sorry for the old man . . . What a lovely brain.'[34] Two years later, in an article attacking Plekhanov bitterly for his policies in the 1905 revolution, Lenin still went out of his way to praise his important earlier theoretical contributions.

Again, in a letter to the editorial board of *Pravda*, written some time after 25 May 1913, Lenin could overlook the past and write: 'He [Plekhanov] is valuable now because he is fighting the enemies of the working-class movement.'[35] Even after 1917, when Plekhanov not only supported the war, but went out of his way, in his paper *Edintsvo*, to accuse Lenin of being a paid German agent, Lenin continued to praise Plekhanov's contributions to marxist theory.

Lenin showed great warmth and tact in helping comrades to develop, and to improve their knowledge. Krupskaya writes:

> I recall Ilyich's attitude towards inexperienced authors. In discussing their work with them he would get right down to the heart of the subject, to the fundamentals and make suggestions for improvement. But he did all this very discreetly, so that these authors hardly noticed that they were being corrected. And Ilyich was very good at helping people in their work. If, for example, he wanted someone to write an article but was not sure whether he would be able to do it properly, he would start a discussion with him, expound his ideas and get the prospective writer interested. After he had sounded him on the subject sufficiently, he would say to him: 'Would you like to write an article on this subject?' And the author would not even have noticed that his preliminary discussion with Ilyich had helped him and that in writing his article he had actually used Ilyich's expressions and turns of phrase.[36]

If Lenin had one weakness, it was that he fell in love with people too easily. 'Vladimir Ilyich was always having these periods of enthusiasm for people. He seemed to discern some valuable quality in a person and clung on to it.'[37] But these enthusiasms did not continue for long. While on first acquaintance Lenin was always ready to 'fall in love' with a new collaborator, after a longer acquaintance he would nearly always discern elements of weakness in him.

His attitude towards a person tended to change radically, depending on whether at the time he was on his side or against him. There was no fickleness in these attachments. The reason why one often finds in Lenin's writings startling contradictions in his comments on people, is that his basic rule was that the needs of the struggle took priority over everything else. Lenin's immense self-control, which allowed him to be objective in evaluating people's contributions, including those of his opponents, his generosity of spirit and exceptional warmth, earned him not only the trust, but also the love of his associates.

After this digression on Lenin's attitude towards his comrades, let us return to the aftermath of the 1903 Congress.

The Madness of the Split

Once while walking, Leo Tolstoy spotted in the distance the figure of a man squatting and gesturing strangely; a madman, he thought – but on drawing nearer he was satisfied that the man was attending to necessary work – sharpening a knife on a stone. Lenin was fond of citing this example. The interminable discussions and factional squabbles at the 1903 Congress looked to an outside observer like the activities of madmen.

It would be hard for an event to appear more trifling or meaningless than this split between the Bolsheviks and Mensheviks. Reading the minutes of the Congress one cannot but be astonished that *this* was a turning point in the history of the Russian labour movement. Even the participants did not believe that the split was of great importance, or that it would last for any length of time. Thus Lunacharsky wrote subsequently:

> The greatest difficulty in that struggle consisted in this, that the second Congress, having split the party, had not yet plumbed the really profound differences between the Martovists on the one hand and the Leninists on the other. These differences still seemed to turn on the one paragraph of the party statutes and the personnel of the editorial board. Many were embarrassed by the insignificance of the reason that led to the split.[38]

Piatnitsky, later a prominent official of the Comintern, but at that time a young workman, writes in his reminiscences:

> I could not understand why petty differences kept us from working together . . . word reached us of differences of opinion within the *Iskra* group itself.
>
> I could hardly believe those rumours. We had expected to hear of important differences with the *Rabochaye Dyeloists* and their supporters; but I personally had not expected any disunion within the *Iskra* group, which I was accustomed to consider as a homogeneous body. The agony of uncertainty lasted for many days. At last the delegates returned from the Congress to Berlin. We heard reports on the Congress from both sides, and immediately each side began agitating for its own line. I was torn between the two. On the one hand I was very sorry that they had offended Zasulich, Potresov . . . and Axelrod, by expelling them from the editorial board of the *Iskra* . . . Moreover, comrades with whom I had been especially close . . . were in the Menshevik camp, whereas I fully endorsed the organizational structure of the party advocated by Comrade Lenin. Logically I was with the majority, but my personal sympathies, if I may so express myself, were with the minority.[39]

The engineer Krzhizhanovsky, who was very close to Lenin in those years, recalls, 'To me personally, the thought about Comrade Martov's opportunism seemed particularly far-fetched.' There is a great deal of such testimony. From Petersburg, from Moscow, from the provinces, came protests and laments. No one wanted to acknowledge the split which had taken place at the congress among the *Iskrists*.[40]

A factory worker wrote to Lenin complaining about the split and 'meaningless faction fight':

> Look comrade, is it a natural state of affairs when all energies are spent on travelling around the committees for the one purpose of talking about the majority and minority? Really, I don't know, is this issue really so important that all energies should be devoted to it and because of it people should look on each other practically as enemies? For that's what it comes down to: if a committee is, let's say, made up of followers of one camp, then nobody from the other camp will ever get into it, no matter how fit he may be for the

work; in fact, he won't get in even if he is essential to the work and it suffers badly without him. I don't mean to say, of course, that the struggle over this issue should be given up altogether, no, only I think it should be of a different kind and should not lead us to forget our principal duty, which is to propagate Social Democratic ideas among the masses; for if we forget that we shall rob our party of its strength. I don't know if it is fair or not, but when I see people trampling the interests of the work in the mud and completely forgetting them, I call them all political intriguers. It really hurts and fills you with alarm for the work when you see the people at the head of it spending their time on something else. When you see that, you ask yourself: is our party doomed to perpetual splits over such trifles, are we incapable of waging the internal and the external struggle at the same time?[41]

Personal bickering and vilification aggravated the split. Years later Lenin could write:

No struggle over principles waged by groups within the Social Democratic movement *anywhere in the world* has managed to avoid a number of personal and organizational conflicts. Nasty types make it their business deliberately to pick on 'conflict' expressions. But only weak-nerved dilettanti from among 'sympathizers' can be embarrassed by these conflicts, can shrug them off in despair or in scorn, as if to say 'it is all a squabble!'[42]

At the time, in 1903, the personal enmity between the contestants added to the confusion.

That Lenin himself was not at all clear about the depth of the split and its future significance was clear from his writings at the time. His uncertainty is revealed partly by the fact that the section of his *Collected Works* covering this period contains an unprecedented number of unmailed letters, undelivered statements and articles drafted but not published. Those that did see the light of day indicate that he did not expect the split with the Mensheviks to continue for long, and did not think it was justified to break up the party over 'trifling' issues. Thus he wrote in a letter to A.N.Potresov (13 September):

I ask myself: over what, in point of fact, would we be parting company as enemies for life? I go over all the events and impressions of the Congress. I realize that I often behaved and acted in a state of frightful irritation, 'frenziedly'; I am quite willing to admit *this fault of mine to anyone*, if that can be called a fault which was a natural product of the atmosphere, the reactions, the interjections, the struggle, etc. But examining now, quite unfrenziedly, the results attained, the outcome achieved by frenzied struggle, I can detect nothing, absolutely nothing in these results that is injurious to the party, and absolutely nothing that is an affront or insult to the minority.[43]

Six months after the Congress he could write: 'the disagreements that divide the two wings at the present time for the most part concern, not questions of programme or tactics, but only organizational questions';[44] 'questions of organization . . . are, of course, less fundamental than questions of tactics, let alone of programme.'[45] 'Formerly we used to differ over major issues, such as might in some cases even justify a split; now we have reached agreement on all major and important points, and are only divided by *shades*, about which we may *and should* argue, but over which it would be absurd and childish to part company.'[46] 'If our party members are to be worthy representatives of the class-conscious militant proletariat, worthy participants in the world working-class movement, they must do their utmost to ensure that no individual differences over the interpretation and methods of realizing the principles of our party programme shall interfere, or be capable of interfering, with harmonious joint work under the direction of our central institutions.'[47]

Lenin wavered for months. Despite the myth propagated by the cult-builders, he was not omniscient, and could not foresee the results of the 'little crack' in the party. His indecision badly affected his nerves. On the eve of the second Congress, Krupskaya remembers: 'Vladimir Ilyich was so overwrought that he developed a nervous illness called "holy fire" which consists in inflammation of the nerve terminals of back and chest . . . On the way to Geneva Vladimir Ilyich was very restless; on arriving there he broke down completely, and had to lie in bed for two weeks.'[48] During the Congress he got into such a state that he stopped sleeping altogether and was extremely restless.[49]

In fact, after every conference Lenin would go off, usually with Krupskaya, on long hiking or cycling expeditions. His self-discipline was so great that there were few indications of the surges of emotion that rocked him. Yet in Krupskaya's memoirs there are constant references to weeks and months of nervous exhaustion.

If he managed to retain his composure and to soldier on, keeping his intellectual honesty, minimally affected by personal upsets and by his nerves and tensions, it was largely due to his life's companion, Krupskaya, whose outstanding personality, devotion to the cause, energy and purity of character, and steadfast love sustained him.

To return to the events which followed the 1903 Congress – it was more than six months later that Lenin finally came to the conclusion that the split was justified and necessary. He stopped hesitating and came out firmly with the argument that the split was a reflection of the differences between the proletarian wing and the petty bourgeois intellectualist wing of the party.

In his 230-page review of the 1903 Congress and its aftermath, called *One Step Forward, Two Steps Back* (written February-May 1904), he says that to 'the individualism of the intellectual, which already manifested itself in the controversy over Paragraph 1, revealing its tendency to opportunist argument and anarchistic phrase-mongering, *all* proletarian organization and discipline seems to be *serfdom*'.[50]

He quotes a letter written to *Iskra* (now a Menshevik paper), which denounced him for visualizing the party as 'an immense factory' headed by a director in the shape of the Central Committee. Lenin's comment is that the writer

> never guesses that this dreadful word of his immediately betrays the mentality of the bourgeois intellectual unfamiliar with either the practice or the theory of proletarian organization. For the factory, which seems only a bogey to some, represents that highest form of capitalist co-operation which

has united and disciplined the proletariat, taught it to organize, and placed it at the head of all the other sections of the toiling and exploited population. And marxism, the ideology of the proletariat trained by capitalism, has been and is teaching unstable intellectuals to distinguish between the factory as a means of exploitation (discipline based on fear of starvation) and the factory as a means of a technically highly developed form of production. The discipline and organization which come so hard to the bourgeois intellectual are very easily acquired by the proletariat just because of this factory 'schooling'.[51]

In attacking the intelligentsia and emphasizing the need for the revolutionary party to discipline it, Lenin quotes at length Kautsky's brilliant characterization of intellectual individualists :

The intellectual is not a capitalist. True, his standard of life is bourgeois, and he must maintain it if he is not to become a pauper; but at the same time he is compelled to sell the product of his labour, and often his labour-power, and is himself often enough exploited and humiliated by the capitalist. Hence the intellectual does not stand in any economic antagonism to the proletariat. But his status of life and his conditions of labour are not proletarian, and this gives rise to a certain antagonism in sentiments and ideas.

As an isolated individual, the proletarian is nothing. His whole strength, his whole progress, all his hopes and expectations are derived from *organization*, when he forms part of a big and strong organism. This is the main thing for him; the individual in comparison means very little. The proletarian fights with the utmost devotion as part of the anonymous mass, without prospect of personal advantage or personal glory, doing his duty in any post he is assigned to with a voluntary discipline which pervades all his feelings and thoughts.

Quite different is the case of the intellectual. He does not fight by means of power, but by argument. His weapons are his personal knowledge, his personal ability, his personal convictions. He can attain to any position at all only through his personal qualities. Hence the freest play for his individuality seems to him the prime condition for successful activity. It is only with difficulty that he submits to being a part subordinate to a whole, and then only from necessity, not from inclination. He recognizes the need of discipline only for the mass, not for the elect minds. And of course he counts himself among the latter ...

Nietzsche's philosophy, with its cult of the superman, for whom the fulfilment of his own individuality is everything and any subordination of that individuality to a great social aim is vulgar and despicable, is the real philosophy of the intellectual; and it renders him totally unfit to take part in the class struggle of the proletariat.

Next to Nietzsche, the most outstanding exponent of a philosophy answering to the sentiments of the intelligentsia is probably Ibsen. His Doctor Stockmann (in *An Enemy of the People*) is not a socialist, as many have thought, but the type of the intellectual, who is bound to come into conflict with the proletarian movement, and with any movement of the people generally, as soon as he attempts to work within it. For the basis of the proletarian movement, as of every democratic movement, is respect for the majority of one's fellows. The typical intellectual à *la* Stockmann regards a 'compact majority' as a monster that must be overthrown.[52]

Lenin concluded that the position taken by Martov and his supporters reflected capitulation before the individualism of the intellectuals. Party rules should aim to discipline these same intellectuals.

It is interesting to compare Lenin's arguments in *What is to be Done?* with *One Step Forward, Two Steps Back.* In the former the target for criticism was the local activist, whose horizon was the narrow one of the circle. Hence the notion that the proletariat 'is spontaneously drawn towards trade unionist consciousness' only, and that the marxist intelligentsia has a central role to play in bringing class and political consciousness to the workers from outside. Now, two years later, in *One Step Forward, Two Steps Back,* the proletarian elements in the party have to impose discipline on the intelligentsia. Times change, the needs of the movement change, and Lenin bends the stick over in order to steer the required course.

Anticipation

The 1903 split was a foretaste of later developments. The political differences between Lenin and Martov, considered in static terms, i.e. mechanically, were too small to justify a split. But when they are looked at from the point of view of their development, i.e. dialectically, it is clear that small differences can become big ones. In the united party, petty bourgeois circles are not completely isolated from working-class circles; one faction tends to gather around itself and become the mouthpiece of a non-proletarian social group, while the other becomes increasingly antagonistic towards these petty bourgeois elements. But in 1903 the differences were solely in the organizational field, and political and programmatic differences had not yet manifested themselves. For this reason Lenin did not, to begin with, consider the split justified. However, the very existence of separate organizations may lead to political differences as policy develops within them, and the *personal* element may play a significant role in shaping policy within each group.

It is true that the two factions in 1903 were not chemically pure in composition. On the side of the Bolsheviks stood Plekhanov, who later became an extreme right-wing Menshevik, and on the side of the Mensheviks stood Trotsky and Rosa Luxemburg. But the character of the factions was basically determined by the two leaders who differed most in their characteristics, Lenin and Martov. The fact that the Bolsheviks were from the beginning called the 'hard ones', and the Mensheviks the 'soft', was a psychological characterization that on the whole fitted the leadership of the two wings of the movement. Everyone spoke of Lenin's hardness, and Martov's softness was no less talked about. Many years after the 1903 Congress Trotsky called Martov 'the Hamlet of Democratic Socialism' : 'his thought lacked the mainspring of will'.[53]

One expression of the difference in psychological traits between Lenin and Martov can be seen in the very choice of the names Bolshevik and Menshevik. Lenin steadfastly held to the title Bolshevik, while Martov meekly carried the label of Menshevik for the rest of his life. Even when Martov had a majority he still called himself a Menshevik !

One of the pamphlets which Martov wrote against Lenin after the second Congress was called 'Once Again in the Minority!' Had Lenin been in a minority on every issue in the Congress as he was on Rule 1, would he have called his group Mensheviks? Of course not. He would probably have called it the 'Hards', 'Orthodox Marxists', 'Revolutionary Social Democrats', or something similar. The names which Martov and Lenin chose were symptomatic: fatalism and submissiveness versus willpower and action. Here the historical and the personal factors became enmeshed.

One certainly could not describe Martov politically in 1903 as a reformist. He showed signs of centrism, which is a general term for very varied tendencies and groupings ranging from reformism to marxism. One of the main characteristics of centrists is their obscuring of the need for a clear demarcation between the vanguard of the class and the mass, of the initiative of the minority and the routine of the majority. Centrism's main drawback is its historical fatalism. Because it is so indefinite in nature, so lacking in clear, sharp character delineation, because it vacillates between marxism and reformism, centrist groupings do not all move in the same direction. Some move leftwards towards marxism and some rightwards towards reformism. In addition, lacking consistency as they do, centrists sometimes move to the left and then later veer to the right. In the process, differentiation takes place in the grouping itself, and splits ensue: some sections move over completely to reformism, while others join the revolutionary wing of the labour movement.

In Tsarist Russia the differentiation between consistent revolutionaries, centrists and reformists was impeded by the autocratic régime itself. In Western Europe the most moderate elements of the labour movement were frankly describing themselves as reformists. But under the Tsarist régime even the most moderate of socialists could not constitute themselves into a party of reform. The 'parliamentary road to socialism' could not attract where parliament did not exist. A semi-parliament at least was needed – the Tsarist Duma of later years – for a parliamentary cretinism to raise its head. Nobody in the Russian socialist movement in 1903 openly unfurled the banner of reformism.

The Bolshevik and Menshevik factions of Russian Social Democracy were heading for a deep schism which would give expression in real political terms to the latent tendencies of the two factions, and which would rule out the possibility of any reconciliation. But this outcome was not foreseen by any of the participants in the quarrels of those days.

It needed the year of revolution of 1905 and the period of reaction of 1907-10 for Menshevism to be fully fashioned. Because the Menshevism of 1903 was largely centrism, the attitude of the Bolsheviks, including Lenin, to the split was very unclear and unstable. A further consequence was that the process of complete separation between Bolshevism and Menshevism took a number of years. To anticipate the story, the following was the history of their relationship:

July-August 1903	official split
Spring 1905	actual split
1906-07	semi-unity
1908-09	split
1910	semi-unity
January 1912	final split.

Bolshevik Leaders Refuse to Split with the Mensheviks

Shortly after the Congress Plekhanov, who had supported Lenin there, changed his mind. He announced that he could not bear to 'fire on his comrades', that 'rather than have a split, it is better to put a bullet in one's brain'. He decided to invite Martov, Axelrod, Zasulich and Potresov to join the editorial board of *Iskra*. Lenin resigned in disgust.

Lenin's immediate reaction was to organize for the convening of a new Congress. Thus on 18 December 1903 he wrote to one of his closest friends, G.M.Krzhizhanovsky:

The only salvation is – a congress. Its watchword: the fight against disrupters. Only by this watchword can we catch out the Martovites, win over the broad masses and save the situation. In my opinion, the only possible plan is this: *for the time being* not a word about the *congress*, complete secrecy. *All, absolutely all,* forces to be sent *into the com-*

mittees and on tours. A fight to be waged for peace, for putting a stop to disruption, for subordination to the Central Committee. Every effort to be made to strengthen the committees with our people. Every effort to be made to catch out the Martovites and *Yuzhny-Rabochy* people in disruption, pin them down by documents and resolutions against the disrupters; resolutions of the committees should pour into the Central Organ. Further, our people should be got into the wavering committees. Winning over the committees with the watchword: against disruption – this is the *most important* task. *The congress must be held not later than January*, therefore set to work energetically. I repeat: either *complete* defeat ... or *immediate preparation for a congress. It must be prepared secretly at first* during a maximum of one month, *after which during three weeks the demands of half the committees to be collected and the congress convened*. Again and yet again – this is the only salvation.[54]

However, it took Lenin eighteen months, until May 1905, to manage to convene the Congress and thus set the seal on the split with the Mensheviks.

He first met resistance to the idea of the new Congress from the Central Committee. Although all its members were Bolsheviks, they were more and more exasperated with the split and were looking for a compromise with the Mensheviks:

> shortly after the January meeting five of the six members of the CC then in Russia expressed their disapproval of Lenin's demand for a new Congress. They also rejected his suggestion that they should co-opt two more members . . . The motives behind the proposal were all too transparent. Their letter ended: 'We all implore the Old Man (Lenin) to give up his quarrel and begin work. We are waiting for leaflets, pamphlets and all kind of advice – the best way of soothing one's nerves and answering slander.'
> But this was a course Lenin had no wish to adopt. 'I am not a machine', he replied, 'and cannot do any work in the present disgraceful state of affairs.'[55]

After months of acrimonious correspondence with its members, by the summer of 1904 he was to all intents and purposes ousted from the CC, although formally still a member. In July 1904 the Central Committee made a move towards a compromise with the Mensheviks: in an announcement published in *Iskra* it recognized the full authority of the editorial board of the paper (made up of the five Mensheviks, including Plekhanov), called on Lenin to rejoin the board, and denounced his agitation for a new, third Congress to settle accounts with the Mensheviks.

Lenin had set up without the knowledge of the CC a body called the Southern Bureau of the CC, under the leadership of V.V.Vorovsky, who was not a CC member. It had no official status, but served Lenin as a means for calling a new Congress. The CC dissolved the Southern Bureau, and deprived Lenin of the powers of foreign representative of the Central Committee, forbidding his writings to be published without their sanction.[56] In place of Lenin they appointed Noskov, a conciliator, as their official foreign representative.

But Lenin did not sit idly while this was happening. With the aid of Krupskaya in Geneva, and a group of supporters operating inside Russia, he built a completely new set of centralized committees, quite regardless of Rule 6 of the party statutes, which reserved to the Central Committee the right to organize and recognize committees. Three conferences of Bolshevik local committees were held in September-December 1904: (1) the Southern (Odessa, Ekaterinoslav, and Nikolayev committees); (2) the Caucasian (Baku, Batum, Tiflis, and Imeretian-Mingrelian committees); and (3) the Northern (St Petersburg, Moscow, Tver, Riga, Norther, and Nizhni-Novgorod committees). At Lenin's suggestion, the conferences elected a Bureau of Majority Committees to prepare and convene the third party Congress. The Bureau, of which Lenin became a member, was formally constituted in December 1904.[57]

A new Congress was first called for by 22 Bolsheviks at a conference, held in Switzerland in September 1904 and attended by 19 people, with 3 others subscribing to the decision. Among the 19 were Lenin, his wife and his sister.

In December 1904 Lenin succeeded in establishing a newspaper of his own, *Vperyod* (Forward), which became the organ of Bolshevism. However, even after this things did not go too well. Thus on 11 February 1905, Lenin wrote to his two close supporters, A.A.Bogdanov and S.I.Gusev:

> Just look at the Bundists: they do not prate about central-ism, but *every one* of them writes to the centre weekly and contact is thus *actually* maintained. You only have to pick up their *Posledniye Izvestia* to see this contact. We, how-ever, here are issuing the sixth number of *Vperyod*, yet one of our editors (Rakhmetov) has not written a single line, either about or for *Vperyod*. Our people 'talk' of extensive literary connections in St Petersburg and in Moscow, and of the Majority's young forces, while we here, *two months* after the issuance of the call for collaboration, . . . have seen or heard nothing from them . . . We did 'hear' from strangers about some sort of alliance between the St Petersburg Com-mittee of the Majority and a group of Mensheviks, but from our own people not a word. We refuse to believe that Bol-sheviks could have taken such an imbecilic, suicidal step. We did 'hear' from strangers about a conference of Social Democrats and the formation of a 'bloc', but from our own people *not a word*, although there are rumours that this is a *fait accompli*.[58]

Resistance to the split was also widespread among the rank and file, and it took months of Herculean effort actually to put into effect the break between Bolsheviks and Men-sheviks in a number of Russian cities. In St Petersburg the party split in autumn 1904, when the Menshevik minority broke away from the local committee: 'many of the district cells even in 1904-05 were of a mixed Bolshevik-Menshevik composition, and many of the rank and file members were neither very conscious of the split nor of its significance'.[59]

In Moscow the formal split did not take place until May 1905. In Siberia and other places the two factions operated within the same organizational structure throughout 1904 and 1905 and continued to do so until the fusion conference held in April-May 1906.

The famous illegal Caucasian printshop, in which Bol-shevik sympathies predominated, continued in 1904 to re-print the Menshevik *Iskra* as well as many Menshevik pamphlets.* 'Our differences of opinion', writes Yenukidze, 'were absolutely not reflected in our work.' Only after the third Congress of the party, i.e. not earlier than the middle of 1905, did the printshop pass into the hands of the Bolshevik Central Committee.[60]

A number of factors worked against the splitting of the RSDLP. First, as we have said, the differences between Bolsheviks and Mensheviks were not at all clear. Secondly, there is always a general popular sentiment in favour of unity. Thirdly, all the important writers and theoreticians apart from Lenin were to be found among the Mensheviks – Plekhanov, Axelrod, Zasulich, Martov, Trotsky and Potresov. As we shall see later, during the years of reaction (1906-10) Lenin also lost the new highly qualified writers who joined the Bolsheviks at the time – Bogdanov, Lunacharsky, Pokrovsky, Rozhkov and Gorky. The Bolsheviks always suffered from the fact that they had far fewer intellectuals and able journalists than the Mensheviks. The reverse side of the coin was that the Mensheviks fell victim to the illusion that their superiority in literary ability guaranteed their future influence in the labour movement.

To add to Lenin's difficulties, in the summer of 1904 *all* the leaders of the socialist movement outside Russia sided with Martov and the Mensheviks. Among these were Karl Kautsky, Rosa Luxemburg and August Bebel. The latter went so far as to say that the 'monstrous scandal' of the Russian party wrangles proved that the behaviour of the Bolsheviks bordered 'on unscrupulous and complete inability' to be leaders of the movement.[61]

---

* This was by far the largest underground printing press in Russia and was literally underground, being in a cellar. The printers were seven self-sacrificing party members. They worked ten hours a day and unlimited hours in emergencies. The cellar was without heat or ventilation. To avoid detection, no one was ever allowed to leave it during the day. At night the printers took it in turns to spend a couple of hours in the open air.

Setbacks in Russia

On 15 August 1904 Lenin wrote to the St Petersburg Bolshevik leadership:

> The state of things in your Committee, which is suffering from a lack of people, lack of literature and complete lack of information, is similar to the state of things in Russia as a whole. Everywhere there is a terrible lack of people . . . complete isolation, a general mood of depression and bitterness, stagnation as regards positive work. Ever since the second Congress, the party is being torn to pieces, and today things have gone very, very far in this respect.[62]

On 22 December 1904 he wrote: 'That our party is seriously ill and has lost a good half of its influence during the past year is known to the whole world.'[63] And on 11 March 1905: 'The Mensheviks at present are stronger than we are. It's going to be a long and hard fight.'[64]

The Bolsheviks undertook very little activity in Petersburg in 1904. During that year they issued only 11 leaflets, compared with 55 in 1903. Between May and November 1904, only one leaflet was issued, in July.[65]

> In January 1905, for the whole of St Petersburg, the Bolsheviks claimed sixty agitators, more than half of whom were 'very young' and presumably new to revolutionary activity. Nevertheless Gusev, secretary of the St Petersburg Committee, considered the Bolsheviks to have a vast conspiratorial organization in the city. These local leaders seem to have been largely students. In the Town district, the fifteen agitators and ten propagandists claimed by the Bolsheviks were 'exclusively students'.[66]

This was the situation in 1904 – the year in which the Russo-Japanese war broke out, which led directly to the revolution.

A similar decline of the party, affecting both Bolsheviks and Mensheviks, took place in Moscow:

> the Social Democrats in Moscow had only a few cells. During the summer and autumn of 1904 the RSDLP in Moscow appeared to be thoroughly routed. Its leaders were in jail and its activities had been brought to an almost complete halt. The leaflets of the Committee are an index of the activity: of 252 leaflets published in *Listovki Moskovskikh*

bol'shevikov v period pervoy russkoy revolyutsii (M. 1955), only 16 were printed in 1904.[67]

On 5 January 1905, four days before the outbreak of the revolution, Krupskaya wrote from Geneva to the Petersburg Committee of the Bolsheviks:

> But where are the proclamations with which the Committee promised to deluge the city? We aren't getting them. Nor any reports. We learned from foreign papers that the Putilov plant was on strike. Do we have connections there? Will it really be impossible to get information about the strike? Only it has to come quickly. Make every effort to arrange for workers themselves to write reports.[68]

Nevskii, quoting this letter, adds: 'One of the greatest proletarian movements was beginning, already its spearhead – the Putilov workers – was fighting capitalists, but the centre abroad learned of these clashes from foreign papers, because the Bolshevik Committee in Petersburg had to devote itself entirely to fighting the conciliationist Menshevik organizations.'[69] In a later passage, Nevskii, no longer blaming the wicked Mensheviks, writes about 'the remoteness of our organization from the broad masses and its ignorance of the life and interests of these masses'.

> Indeed, a vast strike movement was in progress, some unknown tremendous wave was rising, but the Bolshevik Committee was living its own segregated life; having once and for all appraised the Gapon movement as Zubatovite, it was not even able to sense that the strike at the Putilov plant was no common strike but a movement linked by the closest ties to all the Gapon locals, to the whole mighty strike movement of the entire Petersburg proletariat.[70]

A report of the Petersburg Committee to the third Congress (April-May 1905) described the situation in the party:

> The January events caught the Petersburg Committee in an extremely sorry state. Its ties with the working masses had been utterly disorganized by the Mensheviks. We managed to preserve them, with great effort, only in the Town District (this sector has always held to the Bolshevik viewpoint), on Vasil'ev-Ostrov, and in the Vyborg sector. In late December the printing press of the Petersburg Committee

was discovered. By that time the Petersburg Committee consisted of a secretary (through him the Committee communicated with the head of the press and with the finances commission), a chief writer and editor (*otvetstvennyi literator*), a chief organizer, an agitator (he was also the student organizer), and four organizers. There was not a single worker among the members of the Committee. The strike at the Putilov plant caught the Committee unprepared.[71]

The Mensheviks were also having a difficult time. The factional fight damaged both wings of the RSDLP. Years later Martov wrote:

It was necessary for tremendous renewed efforts by the Social Democratic forces in order to make the most of the upsurge in the working-class movement and to guide it to the right path. However the internal fight in the party prevented this possibility. The entire strength of the party was absorbed in this fight and in the winter 1903-04 the organization's activity came to a standstill.[72]

In one district of Petersburg the number of Menshevik circles was reduced from fifteen or twenty at the beginning of 1904 to only four or five by December.[73]

Lack of Centralized Leadership

Throughout 1904 and well into the years of the revolution, Lenin repeatedly complained, in letters to his close supporters in Russia, of lack of central leadership in the country itself, and weakness of communication with the leadership abroad.

In a letter of 11 February 1905 to A.A.Bogdanov and S.I.Gusev, he wrote:

A nice business: we talk of organization, of centralism, while actually there is such disunity, such amateurism among even the closest comrades in the centre, that one feels like chucking it all in disgust.[74]

The Mensheviks have more money, more literature, more transportation facilities, more agents, more 'names', and a larger staff of contributors. It would be unpardonable childishness not to see that.[75]

In a letter of 29 January 1905 to the Secretary of the Majority Committee's Bureau, he wrote: 'I have a great favour to ask you. Please give Rakhmetov a scolding, yes, a good sound scolding.' He had only sent

> two [letters] in thirty days. What do you think of that? Not a sign of him. Not a line for *Vperyod*. Not a word about the work, plans and connections. It's simply impossible, incredible, a disgrace. No. 4 of *Vperyod* will come out in a day or two, and immediately after it (a few days later) No. 5, but without any support from Rakhmetov. Today letters arrived from St Petersburg dated January 10, very brief ones. And no one arranged for good and full letters about the Ninth of January![76]

In a letter to the Central Committee of the RSDLP dated 11 July 1905, Lenin says: 'The general opinion is that there is no Central Committee, that it does not make itself felt, that no one notices it. And the facts confirm this. There is no evidence of the CC's political guidance of the party. Yet all the CC members are working themselves to death! What's the matter?' And he goes on to explain:

> In my opinion, one of the principal causes of it is that there are no regular CC leaflets. Leadership by means of talks and personal contacts at a time of revolution is sheer utopianism. Leadership must be public. *All other* forms of work must be wholly and unconditionally subordinated to this form. A responsible CC litterateur should concern himself first of all with writing (or obtaining from contributors – though the editor himself should always be prepared to write) a leaflet twice a week on party and political topics (the liberals, the Socialist Revolutionaries, the Minority, the split, the *Zemstvo* delegation, the trade unions, etc. etc.) and republishing it in every way, immediately mimeographing in 50 copies (if there is no printing press) and circulating it to the committees for republication. Articles in *Proletary* could, perhaps, sometimes be used for such leaflets – after a certain amount of revision. I cannot understand why this is not being done! Can Schmidt and Werner have forgotten our talks on this? Surely it is possible to write and circulate

at least one leaflet a week? The report on the third Congress has not been reprinted in full anywhere in Russia all this time. It is so outrageous.[77]

Apparently, the CC members completely fail to understand the tasks of 'keeping in the public eye'. Yet without that there is no centre, there is no party! They are working themselves to the bone, but they are working like moles, at secret rendezvous, at meetings with agents, etc., etc. It is a sheer waste of strength! ... The thing is to act, to act *all the time* openly, to stop being dumb. Otherwise we here, too, are completely cut off.[78]

Our CC ... suffers from a lack of tenacity and sensitivity, from inability to take political advantage of every trifle in the party struggle.[79]

Again, in a letter to Lunacharsky of 2 August 1905, Lenin accuses the Bolshevik Central Committee of being much less effective in faction fighting than the Mensheviks. The Mensheviks, he says,

are lively busybodies, brazen as hucksters, well skilled by long experience in demagogy – whereas among our people a kind of 'conscientious stupidity' or 'stupid conscientiousness' prevails. They can't put up a fight, they're awkward, inactive, clumsy, timid ... They're good fellows, but no damn'd good whatever as politicians. They lack tenacity, fighting spirit, nimbleness and speed.[80]

The Central Committee, Lenin complained, also completely neglected the leadership abroad. The Central Committee

has a lofty contempt for us 'foreigners' and keeps all the best people away from us or takes them from here. And we here, abroad, find ourselves behindhand. There is not enough ferment, stimulus or impulse. People are incapable of acting and fighting by themselves. We are short of speakers at our meetings. There is no one to pour cheer into people, to raise key issues, no one capable of lifting them above the Geneva marsh into the sphere of more serious interests and problems. And the whole work suffers. In political struggle a halt is fatal. There are thousands of demands and they are continually increasing.[81]

Priority for the Organization Question

The difference between the concept of centralism expressed in *What is to be Done?* or *Letter to a Comrade on our Organizational Tasks*, and the reality among the Bolsheviks in 1904 and 1905 is remarkable! There was a total cleavage between the ideal of a coherent, efficient party structure as visualized in Lenin's writings, and the ramshackle party organization that existed.

Lenin had to strive with all the power at his command, to build up an organization independent of and in opposition to the Mensheviks, and to create a party machine. He was so absorbed in the struggle against the Mensheviks that, incredible as it may seem, during the whole of the year 1904 there are only three references in his writings to the Russo-Japanese war. The overwhelming dominant theme is the split with the Mensheviks. A whole volume of his *Collected Works*, one of the stoutest, is all but filled with his writings on the Congress and the split, written in the most polemical, hard and irritable fashion.

Was it not madness to concentrate on building a party machine while an earthquake was shaking the state? But Lenin was not one to deviate from a decision arrived at centrally. Since 1900 he had repeated again and again that the key task facing the movement was the building of a revolutionary party. On 21 April 1901, he had written to Plekhanov about 'the priority of organization over agitation at the present time'.[82] In 1902 he rephrased Archimedes: 'Give us an organization of revolutionaries, and we will overturn Russia.'[83]

Unlike Marx and Engels, who lived in a period of expanding capitalism and hence did not emphasize party organization, the immediacy of revolution for Lenin meant that party organization was of cardinal importance. He could never have written, as Marx did to Engels on 11 February 1851:

> I am much pleased with the public and authentic isolation in which we now find ourselves, you and I. It perfectly cor-

responds to our principles and our position. The system of reciprocal concessions, of half-measures tolerated only in order to keep up appearances, and obligation to share in public with all these asses in the general absurdity of the party – all that is done with now.[84]

Nor could he have replied to Marx as Engels did on 12 February 1851:

> We now have a chance again at last ... to show that we need no popularity, no support from any party whatsoever ... from now on we are responsible only to ourselves, and when the moment comes that these gentlemen need us, we shall be in a situation to be able to dictate our own terms. Till then we shall at least have peace. To tell the truth, even a certain loneliness ... How can people like us, who avoid official positions like the plague, ever find ourselves at home in a 'party'? ... The principal thing for the moment is: some way of getting our ideas into print ... What will all the gossip and scandal mean which the whole émigré pack may circulate against you, once you answer them with your political economy?[85]

To a person standing on the sidelines – even to many of those involved – 1903-04 was a period of squabbles, interminable discussions, splits between Bolsheviks and Mensheviks, argument and splits inside the Bolshevik faction itself – at a time when Russia was on the eve of a revolution.

Trotsky at that time considered Lenin's factionalism to be sheer lunacy. In a pamphlet written in April 1904 he states: 'Just at a time when history has placed before us the enormous task of cutting the knot of world reaction, Russian Social Democrats do not seem to care for anything except a petty internal struggle.' What a 'heartrending tragedy' this was, and what a 'nightmarish atmosphere' it created; 'almost everybody was aware of the criminal character of the split'.[86]

But Lenin was absolutely single-minded. Whatever might happen, a revolutionary party had to be built, and urgently. So, consistently, doggedly, relentlessly, in the years 1900 to 1904 Lenin built a party machine. However far it may have been from his ideal model, when the 1905 revolution came he had a machine under his control. He had demonstrated in full measure the political, organizational and administrative talent needed to build such an apparatus.

In the revolution itself, Lenin was to show that if necessary, if the masses went further than the party machine was prepared to move, he would be willing and able to overcome the lagging of the very machine he had built, by mobilizing the energy of rank-and-file workers. But we are anticipating the story.

6

Fighting the Liberals

'When a liberal is abused, he says: Thank God they didn't beat me. When he is beaten, he thanks God they didn't kill him. When he is killed, he will thank God that his immortal soul has been delivered from its mortal clay.'[1]

On 8-9 February 1904 a war broke out between Russia and Japan. One reason for this was to enable the government to use war hysteria against revolutionary stirrings. Prime minister Plehve actually said: 'We need a small victorious war to stem the tide of revolution.'[2]

The liberals were very willing to play the Tsarist game. Their immediate reaction was patriotism. In *Osvobozhdenie*, the paper published abroad by the liberals, Struve, now a liberal stalwart, suggested as a slogan: 'Long live the army!' When the Japanese demonstrated their superior fighting ability on both land and sea the liberals' patriotism weakened somewhat, and they became mildly oppositional. This attitude sharpened after the Japanese were victorious at the battle of Liaoyang in July, when it became apparent that the Russians were not going to win the war, and that the government was clearly in a blind alley. Now the brave leaders of the gentry and the middle classes showed their mettle. *Osvobozhdenie* wrote: 'The occupation of Manchuria and the outlet to the sea were economically nonsensical for Russia.'[3] Their attitude towards the war became defeatist. Defeat would weaken the Tsar and make the autocracy amenable to compromise. 'The Japanese', said a Russian liberal, 'will not enter the Kremlin, but the Russians will.'[4]

Gaining confidence, the liberals started a campaign, using the local organs of self-government, the *Zemstvos*, as their platform. There they aired their grievances and planned a national conference of *Zemstvo* delegates. The conference took place in November, and was followed by banquets of liberal landlords, industrialists, professors, lawyers, doctors, economists, etc. Long-winded speeches were made, plans for constitutional reforms were discussed, protests were aired. It is an interesting question whether the aim was to overthrow Tsarism, or to strike a bargain with it.

The Mensheviks were enthusiastic about these banquets. Their policy was to call on the workers to back the liberals, bolstering their courage while avoiding any extreme action, in case the liberals took fright.

Thus, in November 1904 the editor of *Iskra* sent a letter to all party organizations:

> In the person of the liberal *Zemstvos* and *Dumas* we have to deal with enemies of our enemy, who are not, however, willing or able to go as far in the struggle against him as is required by the interests of the proletariat. But in coming out officially against absolutism and confronting it with demands aimed at its annihilation, by that alone they show themselves to be our allies . . . within the limits of the struggle against absolutism, and particularly in its present phase, our attitude towards the liberal bourgeoisie is defined by the task of imbuing it with more courage and impelling it to join in those demands being put forward by the proletariat led by the Social Democracy.[5]

> We should be making a fatal mistake if we tried by strong measures of *intimidation* to *force* the *Zemstvos* or other organs of the bourgeois opposition to give here and now,

under the influence of *panic*, a formal promise to present our demands to the government. Such a tactic would discredit the Social Democrats, because it would make our entire political campaign a lever for reaction . . .

As regards the present *Zemstvos* . . . our task reduces itself to presenting to them those political demands of the revolutionary proletariat which they must support if they are to have any right to speak in the name of the people and count on the energetic support of the worker masses.[6]

Following up this statement, Axelrod, one of the most important Menshevik leaders, suggested campaign tactics: efforts must be made

to bring the masses into direct contact with the *Zemstvo* Assembly, to concentrate the demonstration before the actual premises where the *Zemstvo* assemblymen are in session. Some of the demonstrators penetrate into the session hall, and at a suitable moment, through the spokesman specially authorized for the purpose, they ask the permission of the Assembly to read out a statement on behalf of the workers. If this is not granted, the spokesman enters a loud protest against the refusal of an Assembly which speaks in the name of the people to hear the voice of the people's genuine representatives.

The executive committee must take measures in advance to ensure that the appearance of several thousand workers outside the building where the *Zemstvo* assemblymen are in session, and of several score or hundred in the building itself, *shall not plunge the* Zemstvoists *into panic fear* under the impact of which they might throw themselves under the shameful protection of the police and Cossacks, thus transforming a peaceful demonstration into an ugly fight and brutal battering, distorting its whole meaning.[7]

The spokesman of Menshevism, Martynov, in his pamphlet *Two Dictatorships* (1904), spelled out the reasoning behind this attitude in similar terms:

The coming revolution will be a revolution of the bourgeoisie; and that means that . . . it will only, to a greater or lesser extent, secure the rule of all or some of the bourgeois classes . . . If this is so, it is clear that the coming revolution can on no account assume political forms *against the will of the whole* of the bourgeoisie, as the latter will be the master of tomorrow. If so, then to follow the path of simply *frightening* the majority of the bourgeois elements would mean that the revolutionary struggle of the proletariat could lead to only one result – the restoration of absolutism in its original form.

The revolutionary's goal, therefore, lay in 'the more democratic "lower" section of society's compelling the "higher" section to *agree* to lead the bourgeois revolution to its logical conclusion.'[8]

The Menshevik paper *Iskra* at the time viewed Russian society and the workers' tasks as follows:

When looking at the arena of struggle in Russia, what do we see? Only two powers: Tsarist autocracy and the liberal bourgeoisie, the latter organized and of tremendous specific weight. The working masses are split and can do nothing; as an independent force we do not exist, and therefore our task consists in the support of the second force – the liberal bourgeoisie; we must encourage it, and on no account frighten it by putting forward the independent demands of the proletariat.[9]

Plekhanov echoed the same idea, writing in 1905:

The sympathy of 'society' is very important for us and we can – or more exactly we *had many chances* to – win it without changing one iota of our programme. But of course, it requires *tact* to make the *possibility a reality*, and that is what we have not always got.

Then the interests of the liberals would indeed 'force' them to 'act jointly with the socialists against the government', because they would cease to meet in revolutionary publications the assurance that the overthrow of absolutism would be the signal for a social revolution in Russia.[10]

Hardly an article came from Plekhanov's pen that did not belabour the Bolsheviks for their tactlessness. Indeed, he wrote a whole series of articles collectively entitled: 'Letters on Tactics and Tactlessness'.[11]

In complete contrast, Lenin always relentlessly denounced the Russian liberal bourgeoisie as a counter-revolutionary force. Of Martynov's campaign tactics for the *Zemstvo* Assembly, he wrote contemptuously in November 1904:

A fine definition of the tasks of the workers' party, I must say! At a time when an alliance of the moderate *Zemstvoists* and the government to fight the revolutionary proletariat is only too clearly possible and probable . . . we are to 'reduce' our task, not to redoubling our efforts in the struggle against the government, but to drawing up casuistic conditions for agreements with the liberals on mutual support.[12]

If we are in a position to organize an imposing mass demonstration of workers in the hall of a *Zemstvo* Assembly, we shall, of course, do so (though if we have forces enough for a mass demonstration it would be much better to 'concentrate' them 'before the premises' not of the *Zemstvo*, but of the police, the gendarmerie, or the censorship). But to be swayed when doing so by considerations like the *Zemstvo*-ists panic fears, and to engage in negotiations on that score, would be the height of ineptitude, and height of absurdity.[13]

What is needed here is not 'negotiations', but the actual mustering of force; not pressure on the *Zemstvoists*, but pressure on the government and its agents.[14]

He pulled no punches in his outspoken analysis of the reasons why the liberals would prove to be reactionary.

The antagonism between the proletariat and the bourgeoisie with us is much deeper than it was in 1789, 1848 or 1871; hence, the bourgeoisie will be more fearful of the *proletarian* revolution and will throw itself more readily into the arms of reaction.[15]

The bourgeoisie as a whole is incapable of waging a determined struggle against the autocracy; it fears to lose in this struggle its property which binds it to the existing order; it fears an all-too-revolutionary action of the workers, who will not stop at the democratic revolution but will aspire to the socialist revolution; it fears a complete break with officialdom, with the bureaucracy, whose interests are bound up by a thousand ties with the interests of the propertied classes. For this reason the bourgeois struggle for liberty is notoriously timorous, inconsistent, and half-hearted.[16]

The Constituent Assembly of the whole people will be just strong enough to make the Tsar grant a constitution, but it will not *and must not* (from the point of view of the bourgeoisie's interests) be any stronger. It must only counterbalance the monarchy, but not overthrow it; it must leave the material instruments of power (the army, etc.) in the hands of the monarchy.[17]

The experience of the 1905 revolution demonstrated even more clearly the bankruptcy of the liberal bourgeoisie, particularly in the question which was crucial for the overwhelming majority of the Russian population, the agrarian question. The liberals were against expropriating the great landowners. Their party, the Cadets, supported the distribution of the crown and monastery lands among the peasants, but agreed to the compulsory expropriation of the landlords' estates only on condition that fair prices were paid to the landlords.[18]

The Cadets were, in fact, largely representatives of the landlord class. Lenin cited evidence for this: the Cadets were a party of the liberal bourgeoisie, liberal landowners and bourgeois intelligentsia. If there were any doubts about the landowner colouring of the Cadets, two facts could be pointed to: (1) the composition of the Cadet group in the first Duma, and (2) the Cadets' draft agrarian programme.[19] On the first point, the facts were as follows:

> of the 153 Cadets in the first Duma, 92 were of the nobility. Of these, 3 owned landed estates between 5,000 and 10,000 *desiatins*;* 8 owned estates from 2,000 to 5,000 *desiatins*; 8 owned estates from 1,000 to 2,000 *desiatins*, and 30 owned estates from 500 to 1,000 *desiatins*. Thus about one-third of the Cadet deputies were big landowners.[20]

Of the agrarian programme of the Cadets Lenin said:

> [It] is in effect, a plan of *the capitalist landlord*, conversion of the peasant into a *Knecht*, and the formation of local land commissions of equal numbers of landlords and peasants with chairmen appointed by the government – all this shows as clearly as can be that Cadet policy in the agrarian question is one of retaining landed proprietorship by *cleansing* it of some of its feudal traits, and by the peasant's ruination through redemption payments and his shackling by government officials.[21]

---

* Desiatin = 2.7 acres

Stolypin* and the Cadets disagreed on *the extent* of the concessions and on the means (crude or more sophisticated) by which reform should be introduced. Both supported the *reform*, that is, they supported the preservation of landlord *domination* through *concessions to the peasants.*[22]

A couple of years later, in March 1908, Lenin argued, in an article entitled 'On the "Nature" of the Russian Revolution', that experience had demonstrated the counter-revolutionary nature of the liberals' attitude to the peasant question:

> At the beginning of 1906, prior to the first Duma, the Cadet leader, Mr Struve, wrote: 'The peasant in the Duma will be a Cadet' ... The monarchist paper proclaimed, 'the *muzhik* will help us out', i.e. that broad representation of the peasants would prove favourable for the autocracy. Such opinions were ... widespread in those days ... But the first *Duma* had dispelled these illusions of the monarchists and *the illusions of the liberals* completely. The most ignorant, undeveloped, politically virgin, unorganized *muzhik* proved to be *incomparably more left* than the Cadets.[23]

He concluded:

> And the whole historic significance of the first period of the Russian revolution may be summed up as follows: liberalism has *already* conclusively demonstrated its counter-revolutionary nature, its incapacity to lead the peasant

---

* The Tsarist prime minister Stolypin's chief claim to fame was the law of November 1906, the main product of the victorious counter-revolution. The law gave a small minority of the peasants of any commune, even against the will of the majority, the right to detach from the communal land a section to be owned independently. Stolypin described his policy as 'banking on the strong ones', i.e. relying on the rich peasant to join forces with the great landlords and the autocracy. 'The natural counter-weight to the communal principle', Stolypin said, 'is individual ownership. The small owner is the nucleus on which rests all stable order in the state.' The aim of Stolypin's agrarian legislation was to turn the kulaks into a new source of social support for the autocracy in the countryside, while preserving the landed estates and forcibly destroying the village communes.

revolution; the peasantry has not *yet* fully understood that it is only along the path of revolution and republic, under the guidance of the socialist proletariat, that a real victory can be won.[24]

Liberalism Shows its True Colours

During the 1905 revolution the political course steered by the liberals was an erratic one. They advanced and retreated, their revolutionary ardour cooling as the revolution advanced, drawing millions of workers and peasants into political and social struggle.

At the beginning of the revolution Struve wrote: 'Every sincere and thinking liberal in Russia demands revolution.'[25] His Cadet Party, and indeed the majority of employers, were sympathetic even to the revolutionary general strike which the workers used as a weapon against Tsarism. Khrustalev-Nosar, then President of the Petrograd Soviet, wrote:

> During the October strike, the employers, not content with putting no obstacle in the way of workers' meetings at the factories, paid 50% wages for the time of the strike; in some of the factories full wages were even paid. No one was sacked for the strike. At the Putilov works and elsewhere the management paid full wages to the delegates for the days they assisted at the meetings of the soviet. The management of the Putilov works was so considerate as to place its steamer at the disposal of the soviet delegates when they went to town.[26]

The editor of *Pravo*, the principal organ of those who soon afterwards formed the Cadet Party, declared: 'The first strike will forever remain a glorious page in the history of the liberation movement, a monument to the great services of the working class in the struggle for the political and social emancipation of the people.'[27] In the same vein, a resolution of the foundation congress of the Cadets declared:

> The demands of the strikers, as they have been formulated by themselves, are mainly confined to the immediate introduction of the basic liberties, the free election of representatives of the people to a constituent assembly on the basis of

universal, equal, direct and secret ballot; and of general political amnesty. There is not the slightest doubt that these demands are identical with those of the Constitutional Democratic (Cadet) Party. In view of this identity of aims the *constituent congress of the Constitutional Democratic Party considers it its duty to express its complete solidarity with the strike movement.* At their own place and with the aid of methods accessible to this party, its members strive to attain the same ends. Like the other groups taking part in the struggle *we emphatically reject the idea of attaining our object by means of negotiations with the government.*[28]

But this sympathy for the revolutionary workers evaporated quickly. It soon became clear that a separation could not be made between the anti-Tsarist demands of the workers and their struggle to improve their conditions of life in opposition to the interests of the employers. The workers who took part in the general strike against the Tsar in October 1905 gained so much confidence in their own power that, a month later, the most advanced section of them, the workers of St Petersburg, came out on strike demanding an eight-hour day. This clearly threatened the employers' pockets, and they reacted immediately. The striking workers were ruthlessly locked out. In November in St Petersburg, 72 factories, with 110,000 workers, were closed, in Moscow 23 factories with 58,634 workers; in other cities the picture was similar.[29] (Being badly organized, the workers were defeated in this clash with the capitalists, their former anti-Tsarist allies.)

All the bourgeois politicians now showed their animosity towards the workers and fear of strikes. Where formerly the strike was commended, it was now called by the Cadet leader Miliukov 'a crime, a crime against the revolution'.[30]

Struve, who at the beginning of 1905 had urged on the revolution, now wrote: 'the pernicious anarchy of the Russian revolution is shown most clearly in the fact that it much more disorganizes than organizes the country, as well as itself'.[31] The bourgeoisie thus turned out to be much more afraid of the revolutionary workers than of counter-revolutionary Tsarism.

Because the Cadets opposed the revolutionary struggle,

their attempt to solve the burning question of the time – the land question – came to nothing. In March 1905 Struve wrote:

> The Russian opposition, being not only democratic, but also moderate-constitutional, must at the present time take as its point of departure the fact that *the agrarian revolution has already begun in the country*. If so, the only intelligent tactic, from all points of view, is to seize hold of the revolution from its beginning and, recognizing the just nature of this revolution, direct it into the channel of lawful social reform.[32]

The programme adopted at the founding congress of the Cadet Party included a demand for a Constituent Assembly (Article 13) and the monarchy was not mentioned at all. But the January 1906 congress changed Article 13, replacing it by a demand for a 'constitutional and parliamentary monarchy'. The Cadets proved, as Lenin had foretold, not to be made of the same stuff as Robespierre and the Jacobins, or Cromwell and his Ironsides.

In Conclusion

Lenin's hatred of the liberals had been seared into his very soul by the experience of his youth. Krupskaya relates:

> Vladimir Ilyich once told me about the attitude of the liberals towards the arrest of his elder brother. All acquaintances shunned the Ulyanov family. Even an aged teacher, who had formerly come every evening to play chess, left off calling. There was no railway at Simbirsk at that time, and Vladimir Ilyich's mother had to go on horseback to Syzran in order to go on to St Petersburg, where her eldest son was imprisoned. Vladimir Ilyich was sent to seek a companion for the journey. But no one wanted to travel with the mother of an arrested man. Vladimir Ilyich told me that this widespread cowardice made a very profound impression upon him at that time. This youthful experience undoubtedly did leave its imprint on Lenin's attitude towards the liberals. It was early that he learned the value of all liberal chatter.[33]

Nor did Lenin forget how the great revolutionary Chernyshevsky in his time had been disgusted by the liberals. Chernyshevsky spoke of the liberals of the sixties as 'wind-

bags, braggarts and fools'. He clearly perceived their dread of revolution, their spinelessness and their servility in the face of Tsarism.

7

The 1905 Revolution
The Rise of Police Trade Unionism

In Chapter 4 we described the stormy rise of a working-class movement in the years 1900-03. Tsarism reacted to this in its usual way, by heavy repression. But it also tried a new method of heading off the revolutionary steam.

In 1901 a police report on the state of labour asserted:

> Agitators, seeking to rewrite their goals, have achieved some success, unfortunately, in organizing the workers to fight against the government. Within the last three or four years the easygoing Russian young man has been transformed into a special type of semi-literate *intelligent*, who feels obliged to spurn religion and family, to disregard the law, and to defy and scoff at constituted authority. Fortunately such young men are not numerous in the factory, but this negligible handful terrorizes the inert majority of workers into following it.[1]

Although this report distorted the real situation, it did point to a real change in the working class: a number of workers had started joining revolutionary groups.

It was to outflank and divert this development that a section of the secret police initiated a new form of police trade unionism: Zubatovism. (Zubatov was Chief of the Moscow Gendarmerie.) As conceived, workers' societies were to be formed with police approval, to provide opportunities for cooperative self-help for workers, and protection against the influence of revolutionaries. Such groups were organized in Moscow, Odessa, Kiev, Nikolayev, and Kharkov.

But the police plans did not work out as expected. The workers used the legal Zubatov organizations to organize strikes and vent their demands. In fact, as the Bolshevik historian M.N.Pokrovsky related, the result of Zubatovism was entirely different to Zubatov's expectations :

> precisely because these workmen were politically so undeveloped, Zubatovism was a tremendous step in the direction of developing their *class* consciousness, in helping them to understand the class opposition between the worker and employer. The whole business did nothing but ape the agitation of the Social Democrats – that was all there was in the idea. In their clumsy imitation of the revolutionary agitators, Zubatov's agents went so far as to promise that the government would soon have the factories taken away from the employers and handed over to the workmen. The government, they said, was ready to do anything for the workers, if they stopped listening to the 'petty intelligentsia'. In some strikes the police actually supported the strikers, paid them relief money, and so on.[2]

A strike led by the Zubatov unions in Odessa in July 1902, unexpectedly for the initiators, drew in the whole of the city and acquired a markedly political character. Mass political strikes in 1903 spread through almost the whole of South Russia (Kiev, Ekaterinoslav, Nikolayev, Elizavetgrad, and other towns). The effect was to turn the Tsarist government against Zubatovism. All the societies, with the exception of those of St Petersburg and Moscow, were disbanded by the end of 1903 and Zubatov was exiled. But Tsarism continued to vacillate, and within a few weeks 'police socialism' was again introduced as a weapon against the revolutionary movements.

The police union in St Petersburg was called the 'Assembly of Russian Factory and Workshop Workers'. It had branches in all the districts of the capital and organized mutual aid and cultural, educational and religious activities. It was led by Father Gapon, a prison chaplain and protégé of Zubatov.

The Gapon movement began as a most 'loyal' undertaking, innocent of the smallest attempts to join in the struggle between labour and capital. Its modest aim was to give workers a chance to gather and soberly spend their free time in edifying pursuits. In the early period, as Gapon wrote subsequently, every meeting at the first tearoom-reading room 'began and closed with prayer'. At the official opening of the Assembly on 11 April 1904, after it had received its statute, a religious service was held, 'God Save the Tsar' was sung three times, and the Assembly sent a telegram to the Minister of the Interior, 'with the respectful request to lay at the feet of His Imperial Majesty the adored Monarch the most submissive feelings of the workers inspired by zealous love for the throne and the fatherland'.[3]

Bloody Sunday

At the end of December 1904 economic unrest disturbed the giant Putilov engineering works in Petersburg, which employed 12,000 workers. The immediate cause was small: four workers had been sacked for belonging to Gapon's organization. On Monday, 3 January 1905, it developed into a strike for the reinstatement of the four workers. This was the modest beginning which led inexorably on to revolution.   .

The experience of the Russian revolution, like the experience of other countries, proves beyond doubt that where the objective conditions of a profound political crisis exist, the tiniest conflict, seemingly remote from the true birthplace of revolution, can act as a spark to kindle an upsurge in public feeling.[3]

It was to the Assembly of Russian Factory and Workshop Workers that the Putilov workers turned for help to reinstate the workers who had been dismissed. The leadership of the Assembly would have lost all credibility if it had not come to the aid of its four sacked members. It could not but tolerate the Putilov workers turning for help to workers of other factories. Accordingly all branches of the Assembly throughout Petersburg held mass meetings. These roused the workers' passions, and rapidly proceeded from the individual incident at the Putilov factory to the general issues facing the

Russian workers – the extremely harsh material conditions and the complete absence of rights.

Under the influence of the euphoria generated by these mass meetings, Gapon suggested adding to the original demand for reinstatement of the four sacked workers and the removal of the foreman responsible a list of other demands which were discussed at length in the Assembly, but which the workers had never before dared to put forward: an eight-hour day, an increase in the minimum daily wage from 60 kopeks to a ruble for men, and from 40 kopeks to 75 for women, the improvement of sanitary facilities and the granting of free medical aid. At this stage of the movement Gapon was successful in influencing the workers to limit their struggle to purely economic demands. He instructed them to tear up, unread, the leaflets that students were distributing, which included among their demands a struggle against Tsarism.

The leaders of the Assembly thought it would be a good idea to have the workers turn to the Tsar for support. The Police Department concurred with this: a few benevolent words from the throne, accompanied by some measures, however small, to ameliorate workers' conditions would be enough, they thought, to stop the movement from going to extremes and would reinforce the myth of the Tsar as the workers' friend. Thus the idea was born of a petition and a solemn procession, carrying the Tsar's portrait, holy icons and church banners. The petition would humbly beg the Tsar for redress of the workers' grievances. Chanting prayers and hymns, the workers would, on bended knee, entrust the petition to the Tsar.

However, while the police were making plans, the Petersburg Social Democrats were acting. After a slow start, they finally intervened actively in the movement, and achieved a measure of success. They sent speakers to the district meetings of the Assembly, and succeeded in introducing resolutions and amendments into the original text of the petition. It was actually the Menshevik Group that displayed this initiative. (We shall deal below with the tactics of the Bolsheviks at the time.) The result was a petition very different from the one originally envisaged by the leaders of the Assembly : a whole string of political demands were included under the influence of the Social Democrats : the eight-hour working day, freedom of assembly for the workers, land for the peasants, freedom of speech and the press, the separation of church and state, an end to the Russo-Japanese war and the convocation of a Constituent Assembly.

The Putilov strike which began on 3 January became by 7 January a general strike of the whole of St Petersburg. Not only all the big factories, but many small workshops came to a standstill; practically all the newspapers stopped publication. Even official reports placed the number of strikers at 100-150,000. 'Russia had never yet witnessed such a gigantic outbreak of the class struggle,' Lenin wrote.[4]

On Sunday, 9 January, 200,000 Petersburg workers marched in an enormous but peaceful procession to the Tsar's Winter Palace, headed by Father Gapon. The Tsar refused to receive the petitioners. The troops guarding the Winter Palace were ordered to fire into the crowd. More than a thousand people were killed and as many as two thousand wounded. Thus the Tsar tried to quell the revolution. The same night the appalled Gapon addressed the crowd; declaring 'We no longer have a Tsar', he called on the soldiers to consider themselves freed from obligation 'to the traitor, the Tsar, who had ordered innocent blood to be spilt.' The workers learned by bitter experience that icons and pictures of the Tsar are less potent than revolvers and guns.

Various interpretations were given to the events of 9 January. The simplest was that of the Ministry of War, which saw in the mass strike the hand (and the finance) of Anglo-Japanese agents.

> The Minister of War went so far as to publish in newspapers and announce by placards that 'Anglo-Japanese provocateurs' were responsible for the strikes among men employed in the manufacture of naval equipment. Even the Holy Synod accepted this interpretation, and, on the 14th, issued a statement deploring the recent disturbances 'provoked with bribes from the enemies of Russia.'[5]

The liberals did not believe in the existence of a revolutionary people, so they explained the events as the natural emanation of Gapon's personality. 'There is not yet such a thing as a revolutionary people in Russia', wrote Peter Struve in his paper *Osvobozhdenie* (Liberation), published abroad, on 7 January 1905, precisely two days before the guards' regiments crushed the Petersburg workers' demonstration.[6]

The liberals persisted for a long time in the belief that the entire secret of the events of 9 January lay in Gapon's personality. They contrasted him with the Social Democrats as though he were a political leader who knew the secret of controlling the masses and they a doctrinaire sect. In doing so they forgot that 9 January would not have taken place if Gapon had not encountered several thousand politically conscious workers who had been through the school of socialism.[7]

Lenin evaluated the events of 9 January very differently. Writing three days after Bloody Sunday, he said:

The working class has received a momentous lesson in civil war; the revolutionary education of the proletariat made more progress in one day than it could have made in months and years of drab, humdrum, wretched existence.[8]

Immediate overthrow of the government – this was the slogan with which even the St Petersburg workers who had believed in the Tsar answered the massacre of 9 January; they answered through their leader, the priest Georgi Gapon, who declared after that bloody day: 'We no longer have a Tsar. A river of blood divides the Tsar from the people. Long live the fight for freedom!'[9]

Writing on 8 February, he reiterated: '9 January 1905 fully revealed the vast reserve of revolutionary energy possessed by the proletariat.' But then he added in sorrow that it revealed 'as well . . . the utter inadequacy of Social Democratic organization'.[10]

Lenin and Gapon

At first the Social Democrats reacted slowly to the Gapon movement. Thus Martov declared:

Strange as it may seem, it must be noted that the revolutionary organizations in Petersburg had overlooked the growth and gradual transformation of the legal workers' organization founded by Father Gapon, which in Autumn 1904 had already changed from the original 'Aid funds for mutual support' into working men's clubs of a kind.

When at the end of December 1904 Gapon's group entered into a full fight against the industrialists as the result of a conflict at the Putilov works, the Social Democrats were completely overtaken by the events.

When at last the Social Democrats influenced by Gapon turned to the workers, they were cold-shouldered. Their leaflets were destroyed by the strikers. Even a gift of 500 rubles from the Social Democratic Committee was 'received unwillingly'.[11]

The isolation of the Petersburg Committee of the Bolsheviks from the developing movement was noted by one of its members, N.V.Doroshenko.

> Until the last days of December, I and my close comrades had had no occasion to visit a single local of the Gapon society. More than that, I do not recall a single conversation with organized workers of the Vasil'ev-Ostrov and the Petersburg sectors about any of our people's having visited the said locals.[12]

In early January the party workers of the Petersburg Committee began to take notice of the Gapon movement:

> The workers, most of whom were unquestionably under Gapon's influence, did not at that time regard Social Democracy as their own party. More than that, it seemed to them that the clear-cut, unambiguous line of Social Democracy hampered them in accomplishing what Gapon was urging them on to. At one of the secret committee rendezvous at which all of us party workers congregated, S.I.Gusev informed us of the steps taken by the Committee and relayed its directive enjoining us to penetrate into the factories to the locals of the Gapon society and *oppose* to Gapon's demands the minimum programme of the party, *exposing* the hopelessness and absurdity of the project of marching to the palace.[13]

Doroshenko himself tried to carry out the assignment of opposing and exposing at a meeting of the Gapon branch in the City sector on 7 January, but was stopped by shouts of 'Enough, go away, don't interfere', and so on. 'It was made impossible for me to continue my speech and I had to leave the hall.'[14] From this meeting he went to a conference of the Petersburg Committee of the Bolsheviks: 'The overall impression was that the conference somehow did not believe that the march to the palace would materialize. The idea was that the government would take steps to nip Gapon's intentions in the bud. Hence, there was at any rate no certainty that mass slaughter would be allowed to occur.'[15]

Finally, however, the Petersburg Committee decided that the party members *should* take part in the 9 January procession.

> To carry out the measures planned by the Petersburg Committee, the committee of the City sector chose as the gathering point for 9 January the corner of Sadovaia and Chernyshev Alley, where the subsector organizers were to come in the morning with their organized circles.

The attendance was pitiful, 'only a small group, some fifteen workers, no more, appeared at the rendezvous'.[16]

Lenin however, realized from the beginning that the Gapon movement would outgrow the intentions of the Tsarist authorities. In an article called 'The St Petersburg Strike' he wrote:

> The strike that began at the Putilov works on 3 January is developing into one of the most imposing manifestations of the working-class movement . . . And now the Zubatov movement is outgrowing its bounds. Initiated by the police in the interests of the police, in the interests of supporting the autocracy and demoralizing the political consciousness of the workers, this movement is turning against the autocracy and is becoming an outbreak of the proletarian class struggle.
>
> The Social Democrats long ago predicted that *such* would be the inevitable outcome of the Zubatov movement in our country. The legalization of the working-class movement, they said, would definitely benefit us Social Democrats. It would draw certain sections of the workers into the movement, especially the backward sections: it would help to rouse those who would not soon, perhaps ever, be roused by

a socialist agitator. And once drawn into the movement and having acquired an interest in their own future, the workers would go further. The legal labour movement would only be a new and broader basis for the Social Democratic labour movement.[17]

A week later, in an article called 'The First Steps', he elaborated on the same theme:

the revolutionary instinct of the working class and the spirit of solidarity would prevail over all petty police ruses. The most backward workers would be drawn into the movement by the Zubatovists, and then the Tsarist government would itself take care to drive the workers farther; capitalist exploitation itself would turn them away from the peaceable and out-and-out hypocritical Zubatov fold towards revolutionary Social Democracy.[18]

Lenin was not only non-sectarian in his attitude to the mass movement which was forming behind Gapon, but even, as was his wont, 'fell in love' with Gapon himself. When Gapon went abroad, Lenin was eager to meet him. The interview left him in no doubt that Gapon was completely sincere. Many years later, after Gapon had been exposed as a police agent and murdered for his crime by a revolutionary, Krupskaya explained Lenin's infatuation thus:

Gapon was a living part of the revolution that was sweeping Russia. He was closely bound up with the working masses, who devotedly believed in him, and Ilyich was agitated about this meeting.
A comrade recently asked with consternation: how could Ilyich ever have anything to do with Gapon?
Of course, one could simply have ignored Gapon, reckoning in advance that nothing good will ever come from a priest. That is what Plekhanov did, for instance, receiving Gapon extremely coolly. But Ilyich's strength lay precisely in the fact that for him the revolution was a live thing, he was capable of discerning its features, grasping all its manifold details, knowing and understanding what the masses wanted. And knowledge of the masses can only be obtained by close contact with them. How could Ilyich pass by Gapon, who stood close to the masses, and had such influence over them?[19]

On 18 January 1905, Lenin wrote:

> We cannot flatly dismiss the idea that Father Gapon may be
> a sincere Christian socialist and that it was Bloody Sunday
> which converted him to the truly revolutionary path. We
> are inclined to support this idea, especially since Gapon's
> letters written after the massacre of 9 January declaring
> that 'we have no Tsar', his call to fight for freedom, etc., are
> facts that speak for his honesty and sincerity.[20]

On 23 April he said about Gapon: 'He impressed me as being
an enterprising and clever man, unquestionably devoted to
the revolution, though unfortunately without a consistent
revolutionary outlook.'[21]

Lenin went out of his way to try to teach Gapon marxism – without success, however. 'I said to him', he told Krupskaya on his return from meeting Gapon, 'don't you take to
flattery, Little Father; study or that's where you'll find yourself – and I pointed under the table.'[22]

Other Bolshevik leaders were far less enamoured of
Gapon. For instance S.I.Gusev, who arrived from Geneva at
the end of December or in early January, and took over as
secretary and leader of the Petersburg Committee, wrote to
Lenin on 5 January about the 'cursed Gapon':

> This Father Gapon is most certainly a Zubatovist of the
> purest water . . . Exposing and fighting Gapon will be the
> basis of the agitation we are hurriedly preparing. We have
> to move all our forces into action, even if we have to
> squander them all on the strike, for the situation obligates
> us to save the honour of Social Democracy.[23]

He did not change his opinion after Bloody Sunday. On
30 January he wrote to Lenin again:

> The workers are also a bit confused (again under the influ-
> ence of the Mensheviks' anti-revolutionary preachings) about
> the (proper) attitude to Gapon. Your article in No. 4 depicts
> the government's role very justly, but you are too lenient
> with Gapon. *He is a shady character.* I have written you this
> several times, and the more I think the more suspicious he
> seems. One cannot call him a mere crank, he was a Zubatov-
> ite and worked with Zubatovites *knowing* what they are
> and *what* they want.[24]

Fighting the Bolsheviks' Sectarian Attitude towards the Trade Unions and the Soviet

On the Social Democratic attitude to the rising trade union movement Lenin had to do battle with his supporters, who had a narrow, sectarian approach. S.I.Gusev, who was close to Lenin and the Bolshevik centre abroad, proposed at a meeting of the Bolshevik Odessa Committee in September 1905 that the Bolsheviks be guided by the following rules in their stand on the trade union question :

1. To expose in our propaganda and agitation all the illusions about trade unions, stressing especially their narrowness in comparison with the ultimate aims of the labour movement.
2. To clarify to the proletariat that a broad and stable development of the trade union movement is unthinkable under an autocratic regime and that such a development requires first of all the overthrow of Tsarist autocracy.
3. To strongly emphasize in propaganda and agitation that the most vital, primary task of the struggling proletariat is to prepare immediately for an armed uprising to overthrow Tsarist autocracy and win a democratic republic.
4. To carry on an energetic ideological struggle against the so-called Mensheviks, who are reverting, on the issue of trade unions, to the narrow erroneous viewpoint of the Economists, which demeans the tasks of Social Democracy and holds back the thrust of the proletarian movement.

But at the same time they ought 'to use every means to insure Social Democratic influence and, if possible, leadership, in all the newly emerging or already existing legal and illegal trade unions.' Some members of the committee could not stomach this last point. An excerpt from the minutes of the meeting records one speaker as saying :

'Comrade S. is overlooking the fact that Point 5 of his resolution flatly contradicts all the preceding points. What do they say? That one must expose, one must destroy, illusions, one must, in short, disarm the trade unions, in other words, demolish them. And Point 5 suddenly speaks of leadership. To me, a trade union has a definite content. If I assume its leadership, I am thereby taking on this content, I must organize funds, and so on. This is a Menshevist misconception.'[25]

Gusev in fact managed to overcome the objections and the resolution was passed unanimously and sent to Lenin in Geneva.

Lenin, however, did not like the resolution at all. On 30 September 1905 he wrote to the Odessa Committee that it was 'highly erroneous'.

> Generally speaking I think we should be careful not to exaggerate the struggle against the Mensheviks on this issue. This is probably just the time when trade unions will soon begin to spring up. We must not stand aloof, and above all not give any occasion for thinking that we ought to stand aloof, but endeavour to take part, to influence, etc. . . . It is important that at the very outset Russian Social Democrats should strike the right note in regard to the trade unions, and at once create a tradition of Social Democratic participation, of Social Democratic leadership.[26]

A few months later he formulated a resolution along the same lines for the Stockholm ('Unification') Congress, of April-May 1906 :

> 1 . . . all party organizations must promote the formation of non-party trade unions, and induce all party members to join the trade unions in their respective trades;
> 2 . . . the party must exert every effort to educate the workers who belong to trade unions in the spirit of a broad understanding of the class struggle and the socialist aims of the proletariat; by its activities to win a virtually leading position in these unions; and lastly to ensure that these unions, under certain conditions, come into direct association with the party – however, without at all expelling non-party members from their ranks.[27]

Even more crucial than this fight against the sectarian attitude of some Bolshevik leaders towards the trade unions, was the battle Lenin waged against practically the whole St Petersburg Committee on the issue of the newly established Soviet. The Petersburg Soviet of Workers' Deputies was the offspring of the general strike of October 1905. This had been sparked off in Moscow by a small strike of printers, who demanded a few kopeks more per thousand letters set and pay for punctuation marks. The strike spread spontaneously throughout the country. The initiative in establishing the Petersburg Soviet was taken by the Mensheviks, who, however, had no conception of the effect which their creation would have in the long run. The Petersburg Committee of the Bolsheviks, for their part, showed extreme hostility towards the Soviet.

P.A.Krasikov is said to have warned Bolshevik agitators against 'this new intrigue by the Mensheviks . . . a non-party Zubatovite committee'.[28] Bogdanov, as head of the Russian Bureau, the foremost Bolshevik leader in Russia itself, argued that the Soviet, which included men of varying political views, could easily become the nucleus of an anti-socialist independent workers' party.[29]

B.I.Gorev, a representative of the Bolshevik Centre in Petersburg, wrote bluntly that 'when the Petersburg Soviet expanded its activity, became a united revolutionary force, the Petersburg Committee took fright'. He based this judgement on a remark by 'Nina L'vovna' (M.M.Essen, an influential member of the Petersburg Committee) and on resolutions passed at some sector meetings:

> I remember 'Nina L'vovna's' words: 'But where do we come in? So we have to reckon with them! The Soviet issues decrees, and we trail behind it, we cannot put through our own decrees', and so on.
> This was also reflected in the resolutions of sector meetings, especially of the Peterburgskaia Storona, where the leaders were Doroshenko . . . and the Bolshevik Mendeleev, now the well-known Menshevik Schwarz-Monoszon. They demanded that the Soviet either turn into a trade union organization or accept our programme and in effect fuse with the party organization.[30]

The Petersburg Committee's attitude to the Soviet was negative. Some members wanted it to be boycotted as unnecessary given the existence of the party, while others advocated joining the Soviet, getting as many Bolsheviks into it as possible, and 'exploding the Soviet from within' – also on the ground that it was 'unnecessary'.[31] At a meeting of the

Bolshevik Executive Committee of the Neva District of Petersburg,

> on 29 October, one of the fifteen members opposed taking part in it at all because the 'elective principle could not guarantee its class consciousness and Social Democratic character'. Four voted against taking part in the Soviet, if it did not accept a Social Democratic programme. Nine were for taking part and two did not vote.[32]

One reason for the Petersburg Bolsheviks' negative attitude to the Soviet in October 1905 was the fact that the Mensheviks' attitude to it was a positive one. 'Denouncing the inconsistency and lack of principles of the Mensheviks, the Bolsheviks intended to boycott the Soviet.'[33]

The Central Committee of the Bolsheviks, then in Petersburg, sent a 'Letter to All Party Organizations' on 27 October, in which it pointed out the danger of

> politically amorphous and socialistically immature workers' organizations created by the spontaneous revolutionary movement of the proletariat . . . Every such organization represents a certain stage in the proletariat's political development, but if it stands outside Social Democracy, it is, objectively, in danger of keeping the proletariat on a primitive political level and thus subjugating it to the bourgeois parties.

One such organization was the Petersburg Soviet of Workers' Deputies. The Central Committee asked the Social Democratic members of the Soviet: (1) to invite the Soviet to accept the RSDRP's programme and, when this was done, to recognize the leadership of the party and 'ultimately dissolve in it'; (2) if the Soviet refused to accept the programme, to leave the Soviet and expose the anti-proletarian nature of such organizations; (3) if the Soviet, while refusing to accept the programme, reserved to itself the right to decide its political stand in every case as it came up, to stay in the Soviet but reserve the right to speak out on 'the absurdity of such political leadership'.[34]

A few days later Comrade Anton (Krasikov), in the name of the Bolsheviks, did propose to the Soviet that it accept the party programme and recognize the party's leader-ship. 'As far as I remember, the debate was very brief. Khrus-talev objected. Krasikov's proposal received hardly any sup-port. But, contrary to Bogdanov's plan, the Bolsheviks did not leave the Soviet.'[35]

It needed Lenin's intervention to call the Bolshevik leadership in Petersburg to order – to pull them back from the abyss of a completely sectarian attitude towards the Sov-iet. He remained abroad for almost a month after its estab-lishment. On his way to Petersburg, where he arrived on 8 November, he spent about a week in Stockholm, where he wrote an article, 'Our Tasks and the Soviet of Workers' Deputies. A Letter to the Editor', intended for the Bolshevik journal *Novaya Zhizn*. In it he says of the issue:

> the Soviet of Workers' Deputies or the party? I think that it is wrong to put the question in this way and that the deci-sion must *certainly* be: *both* the Soviet of Workers' Deputies *and* the party. The only question – and a highly important one – is how to divide, and how to combine, the tasks of the Soviet and those of the Russian Social Democratic Labour Party.
> I think it would be inadvisable for the Soviet to adhere whol-ly to any one party.[36]

The Soviet was carrying on both an economic and a political struggle. On the former Lenin says:

> Should this struggle be conducted only by the Social Demo-crats or only under the Social Democratic banner? I do not think so; I still hold the view I have expressed (in entirely different, now outdated conditions, it is true) in *What is to be Done?*, namely, that it is inadvisable to limit the composi-tion of the trade unions, and hence of those taking part in the trade union, economic struggle, to members of the Social Democratic Party.[37]

And he goes on to deal with the political struggle:

> in this respect, too, I think it inadvisable to demand that the Soviet of Workers' Deputies should accept the Social Demo-cratic programme and join the Russian Social Democratic Labour Party. It seems to me that to lead the political strug-gle, *both* the Soviet ... *and* the party are, to an equal degree, absolutely necessary.[38]

Lenin argues, prophetically, that the Soviet is not only a new form of organization of the proletariat in struggle but also the form of the future revolutionary power of workers and peasants.

> I believe ... that politically the Soviet of Workers' Deputies should be regarded as the embryo of a *provisional revolutionary government*. I think the Soviet should proclaim itself the provisional revolutionary government of the whole of Russia as early as possible, or should *set up* a provisional revolutionary government (which would amount to the same thing, only in another form).[39]

In order to do this the Soviet should broaden its base; it should

> enlist to this end the participation of new deputies not only from the workers, but, first of all, from the sailors and soldiers, who are everywhere seeking freedom; secondly, from the revolutionary peasantry, and thirdly, from the revolutionary bourgeois intelligentsia ... We are not afraid of so broad and mixed a composition – indeed, we want it, for unless the proletariat and the peasantry unite and unless the Social Democrats and revolutionary democrats form a fighting alliance, the great Russian revolution cannot be fully successful.[40]

This important letter was rejected by the editor of *Novaya Zhizn* – it first saw the light of day in *Pravda* thirty-four years later – on 5 November 1940.

Thus, almost from the outset, Lenin's appreciation of the future historical role of the Soviets was much more advanced than that of the participants. For him the Soviet was not only a new form of organization of the proletariat in struggle; it was the form of future workers' power. He did not evolve this idea in a vacuum. He was articulating and generalizing what many workers felt instinctively. The following anecdote from Trotsky's history of the Russian revolution illustrates this grass-roots feeling.

> An old Cossack from Poltava province complained of unjust treatment by the Princes Repnin, who had exploited him as a clerk for twenty-eight years and them dismissed him without cause; the old man was asking the Soviet to negotiate with the Princes on his behalf. The envelope containing this

curious petition was addressed simply to The Workers' Government, Petersburg, yet it was promptly delivered by the revolutionary postal service.[41]*

A year after writing the important article quoted above, and after the experience of the December 1905 uprising in Moscow, Lenin developed further the concept of the inter-relation between the Soviet and the revolutionary government. In the article quoted above he argued that the Soviet was the form of revolutionary government of the future. A year later he argued that the Soviet could not exist independently of the immediate revolutionary situation, but also that it was not able by itself to organize the armed insurrection.

> The experience of October-December has provided very instructive guidance . . . Soviets of Workers' Deputies are *organs of direct mass struggle*. They originated as organs of the *strike* struggle. By force of circumstances they very quickly became the organs of the *general revolutionary* struggle against the government. The course of events and the transition from a strike to an uprising *irresistibly* transformed them *into organs of an uprising*. That this was precisely the role that quite a number of 'Soviets' and 'committees' played in December, is an absolutely indisputable fact. Events have proved in the most striking and convincing manner that the strength and importance of such organs in time of militant action depend *entirely* upon the strength and success of the uprising.
> It was not some theory, not appeals on the part of someone, tactics invented by someone, not party doctrine, but the force of circumstances that led these non-party mass organs to realize the need for an uprising and transformed them into organs of an uprising . . .
> If that is so – and undoubtedly it is – the conclusion to be drawn is also clear : 'Soviets' and similar mass institutions are in themselves *insufficient* for organizing an uprising.

---

* In fact three days after 'Bloody Sunday' Lenin had already put forward the need for popular democratic committees to lead the struggle : 'Revolutionary committees will be set up at every factory, in every district, in every large village. The people in revolt will overthrow all the government institutions of the Tsarist autocracy and proclaim the immediate convocation of a Constituent Assembly.'[42]

They are necessary for welding the masses together, for creating unity in the struggle, for handing on the party slogans (or slogans advanced by agreement between parties) of political leadership, for awakening the interests of the masses, for rousing and attracting them. But they are not sufficient for organizing the *immediate fighting force*, for *organizing an uprising* in the narrowest sense of the word.[43]

This passage shows a marvellous grasp of the strategic inter-relationship of the Soviets and the armed insurrection – and this on the basis of only a few weeks' experience! The story of 1917 is practically told here in a nutshell.

The Soviets comprise practically the whole of the working class. Hence although they rise only in a revolutionary situation, they are not necessarily led by revolutionaries. They may well be led by opponents of the revolution. This was the case in Russia after February 1917 – when they supported the bourgeois provisional government and its imperialist war effort. It was the case in Germany in 1918, when the Workers' Council of Berlin not only excluded Rosa Luxemburg and Karl Liebknecht from membership, but also supported the capitalist government which decapitated the revolution and murdered these two outstanding leaders.

The revolutionary party represents the advanced section of the working class. For workers' power one needs a certain combination of the party and the Soviets. Hence 'Soviets and similar mass institutions are in themselves insufficient for organizing an uprising.' But there is another reason. Even if the Soviets are under the influence of the revolutionary party, as in 1917, they cannot of themselves carry out the insurrection. They lack the homogeneity which is so vital for the abrupt act of armed insurrection, They are needed to impart a legal character to the insurrection. But they are not 'sufficient . . . for *organizing an uprising* in the narrowest sense of the word' – as Lenin put it so clearly, many years before 1917.

It is useful to compare Lenin's clear formulation with an analysis of the lessons of 1905 by Rosa Luxemburg and Leon Trotsky. Rosa Luxemburg, participant in the 1905 revolution, in her magnificent book *The Mass Strike, the Political*

Party and the Trade Unions, does not mention the Soviet at all. Not until 1918 did she appreciate its role as a form of workers' government.

> Rosa Luxemburg did not allocate any governmental role to Soviets ... though she was well aware of their significance; these were spontaneous instruments of the struggle but were not to be incorporated into the permanent institutional structure. This conception of Soviets as a means rather than an end still dominated the early thinking of the *Spartakus-bund* in Germany twelve years later, and it was not until the *Spartakus* leaders had to face the unwelcome demand of the SPD for a constituent assembly that they allocated a more positive and permanent role to the workers' and soldiers' councils – inspired by a Russian example![44]

Trotsky, who was President of the Petrograd Soviet in 1905 and who predicted the socialist content of the future Russian revolution, writing from prison immediately after the revolution, clearly described the governmental role of the Soviet:

> the Soviet really was a workers' government in embryo ... Prior to the Soviet we find among the industrial workers a multitude of revolutionary organizations ... But these were organizations *within the proletariat*, and their immediate aim was to achieve influence over the masses. The Soviet was, from the start, the organization *of the proletariat*, and its aim was the struggle for revolutionary power ... With the Soviet we have the first appearance of democratic power in modern Russian history. The Soviet is the organized power of the mass itself over its separate parts. It constitutes authentic democracy, without a lower and an upper chamber, without a professional bureaucracy, but with the voters' right to recall their deputies at any moment. Through its members – deputies directly elected by the workers – the Soviet exercises direct leadership over all social manifestations of the proletariat as a whole and of its individual groups, organizes its actions and provides them with a slogan and a banner.[45]

Yet, strangely, after some months had elapsed and the Soviets were no longer an immediate presence, Trotsky, reflecting on the lessons of the 1905 revolution, in his *Results and Prospects* (1906), did not even mention the Soviets. He made no effort to identify the form the revolutionary workers' government would take: 'Revolution is first and foremost a question of power, not of the state form (Constituent Assembly, Republic, United States) but of the social content of the government.'[46] He could describe the Soviet which had arisen, but it held no significance for him except as a historical phenomenon.

For the Mensheviks, who brought it into being, the Petersburg Soviet was neither an organization of struggle for power, nor a governmental form. For them it was merely a 'proletarian parliament', an 'organ of revolutionary self-administration', and so on.

8

'Open the Gates of the Party'
Lenin Relies on the Committee-Man

The personification of Lenin's concept of the party member, as described in *What is to be Done?* or in his arguments during the second Congress and its aftermath, was the Bolshevik committee-man. He was the professional revolutionary *par excellence*, leading the life of a hunted agitator and organizer. While at large he spent his whole time organizing strikes, street demonstrations, secret meetings and conferences. Then came prison and exile, followed by escape, and a new bout of activity, interrupted once again by arrest and deportation.

In fact the Mensheviks were no less dependent on the work of the professional revolutionaries than the Bolsheviks, as is shown by the figures given on p. 182. However, in the Menshevik concept of the party, the professional revolutionaries did not have a special role to play. In theory they were on a level with all other socialists – including strikers and socialist intellectuals. But for Lenin they had a very important function to perform. Unlike Martov, Lenin saw his own task not only as that of a political leader of the party, but also as head of the hierarchy of professional revolutionaries.

It was natural for Lenin, whenever he found the other Bolshevik leaders wanting, to try to establish direct contact with members of lower party committees, who were more determined, less vacillating, and whom he encouraged and promoted to higher positions in the faction. He had a very high regard for the committee-man. He prized men and women of action and resolution like I.V.Babushkin, Inessa Armand, G.K.Ordzhonikidze, S.S.Spandarian, M.P.Tomsky, I.V. Stalin, A.I.Rykov, L.B.Krasin, F.I.Goloshchekin, V.K.Taratura, L.P.Serebryakov and many others.

He did not regard the centralized party machine a fetish, or an end in itself, but as a means of increasing the activity, consciousness and organization of the vanguard sections of the working class. In contrast, the committee-men showed clear conservative and élitist characteristics, as can be seen from an appeal written by Stalin on the eve of the 1905 revolution, which reached the following climax: 'Let us stretch out our hands to one another and *rally around the party committees*. We must not forget for a moment *that only the party committees can worthily lead us, only they* will light up our road to the "promised land" called the socialist world'![1]

Compare this with the words of Lenin, written on practically the same day in far-off Geneva. 'Make way for the anger and hatred that have accumulated in your hearts throughout the centuries of exploitation, suffering and grief!' Trotsky quotes these words, and then comments: 'All of Lenin is in that phrase. He hates and rebels together with the masses, feels the rebellion in his bones, and does not ask of those in revolt that they act only with the permission of the "committees".[2]

The committee-men were, in a number of ways, people of sterling character. They devoted their lives to the revolutionary movement and put themselves completely at the disposal of the party. They had no life outside the movement. Because they made great sacrifices, they had strong moral authority. They were always in a position to demand sacrifices from rank-and-file workers, because they set such an example themselves. They acquired great self-assurance, through repeatedly having to take on-the-spot decisions under fire. They were on the whole competent, shrewd, energetic and strong-willed; as complete outlaws, they could not otherwise have survived.

The committee-men kept up their unfaltering activity over months and years. One only has to look down the list of delegates at say, the London fifth Congress (1907) to see a gallery of people who were the backbone of Bolshevism, who carried on the tradition, the continuity of the party.

During the period of reaction, 1906-10, it was not the committee-men who deserted the party in large numbers; they mostly remained loyal. In the struggle a process of selection of cadres took place, and those who were selected were on the whole the committee-men. Unfortunately, however, self-sacrifice and special abilities do not provide a guarantee against the conservatism of the party machine. Herbert Spencer, the well-known naturalist, wisely observed that every organism is conservative in direct proportion to its perfection. Lenin, who knew how to recruit, train and keep the loyalty of the committee-men, had to oppose their conservatism during the revolution of 1905.

Whereas in the years before the 1905 revolution and during the years of reaction following it, the committee-men had a much higher level of activity and consciousness than even the advanced section of the proletariat, at the time of the revolution itself they lagged behind considerably.

To survive during the difficult years of illegality and

suffering, they had had to evolve a discipline, which now became an impediment. Krupskaya summed up the committee-man's characteristics very aptly :

> The 'Komitetchik' [committee-man] was usually a fairly self-assured person, who realized what great influence the work of the committees had over the masses; he generally did not recognize any inner-party democracy whatever. 'This democratism only leads to us falling into the hands of the authorities; we are already quite well enough connected with the movement,' the Komitetchiks would say. And inwardly, these committee members always rather despised 'the people abroad', who, they considered, just grew fat and organized intrigues. 'They ought to be sent to work under Russian conditions' was their verdict. The Komitetchiks did not like to feel the pressure from abroad. At the same time they did not like innovations. They were neither desirous nor capable of adapting themselves to the changing conditions.
> In the period 1904-1905 these members of the committees bore tremendous responsibilities on their shoulders, but many of them experienced the utmost difficulty in adapting themselves to the conditions of increasing opportunities for legal work, and to the methods of open struggle. At the third Congress there were no workers present – or at any rate, not a single prominent worker. On the other hand there were many committee members.[3]

Opening up the Party

In the new times of the revolutionary spring of 1905, Lenin was singing a different tune, and he tried desperately to rid the committee-men of their old habits, their formalism, their cautions and fears, exhorting them to boldness and initiative.

Organize, organize, organize, open the gates of the party to new forces – this was the message he repeated impatiently and urgently. In a letter of 11 February 1905, to A.A.Bogdanov and S.I.Gusev, he wrote :

> Really, I sometimes think that nine-tenths of the Bolsheviks are actually formalists ... We need young forces. I am for shooting on the spot anyone who presumes to say that there are no people to be had. The people in Russia are legion; all

we have to do is to recruit young people more widely and boldly, more boldly and widely, and again more widely and again more boldly *without fearing them*. This is a time of war. The youth – the students, and still more so the young workers – will decide the issue of the whole struggle. Get rid of all the old habits of immobility, of respect for rank, and so on. Form *hundreds* of circles of *Vperyodists* from among the youth and encourage them to work at full blast. Enlarge the committee *threefold* by accepting young people into it, set up half a dozen or a dozen subcommittees, 'co-opt' any and every honest and energetic person. Allow every subcommittee to write and publish leaflets without any red tape (there is no harm if they do make a mistake; we on *Vperyod* will 'gently' correct them). We must, with desperate speed, unite all people with revolutionary initiative and set them to work. Do not fear their lack of training, do not tremble at their inexperience and lack of development . . .

Only you must be sure to organize, organize, and organize *hundreds* of circles, completely pushing into the background the customary, well meant committee (hierarchic) stupidities. This is a time of war. Either you create *new*, young, fresh, energetic battle organizations everywhere for revolutionary Social Democratic work of all varieties among all strata, or you will go under wearing the aureole of 'committee' bureaucrats.[4]

On 25 March 1905 he wrote to the Odessa Committee of the party: 'Are you taking workers into the committee? This is essential, absolutely essential! Why don't you put us in direct contact with workers? Not a single worker writes to *Vperyod*. *This is a scandal*. We need at all costs *dozens* of worker correspondents.'[5]

A short time later, in a pamphlet called *New Times and New Forces*, he called even more vehemently for the party to be opened up. But his appeal met with stubborn resistance from the conservative committee-men.

At the third Congress, in the spring of 1905, Lenin and Bogdanov proposed a resolution urging the party to open its gates wide to workers, who should be brought forward to take a leading role in it, to

make every effort to strengthen the ties between the party and the masses of the working class by raising still wider sections of proletarians and semi-proletarians to full Social Democratic consciousness, by developing their revolutionary Social Democratic activity, by seeing to it that the greatest possible number of workers capable of leading the movement and the party organizations be advanced from among the mass of the working class to membership on the local centres and on the all-party centre through the creation of a maximum number of working-class organizations adhering to our party, by seeing to it that working-class organizations unwilling or unable to enter the party should at least be associated with it.[6]

The debate at the Congress waxed very fierce. The next speaker, Gradov (Kamenev), said : 'I must express my strong opposition to . . . this resolution. As an issue of the relationship of workers and the intelligentsia in party organizations, this question does not exist. (Lenin : It does.) No, it does not : it exists as a demagogic question, that is all.'[7]

The inclusion of workers in local committees was debated with particular heat. Filippov said that there was only one worker in the Petersburg Committee, although work in Petersburg had been going on for fifteen years. (Lenin : Outrageous!)[8] Leskov said that in the Northern Committee things were even worse :

> At one time three of the seven members of our Northern Committee were workers; now not one of the eight committee members is a worker. Very soon this question will become even more complex. The labour movement is growing irresistibly, quite apart from party influence, and the newly emerging masses must be organized. This weakens the ideological influence of Social Democracy.[9]

Osipov reported: 'Not so long ago I toured the Caucasus Committees . . . At the time there was one worker in the Baku Committee, one in the Batum Committee, and none in the Kutais Committee. Only the Tiflis Committee had several . . . Could it be that our Caucasus comrades prefer *intelligenty* committee-men to worker committee-men ?'[10]

Orlovsky commented that 'a workers' party in which leadership is the hereditary property of the intelligentsia is doomed to be anaemic'.[11] A.Belsky (Krasikov) declared : 'In our committees, and I have seen plenty of them in my work, there is some kind of phobia towards workers."[12] Lenin intervened, and the session became even noisier.

> It will be the task of the future centre to reorganize a considerable number of our committees: the inertness of the committee-men has to be overcome. (*Applause and booing.*) I can hear Comrade Segeyev booing while the non-committee-men applaud. I think we should look at the matter more broadly. To place workers on the committees is a political, not only a pedagogical task. Workers have the class instinct, and, given some political experience, they pretty soon become staunch Social Democrats. I should be strongly in favour of having eight workers to every two intellectuals on our committees.[13]

Mikhailov, speaking immediately after Lenin, added fuel to the flames:

> We must see to it that our committees are immediately expanded to fifteen-twenty members, with an elective board. The main contingent of a committee must consist of workers. It is said that we do not have workers capable of sitting on a committee. That is not true. The criterion for admitting workers . . . ought to be different from the one applied to *intelligenty*. There is talk of tempered SDs, but . . . first and second-year students, familiar with Social Democratic ideas from the Erfurt Programme and a few issues of *Iskra*, are already considered tempered SDs. Thus in practice the requirements for *intelligenty* are very low, and for workers they are extremely high. (Lenin: Very true! The Majority of the Delegates: Not true!) The only valid criterion for admitting workers into a committee must be the degree of their influence among the masses. (*Hissing, shouting.*) All workers who are leaders and have been in our circles must be members of our committee. (Right!) I think this is the only way to settle the vexed question between workers and *intelligenty* and to cut the ground from under demagoguery.[14]

Later Lenin returned to the subject:

> I could hardly keep my seat when it was said here that there are no workers fit to sit on the committees. The question is being dragged out; obviously there is something the matter with the party. Workers must be given places on the committees. Oddly enough, there are only three journalists at

the Congress, the others being committee-men: it appears however that the journalists are for placing the workers, whereas the committee-men for some reason are quite wrought up over it.

'Chair-warmers and keepers of the seal' should all be smoked out:

> If this clause constitutes a threat to the committee consisting of intellectuals then I am all for it. A tight hold must always be kept on the intelligentsia. It is always the instigator of all sorts of squabbles.
> One cannot rely on a small periphery of intellectuals, but one can and should rely on hundreds of organized workers.[15]

Most of the delegates to the Congress were committee-men who were opposed to any move which would tend to weaken their authority over the rank and file. Buttressing themselves with quotations from *What is to be Done?*, they called for 'extreme caution' in admitting workers into the committees and condemned 'playing at democracy'. Lenin's resolution was defeated by 12 votes to $9\frac{1}{2}$. It was not the last occasion on which he found himself in a minority among the Bolshevik leaders, and even booed at a Bolshevik Congress.*

The unfortunate Lenin had to persuade his supporters to oppose the line proposed in *What is to be Done?* He denied that he had

> at the second Congress . . . any intention of elevating my own formulations, as given in *What is to be Done?* to 'programmatic' level constituting special principles. On the contrary, the expression I used – and it has since been frequently quoted – was that the 'economists' had gone to one extreme. *What is to be Done?*, I said, straightens out what had been twisted by the 'economists'. I emphasize that just because we were so vigorously straightening out whatever had been twisted, our line of action would always be the straightest.
> The meaning of these words is clear enough: *What is to be*

---

* The opposition of the committee-men to the inclusion of workers in the committees was not limited to the Bolsheviks. The same happened among the Mensheviks.[16]

Done? is a controversial correction of 'economist' distortion and it would be wrong to regard the pamphlet in any other light.[17]

On the idea that socialist consciousness could be brought in only from the 'outside', and that the working class could spontaneously achieve only trade-union consciousness, Lenin now formulated his conclusion in terms which were the exact opposite of those of *What is to be Done?* In an article called 'The Reorganization of the Party' written in November 1905, he says bluntly: 'The working class is instinctively, spontaneously Social Democratic.'[18]

A few years later, in an article commemorating the 1905 revolution, Lenin goes even further in expressing the view that capitalism itself inculcates a socialist consciousness in the working class.

> The very conditions of their lives make the workers capable of struggle and impels them to struggle. Capital collects the workers in great masses in big cities, uniting them, teaching them to act in unison. At every step they come face to face with their enemy – the capitalist class. In combat with this enemy the worker becomes a *socialist*, comes to realize the necessity of a complete abolition of all poverty and all oppression.[19]

This does not mean that Lenin had been wrong in *What is to be Done?* In 1900-03 his emphasis on the need for an organization of professional revolutionaries was perfectly justified. In 1908 he wrote:

> To maintain today that *Iskra* exaggerated (*in 1901 and 1902!*) the idea of an organization of professional revolutionaries is like reproaching the Japanese, *after* the Russo-Japanese war, for having exaggerated the strength of Russia's armed forces, for having prior to the war exaggerated the need to prepare for fighting these forces. To win victory the Japanese had to marshall all their forces against the probable maximum of Russian forces. Unfortunately, many of those who judge our party are outsiders, who do not know the subject, who do not realize that *today* the idea of an organization of professional revolutionaries has al-

ready scored a complete victory. That victory would have been impossible if this idea had not been pushed to the *forefront* at the time, if we had not 'exaggerated' so as to drive it home to people who were trying to prevent it from being realized.[20]

It was not characteristic of Lenin to give up a fight, and a few months after the third Congress, in November 1905, he returned to the issue with increased vigour : the gates of the party should be opened, despite the conservative committee-men : 'rally all the worker Social Democrats round yourselves, incorporate them in the ranks of the party organizations by hundreds and thousands'.[21]

The committee-men were very much afraid of dangers of 'diluting' the party. Lenin countered this opposition to worker recruitment as follows :

> Danger may be said to lie in a sudden influx of large numbers of non-Social Democrats into the party. If that occurred, the party would be dissolved among the masses, it would cease to be the conscious vanguard of its class, its role would be reduced to that of a tail. That would mean a very deplorable period indeed. And this danger *could* undoubtedly become a *very serious* one if we showed any inclination towards demagogy, if we lacked party principles (programme, tactical rules, organizational experience) entirely, or if those principles were feeble and shaky. But the fact is that no such 'ifs' exist ... We have a firmly established party programme which is officially recognized by all Social Democrats and the fundamental propositions of which have not given rise to any criticism (criticism of individual points and formulations is quite legitimate and necessary in any live party). We have resolutions on tactics which were consistently and systematically worked out at the second and third Congresses and in the course of many years' work of the Social Democratic press. We also have some organizational experience and an actual organization, which has played an educational role and has undoubtedly borne fruit.[22]

The party doors should be wide open even to religious workers, if they were opponents of the employers and the government.

To be sure, those workers who remain Christians, who believe in God, and those intellectuals who defend mysticism (fie upon them!), are inconsistent too; but we shall not expel them from the Soviet or even the party, for it is our firm conviction that the actual struggle, and work within the ranks will convince all elements possessing vitality that marxism is the truth, and will cast aside all those who lack vitality. And we do not for one moment doubt our strength, the overwhelming strength of marxists, in the Russian Social Democratic Labour Party.[23]

Non-workers should also be encouraged to join the party.

The urban and industrial proletariat will inevitably be the nucleus of our Social Democratic Labour Party, but we must attract to it, enlighten, and organize all who labour and are exploited, as stated in our programme – all without exception: handicraftsmen, paupers, beggars, servants, tramps, prostitutes – of course, subject to the necessary and obligatory condition that they join the Social Democratic movement and not that the Social Democratic movement join them, that they adopt the standpoint of the proletariat, and not that the proletariat adopt theirs.[24]

In characteristic style, Lenin vehemently reiterated the immediate tasks which he saw facing the movement. During this period he called continually for the party to be opened up to the mass of workers: 'At the third Congress of the party I suggested that there be about eight workers to every two intellectuals in the Party committees.[25] How obsolete that suggestion seems today! Now we must wish for the party organizations to have one Social Democratic intellectual to several hundred Social Democratic workers.'[26]

A year later, in December 1906, he repeated:

It is certainly necessary now to enlarge the party with the aid of *proletarian* elements. It is abnormal that we should have only 6,000 party members in St Petersburg (in St Petersburg Gubernia there are 81,000 workers in factories employing 500 workers and over; in all 150,000 workers); that in the Central Industrial Region we should have only 20,000 party members (377,000 workers in factories employing 500 and over; in all, 562,000 workers). We must *learn* to recruit* five times and ten times as many workers for the party in such centres.

However, Lenin found the going very difficult indeed among the people he himself had organized and trained. The organizational loyalty of the committee-men, which Lenin had cultivated and valued highly, turned into organizational fetishism, and became a serious impediment to Bolshevism.

But Nevertheless it Moves...

Notwithstanding the determined opposition of the committee-men, the Bolshevik Party expanded rapidly in the wake of the revolution and its social composition changed radically.

> On the basis of reports presented to the second Congress, membership of the RSDLP in Russia in 1903 could not have been more than a few thousand, excluding membership of the Bund . . . By the fourth Congress in April 1906, membership had grown, it is estimated, to 13,000 for the Bolsheviks and 18,000 for the Mensheviks. Another estimate (for October 1906) was 33,000 Bolsheviks, 43,000 Mensheviks . . . By 1907 the total membership had increased to 150,000 : Bolsheviks – 46,143, Mensheviks – 38,174, Bund – 25,468, and the Polish and Latvian parts of the party 25,654 and 13,000 respectively.[28]

The Bolsheviks also became largely a party of young people, a factor which more than once helped Lenin to overcome conservative resistance to change in the party. In 1907 the age structure of the 'rank and file' by faction was as follows in percentage :[29]

---

* 'We say "learn to recruit", for the number of Social Democratic workers in such centres is undoubtedly many times the number of party members. We suffer from routine, we must fight against it. We must learn to form, where necessary, *lose Organisationen* – looser, broader and more accessible *proletarian* organizations. Our slogan is : *for a larger Social Democratic Labour Party*, against a non-party labour congress and a non-party party !'[27]

Age	Bolsheviks	Mensheviks	Total
over 30	13	7	20
25-29	8	6	14
20-24	19	6	25
10-19	11	1	12
Total	51	20	71

The 'activists' – defined as propagandists, public speakers, agitators, or members of a local soviet or of an armed (Social Democratic) detachment – were not much older.[30]

Age	Bolsheviks	Mensheviks	Total
over 30	10	10	20
25-29	14	16	30
20-24	25	9	34
10-19	10	0	10
Total	59	35	94

The party leadership was also quite young. Of the leaders of the Bolsheviks in 1907:

the oldest were Krasin, Lenin and Krasikov (all 37). The youngest were Litvinov and Zemlyachka (both 31). The average age of the nine Bolshevik leaders was 34. The Menshevik leaders had an average of 44.[31]

Lenin was both delighted and proud that the party was a party of youth.

We are the party of the future, and the future belongs to the youth. We are a party of innovators, and it is always the youth that most eagerly follows the innovators. We are a party that is waging a self-sacrificing struggle against the old rottenness, and youth is always the first to undertake a self-sacrificing struggle.
No, let us leave it to the Cadets to collect the 'tired' old men of thirty, revolutionaries who have 'grown wise', and renegades from Social Democracy. We shall always be a party of the youth of the advanced class![32]

A few years later, in a letter to Inessa Armand, he wrote: 'The young are the only people worth working on!'[33]

Another factor that helped him to overcome conservative resistance in the party was its largely proletarian composition. The results of the party census in 1922, in which information was given for the Bolshevik membership in 1905, show the following broad occupational division:[34]*

	Workers	Peasants	Office and **shop** workers	Others	Total
Numbers	5,200	400	2,300	500	8,400
% of total	61.9	4.8	27.4	5.9	100

Party cells sprang up in scores of factories. Thus the report of the St Petersburg Committee to the third Congress of the Bolsheviks (May 1905) listed 17 cells in the factories of the Petersburg district, 18 cells in the Vyborg district, 29 in the City district, 20 in the Neva district and 15 circles among the handicraftsmen.[36] Similarly in Moscow at the end of the summer of 1905 the Bolsheviks claimed 40 factory cells.[37]

The facts wholly refute the notion that the party was made up of a handful of intellectuals, a view which prevails among anti-Bolshevik scholars. Thus J.L.H.Keep has asserted that 'the RSDLP, professedly a proletarian party, was in reality an organization of revolutionary intellectuals with only a modicum of popular support.'[38] Lenin wrote in January 1907 that only liars 'can now doubt the *mass proletarian character* of the Social Democratic Party in Russia'.[39]

Over time, the proportion of manual workers increased considerably, not only among the rank and file but also among delegates to party congresses. The social composition of the delegates to four congresses was as follows:

---

* 'This information is based on the evaluation of the members, of whom more than half considered themselves to be "workers". The small number of "peasants" here recorded is evidence that a "peasant" estate classification referred to legal position at birth and not occupation: the bulk of the "peasants" in the movement even in 1905 had already moved from the village to work in the factories.'[35]

Congress	Workers	Peasants	Office workers and others	Unknown
2nd (1903)	3	0	40	8
3rd (1905)	1	0	28	1
4th (1906)	36	1	108	0
5th (1907)	116	2	218	0

Probably the most representative Congress was the fifth, in 1907, at which it was claimed that each delegate represented 500 local party members. The social composition of the Bolshevik and Menshevik delegates in terms of occupation (or former occupation) is shown in the following table:[40]

Occupation	Bolsheviks		Mensheviks	
	Number	%	Number	%
Manual workers	38	36.2	30	31.9
Office and shop workers	12	11.4	5	5.1
'Liberal professions'	13	12.4	13	13.4
Professional revolutionaries	18	17.1	22	22.1
Writers	15	14.3	18	18.6
None	4	3.8	3	3.1
Students	5	4.8	5	5.2
Landowners	0	0.0	1	1.0
Total	105	100.0	97	100.4

The occupation table shows a high degree of similarity between both factions . . . The only differences are in the clerical and manual workers' groups, of which more were Bolsheviks than Mensheviks, and in the professional revolutionaries' group where the Mensheviks had a slightly higher proportion than the Bolsheviks. This last item rebuts the commonly held assertion that the Bolsheviks were a faction of 'professional revolutionaries' in contrast to the Mensheviks.[41]

In Conclusion

Lenin's attitude to organizational forms was always historically concrete, hence its strength. He was never taken in by abstract, dogmatic schemes of organization, but always ready to change the organizational structure of the party to reflect the development of the class struggle.

Organization is subordinate to politics. This does not mean that it has no independent *influence* on politics. But it is, and must be, subordinated to the concrete policies of the day. The truth is always concrete, as Lenin reiterated again and again. And this also applies to the organizational forms needed to undertake the concrete tasks.

Lenin grasped better than anyone else the need for a centralized party organization. However, he saw it not as an aim in itself, but rather as a lever to raise the level of activity and consciousness among the mass of the workers. To make the organization into a fetish, to submit to it although it impeded mass action, went against his grain. When he found it necessary, as in 1905-07, or in 1917, he would appeal to the energy of the masses to overcome the conservatism of the party machine.

9

Lenin on Armed Insurrection

'Major questions in the life of nations are settled only by force.'[1]

For Lenin the armed insurrection was the climax of the revolution. The passive Mensheviks never understood the role of active preparation for an uprising. The old Blanquist putschists spoke only of the technical side of the insurrection, abstracting it completely from the general mass movement, from the daily life of the masses, from their organization and class consciousness. But Lenin referred over and over again to the insurrection as an art that needed active study and execution, but an art related to the general movement of the revolution.

Marx said that revolution was the midwife of a new

society; midwifery has certain specific rules that have to be studied. Lenin posed the question of insurrection in this light, looking at the concrete circumstances of its occurrence. Hence at different periods of his life he posed the question differently.

In 1897 he postponed consideration of the question. In his *Tasks of Russian Social Democrats*, he states that

> to decide at the present time the question of what methods the Social Democracy will resort to for the direct overthrow of the autocracy, whether it will choose an uprising, or a widespread political strike, or some other form of attack, would be akin to generals calling a council of war before they have mustered an army.[2]

The mustering of an army called for general organization, propaganda and agitation. In 1902, in *What is to be Done?*, he dealt with the insurrection in terms of general preparation:

> Picture to yourselves a popular uprising. Probably everyone will now agree that we must think of this and prepare for it. But *how*? Surely the Central Committee cannot appoint agents to all localities for the purpose of preparing the uprising! Even if we had a Central Committee it could achieve absolutely nothing by such appointments under present-day Russian conditions. But a network of agents that would form in the course of establishing and distributing the common newspaper would not have to 'sit about and wait' for the call for an uprising, but could carry on the regular activity that would strengthen our contacts with the broadest strata of the working masses and with all social strata that are discontented with the autocracy, which is of such importance for an uprising. Precisely such activity would serve to cultivate the ability to estimate correctly the general political situation and, consequently, the ability to select the proper moment for an uprising. Precisely such activity would train *all* local organizations to respond simultaneously to the same political questions, incidents and events that agitate the whole of Russia and to react to such 'incidents' in the most vigorous, uniform and expedient manner possible; for an uprising is in essence the most vigorous, most uniform, and most expedient 'answer' of the entire people to the government. Lastly, it is precisely such activity that would train all revolutionary organizations throughout

Russia to maintain the most continuous, and at the same time most secret, contacts with one another, thus creating *real* party unity; for without such contacts it will be impossible collectively to discuss the plan for the uprising and to take the necessary preparatory measures on its eve, measures that must be kept in the strictest secrecy.[3]

The third stage of consideration of the question comes in 1905. After Bloody Sunday, 9 January 1905, Lenin advances insurrection as a direct appeal, in the paper *Vperyod* and at the third Congress in May 1905. In a *Resolution on the Armed Uprising* put at the Congress, he states :

> the third Congress of the RSDLP holds that the task of organizing the proletariat for direct struggle against the autocracy by means of the armed uprising is one of the major and most urgent tasks of the party at the present revolutionary moment.
> Accordingly, the Congress instructs all party organizations :
> (a) to explain to the proletariat by means of propaganda and agitation, not only the political significance, but the practical organizational aspect of the impending armed uprising,
> (b) to explain in that propaganda and agitation the role of mass political strikes, which may be of great importance at the beginning and during the progress of the uprising, and
> (c) to take the most energetic steps towards arming the proletariat, as well as drawing up a plan of the armed uprising and of direct leadership thereof, for which purpose special groups of party workers should be formed as and when necessary.[4]

The armed uprising was central to all the resolutions of the third Congress. Every item on the agenda was debated and decided in the light of it.

A couple of months after the Congress, in his book *Two Tactics of Social Democracy in the Democratic Revolution*, Lenin again emphasized the urgency of preparation for the insurrection :

> Undoubtedly we still have a great deal to do in educating and organizing the working class; but now the gist of the matter is : where should we place the main political emphasis in the work of education and organization? On the trade unions and legally existing associations, or on an insurrec-

tion, on the work of creating a revolutionary army and a revolutionary government? Both serve to educate and organize the working class. Both are, of course, necessary. But in the present revolution the problem amounts to this: which is to be emphasized in the work of educating and organizing the working class, the former or the latter.[5]

A little later he pronounced judgement. 'Major questions in the life of nations are settled only by force.'[6]

On the eve of the armed uprising in Moscow, in December 1905, Lenin made it clear that once the masses are roused to revolution and are ready to act, the party must call for insurrection and explain to the masses the practical steps necessary for its success.

The slogan of insurrection is a slogan for deciding the issue by material force, which in present-day European civilization can only be military force. This slogan should not be put forward until the general prerequisites for revolution have matured, until the masses have definitely shown that they have been roused and are ready to act, until the external circumstances have led to an open crisis. But once such a slogan has been issued ... once the die is cast, all subterfuges must be done with; it must be explained directly and openly to the masses what the practical conditions for a successful revolution are at the present time.[7]

Insurrection as an Art

Again and again, especially after the December 1905 armed struggle in Moscow, Lenin referred to Marx's and Engels' profound 'propositions that insurrection is an art, and that the principal rule of the art is the waging of a desperately bold and irrevocably determined *offensive*'. He emphasized the tremendous importance of military knowledge, military technique and military organization. The workers must learn from the capitalists' knowledge and techniques, and from their own experience in struggle.

In an article called 'Lessons of the Moscow Uprising', written in August 1906 Lenin says:

There have been new advances in military technique in the very recent period. The Japanese war produced the hand grenade. The small-arms factories have placed automatic rifles on the market. Both these weapons are already being successfully used in the Russian revolution, but to a degree that is far from adequate. We can and must take advantage of improvements in technique, teach the workers' detachments to make bombs in large quantities, help them and our fighting squads to obtain supplies of explosives, fuses and automatic rifles.[8]

And on the lessons of the Moscow uprising he writes:

Military tactics depend on the level of military technique. This plain truth Engels demonstrated and brought home to all marxists. Military technique today is not what it was in the middle of the nineteenth century. It would be folly to contend against artillery in crowds and defend barricades with revolvers. Kautsky was right when he wrote that it is high time now, after Moscow, to review Engels' conclusions, and that Moscow had inaugurated *new barricade tactics*. These tactics are the tactics of guerrilla warfare. The organization required for such tactics is that of mobile and exceedingly small units, units of ten, three or even two persons. We often meet Social Democrats now who scoff whenever units of five or three are mentioned. But scoffing is only a cheap way of ignoring the *new* question of tactics and organization raised by street fighting under the conditions imposed by modern military technique. Study carefully the story of the Moscow uprising gentlemen, and you will understand what connection exists between 'units of five' and the question of 'new barricade tactics'.

Moscow advanced these tactics, but failed to develop them far enough, to apply them to any considerable extent, to a really mass extent. There were too few volunteer fighting squads, the slogan of bold attack was not issued to the masses of the workers and they did not apply it; the guerrilla detachments were too uniform in character, their arms and methods were inadequate, their ability to lead the crowd was almost undeveloped. We must make up for all this and we shall do so by learning from the experience of Moscow, by spreading this experience among the masses and by stimulating their creative efforts to develop it still further.[9]

Lenin already saw very clearly that the revolution could not be victorious unless at least a section of the army went over to the side of the revolutionaries. This became even clearer in 1917. But to achieve this the soldiers must be convinced of the readiness of the workers to seize victory even at the cost of their own lives.

> Of course, unless the revolution assumes a mass character and affects the troops, there can be no question of serious struggle. That we must work among the troops goes without saying. But we must not imagine that they will come over to our side at one stroke, as a result of persuasion or their own convictions. The Moscow uprising clearly demonstrated how stereotyped and lifeless this view is. As a matter of fact, the wavering of the troops, which is inevitable in every truly popular movement, leads to a real *fight for the troops* whenever the revolutionary struggle becomes acute ... we shall prove to be miserable pedants if we forget that at a time of uprising there must also be a physical struggle for the troops.
>
> In the December days, the Moscow proletariat taught us magnificent lessons in ideologically 'winning over' the troops, as, for example, on 8 December in Strastnaya Square, when the crowd surrounded the Cossacks, mingled and fraternized with them, and persuaded them to turn back. Or on 10 December, in Presnya District, when two working girls, carrying a red flag in a crowd of 10,000 people, rushed out to meet the Cossacks crying: 'Kill us! We will not surrender the flag alive!' And the Cossacks were disconcerted and galloped away, amidst the shouts from the crowd: 'Hurrah for the Cossacks!' These examples of courage and heroism should be impressed forever on the mind of the proletariat.[10]

Characteristically, Lenin did not limit himself to issuing general slogans, but also attended to practical affairs. He made sure that the combat squads did not remain on paper or become overwhelmed by routine. Immediately after Bloody Sunday he translated into Russian a pamphlet called *On Street Fighting (The Advice of a General of the Commune)* by General Gustave-Paul Cluseret.[11] General Cluseret, during an adventurous life, had participated in the suppression of the Paris workingmen's revolt in June 1848, but had then served with Garibaldi in Italy, later with the North in the American Civil War (where he became a general), and finally became a military leader of the Paris Commune. Lenin also read everything he could find on military science. His favourite authority was Clausewitz, author of the classic study *On War*. Lenin also carefully re-read everything Marx and Engels had written on military matters and insurrection. He was the only Russian émigré leader who reacted in this way to Bloody Sunday.

He propagated the results of his studies amongst his comrades. After receiving a report from the Combat Committee of the Petersburg Committee on the organization of preparations for insurrection, which proposed an organizational scheme, he wrote, on 16 October 1905, warning sharply against constructing pyramids on paper and concocting blueprints:

> Judging by the documents, the whole thing threatens to degenerate into office routine. All these schemes, all these plans of organization of the Combat Committee create the impression of 'red tape' – forgive me my frankness, but I hope that you will not suspect me of fault-finding. Schemes and disputes and discussion about the functions of the Combat Committee and its rights, are of the least value in a matter like this.

What is necessary, above all, is *action*:

> What is needed is furious energy, and again energy. It horrifies me – I give you my word – it horrifies me to find that there has been talk about bombs for *over six months*, yet not one has been made! And it is the most learned of people who are doing the talking.

He recommends the committee to turn to the young people:

> Go to the youth, gentlemen! That is the only remedy! Otherwise – I give you my word for it – you will be too late (everything tells me that), and will be left with 'learned' memoranda, plans, charts, schemes, and magnificent recipes, but without an organization, without a living cause. Go to the youth.[12]

Then Lenin spells out the practical steps necessary:

Form fighting squads *at once* everywhere, among the students, and *especially among the workers*, etc., etc. Let groups be at once organized of three, ten, thirty, etc., persons. Let them arm themselves at once as best they can, be it with a revolver, a knife, a rag soaked in kerosene for starting fires, etc. Let these detachments at once select leaders, and as far as possible *contact* the Combat Committee of the St Petersburg Committee. Do not demand any formalities, and, for heaven's sake, forget all these schemes, and send all 'functions, rights and privileges' to the devil . . . Do not refuse to contact any group, even if it consists of only three persons; make it the one sole condition that it should be reliable as far as police spying is concerned and prepared to fight the Tsar's troops. Let the groups join the RSDLP or *associate* themselves with the RSDLP if they want to; that would be splendid. But I would consider it quite wrong to *insist* on it.

The role of the Combat Committee of the St Petersburg Committee should be to *help* these contingents of the revolutionary army, to serve as a 'bureau' for contact purposes; if in *such a matter* you begin with schemes and with talk about the 'rights' of the Combat Committee, you will ruin the whole cause; I assure you, you will ruin it irreparably.

You must proceed to propaganda on a wide scale. Let five or ten people make the round of *hundreds* of workers' and students' study circles in a week, penetrate wherever they can, and everywhere propose a clear, brief, direct, and simple plan : organize combat groups immediately, arm yourselves as best you can, and work with all your might; we will help you in every way we can, but *do not wait for our help*; act for yourselves.

The principal thing in a matter like this is the initiative of the mass of small groups. They will do everything. Without them your entire Combat Committee is nothing. I am prepared to gauge the efficiency of the Combat Committee's work by the number of such combat groups it is in contact with. If in a month or two the Combat Committee does not have a minimum of 200 or 300 groups in St Petersburg then it is a dead Combat Committee. It will have to be buried. If it cannot muster a hundred or two of groups in seething times like these, then it is indeed remote from real life.

The propagandists must supply each group with brief and simple recipes for making bombs, give them an elementary explanation of the type of the work, and then leave it all to them. Squads must *at once* begin military training by launching operations immediately, at once. Some may at once undertake to kill a spy or blow up a police station, others to raid a bank to confiscate funds for the insurrection, others again may drill or prepare plans of localities, etc. But the essential thing is to begin at once to learn from actual practice: have no fear of these trial attacks. They may, of course, degenerate into extremes, but that is an evil of the morrow, whereas the evil today is our inertness, our doctrinaire spirit, our learned immobility, and our senile fear of initiative. Let every group learn, if it is only by beating up policemen: a score or so victims will be more than compensated for by the fact that this will train hundreds of experienced fighters, who tomorrow will be leading hundreds of thousands.[13]

While Lenin's general approach to the question of an armed insurrection was consistent and concrete in the extreme, the technical advice he gave was faulty, and not suited to the needs of the time. From the measures they took, it seems that he and Leonid Krasin – the Bolshevik chief of the 'fighting groups' whose job was to procure and manufacture arms and prepare for the actual uprising – assumed that street fighting would take the form of mass charges and scuffles at close quarters. They therefore put the emphasis on hand grenades and revolvers. When the uprising did take place in December 1905 in Moscow, these weapons of close fighting were found to be no match for the long-range rifles and artillery of the Tsarist army, as Lenin readily admitted after the event.

In the October 1917 insurrection, Lenin again gave advice which was not tactically appropriate to the concrete situation (for example, to start the uprising in Moscow and not in Petrograd). This advice was fortunately countermanded by Trotsky, who was the actual organizer of the October insurrection. In 1905 Krasin agreed with Lenin's technical advice. From the top of a mountain the high command can see the whole field of struggle quite clearly; but it can easily misjudge what is actually happening or going to happen on the ground, where the combatants are engaged.

An Uprising
Can and Should Be Timed

In February 1905 Lenin was already arguing that the revolutionary leadership not only should be able to time the armed uprising, but has to do so.

> if we have really prepared an uprising, and if a popular uprising is realizable by virtue of the revolutions in social relations *that have already taken place*, then it is quite possible to time the uprising . . . Can the working-class movement be timed? No, it cannot; for that movement is made up of thousands of separate acts arising from a revolution in social relations. Can a strike be timed? It can, . . . *despite* the fact that every strike is the result of a revolution in social relations. When can a strike be timed? When the organization or group calling it has influence among the *masses* of the workers involved and is able correctly to gauge the moment when discontent and resentment among them are mounting.[14]

If a strike needs a resolute leadership to plan actions and to time them, the need is even greater in the case of an armed insurrection. Only a seriously committed revolutionary party is capable of leading a genuine insurrection of the masses, for the masses differentiate clearly between a vacillating and a resolute leadership.

The issue of the timing of an uprising, already acute in February 1905, became central in 1917. During the months of September and October, Lenin implored, castigated and pleaded with the Bolshevik leaders to name the day of the uprising. 'The success of both the Russian and the world revolution depends on two or three days' fighting,' he said.[15]

Lenin's Remarkable
Creative Imagination

Lenin's conclusions on the nature of insurrection were based on the very limited experience of the uprising in Moscow in December 1905. This uprising involved very few workers, and ended after a very short time. One of the leaders of the insurrection wrote in his memoirs: 'The number of armed fighters amounted probably to several hundred. The majority were armed with poor revolvers, but some had Mausers and Winchesters, arms that were quite powerful enough for street fighting.' Another prominent leader made the following assessment:

How many fighters were there in Moscow, you will ask me. At a rough estimate, according to the information I disposed of, there were some 700-800 members of fighting squads armed with revolvers. In the railway district there were not more than 100, in Presnya, Khamovniki and Butyrki including what we had inherited, but not including the Schmidt squad, the number was 180 or 200; the figure includes the 'bulldogs' and revolvers taken from the police and the double barrelled guns received from the inhabitants.[16]

Another leading participant in the insurrection estimated the number of combatants at 2,000.[17]

And if we count all those who served the movement as scouts, revolutionary 'sappers', and ambulance workers (a very dangerous duty in those days, as the Dubasov troops specially singled out all those who helped the wounded), we shall be very near to the figure of 8,000 quoted by Lenin in his speech on the occasion of the twelfth anniversary of our first revolution.[18]

The first barricades were erected on 9 December. The last resistance was crushed eight days later in the Presnya district by the Semyonovsky regiment. From the failure of this uprising Lenin drew one set of conclusions, while Plekhanov, now on the extreme right of the Mensheviks, drew exactly the opposite:

'The political strike, inopportunely begun', said Plekhanov, 'resulted in the armed uprising in Moscow, Rostov, and elsewhere. The strength of the proletariat proved inadequate for victory. It was not difficult to foresee this. And therefore it was wrong to take up arms.' The practical task of the class-conscious elements in the working-class movement 'is to point out to the proletariat its mistake, and to explain to it how risky is the game called armed uprising.' 'We must value the support of the non-proletarian opposition parties, and not repel them by tactless actions.'[19]

In contrast with this complacency and passivity, Lenin's reaction was to call for self-criticism of the leadership, and *a more active attitude* to the question of armed revolt.

The proletariat sensed sooner than its leaders the change in the objective conditions of the struggle and the need for a transition from the strike to an uprising. As is always the case, practice marched ahead of theory. A peaceful strike and demonstrations immediately ceased to satisfy the workers; they asked: What is to be done next? And they demanded more resolute action. The instructions to set up barricades reached the districts exceedingly late, when barricades were already being erected in the centre of the city. The workers set to work in large numbers, but *even this did not satisfy them*; they wanted to know: what is to be done next? – they demanded active measures. In December, we the leaders of the Social Democratic proletariat, were like a commander-in-chief who has deployed his troops in such an absurd way that most of them took no active part in the battle. The masses of the workers demanded, but failed to receive, instruction for resolute mass action.
Thus, nothing could be more short-sighted than Plekhanov's view, seized upon by all the opportunists, that the strike was untimely and should not have been started, and that 'they should not have taken to arms'. On the contrary, we should have explained to the masses that it was impossible to confine things to a peaceful strike and that a fearless and relentless armed fight was necessary.[20]

In Conclusion

In its practical, decisive attitude to the armed uprising, Bolshevism differed radically from Menshevism. As early as March 1904, in a polemic against the Bolshevik *Vperyod*, Martov had written in a leading article that Social Democracy can 'prepare the uprising' in only one sense – by preparing its own forces for an eventual uprising of the masses. The technical side of this preparation, however important it is, must definitely be subordinated to the political side of the matter. And the political preparation of our party and of the whole conscious proletariat for this entirely feasible uprising must, once again, be included in the deepening and broadening of the agitation, in the consolidation and development of the organization of all revolutionary elements of the proletariat.[21] Lenin's reply to Martov was that 'to separate the "technical" side of the revolution from its political side is sheer nonsense'.[22]

In 1907, at the fifth Party Congress in London, Martov demonstrated even more clearly his conception of the party's passive role in an armed insurrection. 'A Social Democratic Party may take part in an armed uprising, may call upon the masses to rise . . . but cannot *prepare* an uprising if it is to remain faithful to its programme of not becoming a party of "putschists".'[23]

Lenin spoke very scornfully of Martov's formula of 'arming the people with a burning desire to arm themselves'. In his very first article after hearing the news of Bloody Sunday, Lenin wrote: 'The arming of the people is an immediate task.' The question of the armed uprising was bound up with the objective of the revolutionaries: did they aim to take power into their own hands or not? As Lenin put it: 'You cannot fight if you do not expect to capture the point you are fighting for.'[24]

It is impossible to wage war consistently while rejecting the idea of victory. The Mensheviks believed that the Russian revolution would bring the liberal bourgeoisie to power. From this derived their passive, irresolute attitude to the question of the insurrection. The Bolsheviks aimed at taking power; hence their decisive, relentless, practical approach to the art of insurrection.

October 1917 was to provide the crucial test of Lenin's concept of the interrelation between the mass movement and the planned, armed insurrection. To achieve the right balance between political leadership and technical planning in an armed insurrection, it must be cautiously prepared and boldly executed. A revolutionary situation is short-lived, and the mood of the masses changes very quickly during such stirring days. The revolutionary party has to decide on the exact day and the exact way of carrying out the insurrection, because it is a question of life and death for the working class.

The accuracy of Lenin's foresight about the nature of the proletarian armed uprising is demonstrated by the following quotation. One could easily mistake the time of writing for 1917, rather than August 1906:

> Let us remember that a great mass struggle is approaching. It will be an armed uprising. It must, as far as possible, be simultaneous. The masses must know that they are entering upon an armed, bloody and desperate struggle. Contempt for death must become widespread among them and will ensure victory. The onslaught on the enemy must be pressed with the greatest vigour; attack, not defence, must be the slogan of the masses; the organization of the struggle will become mobile and flexible; the wavering elements among the troops will be drawn into active participation. And in this momentous struggle, the party of the class-conscious proletariat must discharge its duty to the full.[25]

10

The Argument for a Revolutionary Provisional Government
Bolsheviks and Mensheviks on the Nature of Government Born out of Revolution

The Mensheviks, trailing behind the liberal bourgeoisie, saw the goal of the revolution as a victory of the bourgeoisie at the head of a revolutionary government. Their conference of April-May 1905, meeting in Geneva, passed a resolution 'On Conquering Power and on Participating in the Provisional

Government', which declared that as the revolution was a bourgeois one, its outcome would be a provisional government which would be obliged

> not only to further the development of the revolution but also to combat those of its factors that threaten the foundations of the capitalist system.
>
> This being so, Social Democracy must endeavour to preserve throughout the revolution a position that will best enable it to further the revolution, that will not hamstring it in combating the inconsistent and selfish policies of the bourgeois parties, and that will keep it from dissolving in bourgeois democracy. Therefore Social Democracy must not aim at seizing or sharing power in the provisional government but must remain the party of the extreme revolutionary opposition.

Following this logic to its conclusion, a conference of Mensheviks in the Caucasus stated:

> The Conference believes that the formation of a provisional government by Social Democrats, or their entering such a government would lead, on the one hand, to the masses of the proletariat becoming disappointed in the Social Democratic Party and abandoning it, because the Social Democrats, despite the seizure of power, would not be able to satisfy the pressing needs of the working class, including the establishment of socialism, . . . and, on the other hand, *would cause the bourgeois classes to recoil from the revolution and thus diminish its sweep.*[1]

Against this Lenin argued that one cannot make a revolution if one does not aim at taking state power.

To accomplish the minimum programme of Social Democracy a revolutionary dictatorship was necessary. In his pamphlet *Social Democracy and the Provisional Revolutionary Government* (written in March-April 1905) Lenin argued that:

> rejecting the idea of the revolutionary-democratic dictatorship in the period of the autocracy's downfall is tantamount to renouncing the fulfilment of our minimum programme. Indeed, let us but consider all the economic and political transformations formulated in that programme – the demand for the republic, for arming the people, for the separa-

tion of the church from the state, for full democratic liberties, and for decisive economic reforms. Is it not clear that these transformations cannot possibly be brought about in a bourgeois society without the revolutionary democratic dictatorship of the lower classes?[2]

He further developed the same idea in his book *Two Tactics of Social Democracy in the Democratic Revolution* (June-July 1905):

> the only force capable of gaining 'a decisive victory over Tsarism' is the *people*, i.e. the proletariat and the peasantry . . . 'The revolution's decisive victory over Tsarism' means the establishment of the *revolutionary-democratic dictatorship of the proletariat and the peasantry.*

This was the aim of the revolution. He continued:

> And such a victory will be precisely a dictatorship, i.e. it must inevitably rely on military force, on the arming of the masses, on an insurrection, and not on institutions of one kind or another established in a 'lawful' or 'peaceful' way. It can only be a dictatorship, for realization of the changes urgently and absolutely indispensable to the proletariat and the peasantry will evoke desperate resistance from the landlords, the big bourgeoisie, and Tsarism. Without a dictatorship, it is impossible to break down that resistance and repel counter-revolutionary attempts.[3]

To the argument of the Geneva conference quoted above, Lenin replied:

> Just imagine; these people will not enter a provisional government because that would cause the bourgeoisie to recoil from the revolution, thereby diminishing the sweep of the revolution! Here, indeed, we have the new-*Iskra* philosophy as a whole, in a pure and consistent form: since the revolution is a bourgeois revolution, we must bow to bourgeois philistinism and make way for it. If we are even in part, even for a moment, guided by the consideration that our participation may cause the bourgeoisie to recoil, we thereby simply hand over leadership of the revolution entirely under the tutelage of the bourgeoisie (while retaining complete 'freedom of criticism'!) compelling the proletariat to be moderate and meek, so that the bourgeoisie should not recoil.[4]

Bolsheviks and Mensheviks in Agreement on the Bourgeois Nature of the Revolution

The Bolsheviks and the Mensheviks disagreed about the nature of the government that would and should come out of the revolution. The Bolsheviks called for a democratic dictatorship of workers and peasants, while the Mensheviks hoped for a bourgeois government. But on one point both wings of Russian Social Democracy agreed: that the coming revolution would be a *bourgeois* revolution. By this was meant a revolution resulting from a conflict between the productive forces of capitalism on the one hand, and the autocracy, landlords and other relics of feudalism on the other.

That this was the view of the Mensheviks needs no repetition. But that Lenin at the time held the same opinion, and that he held to it for many years afterwards, needs some demonstration, especially in the light of the actual victory of the October revolution, which went far beyond the limits of a bourgeois revolution.

Thus Lenin wrote about the future Russian revolution in *Two Tactics of Social Democracy in the Democratic Revolution*:

> At best, it may bring about a radical redistribution of landed property in favour of the peasantry, establish consistent and full democracy, including the formation of a republic, eradicate all the oppressive features of Asiatic bondage, not only in rural but also in factory life, lay the foundation for a thorough improvement in the conditions of the workers and for a rise in their standard of living, and – last but not least – carry the revolutionary conflagration into Europe. Such a victory will not yet by any means transform our bourgeois revolution into a socialist revolution; the democratic revolution will not immediately overstep the bounds of bourgeois social and economic relationships.[5]

Again, 'this democratic revolution in Russia will not weaken but strengthen the domination of the bourgeoisie'.[6]

In view of Russia's backwardness and the smallness of her working class he rejected the absurd and semi-anarchist ideas of giving immediate effect to the maximum programme, and the conquest of power for a socialist revolution. The degree of Russia's economic development (an objective condition), and the degree of class-consciousness and organization of the broad masses of the proletariat (a subjective condition inseparably bound up with the objective condition) make the immediate and complete emancipation of the working class impossible. Only the most ignorant people can close their eyes to the bourgeois nature of the democratic revolution which is now taking place . . . Whoever wants to reach socialism by any other path than that of political democracy, will inevitably arrive at conclusions that are absurd and reactionary both in the economic and the political sense.[7]

Further, 'we marxists should know that there is not, nor can there be, any other path to real freedom for the proletariat and the peasantry, than the path of bourgeois freedom and bourgeois progress.'[8]

In the same book Lenin makes it clear that the programme of the revolution should be limited to reform within the framework of capitalism :

a programme of action that will conform with the objective conditions of the present period and with the aims of proletarian democracy. This programme is the *entire* minimum programme of our party, the programme of the immediate political and economic reforms which . . . can be fully realized on the basis of the existing social and economic relationships.[9]

Lenin did not change this opinion until after the revolution of February 1917. In *The War and Russian Social Democracy* (September 1914), for example, he was still writing that the Russian revolution must limit itself to 'the three fundamental conditions for consistent democratic reform, viz., a democratic republic (with complete equality and self-determination for all nations), confiscation of the landed estates, and an eight-hour working day'.[10]

It is clear, moreover, from all Lenin's writings up to 1917 that he anticipated that a whole period would elapse between the coming bourgeois revolution and the proletarian, socialist revolution. His treatment of the agrarian problem, as we shall see in Chapter 11, illustrates this point. Nationalization of the land, he insisted, was not a socialist, but a capitalist demand, albeit one which, in clearing the way for capitalist development, would lead to a rapid increase in the number of proletarians and a sharpening of the class struggle. It would make possible the 'American path of capitalist development' – that is, development unfettered by any remnants of feudalism. The abolition of private property in land was the maximum of what can be done in bourgeois society for the removal of all obstacles to the free investment of capital in land and to the free flow of capital from one branch of production to another. 'Nationalization makes it possible to tear down *all* the fences of land ownership to the utmost degree and to "clear" all the land for the *new system of economy* suitable to the requirements of capitalism.'[11]

Clearly, if Lenin had foreseen that the bourgeois revolution would develop into the socialist revolution, there would have been no reason for him to have emphasized such arguments as these for nationalization of the land.

Trotsky

Trotsky, like Lenin, was convinced that the liberal bourgeoisie could not carry out any revolutionary task consistently, and above all that the agrarian revolution, a fundamental element in the bourgeois revolution, could be carried out only by an alliance of the working class and the peasantry. 'The agrarian problem in Russia is a heavy burden to capitalism: it is an aid to the revolutionary party and at the same time its greatest challenge: it is the stumbling block for liberalism, and a *memento mori* for counter-revolution.'[12] But he differed fundamentally from Lenin in his view of the nature of the coming Russian revolution.

In all the revolutions since the German Reformation the peasants had supported one faction or another of the bourgeoisie, but in Russia the strength of the working class and the conservatism of the bourgeoisie would force the peasantry to support the revolutionary proletariat. Although in the revolution against the Tsar and the great landowners an alliance would be forged between the workers and the majority of the peasants, the subsequent government would not be a coalition of two *independent* forces, but would be led by the proletariat. In no uncertain terms Trotsky argued that the revolution could not therefore confine itself to the carrying out of bourgeois democratic tasks, but must proceed immediately to carry out proletarian socialist measures :

> The proletariat grows and becomes stronger, with the growth of capitalism. In this sense the development of capitalism is also the development of the proletariat towards dictatorship. But the day and the hour when power will pass into the hands of the working class depends directly not upon the level attained by the productive forces but upon relations in the class struggle, upon the international situation, and, finally, upon a number of subjective factors : the traditions, the initiative and the readiness to fight of the workers ... To imagine that the dictatorship of the proletariat is in some way automatically dependent on the technical development and resources of a country is a prejudice of 'economic' materialism simplified to absurdity. This point of view has nothing in common with marxism.
> In our view, the Russian revolution will create conditions in which power can pass into the hands of the workers – and in the event of the victory of the revolution it must do so – *before* the politicians of bourgeois liberalism get the chance to display to the full their talent for governing.[13]

> In the event of a decisive victory of the revolution, power will pass into the hands of that class which plays a leading role in the struggle – in other words, into the hands of the proletariat.[14]

> *The proletariat in power will stand before the peasant as the class which has emancipated it.*[15]

> But is it not possible that the peasantry may push the proletariat aside and take its place? That is impossible. All historical experience protests against this assumption. Historical experience shows that the peasantry are absolutely incapable of taking up an *independent* political role. The history of capitalism is the history of the subordination of the country to the town.[16]

> The political domination of the proletariat is incompatible with its economic enslavement. No matter under what poli-

tical flag the proletariat has come to power, it is obliged to take the path of socialist policy. It would be the greatest utopianism to think that the proletariat, having been raised to political domination by the internal mechanism of a bourgeois revolution can, even if it so desires, limit its mission to the creation of republican-democratic conditions for the social domination of the bourgeoisie ... The barrier between the 'minimum' and the 'maximum' programme disappears immediately the proletariat comes to power.[17]

There was another important element in Trotsky's theory of the permanent revolution, namely the international character of the coming Russian revolution. He believed that it would begin on a national scale, but could be completed only by the victory of the revolution in the more developed countries:

But how far can the socialist policy of the working class be applied in the economic conditions of Russia? We can say one thing with certainty – that it will come up against political obstacles much sooner that it will stumble over the technical backwardness of the country. *Without the direct state support of the European proletariat the working class of Russia cannot remain in power and convert its temporary domination into a lasting socialistic dictatorship.* Of this there cannot for one moment be any doubt. But on the other hand there cannot be any doubt that a socialist revolution in the West will enable us directly to convert the temporary domination of the working class into a socialist dictatorship.[18]*

---

* This aspect of Trotsky's theory was a development of Marx's analysis of the German revolution of 1848. Even before that revolution, the *Communist Manifesto* had predicted that because of the 'advanced conditions' and 'developed proletariat' of Germany, 'the bourgeois revolution in Germany' would be 'but the prelude to an immediately following proletarian revolution'. And after the defeat of 1848 Marx stated that, faced with the incapacity of the bourgeoisie to carry out the anti-feudal revolution, the working class had to struggle for the growth of the bourgeois revolution into the proletarian, and of the national revolution into the international revolution.
In an address to the central council of the Communist League (March 1850) Marx said: 'While the democratic

There is no doubt that Trotsky's perspective on the Russian revolution was proved in 1917 to be absolutely correct. He was proved right in relation not only to the Mensheviks, but also to Lenin's 1905-16 perspectives for a democratic dictatorship of workers and peasants. However, despite his clear vision of future developments, Trotsky badly misjudged the *concrete* prospects for the development of Bolshevism versus Menshevism. From an abstract standpoint the Bolsheviks, claiming the Russian revolution to be a bourgeois revolution, were no less in error than the Mensheviks. Both were bound, in Trotsky's view, to become obstacles in the path of the revolutionary. Thus, he wrote in 1909, in an article entitled 'Our Differences', published in Rosa Luxemburg's Polish marxist journal *Przeglad social-demokratyczny*:

> Whereas the Mensheviks, proceeding from the abstract notion that 'our revolution is a bourgeois revolution', arrive at the idea that the proletariat must adapt all its tactics to the behaviour of the liberal bourgeoisie in order to ensure the transfer of state power to that bourgeoisie, the Bolsheviks proceed from an equally abstract notion – 'democratic dictatorship, not socialist dictatorship' – and arrive at the idea of a proletariat in possession of state power imposing a bourgeois-democratic limitation upon itself. It is true that the difference between them in this matter is very considerable; while the anti-revolutionary aspects of Menshevism have already become fully apparent, those of Bolshevism are likely to become a serious threat only in the event of victory.[20]

---

petty bourgeois wish to bring the revolution to a conclusion as quickly as possible ... it is our interest and our task to make the revolution permanent, until all more or less possessing classes have been displaced from domination, until the proletariat has conquered state power, and the association of the proletarians, not only in one country but in all the dominant countries of the world, has advanced so far that competition among the proletarians of these countries has ceased and that at least the decisive productive forces are concentrated in the hands of the proletarians.' Marx ended his address with the phrase : 'Their (the workers') battle-cry must be : the permanent revolution!'[19]

But Trotsky misjudged Lenin, whose 1905 perspective, as described above, included not only the *limitation* of the coming revolution to the bourgeois democratic tasks, but also its inner dynamic of independent working-class action. And when it came to the test in 1917, Bolshevism, after an internal struggle, overcame its bourgeois democratic crust. Lenin discovered that a revolutionary army with a limited programme can overcome the limits of the programme, so long as it is authentically revolutionary, independent and hegemonic in the struggle. *On s'engage, et puis ... on voit.*

In Lenin's position regarding the prospects of the Russian revolution there was a contradiction, between the bourgeois democratic tasks of the revolution and its proletarian leadership. The first element does not differentiate between Bolshevism and Menshevism, while the latter does so in a fundamental way.

> The Bolsheviks claimed for the proletariat the role of *leader* in the democratic revolution. The Mensheviks reduced its role to that of an 'extreme opposition'. The Bolsheviks gave a positive definition of the class character and class significance of the revolution, maintaining that a victorious revolution implied a 'revolutionary-democratic dictatorship of the proletariat and the peasantry'. The Mensheviks always interpreted the bourgeois revolution so incorrectly as to result in their acceptance of a position in which the role of the proletariat would be subordinate to and dependent on the bourgeoisie.[21]

> Social Democrats . . . rely wholly and exclusively on the activity, the class-consciousness and the organization of the proletariat, on its influence among the labouring and exploited masses.[22]

> From the proletarian point of view hegemony in a war goes to him who fights most energetically, who never misses a chance to strike a blow at the enemy, who always suits the action to the word, who is therefore the ideological leader of the democratic forces, who criticizes half-way policies of every kind.[23]

From the independence and hegemony of the proletariat in the bourgeois revolution it is only one step to Lenin's proposition that in the process of the revolution the proletariat may *overstep* bourgeois democratic limitations : 'from the democratic revolution we shall at once and precisely in accordance with the measure of our strength, the strength of the class conscious and organized proletariat, begin to pass to the socialist revolution. We stand for uninterrupted revolution. We shall not stop half-way.'[24]

In short, Lenin poses two different answers to the question : what happens after the victory of the revolution? The first, to be found mainly in *Two Tactics* and in his writings between 1905 and 1907 is that there will be a period of capitalist development. The second can be summed up as : Let us take power, and then we shall see.

Trotsky misjudged Lenin's stand because he did not grasp it dialectically. One must take into account the dynamic forces which Lenin was relying on and shaping : the proletariat's fight against Tsarism and against its accomplices, the liberal bourgeoisie; the proletariat's struggle as the spearhead of the peasantry; the proletariat leading an armed insurrection; the marxist party fighting for the conquest of power and so on. In this algebra of revolution, the real value of the unknown or doubtful element in Lenin's equation – how far the revolution would go beyond the minimum programme – would be decided largely by the dynamic of the struggle itself.

Above all Trotsky's genius for graphic abstract generalization misled him. He failed to judge the merits of Bolshevism in terms not only of the different programmes, but also of the people, collected, organized, and trained, behind the programmes. So one finds that in the whole of his book on the history of the 1905 revolution, he does not once mention the Bolsheviks or Lenin. Much later he admitted :

> Having stood outside both of the two factions in the period of emigration, the author did not fully appreciate the very important circumstance that in reality, along the line of the disagreement between the Bolsheviks and Mensheviks, there were being grouped inflexible revolutionaries on the one side and, on the other, elements which were becoming more and more opportunist and accommodating.[25]

One must remember that, to add to the misunderstandings between Trotsky and Lenin, Lenin himself probably did not read 'Results and Prospects' before 1919. The first edition of 1906 was confiscated by the police. It is true that he referred to the work a couple of times, but the fact that he never quoted it – and his habit was to quote and requote in his polemics – leads one to believe that his first reading was of the second edition.

In conclusion we may say that Lenin's abstract, algebraic formula of the democratic dictatorship was translated in life into the language of arithmetic and that the conclusions drawn were the result of the sum total of the activity of the Bolshevik Party leading the working class.

11

The Muzhik in Rebellion
The Peasants Enter the Arena

The decisive struggles of the revolution took place in the towns, but these were followed by widespread uprisings of the rural population. After the spring of 1905 peasant struggles developed throughout the countryside. Peasants seized landowners' land, ransacked their estates, took their grain and cattle. One historian described the movement thus:

> South of Moscow, in the depths of the black-soil region, lies the *gubernia* of Kursk, and here began the first important agrarian disturbances of the revolutionary period. On the night of 6 February 1905, there was a great stir in the village of Kholzovki, a great tramping and creaking along the road which led to the estate of a certain Popov, much chopping and crashing in his forests, and then a heavier creaking along the homeward road to the village. When the guards appeared, it was too late; the peasants had already cut a large

quantity of timber, and now they offered 'armed resistance to the police' – though with what result, the chronicle does not say. From Kholzovki the disturbances spread to the surrounding communes, as though according to a plan already agreed upon – or so says the Department of Police. Of an evening, the peasants wait for the order to get under way. Then somewhere on the horizon a signal-fire would be lighted, and with a great outcry and a promiscuous discharge of fire-arms, the peasants would rattle off along the road to the estate selected for that evening's pillaging, where they would take whatever they could cart away, and then return home again. Detachments of soldiers were marched into the district, but the disorders spread to four other *uezds* or counties before they could be halted.[1]

During the summer of 1905 there were peasant riots in 60 districts of 27 provinces. In the last three months of the year peasant risings occurred in 300 districts of 47 provinces.[2]

The peasant movement was at its most violent in the underprivileged central region, where the wrecking of landowners' homes and property was devastating. Strikes and boycotts were practised principally in the south; and in the north, where the movement was weakest, the felling of forests was its most common form of expression. Wherever economic discontent began to be mixed with radical political demands, the peasant refused to recognize the administrative authorities and to pay taxes.[3]

The most stormy events . . . occurred in Saratov province at the end of 1905. Not a single passive peasant was left in the villages which were drawn into the movement; all were involved in the rising. The landowners and their families were expelled from their homes, all movable property was shared out, the cattle were led away, the labourers and house servants were paid off and, finally, the 'red cockerel' was set on the buildings. (That is, they were set on fire.) Armed detachments headed the peasant 'columns' carrying out these raids. The village police and watchmen made themselves scarce, and in certain places were arrested by the armed peasants. The landlord's buildings were set on fire to make it impossible for the landlord to return to his lands after a certain time; but there was no violence.[4]

Peasants' revolts continued throughout Russia from the autumn of 1905 to the autumn of 1906. Their aim was to get rid of the inheritance of feudal relations of property and production. The agrarian problem had dominated the national life of Russia for decades, and peasant revolts had occurred again and again over a long period. A revolutionary peasant movement with a long tradition and widespread influence among the masses had in fact existed for a very long time.

The peasants, it should be understood, were not an integrated class, but a social group differentiated into contradictory classes: there was the rich peasant – the kulak – the middle peasant, and lastly the poor peasant and agricultural worker.

Lenin summed up the class divisions of the Russian agricultural population in European Russia in 1905 in the table below.[5]

Group	Number of holdings (millions)	Total area of land (million desiatins)	Average des. per holding
(a) Ruined peasantry crushed by feudal exploitation	10.5	75.0	7.0
(b) Middle peasantry	1.0	15.0	15.0
(c) Peasant bourgeoisie and capitalist landownership	1.5	70.0	46.7
(d) Feudal latifundia	0.03	70.0	2,333.0
Total	13.03	230.0	17.6
Not classified according to holdings	—	50	—
Grand Total	13.03	280.0	21.4

This basic division of the land between a few landlords at one extreme and masses of poor peasants at the other – 'about 330 poor peasant families for each big landlord' – lay behind the appalling technical backwardness of agriculture, the oppressed and downtrodden position of the mass of the peasantry, and the endless variety of their feudal corvée exploitation.

Under the corvée system of farming the peasant allotment was a means of supplying the landlord cheaply with

farm hands, implements and livestock. The system was particularly widespread in the central *gubernias* of European Russia, the heartland of Russian agriculture. The main feature of
the system was labour rent, of which one form was the pre-
payment of peasants during the winter for work that they
would carry out later in the summer. In winter the peasants
were badly in need of cash and were compelled to accept ex-
tortionate terms. Another form of labour rent was the 'com-
posite labour service', under which the peasants committed
themselves – for money or in return for the land rented to
them – to till one *desiatin* of the landlord's spring crop, one
desiatin of his winter crop and sometimes also one *desiatin*
of meadow land, all with their own implements and horses.

The 'cut-off' lands (*otrezki*), a major grievance of the
peasantry, were used for similar exploitation. These lands,
stolen by the landlords during the 1861 'emancipation' of the
serfs, constituted something like a fifth of the peasants' original holdings. Furthermore, it was the best quality land
which was taken from the peasant, and he was thus deprived
of meadows and pastures, and of access to woods and rivers.
He was also required to pay for his allotment. He could do
so by giving labour to the landlord, or by making a money
payment which considerably exceeded the rental value of
the allotment (by as much as 50-75 per cent). The peasant
could terminate this obligation by making a 'redemption
payment' which was in excess of the market value of the
land. By 1905 the landlords had acquired 1.9 milliard rubles
in redemption dues and interest which, taking into account
the devaluation of the ruble in the previous 44 years, was
nearly three times the market value of the land. The need to
work off these obligations put the peasants very much under
the landlords' yoke. To add insult to injury, many peasants
now had to work on the 'cut-offs'.

The peasant allotments were tiny plots of land, consisting mostly of several scattered narrow strips and distin-
guished by soil of the poorest quality, the best having been
taken by the landlords in 1861, and what was left being exhausted.

The chains of bondage were strengthened by the institution of the village *commune*. This enforced communal use of the land, characterized by compulsory crop rotation and undivided woods and pastures. Its principal feature was collective liability for the fulfilment of all kinds of services and payments to the landlords and the state, periodical redistribution of the land with no right to refuse the allotment given, and prohibition of its purchase and sale. The village commune was used by the large landlords to intensify feudal oppression and to squeeze land redemption and other payments from the peasants.

Marxism and the Peasantry

From its earliest beginnings in Russia the marxist movement recognized the vital importance of the agrarian question, especially the peasant question. The very first draft programme of the Russian marxists, published by the Emancipation of Labour Group in 1885, demanded

> A radical revision of our agrarian relations, i.e. of the terms on which the land is to be redeemed and allotted to the peasant communities. The right to refuse their allotments and to leave the commune to be granted to those peasants who may find it advantageous to do so, etc.[6]

That was all the programme said. Years later Lenin commented: 'The error of that programme is not that its principles or partial demands were wrong. No . . . The error of that programme is its abstract character, the absence of any concrete view of the subject. Properly speaking it is not a programme, but a marxist declaration in the most general terms.'[7] But he hastened to add:

> Of course, it would be absurd to put the blame for this mistake on the authors of the programme, who for the first time laid down certain principles long before the formation of a workers' party. On the contrary it should be particularly emphasized that in that programme the inevitability of a 'radical revision' of the Peasant Reform was recognized twenty years before the Russian revolution.[8]

Very early in his political life, Lenin had made a close

study of rural life. His earliest preserved writing is 'New Economic Developments in Peasant Life', written in the spring of 1893. In 1899 he published his first major theoretical work. Researched and written in prison and while in exile in Siberia this was called 'The Development of Capitalism in Russia.' Two-thirds of this work is devoted to a brilliant and thoroughly documented analysis of capitalist evolution in the Russian countryside, the decay of the feudal economy and the complex variety of transitional formations which had evolved. This theoretical study provided the groundwork for the practical development of an agrarian policy, strategy and tactics for the Russian marxists.

His first effort to elaborate an agrarian programme was his article 'The Workers' Party and the Peasantry' (1901), which may be regarded as the first rough draft of the agrarian programme of the RSDLP. It was adopted by the second Congress of the party (1903). The central demands for the agrarian revolution were:

> the immediate and complete abolition of redemption payments and quit-rents, and the demand for the return to the people of the hundreds of millions which the Tsarist government has extorted from them in the course of the years to satisfy the greed of the slaveowners . . . restitution to the peasants of the land of which they have been deprived, a condition that still binds them to forced labour, to the rendering of corvée-service, i.e. that virtually keeps them in a state of serfdom.[9]

In the process of developing the agrarian programme for the second Congress, Lenin formulated guidelines aimed at the abolition of all feudal relations in the countryside.

> *First*. The agrarian revolution will necessarily be a part of the democratic revolution in Russia. The content of this revolution will be the liberation of the countryside from the relations of semi-feudal bondage. *Second*. In its social and economic aspect, the impending agrarian revolution will be a bourgeois-democratic revolution; it will not weaken but stimulate the development of capitalism and capitalist class contradictions.[10]

In addition to the non-controversial demands which

Lenin never amended – abolition of the social-estate taxation of the peasants, reduction of rents, freedom to use land at will – the agrarian programme adopted at the second Congress contained a number of clauses demanding the refunding of land redemption payments and the restitution of cut-off lands. The latter (Clause 4 of the Programme) was a key demand. It was justified as a means of eliminating one of the surviving features of feudalism :

> wherever the half-hearted nature of our Peasant Reform has led to serf-owning forms of farming surviving to this day, with the aid of land cut off from the peasants' lands, the peasants are given the right to do away with these survivals once and for all, even by means of expropriation, the right to the *restitution of the cut-off lands*.[11]

And Lenin reiterated and emphasized this point : 'We maintain and shall endeavour to prove, that the demand for the restitution of the cut-off lands is the maximum that we can at present advance in our agrarian programme.'[12] At the time, he argued that to go beyond the restitution of cut-off land would simply be to support small-scale farming against large-scale farming.

> Generally speaking, it is not at all the task of the Social Democrats to develop, support, consolidate, let alone, multiply, small-scale farming and small property.[13]

> *Generally* speaking, it is reactionary to support small property *because* such support is directed against large-scale *capitalist* economy and, consequently, retards social development, and obscures and glosses over the class struggle. In this case, however, we want to support small property not against capitalism but against serf-ownership.[14]

What about land nationalization? At that time – in 1902 – Lenin's position was clear. 'The demand for nationalization of the land, while quite valid in principle and quite suitable at certain moments, is politically inexpedient at the present moment.'[15] If the aim of the agrarian revolution was to eliminate feudal relations, then not *all* the landowners' land should be taken away from them, in particular not the part used for capitalist farming and employing wage labour.

Lenin Learns from Gapon

However, the breadth and depth of the peasant uprising in the 1905 revolution made it clear that Lenin's 1903 programme was far too conservative. It is quite interesting to see how eager he was to find out about the mood of the peasants at the time and, whether the demand for restitution of cut-off lands suited these moods, even from the priest Gapon, and from an accidental visitor, a sailor named Matinshenko. Krupskaya relates how a student sitting in Lenin's room

> commenced a dissertation on why the Social Democratic programme was correct, expounding it point by point, with the ardour of the novice . . . The young chap went on reading out the Programme. At that moment Gapon and Matinshenko came in. Just as I was about to get tea for them as well, the young man arrived at the paragraph dealing with the restoration of the 'pieces of land' to the peasants. After reading this point, he explained that the peasants could not go farther than the fight for this land, whereupon Gapon and Matinshenko became infuriated and shouted: 'All land to the people!'[16]

This must have made a big impression on Lenin, for Krupskaya goes on to relate:

> At the December conference in Tammerfors, Ilyich tabled a motion to drop completely from the programme this point on the peasants' land. In its place a paragraph was inserted on the support to be given to the revolutionary measures of the peasantry, including even confiscation of landowners' estates and official, church, monastic, and crown lands.[17]

He made no attempt to cover up his own past errors:

> The 1903 programme attempts to define concretely the nature and terms of the 'revision' about which the Social Democrats in 1885 spoke only in a general way. That attempt – in the main item of the programme, dealing with the cut-off lands – was based upon a tentative distinction between lands which serve for exploitation by means of serfdom and bondage (lands 'cut off' in 1861) and lands which are exploited in a capitalist manner. Such a tentative distinction was quite fallacious, because, in practice, the peasant mass movement could not be directed against particular categories of landlord estates, but only against landlordism in general.[18]

Without the experience of a mass – indeed, more than that, – of a nationwide peasant movement, the programme of the Social Democratic Labour Party *could not* become concrete.[19]

In 1903, when the second Congress of our party adopted the first agrarian programme of the RSDLP, we did not yet have such experience as would enable us to judge the character, breadth, and depth of the peasant movement. The peasant risings in South Russia in the spring of 1902 remained sporadic outbursts. One can therefore understand the restraint shown by the Social Democrats in drafting the agrarian programme.[20]

After 1905 there was no justification at all for continuing with this narrowness and conservatism : 'at the present time to reject the demand for confiscation of all the landed estates would obviously mean restricting the scope of a social movement which has taken definite shape'.[21]

At the Tammerfors conference of the Bolsheviks (12-17 December 1905), Lenin put forward the following resolution:

The conference holds that it is desirable to amend the agrarian programme of our party as follows: to delete the clause on cut-off lands; to declare, instead, that the party supports the revolutionary measures of the peasantry, including the confiscation of all state, church, monastery, crown and privately-owned land.[22]

For Nationalization of the Land

Lenin went on from this to a further revision of the agrarian programme, in which he raised the slogan of nationalization of all the land. In his pamphlet *Revision of the Agrarian Programme of the Workers' Party*, written in March 1906, he said :

If . . . the decisive victory of the present revolution in Russia brings about the complete sovereignty of the people, i.e. establishes a republic and a fully democratic state system, the party will seek the abolition of private ownership of land and the transfer of all the land to the whole people as common property.[23]

The strength of the peasant movement against the land-owners also taught Lenin that in 1903 he had over-estimated the extent to which capitalist development had taken hold in the countryside. Feudal relations were not mere remnants, as he had then assumed, but exercised great influence throughout the rural situation. In his book *The Agrarian Programme of Social Democracy in the First Russian Revolution 1905–1907*, he points this out.

> the mistake of our cut-off-lands programme of 1903 . . . was due to the fact that while we correctly defined the *trend* of development, we did not correctly define the *moment* of that development. We assumed that the elements of capitalist agriculture had already taken full shape in Russia, both in landlord farming (minus the cut-off lands and their conditions of bondage – hence the demand that the cut-off lands be returned to the peasants) and in peasant farming, which seemed to have given rise to a strong peasant bourgeoisie and therefore to be incapable of bringing about a 'peasant agrarian revolution'. The erroneous programme was the result . . . *of an over-estimation of the degree* of capitalist development in Russian agriculture. The survivals of serfdom appeared to us then to be a minor detail, whereas capitalist agriculture on the peasant allotments and on the landlords' estates seemed to be quite mature and well-established . . . We rectified the mistake by substituting for the partial aim of combating the *survivals of the old* agrarian system, the aim of combating *the old agrarian system as a whole*. Instead of purging landlord economy, we set the aim of *abolishing* it.[24]

Learn from the Dark Muzhik

During the years of the revolution, 1905-07, Lenin considered it important to learn from the Russian muzhik. Even the monarchist peasant representatives in the Tsarist Duma taught Lenin that deep beneath the conservative shell there was in fact a revolutionary kernel. He quotes with enthusiasm the speech of the monarchist right-wing peasant Storchak to the Tsarist Duma :

> He begins his speech by repeating in full the words of Nicholas II about 'the sacred rights of property', the impermissibility of their 'infringement', etc. He continues : 'May God

grant the Emperor health. He spoke well for the whole people' . . . And he finishes: 'But if His Majesty said that there should be justice and order, then, of course if I am sitting on 3 *desiatins* of land, and next to me there are 30,000 *desiatins* that is not order and justice.'[25]

And Lenin comments:

an ignorant peasant . . . is as innocent as a babe unborn and amazingly ignorant politically. The link between the monarchy and 'order', i.e. the disorder and injustice which protect the owners of 30,000 *desiatins*, is not clear to him.[26]
Storchak, and the deputies who at bottom share his views – the priest Titov, Andreichuk, Popov IV and Niktyuk – express the revolutionary temper of the peasant mass unconsciously, spontaneously, afraid themselves not only to speak out, but even to think out what their words and proposals imply.[27]

He goes on to quote other peasant speakers in the Duma:

Tomilov: 'The only way out . . . in our opinion, is this: the land should be redistributed at once, in all the village communes of Russia, on the basis of a census similar to those previously carried out; this census should establish the number of male persons as on 3 November 1905.
The fond dream of the peasant is to get land and freedom, but we have heard that so long as the present government is in power, landed property is inviolable. (*Voices in the Centre: 'Private property.'*) Yes, private, noblemen's property. (*Voices in the Centre: 'And yours too.'*) As far as we are concerned, we are prepared to give up our allotments . . . I will say that the peasants in any village are willing to give up their allotments, unit for unit, and to become equal. The statement of the representative of the Ministry amounts to this, that so long as power has not passed into the hands of the peasantry and the people generally, the peasants will not see either the land or political liberties. Thank you for your frankness, though we knew it already.'[28]

Petrov III: 'Remember, gentlemen, the times of the reign of Alexei Mikhailovich, and the protest of the peasant people which expressed itself in the movement under the leadership of Razin.* (*Voices on the Right: 'O-ho!'*) . . . The people most strongly expressed its demands in 1905. Then, too, poverty made the people come out into the street and say their imperious say about what they needed . . . All the land must pass into equalized tenure of all the people . . . I am of course an opponent of private property in land . . . and I say that the working people will not get an easier time until all the land passes into their hands . . . I am absolutely convinced you will see once again the depths of the sea of life disturbed. And then the saying of the Testament will come true: he who lifts the sword shall perish by the sword (*laughter on the Right*). The Trudovik [peasant] group has not changed its ideals and has not changed its aspirations . . . We . . . say: all the land to those who work on it, and all power to the working people!'

Merzlyakov: 'The land must belong to those who till it . . . Only there mustn't be any land racket in Russia, and the land should belong to those who till it by their own labour.'[29]

The peasant Nechitailo says: 'The people who have drunk the blood and sucked the brains of the peasants call them ignorant.' Golovin interrupted: The landlord can insult the peasant, but the peasant insulting the landlord? 'These lands that belong to the people – we are told: buy them. Are we foreigners, who have arrived from England, France, and so forth? This is our country, why should we have to buy our own land? We have already paid for it ten times over with blood, sweat, and money.'

Here is what the peasant Kirnosov (Saratov Gubernia) says: 'Nowadays we talk of nothing but the land; again we are told: it is sacred, inviolable. In my opinion it cannot be inviolable; *if the people wish it, nothing can be inviolable. (A voice from the Right:* 'Oh-ho!'*)* Yes, oh-ho! *(Applause on the Left.)* Gentlemen of the nobility, do you think we do not know when you used us as stakes in your card games, when you bartered us for dogs? We do. It was all your sacred, inviolable property . . . You stole the land from us . . . The peasants who sent me here said this: The land is ours. We have come here not to buy it, but to take it.'

Here is what the peasant Vasyutin (Kharkov Gubernia) says: 'We see here in the person of the Chairman of the Council of

* Razin Stepan was the outstanding leader of the peasant revolt in Russia against the feudal oppression and serfdom which took place in 1667-71.

Ministers, not the minister of the whole country, but the minister of 130,000 landlords. Ninety-million peasants are nothing to him ... You [addressing the Right] are exploiters, you lease your land out at exorbitant rents and skin the peasant alive ... Know that if the government fails to meet the people's needs, the people will not ask for your consent, they will take the land ... I am a Ukrainian [he relates that Catherine made Potemkin a gift of a little estate of 27,000 *desiatin* with 2,000 serfs] ... Formerly land was sold at 25 to 50 rubles per *desiatin*, but now the rent is 15 to 30 rubles per *desiatin*, and the rent of hayland is 35 to 50 rubles. I call that fleecery. *(A voice from the Right:* 'What? Fleecery?' *Laughter.)* Yes, don't get excited *(applause on the Left)*; I call it skinning the peasants alive.'[30]

Lenin comments on the peasant deputies' speeches that they

express the spirit of the peasants' mass struggle outspokenly ... the speeches of the Trudovik peasants, who state their views forthrightly [are] conveying the moods and aspirations of the masses with amazing precision and liveliness, mixing up programmes (some speak of their sympathy with the Bill of the 42 peasants, others of sympathy with the Cadets), but all the more strongly expressing what lies deeper than any programmes.[31]

He goes even further and sees much greater revolutionary fervour in the speeches of the peasants' deputies than in those of the Social Democrat workers' deputies.

Comparing the speeches of the revolutionary peasants in the second Duma with those of the revolutionary workers, one is struck by the following difference. The former are imbued with a far more spontaneous revolutionary spirit, a passionate desire to destroy the landlord régime immediately, and immediately to create a new system. The peasant is eager to fling himself upon the enemy at once and to strangle him.[32]

Lenin showed a remarkable freedom from dogmatism, and a feeling for the real heartbeat of the mass movement, even if it was to be found in the chest of a monarchist peasant!

Bolsheviks, Mensheviks and the Peasantry

During the elections to the second Duma a fierce struggle went on between the two wings of Social Democracy, Mensheviks and Bolsheviks, on the question of whether to enter into an alliance with the Cadets, or with the Trudoviks against the Cadets.

As early as 1892 Plekhanov had argued that the peasant in Russia, as in the West, was fundamentally conservative. 'Apart from the bourgeoisie and the proletariat, we perceive no social forces in our country in which opposition or revolutionary groups could find support.'[33]

In a pamphlet entitled *The Duty of Socialists in the Famine*, Plekhanov wrote:

> The proletarian and the *muzhik* are real political antipodes. The historical role of the proletariat is as revolutionary as that of the *muzhik* is conservative. It was upon the peasants that Oriental despotisms sustained themselves unchanged for thousands of years. In a comparatively short time the proletariat has shaken the whole foundation of Western European society. And in Russia its development and political education is progressing incomparably more rapidly than it did in the West.[34]

This line of argument influenced the Mensheviks' attitude to the liberal party – the Cadets – on the one hand, and the peasant party – the Trudoviks – on the other.

The Menshevik D.Koltsov argued the case for an alliance with the Cadets as against an alliance with the Trudoviks in the following terms:

> With whom have the Social Democrats the greater number of points of contact, with urban or rural democracy? From whom can Social Democracy the sooner expect support in its struggle against cultural, religious, national and other prejudices? Who will the sooner support all measures likely to liberate the productive forces? It is only necessary to raise these questions, which are basic in Social Democratic policy, for the answer to be clear of itself. Everything in the *Communist Manifesto* concerning the revolutionary role of the bourgeois remains as true in the twentieth century as it

was in the nineteenth, as true for Russia as it was for England . . . As far as rural democracy is concerned it will in many cases defend old, outworn modes of production and social organization, despite its revolutionary gallop.[35]

Lenin opposed this argument as follows:

The Bolshevik wing of the party, regards the liberals as representatives of big industry, who are striving to put an end to the revolution as quickly as possible for fear of the proletariat, and are entering into a compromise with the reactionaries. This wing regards the Trudoviks as revolutionary petty-bourgeois democrats, and is of the opinion that they are inclined to adopt a radical position on a land question of such importance to the peasantry, the question of the confiscation of the landed estates. This accounts for the tactics of the Bolsheviks. They reject support for the treacherous liberal bourgeoisie, i.e. the Cadets, and do their utmost to get the democratic petty bourgeoisie away from the influence of the liberals; they want to draw the peasant and the urban petty bourgeois away from the liberals and muster them behind the proletariat, behind the vanguard, for the revolutionary struggle.[36]

one Cadet stated that a right-wing peasant was more left than the Cadets. Yes, on the agrarian question the stand of the 'right' peasants in all three Dumas has been more left than the Cadets', thereby proving that the monarchism of the muzhik is naïveté that is dying out, in contrast to the monarchism of the liberal businessmen, who are monarchists through class calculation.[37]

In the anti-feudal, democratic revolution, Lenin favoured an alliance of the proletarian party with the petty bourgeois peasant democratic parties:

the revolutionary-democratic parties and organizations (the Socialist-Revolutionary Party, the Peasant Union, some of the semi-trade union and semi-political organizations, etc.) most closely express the interests and point of view of the broad masses of the peasantry and petty bourgeoisie, strongly opposing landlordism and the semi-feudal state, consistently striving for democracy and clothing their virtually bourgeois-democratic aims in a more or less nebulous socialist ideology; and the Social Democratic Party deems it possible and necessary to enter into fighting agreements with these parties, while at the same time systematically exposing their pseudo-socialist character and combating their attempts to obscure the class antithesis between the proletarian and the small proprietor.[88]

Let us hasten and make clear that for Lenin the slogan of land nationalization did not mean going beyond the bourgeois democratic revolution. He explains that there are two paths open to capitalist development in the Russian countryside: the first impeded and distorted by feudal survivals – which he called the Prussian path – the second free of all relics of serfdom – which he called the American path of development:

> In the first case feudal landlord economy slowly evolves into bourgeois, Junker landlord economy, which condemns the peasants to decades of most harrowing expropriation and bondage, while at the same time a small minority of *Grossbauern* ('big peasants') arises . . . To facilitate the development of the productive forces (this highest criterion of social progress) we must support not bourgeois evolution of the landlord type, but bourgeois evolution of the peasant type. The former implies the utmost preservation of bondage and serfdom (remodelled on bourgeois lines), the least rapid development of productive force, and the retarded development of capitalism; it implies infinitely greater misery and suffering, exploitation and oppression for the broad mass of the peasantry and, consequently, also for the proletariat. The second type implies the most rapid development of the productive forces and the best possible (under commodity production) conditions of existence for the mass of the peasantry. The tactics of Social Democracy in the Russian bourgeois revolution are determined not by the task of supporting the liberal bourgeoisie, as the opportunists think, but by the task of supporting the fighting peasantry.[39]

Revolutionaries ought to aim at leading Russia along the American path. Therefore they must support land nationalization as the most extreme and consistent way of getting rid of surviving features of feudalism. 'In the Russian revolution the struggle for the land is nothing else than a struggle for the renovated path of capitalist development. The consistent slogan of such a renovation is – nationalization of the land.'[40]

In support of his thesis Lenin refers to Marx, who 'allowed the possibility of, and sometimes directly advocated, the nationalization of the land, not only in the epoch of the bourgeois revolution in Germany in 1848, but also in 1846 for America, which, as he most accurately pointed out at that time, was only just starting its "industrial" development'.[41]

A couple of years later, in 1908, Lenin reiterates this view :

> There is nothing more erroneous than the opinion that the nationalization of the land has anything in common with socialism, or even with equalized land tenure. Socialism, as we know, means the abolition of commodity economy. Nationalization on the other hand, means converting the land into the property of the state, and such a conversion does not in the least affect private farming on the land.[42]

Nationalization of the Land: the First Step towards Socialism?

Lenin went into great detail to explain why land nationalization was part and parcel of the bourgeois revolution. For instance, in his book *The Agrarian Programme of Social Democracy in the First Russian Revolution 1905–1907*, written in November-December 1907, he says :

> After the period of revolutionary nationalization the demand for division may be evoked by the desire to consolidate to the greatest possible degree the new agrarian relations, which meet the requirements of capitalism. It may be evoked by the desire of the *given* owners of land to increase their incomes at the expense of the rest of society. Finally, it may be evoked by the desire to 'quieten' (or, plainly speaking, to put down) the proletariat and the semi-proletarian strata, for whom nationalization of the land will be an element that will 'whet the appetite' for the socialization of the whole of social production.[43]

> nothing is capable of so thoroughly sweeping away the survivals of medievalism in Russia, of so thoroughly renovating the rural districts, which are in a state of Asiatic semi-decay, of so rapidly promoting agricultural progress, as nationalization. Any other solution of the agrarian question in the revolution would create less favourable starting-points for

further economic development.

The moral significance of nationalization in the revolutionary epoch is that the proletariat helps to strike a blow at 'one form of private property' which must inevitably have its repercussion all over the world.[44]

But land nationalization, while part and parcel of the bourgeois revolution, can, depending on the balance of class forces, be a springboard in the struggle for socialism in the countryside. In September 1917, in a postscript to the second edition of *The Agrarian Programme of Social Democracy* (the first edition of 1908 was confiscated by the police) Lenin wrote: 'nationalization of the land is not only "the last word" of the bourgeois revolution, but also *a step towards socialism'*.[45]

In all his forecasts about the Russian revolution Lenin displayed a complete lack of dogmatism and the greatest readiness to push the revolution beyond its bourgeois limitations into an immediate and uninterrupted struggle for socialism.

The Proletariat Versus the Peasantry

Throughout the development of the agrarian policy of the party there are two central points in Lenin's thinking: (1) the working class must lead the peasantry; (2) the workers' party has to keep itself independent and clearly demarcated from the peasantry:

> supporting the revolutionary peasant, the proletariat must not for a moment forget about its own class independence and its own special class aims. The peasant movement is the movement of another class. It is not a proletarian struggle, but a struggle waged by small proprietors. It is not a struggle against the foundations of capitalism, but a struggle to cleanse them of all survivals of serfdom.[46]
>
> We stand by the peasant movement to the end; but we have to remember that it is the movement of another class, *not the one* which can and will bring about the socialist revolution.[47]
>
> Without the initiative and guidance of the proletariat the peasantry counts for nothing.[48]

Lenin discussed the possible development of an independent peasant party, in the form of a coalition of Trudoviks and Socialist-Revolutionaries, but he doubted their stability and ability to achieve homogeneity.

No-one at this stage can tell what forms bourgeois democracy in Russia will assume in the future. Possibly, the bankruptcy of the Cadets may lead to the formation of a peasant democratic party, a truly mass party, and not an organization of terrorists such as the Socialist-Revolutionaries have been and still are. It is also possible that the objective difficulties of achieving political unity among the petty bourgeoisie will prevent such a party from being formed and, for a long time to come, will keep the peasant democracy in its present state as a loose, amorphous, jelly-like Trudovik mass.[49]

The Trudoviks are definitely not fully consistent democrats. The Trudoviks (including the Socialist-Revolutionaries) undoubtedly vacillate between the liberals and the revolutionary proletariat. Such vacillation is by no means fortuitous. It is an inevitable consequence of the very nature of the economic condition of the small producer. On the one hand, he is oppressed and subject to exploitation. He is unconsciously impelled into the fight against this position, into the fight for democracy, for the ideas of abolishing exploitation. On the other hand, he is *a petty proprietor*. In the peasant lives the instinct of a proprietor – if not of today, then of tomorrow. It is the proprietor's, the owner's instinct that repels the peasant from the proletariat, engendering in him an aspiration to become someone in the world, to become a bourgeois, to hem himself in against all society on his own plot of land, on his own dungheap.[50]

the democratic elements of the peasantry . . . [are] incapable of forming a solid organization.[51]

So Wrong and So Right

The victory of 1917 proved Lenin wrong about the Russian revolution in two major respects – his arguments that it would be a bourgeois revolution and that nationalization of the land would be a springboard for wider and speedier capitalist economic development. How then did Lenin manage to play so decisive a role in the victory of this same revolution?

The answer is basically that even in his mistakes regarding perspectives, there was a central core of strategy and tactics that led directly to just such a victory of the proletarian revolution:

> even if our revolution is bourgeois in its economic content (this cannot be doubted), the conclusion must not be drawn from it that the leading role in our revolution is played by the bourgeoisie, that the bourgeoisie is its motive force. Such a conclusion, usual with Plekhanov and the Mensheviks, is a vulgarization of marxism, a caricature of marxism. The leader of the bourgeois revolution may be either the liberal landlord together with the factory-owner, merchant, lawyer, etc., or the proletariat together with the peasant masses. In both cases the bourgeois character of the revolution remains, but its scope, the degree of its advantage to the proletariat, the degree of its advantage to socialism (*that is*, to the rapid development of the productive forces, first and foremost) are *completely different* in the two cases.
>
> From this, the Bolsheviks deduce the *basic* tactics of the socialist proletariat in the bourgeois revolution – to carry with them a democratic petty bourgeoisie, draw them away from the liberals, paralyse the instability of the liberal bourgeoisie, and develop the struggle of the *masses* for the complete *abolition* of all traces of serfdom, including landed proprietorship.[52]

Lenin consistently argued that although the revolution was bourgeois-democratic by nature, the peasantry must show the maximum initiative and democracy, by creating independent local organizations for struggle without waiting for deliverance from above, even from national institutions born of the revolution, such as the future Constituent Assembly.

> There is only one way to make the agrarian reform, which is unavoidable in present-day Russia, play a revolutionary-democratic role: it must be effected on the revolutionary initiative of the peasants themselves, despite the landlords and the bureaucracy, and despite the state, i.e. it must be effected by revolutionary means ... And this is the road we indicate when we make our prime demand the establishment of revolutionary peasant committees.[53]

Marx argued after the experience of the Paris Commune

that 'the working class cannot simply lay hold of the ready-made state machinery and wield it for its own purpose'; the proletariat has 'to smash it and this is the precondition for every real people's revolution'. Lenin's argument echoed this: 'The peasantry cannot carry out an agrarian revolution without abolishing the old régime, the standing army and the bureaucracy, because all these are the most reliable mainstays of landlordism, bound to it by thousands of ties.'[54]

Moreover, even if the revolution was only bourgeois-democratic, it still had an international character:

> the Russian revolution can achieve victory by its own efforts, but it cannot possibly hold and consolidate its gains by its own strength. It cannot do this unless there is a socialist revolution in the West ... After the complete victory of the democratic revolution the small proprietor will inevitably turn against the proletariat; and the sooner the common enemies of the proletariat and of the small proprietors, such as the capitalists, the landlords and the financial bourgeoisie, and so forth are overthrown, the sooner will this happen. Our democratic republic has no other reserve than the socialist proletariat in the West.[55]

A relentless struggle against the liberal bourgeoisie; mistrust of the vacillating peasant party and independence from it; the call for direct action on the part of the peasants; the fight to smash the old bureaucratic police state machine; and the emphasis on the international character of the revolution – all these ideas rooted in the 1905-07 revolution, were central to the policies that led to the victory of 1917. Their bourgeois-democratic wrapping was to be discarded in the storm of future battles. Unfortunately the contradiction between the consistent revolutionary kernel of Lenin's policies in 1905 and afterwards and its bourgeois-democratic shell was to be a factor in the party crises and the paralysis of the Bolshevik leadership days and weeks after the February revolution of 1917, before Lenin returned to Russia to counter his own 'old Bolshevik' formulation.

12
The Great Dress Rehearsal

Although it ended in defeat the 1905 revolution was extremely important in revealing the interests and aims of the different social classes, their respective strengths and weaknesses, their relative importance in Russian society, and the changing relationships between them. It also provided a searching, although not final, test for the main existing parties.

The years of revolution and decline – 1905-07 – were in Lenin's eyes a tremendous opportunity for millions to obtain experience, to learn a lesson that would enter into the life-blood, into the nervous system, into the hearts and brains of the people.

The real nature of class and party were clearly exposed. All the parties completed the 'foetal stage of their development' during this period.

> For the first time the classes have achieved a definite cleavage and taken shape in open political struggle during this period: the political parties which now exist . . . express with previously unheard-of exactness the interests and viewpoint of classes which during the three years have matured a hundred times more than during the preceding half-century.[1]

First of all 'society' exposed itself. The liberals showed their true colours.

> What before the revolution was known as liberal and liberal-Narodnik 'society', or the spokesman and 'enlightened' part of the 'nation' at large – the broad mass of well-to-do, noblemen's and intellectuals' 'opposition', which seemed to be something integral, and homogeneous, permeating the Zemstvos, the universities, all the 'decent' press, etc., etc. – has displayed itself in the revolution as the ideologues and supporters of the bourgeoisie, and has taken up what all can

recognize now as a *counter-revolutionary* position in respect of the *mass* struggle of the socialist proletariat and the democratic peasantry. The counter-revolutionary liberal bourgeoisie has come into existence and is growing.[2]

Above all the stormy events exposed the role of the proletariat in the revolution.

The leading role of the proletarian masses all through the revolution and in all the fields of struggle, from demonstrations, through insurrection, to (in chronological order) 'parliamentary' activity, has become apparent for all to see during this period, if we look over it as a whole.[3]

The revolution was a magnificent mass school.

Millions among the population have gained practical *experience*, in the most varied forms, of a genuinely mass and directly revolutionary struggle, including a 'general strike', the expulsion of landowners, the burning of their country-houses, and open armed uprising.[4]

The best education is gained through struggle. In a lecture on the 1905 revolution delivered at a meeting of young workers in Zurich on 9 January 1917, Lenin said:

When the bourgeois gentry and their uncritical echoers, the social-reformists, talk priggishly about the 'education' of the masses, they usually mean something schoolmasterly, pedantic, something that demoralizes the masses and instils in them bourgeois prejudices.

The real education of the masses can never be separated from their independent political, and especially revolutionary struggle. Only struggle educates the exploited class. Only struggle discloses to it the magnitude of its own power, widens its horizon, enhances its abilities, clarifies its mind, forges its will.[5]

It is in this awakening of tremendous masses of the people to political consciousness and revolutionary struggle that the historic significance of 22 January 1905 lies.[6]

Although the workers had not won the revolution, the revolution had won the workers.

By the heroic struggle it waged during the course of the three years [1905-07] the Russian proletariat won for itself and for the Russian people gains that took other nations decades to win. It won the *emancipation* of the working masses *from the influence* of treacherous and contemptibly impotent *liberalism*. It won *for itself the hegemony* in the struggle for freedom and democracy as a precondition of the struggle for socialism. It won for all the oppressed and exploited classes of Russia the *ability* to wage a revolutionary mass struggle, without which nothing of importance in the progress of mankind has been achieved anywhere in the world.[7]

The mass of workers would never forget 1905:

Just wait, 1905 will come again. That is how the workers look at things. For them that year of struggle provided a model of *what has to be done*. For the intellectuals and the renegading petty bourgeois it was the 'insane year', a model of *what should not be done*. For the proletariat, the working over and critical acceptance of the experience of the revolution must consist in learning how to apply the *then* methods of struggle *more successfully*, so as to make the same October strike struggle and December armed struggle more massive, more concentrated and more conscious.[8]

It is said that beaten armies learn well . . . there is one gain from the first years of the revolution and the first reverses in mass revolutionary struggle about which there can be no doubt. It is the mortal blow struck at the former softness and flabbiness of the masses. The lines of demarcation have become more distinct. The cleavage of classes and parties has taken place.[9]

The revolution had moulded each of the main political parties into a permanent shape which the vicissitudes of the struggle could never entirely change.

in the periods of direct revolutionary struggle deep and lasting foundations of class groupings are laid, and division into large political parties take place, which thereafter persist even in very long periods of stagnation. Some parties may go underground, give no sign of life, disappear from the front of the political stage: but at the slightest revival the main political forces inevitably will give signs of themselves again. Perhaps in an altered form but with the same character and direction of their activity, so long as the objective tasks of the revolution, which has suffered defeat to this or that extent, are not fulfilled.[10]

Lenin's Stress on the Initiative of the Masses

What 1905 meant, more than anything, to Lenin was the practical confirmation of his belief in the tremendous creative abilities of the working class.

In *The Victory of the Cadets and the Tasks of the Workers' Party*, written in March 1906, he says:

> it is just the revolutionary periods which are distinguished by wider, richer, more deliberate, more methodical, more systematic, more courageous and more vivid making of history than periods of philistine, Cadet, reformist progress. But the Liberals turn the truth inside out! They palm off paltriness as magnificent making of history. They regard the inactivity of the oppressed or downtrodden masses as the triumph of 'system' in the work of bureaucrats and bourgeois. They shout about the disappearance of intellect and reason when, instead of the picking of draft laws to pieces by petty bureaucrats and liberal *penny-a-liner* journalists, there begins a period of direct political activity of the 'common people', who simply set to work without more ado to smash all the instruments for oppressing the people, seize power and take what was regarded as belonging to all kinds of robbers of the people – in short, when the intellect and reason of millions of downtrodden people awaken not only to read books, but for action, vital human action, to make history.[11]

And again:

> the organizing abilities of the people, particularly of the proletariat, but also of the peasantry, are revealed a million times more strongly, fully and productively in periods of revolutionary whirlwind than in periods of so-called calm (dray-horse) historical progress.[12]

Years later, Lenin returned to the same theme: 'A democrat . . . whatever illusion he may at times entertain regarding the interests and aspirations of the masses . . . has *faith* in the masses, in the *action* of the masses, in the legitimacy of their sentiments and the expediency of their methods of struggle.'[13]

In the Zurich lecture already referred to, Lenin said about 1905 that it:

does show how great the dormant energy of the proletariat can be. It shows that in a revolutionary epoch – I say this without the slightest exaggeration, on the basis of the most accurate data of Russian history – the proletariat *can* generate fighting energy *a hundred times greater* than in ordinary, peaceful times. It shows that up to 1905 mankind did not yet know what a great, what a tremendous exertion of effort the proletariat is, and will be, capable of in a fight for really great aims, and one waged in a really revolutionary manner![14]

Learn from the Masses

We have seen that the Bolshevik Party lagged behind the masses between 9 January and the establishment of the Petersburg Soviet. Lenin always emphasized that the party must rely on the masses: 'the slogans of the revolutionaries not only evoked a response but actually *lagged* behind the march of events. January 9 and the mass strikes that followed it, and the Potemkin were all events which were in advance of the direct appeals of the revolutionaries.'[15]

The central role of the party was 'to give full scope to the revolutionary creative activity of the masses, who participate but little in this activity in time of peace, but who come to the forefront in revolutionary epochs,'[16] to realize 'that the political consciousness of the masses is the main force',[17] to prize 'above everything the development of the political and class-consciousness of the masses'.[18]

The party must always be with the masses in struggle, whether in victory or defeat, whether they act correctly or commit blunders. As Lenin put it many years later, after the victory of the October revolution:

Unbreakable ties with the mass of the workers, the ability to agitate unceasingly among them, to participate in every strike, to respond to every demand of the masses – this is the chief thing for a Communist Party.[19]

Mistakes are inevitable when the masses are fighting, but the communists *remain with the masses*, see these mistakes, explain them to the masses, try to get them rectified, and strive perseveringly for the victory of class-consciousness over spontaneity.[20]

When Lenin talked about the fighting masses, he did not necessarily mean the majority of the working class. A revolutionary party has to be based in the working class, but not necessarily in the class as a whole. For a whole historical period it may be established only among a minority of the class – its vanguard. As Lenin wrote on 22 August 1907:

> Not to support a movement of the avowedly revolutionary minority – means, in effect, rejecting all revolutionary methods of struggle. For it is absolutely indisputable that those who participated in the revolutionary movement throughout 1905 were the *avowedly revolutionary minority*: it was because the masses who were fighting were in a minority – they were nonetheless masses for being in a minority – that they did not achieve full success in their struggle. But all the successes which the emancipation movement in Russia did achieve, all the gains it did make, were *wholly and without exception* the result of this struggle of the masses alone, who were in a minority.[21]

In January 1905 most workers thought that the Tsar could be spoken to like a decent person. 'Bloody Sunday' opened the eyes of millions. In October the same workers believed that to shake a fist at the Tsar would be enough to force him to grant concessions. The general strike of October proved to them that this was not so. The use of arms was the next step. But again this idea was not accepted by the majority of the working class. Only a minority of Moscow workers participated in the December armed uprising.

The revolutionary party, rooted in the advanced section of the class, learns from the workers in the struggle, and teaches them at one and the same time.

1905 — School for Bolsheviks

The revolution of 1905 was also a great school for the revolutionary workers' party. The revolution is the best test of theories and programmes. It destroys every kind of political ambiguity and fiction. Revolution demands ideological irreconcilability. It purges the consciousness of the advanced workers of routine, inertia and irresolution. At the same time it demands from the party, because of the sharp changes in direction the struggle takes, remarkable tactical skills and adaptability to the swiftly changing needs of the movement.

The revolution threw into sharp relief not only the relation of the vanguard party to the class, but also that of the party leader to the party. In 1905 Lenin's leadership of his own faction was on the whole incontestable. But it demanded from him a continuous effort of thought and organization – he had, in a sense, to reaffirm his leadership and reconquer his party every day. On the evidence of 1905, supported by the experience of 1917, one could write instructive chapters on what happened to the leadership of the Leninists without Lenin. If 1905 steeled the Bolsheviks, even more so did it steel Lenin. His ideas, programme and tactics were put to the stiffest test during those days.

Lenin was quite clear about the leading role of the proletariat and its independence from the liberals, about the role of the Soviet as the form of organization of the revolutionary struggle and as the form of the revolutionary government of the future, about the art of insurrection. The 1905 revolution failed *in spite* of Lenin's correct tactics and strategy. It failed because the proletariat and its party were insufficiently developed. 1905 was for Lenin a magnificent training school, preparing him and his party for the great days of 1917.

In the same way as Marx and Engels in the years of dull 'normalcy' looked back again and again to 1848 as the point from which to determine the future pattern of the revolutionary workers' movement, so Lenin in the coming years looked back to 1905. The mass revolutionary struggle of this period was the point of departure for his formulation and reformulation of the strategy and tactics of Bolshevism.

13

Dark Reaction Victorious

The Revolution Still Advancing

Although the revolution had been in decline for several months and reaction had set in, Lenin continued to believe that it was still on the upswing. Thus, soon after the defeat of the December 1905 insurrection he wrote:

> What is the state of the democratic revolution in Russia? Is it defeated, or are we merely passing through a temporary lull? Was the December uprising the climax of the revolution, and are we now rushing headlong towards a 'Tsarist Constitution' regime? Or is the revolutionary movement, on the whole, not subsiding, but rising, in preparation for a new outbreak, using the lull to muster new forces, and promising, after the first unsuccessful insurrection, a second, with much greater chance of success?[1]

And he answered these questions in the following way:

> The new outbreak may not take place in the spring; but it is approaching, and in all probability is not very far off. We must meet it armed, organized in military fashion, and prepared for determined offensive operations.

In accordance with this, the Bolshevik conference that assembled in Tammerfors (Finland) on 12-17 December 1905 also

> counselled all party organizations to make broad use of the electoral assemblies not in order to bring about, in submitting to the police restrictions, any elections to the Duma, but to broaden the revolutionary organization of the proletariat and to agitate in all strata of the people for an armed uprising. The uprising must be prepared at once, without delay, and organized everywhere, for only its victory will give us the possibility of convoking a genuine popular representation, that is, a freely elected Constituent Assembly on the basis of a universal, direct, equal and secret ballot.[2]

Three months later, in a draft resolution written for the Unity Congress of the RSDLP, Lenin was still insisting that the uprising was an immediate prospect: 'at the present time armed uprising is not only the necessary means of fighting for freedom, but a stage actually reached by the movement'.[3]

At the beginning of June 1906 he wrote: 'It is quite evident that we are now passing through one of the most important periods of the revolution. Signs of a revival of the broad, mass movement against the old order have been visible for a long time. Now this revival is reaching its climax.'[4] And in July he still saw the revolution rising: 'The possibility of simultaneous action all over Russia is increasing. The probability of all partial uprisings merging into one is increasing. The inevitability of a political strike and of an uprising as a fight for power is felt as never before by large sections of the population.'[5]

However, six months later, at the beginning of December, he revised his estimate of the situation. And without making any apology, he explained why he had lagged behind others – the Mensheviks above all – who had declared the revolution defeated months before:

> the marxist is the *first* to foresee the approach of a revolutionary period, and already begins to rouse the people and to sound the tocsin while the philistines are still wrapt in the slavish slumber of loyal subjects. The marxist is therefore the *first* to take the path of direct revolutionary struggle . . . The marxist is the *last* to leave the path of direct revolutionary struggle, he leaves it only when all possibilities have been exhausted, when there is not a *shadow* of hope for a shorter way, when the basis for an appeal to prepare for mass strikes, an uprising, etc., is obviously disappearing. Therefore a marxist treats with contempt the innumerable renegades of the revolution who shout to him: we are more 'progressive' than you, we were the first to renounce the revolution! We were the first to 'submit' to the monarchist constitution![6]

A revolutionary cannot accept the defeat of the revolution until objective facts leave no room for doubt. The revolutionaries are the last to leave the battlefield.

Wrong Perspective

There was an international slump in 1907, which Lenin expected to bring about a revival of the revolutionary struggle. Thus in a draft resolution for the fifth Congress of the RSDLP, he wrote: 'a number of facts testify to the extreme intensification of destitution among the proletariat and also of its economic struggle . . . this economic movement must be regarded as the main source and foundation of the entire revolutionary crisis that is developing in Russia'.[7]

The view that an economic crisis heightens the revolutionary struggle was generally accepted by Russian marxists. The only exception was Trotsky, and he was proved absolutely right.

> After a period of big battles and defeats, a crisis has the effect of depressing rather than arousing the working class. It undermines the workers' confidence in their powers and demoralizes them politically. Under such conditions, only an industrial revival can close the ranks of the proletariat, pour fresh blood into its veins, restore its confidence in itself and make it capable of further struggle.[8]

In retrospect Trotsky could correctly say:

> The world industrial crisis, which broke out in 1907, extended the prolonged depression in Russia for three additional years, and far from inspiring the workers to engage in a new fight, dispersed them and weakened them more than ever. Under the blows of lockouts, unemployment and poverty, the weary masses became definitely discouraged. Such was the material basis for the 'achievements' of Stolypin's reaction. The proletariat needed the resuscitative font of a new industrial resurgence to revive its strength, fill its ranks, again feel itself the indispensable factor in production and plunge into a new fight.[9]

Reaction Victorious

1907-10 were years of dreadful reaction. The retreat of the labour movement can be measured by the catastrophic decline in the strike movement after the peak of 1905.[10]

Year	Number of workers on strike (in thousands)	Percentage of all workers
1895-1904 (average)	431	1.46-5.10
1905	2,863	163.8
1906	1,108	65.8
1907	740	41.9
1908	176	9.7
1909	64	3.5
1910	47	2.4

'In 1908, and even more 1909, the number of strikers was far smaller even than the average of the ten years prior to the revolution.'[11] The decline in *political* strikes was especially marked. Figures for strike-days were as follows:[12]

Year	Total strike-days	Political strike-days
1895-1904 (total)	2,079,408	
1905	23,609,387	7,569,708
1906	5,512,749	763,605
1907	2,433,123	521,647
1908	864,666	89,021

The decline of the revolution left the initiative completely in the hands of the Tsarist government and mass White terror took place.

During the dictatorship of Stolypin over 5,000 death sentences were passed and over 3,500 persons were actually executed – this was at least three times as many as during the whole period of the mass movement (not including of course shootings without trial, after the suppression of the armed insurrection).[13]

Disintegration of the Labour Movement

Once the revolutionary movement was on the decline, and the Tsarist government had regained its confidence, the process of disintegration of the labour movement proceeded rapidly. After it was beaten in battle, the decline in morale intensified and the retreat turned into a complete rout. Workers showed no capacity for further resistance. The whole movement fell to pieces.

In March 1908 Lenin wrote:

> More than six months have passed since the reactionary coup of 3 June, and beyond doubt this first half-year has been marked by a considerable decline and weakening of all revolutionary organizations, including that of the Social Democrats. Wavering, disunity and disintegration – such have been the general feature of this half-year.[14]

But he did not surrender easily. He clutched at any straw which might indicate an upturn in the movement – such as an increase in illegal publications or the persistence of local and factory groups. In January 1909 he hopefully proclaimed: 'The recent All-Russian Conference of the Russian Social Democratic Labour Party has led the party out on to the road, and evidently marks a turning-point in the development of the Russian working-class movement after the victory of the counter-revolution.'[15]

But his optimism was totally baseless, and the indications of an upturn unfounded. In actual fact, at the conference Lenin referred to – held in December 1908 – there were only four delegates from Russia.[16] Stalin described the situation at the time in an article called 'The Crisis in the Party and our Tasks':

> It is no secret to anyone that our party is passing through a severe crisis. The party's loss of members, the shrinking and weakness of the organizations, the latter's isolation from one another, and the absence of co-ordinated party work – all show that the party is ailing, that it is passing through a grave crisis.
> The first thing that is particularly depressing the party is the isolation of its organizations from the broad masses. At one time our organizations numbered thousands in their ranks and they led hundreds of thousands. At that time, the party had firm roots among the masses. This is not the case now. Instead of thousands, tens and at best hundreds, have remained in the organizations. As regards leading hundreds of thousands, it is not worth speaking about . . . It is sufficient to point to St Petersburg, where in 1907 we had about 8,000

members and where we can now scarcely muster 300 to 400, to appreciate at once the full gravity of the crisis. We shall not speak of Moscow, the Urals, Poland, the Donets Basin, etc., which are in a similar state.

But that is not all. The party is suffering not only from isolation from the masses, but also from the fact that its organizations are not linked up with one another, are not living the same party life, are divorced from one another. St Petersburg does not know what is going on in the Caucasus, the Caucasus does not know what is going on in the Urals, etc., each little corner lives its own separate life. Strictly speaking, we no longer have a single party living the same common life that we all spoke of with such pride in the period from 1905 to 1907.[17]

The movement was in actual fact in complete disarray. For instance in the summer of 1905 the Moscow district had 1,435 members.[18] The figure rose in mid-May 1906 to 5,320.[19] But by mid-1908 it had dropped to 250, and six months later it was 150. In 1910 the organization ceased to exist, when the District Secretary's job fell into the hands of one Kukushkin, an agent of the *okhrana*, the secret police.[20]

The first to leave the sinking ship were the intellectuals. In March 1908 Lenin commented on 'the flight of the intellectuals from the party', and quoted a number of correspondents to support this statement.

'Recently *through lack* of intellectual workers the area organization has been dead', writes a correspondent from the Kulebaki Works (Vladimir area organization of the Central Industrial Region). 'Our ideological forces are melting away like snow', they write from the Urals. 'The elements who avoid illegal organizations in general ... and who joined the party only at the time of the upsurge and of the *de facto* liberty that then existed in many places, have left our party organizations.' And an article in the Central Organ entitled 'Questions of Organization' sums up these reports and others which we do not print, with the words: 'The intellectuals, as is well known, have been deserting in masses in recent months.'[21]

A year later, at the end of January 1909, Lenin described the sad state of the movement in the following words:

A year of disintegration, a year of ideological and political disunity, a year of party driftage lies behind us. The membership of all our party organizations has dropped. Some of them – namely, those whose membership was least proletarian – have fallen to pieces.

The main cause of the party crisis . . . is the wavering intellectual and petty-bourgeois elements, of which the workers' party had to rid itself; elements who joined the working-class movement mainly in the hope of an early triumph of the bourgeois-democratic revolution and could not stand up to a period of reaction. Their instability was revealed both in theory ('retreat from revolutionary marxism') . . . and in tactics (the 'whittling down of slogans') as well as in party organization.[22]

In a letter to Maxim Gorky written in February or early March 1910, he once again noted 'the tremendous decline among the organizations everywhere, almost their cessation in many localities. The wholesale flight of the intelligentsia. All that is left are workers' circles and isolated individuals. The young, inexperienced worker is making his way forward with difficulty.'[23]

In October of the same year he wrote:

The deep crisis of the workers' movement and the Social Democratic Party in Russia still continues. Disintegration of the party organizations, an almost universal exodus of the intellectuals from them, confusion and wavering among the Social Democrats who have remained loyal, dejection and apathy among fairly wide sections of the advanced proletariat, uncertainty as to the way out of this situation – such are the distinguishing features of the present position.[24]

In December he complained that 'the Russian Collegium of the Central Committee had not met once during the year'.[25] In May 1911 he wrote: 'At present the *real* position of the party is such that almost everywhere in the localities there are informal, extremely small and tiny party workers' groups and nuclei that meet regularly. They are not connected with each other. Very rarely do they see any literature.'[26]

The activities of *agents provocateurs* contributed to the disintegration of the movement. In 1910 and early 1911 all

Bolshevik members of the Central Committee working in Russia were arrested.[27]

The *okhrana* infiltrated almost all the party organizations and an atmosphere of suspicion and mutual distrust thwarted all initiative. At the beginning of 1910, after a number of well-calculated arrests, the *provocateur* Kukushkin became head of the Moscow district organization. 'The ideal of the *okhrana* is being realized', wrote an activist. 'Secret agents are at the head of all the Moscow organizations.' The situation in Petersburg was not much better. 'The leadership seemed to have been routed, there was no way of restoring it, provocation gnawed away at our vitals, organizations fell apart.' Not a single conference was held abroad with representatives of the Russian party that was not attended by at least one *okhrana* agent.

In 1912, when the legal Bolshevik daily *Pravda* was founded in Petersburg, two police agents, Miron Chernomazov and Roman Malinovsky, were on the editorial staff, the former as an editor and chairman of the editorial board, the latter as contributing editor and treasurer. From Malinovsky the police obtained a complete list of people who contributed donations to the paper and a complete list of subscribers. Malinovsky was also chairman of the Bolshevik group in the Duma, and a member of the Central Committee. Lenin admired him. '*For the first time* we have among our people in the Duma an *outstanding* workers' leader.'[28] He used to call him abroad for the most confidential meetings, and revealed important secrets to him.

Zinoviev, who was very close to Lenin, was later so say: 'at this unhappy period the party as a whole ceased to exist'.[29]

Life in Exile Is Unbearable

During the period of reaction life for revolutionaries abroad became almost intolerable. Walking the Geneva streets Lenin murmured, 'I feel just as if I'd come here to be buried.' Krupskaya, commenting on this, says, 'Our second period of emigration . . . was ever so much harder than the first.'[30]

Lenin's first stay abroad lasted five years, but they were years of a rising movement, years of hope. The second lasted ten, beginning with the reaction and the disintegration of the movement.

Isolated and impotent, the émigrés became involved in furious quarrels, denounced one another bitterly, accused everybody of being traitors, and blamed one another for their terrible defeats. Lenin described the torment:

> there is much that is painful in the life of the exiles . . . There is more poverty and want among them than elsewhere. The proportion of suicides is particularly great among them, and the proportion of those among them whose whole being is one bundle of sick nerves is incredibly, monstrously great. Indeed, how could things be different with tormented people?[31]

He wrote to his sister Maria on 14 January 1908: 'We have been hanging about in this damned Geneva for several days now . . . It is an awful hole, but there is nothing we can do. We shall get used to it.'[32]

Some ten months later planning to leave for Paris he wrote to his mother: 'We hope that a big city will put some life into us all; we are tired of staying in this provincial back-water.'[33]

Yet another year later, in February 1910 he wrote: 'Paris is a rotten hole in many respects . . . I am still unable to adapt myself *fully* to it (after living *here* for a year! . . .)'[34]

In the autumn of 1911, when Anna came to visit him in Paris, he could not conceal from her that the second emigration had been extremely painful. 'His state of mind was noticeably less gay . . . One day when we were walking together, he said to me: "Will we be able to live until the next revolution?"'[35]

On 11 April 1910, he wrote to Gorky, 'Life in exile is now a hundred times harder than it was before the revolution. Life in exile and squabbling are inseparable.'[36]

On the domestic level, poverty dogged their lives. Krupskaya recollected:

> we were so poor. Workers managed to eke out a livelihood somehow or other, but the conditions of the intellectuals

were very bad. It was not always possible to become a worker. To live at the expense of the exiles' funds . . . and to feed in the exiles' dining-room was humiliating. I remember several sad cases. One comrade tried to become a French polisher, but it was not easy to learn the trade, and he was forced to change his jobs frequently. He lived in a working-class district far from where the other exiles lived. At last he became so weak from lack of food that he could not leave his bed and wrote to us asking for money. He asked, however, that it should not be brought directly to him but left with the concierge.

Nikolai Vasilievich Sapozhkov (Kuznetsov) had a hard time. He and his wife found work at painting pottery, but they earned very little and one could see this giant of a man positively withering away; his face became furrowed with wrinkles as a result of slow starvation, although he never complained of his condition. There were many cases like that. The saddest case of all was that of Comrade Prigara, who had taken part in the Moscow uprising. He lived somewhere in a working-class suburb, and the comrades knew little about him. One day he came to us and began to talk excitedly and incoherently about chariots filled with sheaves of corn and about beautiful girls standing on the chariots, etc., etc. It was obvious that the man was insane. Our first thought was that it was due to starvation. Mother began to prepare something to eat for him. Ilyich, his face pale with pity, remained with Prigara while I ran to call a friend of ours who was a mental specialist. The latter came, had a talk with the sick man, and said that it was a serious case of insanity, brought on by starvation. The case was not critical he said, but it would develop into a persecution mania and the patient was likely to commit suicide. He had to be watched. We did not even know his address. Brittman went to see him home, but on the way he disappeared. We roused our group and organized a search, but in vain. Later his corpse was found in the Seine with stones tied to his neck and feet – he had committed suicide.[37]

Bad Communications with Russia

Their isolation from the tiny movement that survived in Russia added to the strain on the life and nerves of Lenin and his co-workers abroad. Communications between Lenin and the underground had always been poor, but in the period of reaction they deteriorated still further, until they became practically non-existent.

Most of the personal contacts Lenin had had were made at party or factional gatherings. But these were now very badly attended by delegates from inside Russia. The December 1908 conference, as we have already mentioned, drew only four Russian delegates. The next assembly, 'The Enlarged Editorial Board of *Proletarii*', held six months later, in June 1909, was attended by five delegates from Russia : three from the same areas as the December conference, and two who had escaped from Siberia and were thus somewhat out of touch.

> Gorky, who was politically opposed to Lenin at this time although the two men corresponded frequently, was somewhat more successful at his school, which opened in Capri in August 1909. Yet even this event was attended by only thirteen Russian committee-men. It did enable Lenin to broaden his contacts somewhat, as five students and one organizer walked out of the school in November as 'Leninists' and came to Paris to meet Lenin. The other eight students followed suit when the school finished in December.
> Thus from December 1908 to December 1909 Lenin met just twenty-two Russian committee-men. During the next fifteen months, up to Lenin's own school at Longjumeau held in the Spring of 1911, he met no Russian committee-men at all. In December 1910, he had attempted 'to repeat the Capri experiment' with the students at the school that Bogdanov and Lunacharsky, also at this time opposed to Lenin, had organized at Bologna, but his attempt failed completely.[38]

Correspondence with Russia was also very irregular. Before the 1903 conference Lenin wrote some 300 letters a month to Russia, but now his correspondence dried up almost completely. The *Collected Works* (fifth Russian edition), which contain his letters for this period, reproduce or refer to very, very few letters into Russia : 9 for the whole of 1909, 15 for 1910, 7 for 1911, and 8 for the first half of 1912. (The number increases appreciably after this : 31 for the second half of 1912, 43 for 1913, 35 for the first 7 months of 1914.)[39]

To make matters worse, the Russian correspondents were often not very helpful. They often wrote in very obscure language, either genuinely to fool the censors, or as a pretext when they either had nothing to report, or wished to obscure the real situation. Thus Lenin complains 'Nikolai has sent in a letter full of joyful exclamations, but absolutely useless' and 'instead of letters you send us various telegraphically brief exclamations which are quite incomprehensible' and 'I have received your two letters and am very much surprised by them. What could seem simpler than writing to us simply and clearly what the matter is.'[40] They frequently did not write at all, and scattered through Lenin's letters from 1909 to 1916 are remarks like 'it is a pity that we did not receive any news from you earlier – we are terribly cut off here, we tried to make contact with you and Vyach, but were unsuccessful',[41] or 'Dear comrades, we have had no news from you for a long time' (this to the Russian Bureau of the Central Committee!);[42] these individual remarks are summed up in the plea, 'For God's sake give us more contacts. Contacts, contacts, contacts, this is what we have not got.'[43]

The difficulties were increased by the fact that the system of distribution of the Bolshevik newspapers, which until 1910 were all produced abroad, broke down after 1905 and was never properly re-established. Hardly any copies managed to be smuggled into Russia. In addition, the committeemen often complained that the journals published abroad were so out of touch with affairs at home that they were practically useless. In 1909 Stalin wrote that

> the organs that are published abroad, apart from the fact that they reach Russia in extremely limited quantities, naturally lag behind the course of party life in Russia, are unable to note in time and comment on the questions that excite the workers and, therefore, cannot link our local organizations together by permanent ties.[44]

This is a good example of the thinking of a 'practical' activist, proud of the organizational work he has carried out under difficult conditions and contemptuous of the émigré discussion groups which he has 'outgrown'. It was echoed by Piatnitsky at the Prague conference in 1912: 'I attacked the editorial board violently because it sometimes forgot that the Central Organ – the *Sotsial-demokrat* – existed not only for the comrades abroad who were familiar with all the party quarrels, but mainly for the comrades in Russia.'[45]

Dr N.A.Semachko, himself an émigré, wrote after the revolution, 'usually émigré disputes were seen as the clashes of *has-beens* cut off from life. To a significant extent even I who directly participated in these disputes thought like this.'[46] One of the seven members of the Central Committee, Suren Spandarian, at the January 1912 conference which elected him, expressed doubts about the need for émigré groups at all: 'Let those who wish to work . . . come into Russia with me.'[47]

Lenin Teaches How to Retreat

To lead an army in retreat is usually a far more difficult task than to lead one which is on the offensive. Without doubt one of the most difficult chapters in the history of Bolshevism was that of the years of reaction, years in which Lenin was more isolated than ever before or afterwards. Many years later, he could look back and observe that revolutionary leaders need to learn how to retreat.

> The revolutionary parties had to complete their education. They were learning how to attack. Now they had to realize that such a knowledge must be supplemented with the knowledge of how to retreat in good order. They had to realize – and it is from bitter experience that the revolutionary class learns to realize this – that victory is impossible unless one has learned how to attack and retreat properly.

And with justified pride he went on to recount:

> Of all the defeated opposition and revolutionary parties, the Bolsheviks effected the most orderly retreat, with the least loss to their 'army', with its core best preserved, with the least significant splits (in point of depth and incurability), with the least demoralization, and in the best condition to resume work on the broadest scale and in the most correct

and energetic manner. The Bolsheviks achieved this only because they ruthlessly exposed and expelled the revolutionary phrase-mongers, those who did not wish to understand that one had to retreat, that one had to know how to retreat.[47]

In concrete terms, to retreat meant to withdraw from the field of the direct, open, revolutionary struggle, and instead 'to work legally in the most reactionary of parliaments, in the most reactionary of trade unions, co-operative and insurance societies and similar organizations'.[48]

The Attitude to the Duma Elections

For several years (1906-10) the question of what attitude to take towards the Duma was of central importance. This problem led Lenin into disagreement both with the majority of his own faction – the Bolsheviks – and, for different reasons, with the Mensheviks.

The issue came up as early as May 1905, before either the Bolshevik Congress or the Menshevik Conference, when it was announced that the Tsar had instructed the new minister of the interior, Bulygin, to work out a draft for a consultative representative assembly. The Mensheviks favoured participation in the elections. They did not alter their position even when on 6 August the statutes of the Duma were published, making it clear that it would have very limited power and that the election process itself would be very undemocratic. Voters were to be divided according to social 'estates', with extremely limited representation for the workers, and there were to be many stages in the election process. The Bolsheviks came out in favour of an 'active' boycott of the elections.

At the beginning of September 1905 a conference of all Social Democrats – Bolsheviks, Mensheviks, Latvian Social Democrats, Polish Social Democrats, the Jewish Bund and the Revolutionary Ukrainian Party – decided, with the exception of the Mensheviks' representatives, to support the boycott. Lenin explained what it implied in an article called 'The

Boycott of the Bulygin Duma and Insurrection', written in August 1905. 'As distinct from passive abstention, an active boycott should imply increasing agitation tenfold, organizing meetings everywhere, taking advantage of election meetings, even if we have to force our way into them, holding demonstrations, political strikes, and so on and so forth.'[49]

On 11 December a statute was published containing a new electoral law. This, while confirming the division of the voters into social 'estates' and the many stages of the election, made significant concessions in the direction of workers' and peasants' representation. It greatly increased the numbers of representatives to be elected by the workers, and even more so by the peasants. Nevertheless, the plural voting for the wealthier sections of society and the indirect elections were openly undemocratic, weighting the system so as to give more representation to landlords than to peasants; workers and peasants were to vote separately from the other classes of the population.

> It allowed for one elector to every 2,000 voters in the landowner curia, one to each 7,000 in the urban curia, i.e. the vote of a landlord was equal to three votes by the urban bourgeoisie, 15 peasant votes and 45 workers' votes. The electors from the worker curias constituted only 4 per cent of the electors who elected deputies to the state Duma.[50]

When Lenin argued for an active boycott of the election to the Duma he made it clear that the tactic was based on his assumption that the revolution was going to continue to gather momentum. He wrote, 'an active boycott . . . is unthinkable without a clear, precise, and immediate slogan. Only an armed uprising can be that slogan.'[51] After the defeat of the Moscow uprising in December 1905, he continued to argue in favour of the boycott, on the ground that the revolution had been halted only temporarily and a further uprising was not far off.

Eventually, both the Bolsheviks and the Mensheviks, who had changed their minds, boycotted the elections to the Duma, but individual Social Democrats ran in defiance of party instructions. Many of them were reasonably successful, which brought a hasty admission from the Mensheviks that they had made a mistake in boycotting the elections. When the Duma assembled on 28 April 1906 a number of Social Democrats were among the deputies. Fourteen of them were organized into a separate Social Democratic Group. In later elections the Georgian Mensheviks succeeded in getting a further five members elected.

In May Lenin remarked on this election victory in an article entitled 'The Social Democratic Election Victory in Tiflis':

> We welcome the successes of our comrades in the Caucasus . . . Our readers know that we were in favour of boycotting the Duma . . . But it goes without saying that, if real party Social Democrats have now been elected to the Duma on really party lines, all of us, as members of a united party, will do all we can to help them to fulfil their arduous duties.[52]

When the Stockholm Congress of the RSDLP (April/ May 1906) assembled, the Menshevik delegates from Transcaucasia proposed that the party should give up its boycott and nominate candidates to the elections that were still pending. The Bolshevik faction accused the Mensheviks of betrayal. But to their consternation they found that Lenin was the only Bolshevik delegate to side with the Mensheviks. In fact he ignored faction discipline and voted with the Mensheviks.

At the end of June 1906 he wrote, justifying his new position,

> does the fact that we boycotted the Duma *necessarily* mean that we must not form our party group in the Duma? Not at all. The boycotters who . . . think so, are mistaken. We were obliged to do – and did – everything in our power to prevent the convocation of a sham representative body. That is so. But since it has been convened in spite of all our efforts, we cannot shirk the task of utilizing it.[53]

On 12 August he came out unequivocally for an end to the boycott:

> The left-wing Social Democrats must reconsider the question of boycotting the state Duma. It should be borne in mind that we have always presented this question concretely, and in connection with a definite political situation.[54]

The time has now come when the revolutionary Social Democrats must cease to be boycottists. We shall not refuse to go into the second Duma when (or 'if') it is convened. We shall not refuse to utilize this arena, but we shall not exaggerate its modest importance; on the contrary, guided by the experience already provided by history, we shall entirely subordinate the struggle we wage in the Duma to another form of struggle, namely, strikes, uprisings, etc.[55]

After making this change in his line Lenin found himself isolated from the other Bolsheviks. At the third conference of the RSDLP, in Kotka (Finland), on 21-23 July 1907, he proposed a resolution against the boycott (the official spokesman of the Bolsheviks – Bogdanov – put a resolution in favour of it). Not one Bolshevik delegate supported Lenin. Instead they accused him of betraying Bolshevism.

Lenin's draft resolution stated :

Whereas,
(1) active boycott, as the experience of the Russian revolution has shown, is correct tactics on the part of the Social Democrats only under conditions of a sweeping, universal, and rapid upswing of the revolution, developing into an armed uprising, and only in connection with the ideological aims of the struggle against constitutional illusions arising from the convocation of the first representative assembly by the old regime;
(2) in the absence of these conditions correct tactics on the part of the revolutionary Social Democrats call for participation in the elections, as was the case with the second Duma.[56]

Lenin was not concerned about the fact that he reached the conclusion that it was necessary to cease boycotting the Duma elections later than the Mensheviks. On the contrary, a 'mistake' of this sort was no mistake at all. 'The revolutionary Social Democrats must be *the first* to take the line of the most resolute, the most direct struggle . . . and must be *the last* to adopt more circuitous methods of struggle.'[57]

He also understood very well that the Bolsheviks arguing for a continuation of the boycott included many of the best revolutionary fighters, and that they argued as they did with the best intentions.

There is no doubt that, in many cases, sympathy for the boy-cott is created precisely by these praiseworthy efforts of revolutionaries to foster a tradition of the finest period of the revolutionary past, to light up the cheerless slough of the drab workaday present by a spark of bold, open and reso-lute struggle. But it is just because we cherish this concern for revolutionary traditions that we must vigorously protest against the view that by using one of the slogans of a parti-cular historical period the essential conditions of the period can be restored. It is one thing to preserve the traditions of the revolution, to know how to use them for constant pro-paganda and agitation and for acquainting the masses with the conditions of a direct and aggressive struggle against the old regime, but quite another thing to repeat a slogan divorced from the sum total of the conditions which gave rise to it and which ensured its success and to apply it to essentially different conditions.[58]

Lenin demanded from the Bolsheviks a readiness to face realities: 'since the accursed counter-revolution has driven us into this accursed pigsty, we shall work there too for the benefit of the revolution, without whining, but also without boasting'.[59]

Many years later, looking back, he said,

compromises are often unavoidably forced upon a fighting party by circumstances . . . The task of a truly revolutionary party is not to declare that it is impossible to renounce all compromises, but to be able, *through all compromises*, when they are unavoidable, to remain true to its principles, to its class, to its revolutionary purpose, to its task of paving the way for revolution and educating the mass of the people for victory in the revolution.

To agree . . . to participate in the third and fourth Dumas was a compromise, a temporary renunciation of revolution-ary demands. But this was a compromise absolutely forced upon us, for the balance of forces made it impossible for us for the time being to conduct a mass revolutionary struggle, and in order to prepare this struggle over a long period we *had* to be able to work even from *inside* such a 'pigsty'. History has proved that this approach to the question by the Bolsheviks as a party was perfectly correct.[60]

14

Strategy and Tactics (Lenin learns from Clausewitz)

The twenty years 1894-1914 saw an enormous growth in the maturity of the Russian labour movement. This development was a living school for tactics and strategy. Lenin, its greatest product, grew with the movement, influenced it and was influenced by it. These two decades constituted a long preparation, for him and for the working class as a whole, for the greatest test in both tactics and strategy – that of the terrible slaughter of the war, and its termination by the revolution. The most intensive lessons of this preparatory period were provided by the 1905 revolution and its aftermath.

Marxism - Science and Art

As we have noted, when the 1905 revolution broke out, Lenin hastened to study the military writings of Karl von Clausewitz, which influenced him considerably in formulating his political tactics and strategy.

Clausewitz, the great philosopher of war, who drew his inspiration from Napoleon, defined tactics as 'the theory of the use of military forces in combat', and strategy as 'the theory of the use of combat for the object of the war'. Lenin defined the relation between revolutionary tactics and revolutionary strategy in terms very similar to those of Clausewitz. The concept of tactics applies to measures that serve a single task or a single branch of the class struggle. Hence Lenin speaks about the tactics needed, say, during the January days of 1905, or in relation to Gapon. He also speaks about trade union tactics, parliamentary tactics, and so on. Revolutionary strategy encompasses a combination of tactics which by their association and growth lead to the working-class conquest of power.

The Second International, emerging during the period of the slow, organic, systematic growth of capitalism and the labour movement, in practice limited itself to the question of tactics : the tasks of the day-to-day struggle for reforms in the trade unions, in parliament, local government bodies, co-operatives, etc. The Russian revolutionary movement, which developed in very stormy times, when the direction of events was often rapidly changing, had to face up to the larger issue of strategy and its relation to tactics. No-one was more competent to develop this question than Lenin, who knew better than anyone else how to raise marxism from the level of a science to that of an art.

Marxism is constantly referred to as a science, but as a guide to action it must also be an art. Science deals with what exists, while art teaches us how to act. Lenin's main contribution is in developing marxism as an art. If Marx had died without participating in the founding of the First International he would still be Marx. If Lenin had died without establishing the Bolshevik Party, giving a lead in the 1905 and later in the 1917 revolutions, and founding the Communist International, he would not have been Lenin.

To advance from theory to practice, from science to art, Lenin had to demonstrate the dialectical relation between them – what is common to both and what distinguishes one from the other.

> 'Our theory is not a dogma, but a guide to action,' Marx and Engels always said, ridiculing the mere memorizing and repetition of 'formulas', that at best are capable only of marking out *general* tasks which are necessarily modifiable by the *concrete* economic and political conditions of each particular *period* of the historical process.[1]

There is an enormous difference between the *general* laws of motion of society and the actual concrete historical conditions, for life is infinitely more complicated than any abstract theory. With so many factors interacting, book knowledge alone is no basis for a knowledge of reality. Lenin loved to repeat, 'Theory, my friend, is grey, but green is the eternal tree of life.' Living reality is always richer in developments, in probabilities, in complications, than any theoretical concept or prognosis, and Lenin therefore derided those who turned marxism into an icon: 'An icon is something you pray to, something you cross yourself before, something you bow down to; but an icon has no effect on practical life and practical politics.'[2] He wrote bitterly in a letter to Inessa Armand, 'People for the most part (99 per cent of the bourgeoisie, 98 per cent of the liquidators, about 60-70 per cent of the Bolsheviks) don't know how to *think*, they only *learn words by heart*.'[3]

The main obstacle to a non-dogmatic understanding of marxism, to its use as a guide to action, is the inclination to substitute the abstract for the concrete. This is one of the most dangerous errors, especially in a pre-revolutionary or revolutionary situation, when historical development is erratic, full of jumps, retreats and sharp turns.

> There is no such thing as abstract truth. Truth is always concrete.[4]

> any abstract truth becomes an empty phrase if it is applied to *any* concrete situation. It is indisputable that 'every strike conceals the hydra of the social revolution'. But it is nonsense to think that we can stride directly from a strike to the revolution.[5]

> every general historical statement applied to a particular case without a special analysis of the conditions of that particular case becomes an empty phrase.[6]

At the same time a clear scientific understanding of the *general* contours of historical development of the class struggle is essential for a revolutionary leader. He will not be able to keep his bearings and his confidence through the twists and turns of the struggle unless he has a general knowledge of economics and politics. Therefore Lenin repeated many times that strategy and tactics must be based 'on an exact appraisal of the *objective* situation',[7] while at the same time being 'shaped after analysing class relations *in their en-*

tirety'.[8] In other words they must be based on a clear, confident, theoretical analysis – on science.

Theoretical scepticism is incompatible with revolutionary action. 'The important thing is to be confident that the path chosen is the right one, this confidence multiplying a hundredfold revolutionary energy and revolutionary enthusiasm, which can perform miracles.'[9]

Without understanding the laws of historical development, one cannot maintain a persistent struggle. During the years of toil and disappointment, isolation and suffering, revolutionaries cannot survive without the conviction that their actions fit the requirements of historical advance. In order not to get lost on the twists and turns of the long road, one must stand firm ideologically. Theoretical scepticism and revolutionary relentlessness are not compatible. Lenin's strength was that he always related theory to the processes of human development. He judged the importance of every theoretical notion in relation to practical needs. Likewise he tested every practical step for its fit with marxist theory. He combined theory and practice to perfection. It was hardly an exaggeration for the Bolshevik historian M.N.Pokrovsky to write, 'You will not find in Lenin a single purely theoretical work; each has a propaganda aspect.'[10]

Lenin believed in improvisation. But in order for this not to degenerate into simply the shifting impressions of the day, it had to be blended into a *general perspective* based on well thought-out theory. Practice without theory must lead to uncertainty and errors. On the other hand, to study marxism apart from the struggle is to divorce it from its mainspring – action – and to create useless bookworms. Practice is clarified by revolutionary theory, and theory is verified by practice. The marxist traditions are assimilated in the minds and blood of men only by struggle.

Theory is the generalization of the practice of the past. Hence, as Gramsci so well put it, 'ideas are not born of other ideas, philosophies of other philosophies; they are a continually renewed expression of real historical development'.[11] To adapt oneself to any new situation without losing one's own identity, one needs unity of theory and practice.

Lenin knew that no revolutionary organization can survive without a permanently creative ideological laboratory. He always tried to find an eventual political use for his research. But while he was actually engaged in it, he did not hesitate to take months at a time off from practical politics in order to immerse himself in the British Museum or the Bibliothèque Nationale.*

The programme of the party – its basic principles – takes as a point of departure the historical potentialities of the working class, i.e. it is derived from the material conditions of society in general, and from the position of the working class within it in particular. Strategy and tactics, however, take as their point of departure not the material world as such, but the consciousness of the workers. If consciousness – what Marx called the ideological superstructure – reflected the material base directly, then tactics and strategy could be derived directly from the party programme. However, the derivation is in fact indirect, complicated, influenced by the traditions and experience of the workers, including the activities of the party itself. A revolutionary party in principle opposes the wages system, but tactically it is far from indifferent to the struggle of the workers for higher wages.

A revolutionary leadership needs not only an understanding of the struggle as a whole, but the capacity to put forward the right slogans at every turning point. These do not derive simply from the party programme, but must fit the circumstances, above all the moods and feelings of the masses, so that they can be used to lead the workers forward. Slogans must be appropriate not only to the general direction of the revolutionary movement, but also to the level of consciousness of the masses. Only through the *application* of the

---

* In his reminiscences M.N.Pokrovsky relates how the Bolsheviks sent a delegation of which Pokrovsky himself was a member to Lenin in 1908 asking him to give up his philosophical studies and return to practical politics. Lenin, however, refused.[12]

general line of the party does its real value become manifest. The organic unity of general theory and particular tactics was at the heart of Lenin's struggle and work style.

> Without a programme a party cannot be an integral political organism capable of pursuing its line whatever turn events may take. Without a tactical line based on an appraisal of the current political situation and providing explicit answers to the 'vexed problems' of our times, we might have a circle of theoreticians, but not a functioning political entity.[13]

The only way to verify the correctness of a strategic plan, or a tactic, is by the test of practice, by checking it against the experience of the actual development of the class struggle:

> decisions made with regard to tactics must be *verified* as often as possible in the light of new political events. Such verification is necessary from the standpoint of both theory and practice: from the standpoint of theory in order to ascertain in fact whether the decisions taken have been correct, and what amendments to these decisions subsequent political events make necessary; from the standpoint of practice in order to learn how to use the decisions as a proper guide, to learn to consider them as directives for practical application.[14]

Trotsky expressed the same idea very aptly when he said, 'the fundamental Bolshevist prejudice consists precisely in the idea that one can only learn to ride when one is sitting firmly on a horse'.[15] Only in the struggle itself can one learn strategy and tactics. Again and again Lenin quoted Napoleon saying: 'On s'engage et puis . . . on voit.' Rendered freely this means 'First engage in a serious battle, and then see what happens.'

In war, and especially in the class war in a revolutionary period, the unknowns, not only in the enemy camp, but also in one's own, are so numerous that sober analysis has to be accompanied by daring improvisation based largely on intuition, on an active, creative imagination.

Marxism differs from all other socialist theories in the remarkable way it combines complete scientific sobriety in the analysis of the objective state of affairs and the objective course of evolution, with the most emphatic recognition of the importance of the revolutionary energy, revolutionary creative genius and revolutionary initiative of the masses – and also, of course, of individuals, groups, organizations and parties that are able to discover an active contact with one or another class.[16]

Lenin constantly stressed that it was necessary to be aware of the thoughts and sentiments of the masses, and he himself excelled in this. As Trotsky said, 'The art of revolutionary leadership in its most critical moments consists nine-tenths of knowing how to sense the mood of the masses. An unexcelled ability to detect the mood of the masses was Lenin's greatest power.'[17]

Only in the struggle itself can the party find out what the masses really think and are able to accomplish. Marxism accepts neither mechanistic determinism, fatalism, nor voluntaristic self-will. Its basis is materialistic dialectics and the principle that the masses discover their own abilities through action. There is nothing in common between Lenin's realism, and pedestrian, passive *Realpolitik*. Against the latter must be counterposed, as Lenin put it, 'the revolutionary dialectics of marxist realism, which emphasize the urgent tasks of the advanced class, and discover in the existing state of things those elements that will lead to its overthrow'.[18] He was well aware that a sober assessment of the real forces is necessary, and that the revolutionary party itself is a central factor in the balance of forces. The boldness of the party gives confidence to the workers, while irresoluteness may lead the masses into passivity and moods of depression. The only way to determine the balance of forces, and the willingness of the masses to struggle, is by action in which the party gives a lead.

As the revolutionary struggle develops and changes, one must beware of clinging to tactics which have outlasted their usefulness. The most dangerous, devastating mistake a revolutionary leader can commit is to become a captive of those formulae of his that were appropriate yesterday, but do not fit today's different balance of forces. Too often it happens that, when history takes a sharp turn, even progressive parties are for a time unable to adapt themselves to the new situation and repeat slogans which were formerly correct but have now lost all meaning – losing it as 'suddenly' as the sharp turn in history was 'sudden'.

In revolutionary life, the question of timing is crucial. One must determine as exactly as possible the pace at which the revolution is developing. Without this no realistic tactics are possible. In fact, one's perspectives regarding the tempo of events will never be absolutely accurate, and one will have to introduce, as quickly as possible, the necessary correction in timing.

For the tactics and strategy of the party to fit its general principles, they must be clear and straightforward. For the masses to understand the politics of the revolutionary party they must not be overwhelmed by detail, distracting attention from the central core of party policy. The policy of the party must be expressed in a small number of simple and clear slogans. 'A straight policy is the best policy. A policy based on principles is the most practical policy.'[19]

> in the final analysis broad, principled politics are the only real, practical politics . . . anybody who tackles the partial problems without having previously settled general problems, will inevitably and at every step 'come up against' those general problems without himself realizing it. To come up against them blindly in every individual case means to doom one's politics to the worst vacillation and lack of principle.[20]

> A line of conduct can *and should* be grounded in theory, in historical references, in an analysis of the entire political situation, etc. But in all these discussions the party of a class engaged in a struggle should never lose sight of the need for absolutely clear answers – *which do not permit of a double interpretation* – to concrete questions of our political conduct: 'yes' or 'no'? Should this or that be done right now, at the given moment, or should it not be done?[21]

One must calculate the relation of forces extremely

soberly and then, once a decision has been taken, act decisively. 'There is no man more faint-hearted than I am, when I am working out a military plan', wrote Napoleon to General Berthier. 'I exaggerate all dangers and all possible misfortunes . . . When my decision is taken everything is forgotten except what can assure its success.'

After quoting this statement, Trotsky comments,

> Except for the pose involved in the inappropriate word faint-hearted, the essence of this thought applies perfectly to Lenin. In deciding a problem of strategy he began by clothing the enemy with his own resolution and far-sightedness. The tactical mistakes of Lenin were for the most part by-products of his strategic power.[22]

The formulation of a bold design on the basis of the least favourable premises was characteristic of Lenin.

'Seizing the Key Link'

Lenin teaches us that in the complicated chain of political action one must always identify the central link at the moment in question, in order to seize it and give direction to the whole chain.

> *Every* question 'runs in a vicious circle' because political life as a whole is an endless chain consisting of an infinite number of links. The whole art of politics lies in finding and taking as firm a grip as we can of the link that is least likely to be struck from our hands, the one that is most important at the given moment, the one that most of all guarantees its possessor the possession of the whole chain.[23]

He often returned to this metaphor and in practice always obeyed the rule which it illustrated; during the most critical periods he was able to set aside all the secondary factors, and grasp the most central one. He brushed aside anything that could directly or indirectly divert him from the main issue. As Trotsky aptly put it,

> when the critical hurdle was happily cleared, Lenin would still now and again exclaim : 'And yet we quite forgot to do this or that . . .' Or 'we missed an opportunity because we were so preoccupied by the main thing . . .' Someone would

answer him: 'But this question had been posed, and this proposal had been made, only you did not want to hear anything!'

'Didn't I? Impossible!' he would say, 'and I don't remember a thing.'

At that point he would burst out laughing, with malicious laughter in which there was an admission of 'guilt'; and he would make a characteristic gesture of raising his arm and moving it helplessly down, as if resigned: well, one cannot do everything. This 'shortcoming' of his was only the obverse side of his talent to mobilize, to the utmost degree, all his inner forces. Precisely this talent made of him the greatest revolutionary in history.[24]

Again Trotsky writes:

Vladimir Ilyich was often criticized by many comrades, and by myself among them, for seemingly not paying attention to secondary matters and certain side issues. I should think that in times of 'normal' slow development this might have been a defect in a political leader; but in this lay Comrade Lenin's pre-eminence as the leader of a new epoch, in which all that is inessential, all that is incidental and secondary recedes into the background, becomes overshadowed, and what remains is only the basic irreconcilable class antagonism in the acute form of civil war. It was Lenin's peculiar gift, which he possessed to the highest degree, that with his intense revolutionary gaze, he could see and point out to others what was most important, most necessary, and most essential. Those comrades who, like myself, were given the chance to observe Lenin's activity and the working of his mind at close quarters, could not help but enthusiastically admire – yes, I repeat, enthusiastically admire – the perspicacity, the acuteness of his thought which rejected all that was external, accidental, superficial, and reached to the heart of the matter and grasped the essential methods of action.[25]

He did commit tactical errors – largely because of his concentration on the essential link and because of his long absences from the scene of action. But the other side of the coin was his magnificent strategic grasp. Party strategy was ruthlessly defined from a distance, even if tactical errors of judgement were involved.

In principle Lenin was right when he insisted on 'bending the stick', one day in one direction, another in the opposite. If all aspects of the workers' movement had been equally developed, if balanced growth had been the rule, then 'stick bending' would have a deleterious effect on the movement. But in real life the law of uneven development dominates. One aspect of the movement is decisive at any particular time. The key obstacle to advance may be a lack of party cadres, or, on the contrary, the conservatism of the party cadres may cause them to lag behind the advanced section of the class. Perfect synchronization of all elements would obviate the need for 'bending sticks', but would also render a revolutionary party or a revolutionary leadership superfluous.

Intuition and Courage

The most sober evaluation of the objective situation does not in itself suffice to develop a revolutionary strategy and tactics. Above all a revolutionary leader must be endowed with a very keen intuitive sense.

In a revolutionary situation, where so much is unknown and so much is open to chance, to complications, a strong will is not enough. What is necessary is the capacity to grasp the whole situation quickly, so as to be able to distinguish the essential from the inessential, to fill in the missing parts of the picture. Every revolution is an equation with many unknowns. Hence a revolutionary leader has to be endowed with a highly realistic imagination.

Apart from a very short interruption in 1905, Lenin spent the fifteen years preceding the revolution abroad. His feeling for reality, his grasp of the mood of the workers, did not diminish over time, but increased. His realistic imagination was rooted in deep theoretical understanding, a good memory, and creative thinking. It was nourished by occasional meetings with individuals who came to see him in exile.

His revolutionary intuition was uncanny. Here is just one example, showing how he managed to visualize a whole social-political situation from a single sentence spoken by a worker, which would probably have passed unnoticed by anyone else.

> After the July days, thanks to the extremely solicitous attention with which the Kerensky government honoured me, I was obliged to go underground ... In a small working-class house in a remote working-class suburb of Petrograd, dinner is being served. The hostess puts bread on the table. The host says: 'Look what fine bread. "They" dare not give us bad bread now. And we had almost given up even thinking that we'd ever get good bread in Petrograd again.'
> I was amazed at this class appraisal of the July days. My thoughts had been revolving around the political significance of those events, weighing the role they played in the general course of events, analysing the situation that caused this zigzag in history and the situation it would create, and how we ought to change our slogans and alter our Party apparatus to adapt it to the changed situation. As for bread, I who had not known want, did not give it a thought. I took bread for granted ...
> This member of the oppressed class, however, even though one of the well paid and quite intelligent workers, takes the bull by the horns with that astonishing simplicity and straightforwardness, with that firm determination and amazing clarity of outlook from which we intellectuals are so remote as the stars in the sky. The whole world is divided into two camps: 'us', the working people, and 'them', the exploiters. Not a shadow of embarrassment over what had taken place; it was just one of the battles in the long struggle between labour and capital. When you fell trees, chips fly.
> 'What a painful thing is the "exceptionally complicated situation" created by the revolution,' that's how the bourgeois intellectual thinks and feels.
> 'We squeezed "them" a bit; "they" don't dare to lord it over us as they did before. We'll squeeze again – and chuck them out altogether,' that's how the worker thinks and feels.[26]

Krupskaya was absolutely right when she wrote: 'Ilyich always had a kind of special instinct – a profound comprehension as to what the working class was experiencing at a given moment.'[27] Intuition is especially vital in grasping the feelings of the masses at the most dramatic points of history, and Lenin excelled in this. 'The ability to think and feel for and with the masses was characteristic of him to the highest degree, especially at the great political turning points.'[28]

Once the decision on certain tactics has been taken, the revolutionary leader must show no hesitation; he must have supreme courage. In this Lenin was certainly not lacking; M.N.Pokrovsky well describes this characteristic quality.

Now, when we are looking into the past, it seems to me that one of the basic characteristics of Lenin was his tremendous political courage. Political courage is not the same as bravery and defiance of danger. Among revolutionaries there has been no lack of brave people unafraid of the rope and the gallows or of Siberia. But these people were afraid of taking upon themselves the burden of great political decisions. It was always clear that Lenin never feared to take upon himself the responsibility for decisions, no matter how weighty. In this respect he would never shrink from any risk and took responsibility for moves which involved not only his person and the fate of his party, but also the fate of the whole country and, to a certain degree, the fate of the world revolution. This was so peculiar a phenomenon that he always had to begin his action with a very small group of people, because only very few were bold enough to follow him right from the start.[29]

Many a 'marxist' has tried to avoid the obligation to reach important decisions by giving marxism a fatalistic nature. This was characteristic of the Mensheviks. In every crisis they showed doubt, hesitation and fear. A revolution, however, is the most ruthless method of solving social questions. And indecisiveness is the worst possible condition at a time of revolution. Lenin was the most consistent of revolutionaries. He was supreme in his boldness of decision, in his readiness to assume responsibility for the greatest actions.

The Dream and the Reality

To carry out revolutionary strategy and tactics one must be not only a realist, but also a dreamer. Many writers describe Lenin as a realist and not a romantic, which is to do him an injustice. One cannot be a revolutionary without the inspiration of a great dream.

'There are rifts and rifts,' wrote Pisarev of the rift between dreams and reality. 'My dream may run ahead of the natural

march of events or may fly off at a tangent in a direction in which no natural march of events will ever proceed. In the first case my dream will not cause any harm; it may even support and augment the energy of the working men . . . There is nothing in such dreams that would distort or paralyse labour-power. On the contrary, if man were completely deprived of the ability to dream in this way, if he could not from time to time run ahead and mentally conceive, in an entire and completed picture, the product to which his hands are only just beginning to lend shape, then I cannot at all imagine what stimulus there would be to induce man to undertake and complete extensive and strenuous work in the sphere of art, science, and practical endeavour . . . The rift between dreams and reality causes no harm if only the person dreaming believes seriously in his dream, if he attentively observes life, compares his observations with his castles in the air, and if, generally speaking, he works conscientiously for the achievement of his fantasies. If there is some connection between dreams and life then all is well.'
Of this kind of dreaming there is unfortunately too little in our movement. And the people most responsible for this are those who boast their sober views, their 'closeness' to the 'concrete'.[30]

Lenin subordinated his own romantic streak to the need for action. He despised the unworldliness of the Russian intelligentsia. Again and again he referred contemptuously to Oblomov, the hero of the famous novel of the same name by Goncharov, a 'superfluous man', always dreaming of great deeds, but too slothful and enervated to carry them out.

Ferdinand Lassalle expressed the fundamental requirement of revolutionary politics well. 'Every great action begins with a statement of what is.' Lenin often used to repeat in English, 'Facts are stubborn things.' 'Marxism', he said, 'takes its stand on the facts, and not on possibilities. A marxist must, as the foundation of his policy, put *only* precisely and unquestionably demonstrated facts.'[31] He was always searching for the bridge from the actual to the possible. He was not afraid to look straight into the abyss between the greatness of the tasks facing the movement, and the *actual* poverty of the same movement. His feet were on the ground, but his head was in the sky.

The Party as a School of Strategy and Tactics

Questions of revolutionary strategy and tactics held a meaning for Lenin only if the possibility of implementing them, through the revolutionary party, was a real one. He saw the party as a school for strategy and tactics, a combat organization for the conquest of power by the working class.

How can the revolutionary leadership learn from the masses and know what they think and feel, unless it forms an integral part of these masses, listening to them at their workplaces, in the streets, in their homes, in their eating places? To teach the masses, the leadership must learn from them. This Lenin believed and practised all his life.

The party must not lag behind the advanced section of the class. But it must not be so far ahead as to be out of reach. It must stand at its head and be rooted in it:

> to be successful, all serious revolutionary work requires that the idea that revolutionaries are capable of playing the part only of the vanguard of the truly virile and advanced class must be understood and translated into action. A vanguard performs its task as vanguard only when it is able to avoid being isolated from the mass of the people it leads and is able really to lead the whole mass forward.[32]

The need for a revolutionary party, as we have already pointed out, is a reflection of the unevenness of consciousness in the working class. At the same time, however, the party exists in order to hasten the overcoming of this unevenness, by raising consciousness to the highest possible level. Adaptation to the average, or even to the lowest level of consciousness of the class, is in the nature of opportunism. Organizational independence and isolation from the most advanced section of the proletariat, on the other hand, is the road to sectarianism. Raising the advanced section to the highest possible level under the prevailing circumstances – this is the role of the really revolutionary party.

To learn from the masses the party must also be able to learn from its own mistakes, to be very self-critical.

A political party's attitude towards its own mistakes is one of the most important and surest ways of judging how earnest the party is and how it fulfils *in practice* its obligations towards its *class* and the *working people*. Frankly acknowledging a mistake, ascertaining the reasons for it, and thrashing out the means of its rectification – that is the hallmark of a serious party; that is how it should perform its duties, and how it should educate and train its *class*, and then the *masses*.[33]

The fighting party of the advanced class need not fear mistakes. What it should fear is persistence in a mistake, refusal to admit and correct a mistake out of a false sense of shame.[34]

The masses must be involved in correcting party mistakes. Thus on 21 January 1905 Lenin wrote:

We Social Democrats resort to secrecy from the Tsar and his bloodhounds while taking pains that the people should know everything about our party, about the shades of opinion within it, about the development of its programme and policy, that they should even know what this or that Party Congress delegate said at the Congress in question.[35]

Open debate is even more vital and essential during a period of direct revolutionary struggle, as Lenin wrote in a leaflet on 25-26 April 1906.

In a revolutionary epoch like the present, all theoretical errors and tactical deviations of the party are most ruthlessly criticized by experience itself, which enlightens and educates the working class with unprecedented rapidity. At such a time, the duty of every Social Democrat is to strive to ensure that the ideological struggle within the party on questions of theory and tactics is conducted as openly, widely and freely as possible, but that on no account does it disturb or hamper the unity of revolutionary action of the Social Democratic proletariat.[36]

He urged repeatedly that debate should not be limited to inner party circles, but should be carried on publicly so that non-party people could follow it.

Our party's serious illness is the growing pains of a *mass* party. For there can be no mass party, no party of a class, without full clarity of essential shadings, without open struggle between various tendencies, without informing the *masses* as to which leaders and which organizations of the party are pursuing this or that line. Without this, a party worthy of the name cannot be built.[37]

Again,

Criticism within the limits of the *principles* of the party programme must be quite free (we remind the reader of what Plekhanov said on this subject at the second Congress of the RSDLP) not only at party meetings, but also at public meetings. Such criticism or such 'agitation' (for criticism is inseparable from agitation) cannot be prohibited.[38]

There is a dialectical relationship between democracy within the party and the party's roots in the class. Without a correct class policy and a party composed of proletarians, there is no possibility of healthy party democracy. Without a firm working-class base all talk of democracy and discipline in the party is meaningless verbiage. At the same time, without party democracy, without constant self-criticism, development of a correct class policy is impossible.

We have more than once already enunciated our theoretical views on the importance of discipline and on how this concept is to be understood in the party of the working class. We defined it as: *unity of action, freedom of discussion and criticism.* Only such discipline is worthy of the democratic party of the advanced class.[39]

the proletariat does not recognize unity of action without freedom to discuss and criticize.[40]

If democracy is essential in order to assimilate the experience of the struggle, centralism and discipline are necessary to lead the struggle. Firm organizational cohesion makes it possible for the party to act, to take initiatives, to direct the action of the masses. A party that is not confident in itself cannot win the confidence of the masses. Without a strong party leadership, having the power to act promptly and direct the activities of the members, a revolutionary party cannot exist. The party is a centralist organization which leads a determined struggle for power. As such it needs iron discipline in action.

Clausewitz on the Art of War

At the beginning of this chapter we mentioned that Lenin's concept of strategy and tactics was profoundly influenced by the writings of Clausewitz. One has only to quote from Clausewitz to perceive a startling similarity in formulation and attitude.

Clausewitz begins his book *On War* by arguing that there is a radical difference between the abstract concept of war and actual concrete wars. Real war is different from abstract war, says Clausewitz, because idealized conditions are never realized. Events are governed not only by simple causality, but by the intersection of different chains of causes and effects; chance plays a great role; psychological factors are important determinants of decisions taken by men, and so on. Clausewitz classifies all these circumstances under the heading 'friction', an obvious allusion to the analogous concept in physics which explains the discrepancy between real and idealized mechanical processes. Only by taking 'friction' into account can one grasp the relation between the real war and the abstract one, between experience and theory. This is the source of the 'difference between the reality and the conception' of war, and 'the influence of particular circumstances'.[41]

In order to bring the concept into line with the real world one needs to 'fall back upon the corresponding results of experience; for in the same way as many plants only bear fruit when they do not shoot too high, so in the practical arts the theoretical leaves and flowers must not be made to sprout too far, but kept near to experience, which is their proper soil'.[42]

The art of war depends on many sciences – physics, geography, psychology, etc. – but it is nevertheless an *art*. The great war leader is one who manages to learn how to use these sciences for the specific task of crushing the enemy. Because of the complexity of war, the commander needs, above all, experience and strong will-power on the one hand, and intuition and imagination on the other.

every war is rich in particular facts, while at the same time each is an unexplored sea, full of rocks which the general may have a suspicion of, but which he has never seen with his eye, and round which, moreover, he must steer in the night. If a contrary wind also springs up, that is, if any great accidental event declares itself adverse to him, then the most consummate skill, presence of mind, and energy are required ... The knowledge of this friction is a chief part of that so often talked of, experience in war, which is required in a good general. Certainly he is not the best general in whose mind it assumes the greatest dimensions, who is most over-awed by it ... but a general must be aware of it that he may overcome it, where that is possible, and that may not expect a degree of precision in results which is impossible on account of this very friction. Besides, it can never be learnt theoretically; and if it could, there would still be wanting that experience of judgement which is called tact.[43]

Clausewitz formulated very well the relation between tactics and strategy.

Strategy is the employment of the battle to gain the end of the war; it must therefore give an aim to the whole military action, which must be in accordance with the object of the war; in other words, strategy forms the plan of the war; and to this end it links together the series of acts which are to lead to the final decision, that is to say, it makes the plans for the separate campaigns and regulates the combats to be fought in each. As these are all things which to a great extent can only be determined on conjectures some of which turn out incorrect, while a number of other arrangements pertaining to details cannot be made at all beforehand, it follows, as a matter of course, that strategy must go with the army to the field in order to arrange particulars on the spot, and to make the modifications in the general plan which incessantly become necessary in war. Strategy can therefore never take its hand from the work for a moment.[44]

Tactics must be subordinated to strategy. A successful series of tactical moves may however necessitate a change in strategy.

... the great point is to keep the overruling relations of both parties in view. Out of them a certain centre of gravity, a centre of power and movement, will form itself, on which everything depends; and against this centre of gravity of the enemy, the concentrated blow of all the forces must be directed.

The little always depends on the great, the unimportant on the important, and the accidental on the essential. This must guide our view.[45]

... the superiority at the decisive point is a matter of capital importance and ... this subject, in the generality of cases, is decidedly the most important of all.[46]

Clausewitz's undogmatic mind made it possible for him to grasp clearly the relationship between the idealized model and the reality which it is intended to represent. He understood the organic relations between theory and practice in the development of both. He underlined the connection between the sciences whose adaptation is necessary for successful leadership in war, and the art of war. Above all he understood the great importance of the genius of intuition supported by a clear scientific conceptual notion.

Clausewitz's ideas influenced Friedrich Engels' military writings, and both Clausewitz and Engels greatly influenced Lenin. Lenin's genius is that these concepts of tactics and strategy, with their complex integration of experience, science, and art, not only became part of his thinking but also entered into his blood. Instinctively, quickly, Lenin developed the most effective strategy and tactics and his willpower matched his intellect.

His powers as a strategist and tactician blossomed in the 1905 revolution and demonstrated their complete mastery twelve years later in the victory of the October revolution of 1917.

15
Semi-Unity with the Mensheviks

During the stormy months of the 1905 revolution, the Menshevik Party was disorganized and in a state of flux. It was composed mainly of centrist elements, and intoxicated by the events, moved on the whole very much to the left, abandoning its allegiance to the liberals and making common cause with the Bolsheviks:

> many Mensheviks began to lose faith in the bourgeois revolution. They dismissed the bourgeois either as treacherous and counter-revolutionary or as virtually non-existent, and like the Bolsheviks they prepared for a seizure of power and the establishment of a revolutionary provisional government. As Dan wrote to Kautsky: '*Man lebt hier wie im Taumel, die revolutionäre Luft wirkt wie Wein*' (One lives here as if in delirium, revolutionary air has an effect like wine.)[1]

The editors of the Menshevik paper *Nachalo* were Trotsky and Parvus. Relations between the paper and the Bolshevik *Novaya Zhizn*, according to Trotsky, were

> most friendly. They engaged in no polemics against each other. 'The first number of the *Nachalo* has come out,' wrote the Bolshevik *Novaya Zhizn*. 'We welcome a comrade in the struggle. The first issue is notable for the brilliant description of the October strike written by Comrade Trotsky.' People don't write in this way when they are fighting with each other. But there was no fighting. On the contrary, the papers defended each other against bourgeois criticism. The *Novaya Zhizn*, even after the arrival of Lenin, came out with a defence of my articles on the permanent revolution. Both newspapers, as well as the two factions, followed the line of the restoration of party unity. The Central Committee of the Bolsheviks, with Lenin participating, passed a unanimous resolution to the effect that the split was merely the result of the conditions of foreign exile, and the events of the revolution had deprived the factional struggle of any reasonable

grounds. I defended the same line in the *Nachalo*, with only a passive resistance from Martov.[2]

Years later, Lenin could still write, 'Remember *Nachalo* . . . Remember articles in the spirit of "Witte Is the Agent of the Bourse, Struve Is the Agent of Witte". Those were excellent articles! And those were excellent times – we did not then disagree with the Mensheviks in our assessment of the Cadets.'[3] The right-wing Menshevik Chervanin ruefully remembered 1905-06: 'the Mensheviks had fallen under the influence of the revolutionary intoxication of the Bolsheviks, by taking part in the November strike in St Petersburg, the forcible introduction of the eight-hour day and the boycott of the first Duma'.[4]

The Contemporary Situation and the Possible Future

In Moscow the Mensheviks were very much to the fore in the revolutionary workers' struggle. At a meeting of the Moscow Soviet on 6 December they enthusiastically supported a resolution for a general strike and armed uprising.[5] A few days later they issued leaflets in support of the armed uprising.[6] This is how one Menshevik leader, Martynov, summed up their behaviour in 1905, 'We said to ourselves then: *Le vin est tiré, il faut le boire* – Since the wine is poured, it will have to be drunk. At decisive moments one is forced to act firmly, with no time to analyze.' But the Mensheviks were influenced by events, rather than trying to direct them. 'The difference, however', continued this Menshevik leader, 'was that we considered our situation as one forced upon us, while the Bolsheviks strove for it and regarded it as natural.'[7] A few months later Martynov was already recanting the 'madness' of 1905! Martov's reaction was characteristic. In February 1906 he complained in a letter to Axelrod, 'For two months now . . . I have not been able to finish any of the writing I have started. It is either neurasthenia or mental fatigue – but I cannot gather my thoughts together.' 'Martov did not know what to call his illness in 1906', Trotsky wrote after 1917, when this letter became public, 'but it has a quite definite name : Menshevism', and he adds, 'In an epoch of revolution, opportunism means, first of all, vacillation and inability "to gather one's thought".'[8]

Lenin hoped that the pressure of revolutionary events would continue to move the Mensheviks leftwards. From February 1905 onwards he called for unity between Bolsheviks and Mensheviks. In November he said :

> It is no secret to anyone that the vast majority of Social Democratic workers are exceedingly dissatisfied with the split in the Party and are demanding unity. It is no secret to anyone that the split has caused a certain cooling-off among Social Democratic workers (or workers ready to become Social Democrats) towards the Social Democratic Party.
>
> The workers have lost almost all hope that the party 'chiefs' will unite of themselves. The need for unity was formally recognized both by the third Congress of the RSDLP and by the Menshevik conference held last May. Six months have passed since then, but the cause of unity has made hardly any progress. No wonder the workers are beginning to show signs of impatience.[9]

In fact, quite independently of central policy, and on their own initiative, Bolshevik and Menshevik branches had been combining together all over Russia. In the summer of 1905 there was a spate of mergers between Bolshevik and Menshevik committees. Thus Piatnitsky recalls how unity between the Bolsheviks and the Mensheviks was brought about in Odessa in November 1905, some six months before the official unification of the two parties on a national scale.

> About this time the Bolshevik Leva (Vladimirov), an agent of the Central Committee, came from St Petersburg with the proposal of uniting with the Mensheviks at all costs, without waiting for the union of the two centres above. He was supported by the Bolshevik Baron (Edward Essen), who had arrived at Odessa before the pogrom. Their proposal met with a warm response from among the party members, the Mensheviks as well as the Bolsheviks. That was easy to understand: that our few available forces were weak and scattered had become apparent to every party member dur-

ing the pogrom. At the general meeting of the members of the Odessa organization, where Comrade Gusev read a report on the form our organization should take after the Manifesto of 17 October, Comrades Leva and Baron spoke for immediate union with the Mensheviks. The committee did not object to union, but was definitely against the method of union from below. The Odessa Committee was part of the Bolshevik Party, at the head of which stood the Central Committee and the Central Organ elected at the third Party Congress. How, in that case, could Odessa unite with the Mensheviks without the knowledge and consent of the Central Committee of our party? Baron and Leva, on the other hand, stood for union without the consent of the Central Committee, in order to bring pressure to bear from below. It was obvious to the committee that the proposal of union would be passed by a great majority at the party meetings of both the Bolsheviks and Mensheviks, for wherever the advocates of immediate unity spoke they were supported almost unanimously. Therefore the Bolshevik committee was forced to work out the terms of the union which they themselves were against.[10]

Between 23 April and 8 May 1906 a 'Unification' Congress was held in Stockholm. The 'united' party which resulted included not only the Bolsheviks and Mensheviks (altogether some 70,000 members), but also the Jewish Bund (33,000 members), the Polish Social Democrats, under Rosa Luxemburg's leadership (28,000 members) and the Lettish Social Democrats (13,000 members).

In April 1906, Lenin argued that the differences between the Mensheviks and the Bolsheviks were becoming smaller in practice and that unity between them was more necessary than ever.

Indeed, if we examine the question in the light of the deviations that the Social Democratic movement has made from its ordinary, 'normal' course, we shall see that even in this respect there was *more* not less solidarity and ideological integrity among the Social Democrats in the period of 'revolutionary whirlwind' than there was before it. The tactics adopted in the period of 'whirlwind' did not further estrange the two wings of the Social Democratic Party, but brought them closer together. Former disagreements gave way to unity of opinion on the question of armed uprising. Social Democrats of both factions were active in the Soviet of Workers' Deputies, these peculiar instruments of embryonic revolutionary authority; they drew soldiers and peasants into these Soviets, they issued revolutionary manifestos jointly with the petty-bourgeois revolutionary parties. Old controversies of the pre-revolutionary period gave way to unanimity on practical questions. The upsurge of the revolutionary tide pushed aside disagreements, compelling Social Democrats to adopt militant tactics; it swept the question of the Duma into the background and put the question of insurrection on the order of the day; and it brought closer together the Social Democrats and revolutionary bourgeois democrats in carrying out immediate tasks. In *Severny Golos*, the Mensheviks, jointly with the Bolsheviks, called for a general strike and insurrection; and they called upon the workers to continue this struggle until they had captured power. The revolutionary situation itself suggested practical slogans. There were arguments only over matters of detail in the appraisal of events: for example, *Nachalo* regarded the Soviets of Workers' Deputies as organs of revolutionary local self-government, while *Novaya Zhizn* regarded them as embryonic organs of state power that united the proletariat with the revolutionary democrats.

Nachalo inclined towards the dictatorship of the proletariat. *Novaya Zhizn* advocated the democratic dictatorship of the proletariat and the peasantry. But have not disagreements of this kind been observed at every stage of development of every socialist party in Europe?[11]

Lenin, however, was not deceived into thinking that the Mensheviks could be relied on completely, and did not wish to dissolve his faction in the united party. On the eve of the 'Unification' Congress he explained to Lunacharsky, 'If we have a majority in the Central Committee we will demand the strictest discipline. We will insist that the Mensheviks submit to party unity. So much the worse for them if their petty-bourgeois nature will not allow them to go along with us. Let them assume responsibility for splitting the party.'

'But what if we remain in the minority?' asked Lunacharsky, 'Shall we be forced to submit to them?'

Lenin smiled and replied: 'We won't permit the idea of

unity to tie a noose round our necks and we shall under no circumstances permit the Mensheviks to lead us by the rope.'[12]

Lenin did believe that the pressure of events would ensure that the Mensheviks were pushed leftwards. He persisted in this belief even when, at the end of 1906, they entered into an election alliance with the Cadets, a move which he strongly condemned. Thus he wrote in November 1906,

> Does the sanction by Social Democrats of blocs with the Cadets necessitate a complete severance of organizational relations, i.e. a split? We think *not*, and all Bolsheviks think the same way. In the first place the Mensheviks are only just setting their feet, unsteadily and uncertainly, on the path of practical opportunism *en grand* . . . Secondly – and this is far more important – the objective conditions of the proletarian struggle in Russia today irresistibly provoke *definite* and decisive steps. Whether the tide of revolution rises very high (as we expected) or completely subsides (as some Social Democrats think it will, though they are afraid to say so), in *either* case the tactics of blocs with the Cadets will inevitably be scattered to the winds, and that in the not very distant future. Therefore, our *duty* at the present time is to avoid intellectualist hysteria and preserve party unity, trusting to the staunchness and sound class instinct of the revolutionary proletariat.[13]

He believed that 'The Menshevik comrades will . . . go through the purgatory of blocs with the bourgeois opportunists and return to revolutionary Social Democracy'.[14]

Meanwhile, the Tammerfors conference of the party (3-7 November 1906) decided, under Menshevik influence, to enter an electoral bloc with the Cadets. Lenin's reaction was that local party organizations should be free to oppose this in their own areas. 'In the present election campaign, the decision of the Mensheviks and the Central Committee in favour of blocs is not binding in practice on the local organizations, and does not commit the party as a whole to these shameful tactics of blocs with the Cadets.'[15]

> All the delegates at the conference agreed that its decisions were *not binding* and committed nobody in any way, for a conference is an advisory, not a deciding body. Its delegates were not democratically elected, but were chosen by the

Central Committee from local organizations selected by it, and in a number which it specified.[16]

Of the decisions he said, 'Within what limits are they binding in regard to this particular question? Obviously, within the limits of the decisions of the Congress and within the limits of the autonomy of the local party organizations that is recognized by the Congress.'[17]

What had happened to the democratic centralism so dear to Lenin? For years he had argued for the subordination of the lower organs of the party to the higher, and against the federal concept of the party. In *One Step Forward, Two Steps Back*, written in February-May 1904, he had said that 'the undoubted tendency to defend *autonomism against centralism*, . . . is a fundamental characteristic of opportunism in matters of organization'.[18]

For Lenin, however, organizational methods were totally subordinate to political ends, and he was prepared to propose rules of organization for the united party in 1906 quite different from those he had hitherto put forward. Quite unashamedly he explained shortly afterwards:

> The rules of our party very definitely establish the democratic organization of the party. The whole organization is built from below upwards, on an elective basis. The party rules declare that the local organizations are independent (autonomous) in their local activities. According to the rules, the Central Committee co-ordinates and directs all the work of the party. Hence it is clear that it has no right to interfere in determining the *composition* of local organizations. Since the organization is built from below upwards, interference in its composition from above would be a flagrant breach of democracy and of the party rules.[19]

He gave a new twist to the concept of party discipline.

> *After* the competent bodies have decided, *all* of us, as members of the party, must *act as one man*. A Bolshevik in Odessa must cast into the ballot box a ballot paper bearing a Cadet's name even if it sickens him. And a Menshevik in Moscow must cast into the ballot box a ballot paper bearing only the names of Social Democrats, even if his soul is yearning for the Cadets.[20]

A couple of months later, in January 1907, Lenin went so far as to argue for the institution of a *referendum* of all party members on the issues facing the party – certainly a suggestion which ran counter to the whole idea of democratic centralism.

> In order that the settlement of a question may be really democratic, it is not enough to call together the elected representatives of the organization. It is necessary that *all* the members of the organization, in electing their representatives, should at the same time *independently and each for himself*, express their opinion on the point at issue before the whole organization.[21]

Although he agreed that it would be impossible to decide all political questions by referendum, 'the most important questions, and especially those which are directly connected with some definite action by the *masses themselves*, must, for the sake of democracy, be settled not only by sending representatives, but also by canvassing the opinion of all members of the party'.[22]

To sum up, during the year of the revolution, the Mensheviks were largely borne along on the wave of events, while different trends in Menshevism became differentiated from each other. On the right were people like Plekhanov, Axelrod and Martov, who were inclined towards the Cadets, and wedded to the concept of a bourgeois revolution led by the liberals. On the left stood people like Trotsky and Parvus, and Lenin hoped that processes would take place amongst the Mensheviks similar to those which many years later enabled the Communist International to be formed – the movement of large numbers of centrist elements to the left. He drew a distinction between the centrism of the Menshevik workers and the incurable professional centrism of many leaders. While standing firm against the Menshevik right, and against the convinced centrists, he still believed that the tightly knit group of hard-line Bolsheviks would be more effective in pulling over the centrist elements if they made up a faction in a united party than if they existed as a completely separate group.

16

Lenin Expels
the Ultra-Leftists

Lenin had difficulties to contend with within the Bolshevik group itself. The question of the boycott was not
shelved even after the second Duma elections, in which the
RSDLP participated fully. These elections resulted in a considerable success for the party: 65 Social Democratic deputies were elected, including 18 pro-Bolsheviks.[1]

However, on 3 June 1907 Prime Minister Stolypin dissolved the second Duma, and issued a new and highly unrepresentative electoral decree designed to rid the government of the opposition majority. The new regulations entitled the landowner curia to elect one elector for every 230
persons, the first urban curia one for every 1,000, the second
urban curia one for every 15,000, the peasant curia one for
every 60,000 and the worker curia one for every 125,000.
The landlords and the bourgeoisie elected 65 per cent of the
electors, the peasants 22 per cent (instead of the former 42
per cent) and workers 2 per cent (as against 4 per cent previously). The law disfranchised the indigenous population of
Asian Russia and the Turkic peoples of the Astrakhan and
Stavropol *gubernias*, and cut by half the proportion of representatives for the population of Poland and the Caucasus. All
non-Russian speakers were disfranchised. The result was
greatly to increase the proportion of members of the Duma
representing the landlords and the commercial and industrial
bourgeoisie, while sharply reducing the proportion of peasant
and workers' deputies, which was already small.

The boycott question, so recently resolved, was immediately revived. Local Bolshevik organizations voted over-
whelmingly in favour of resuming the boycott of the Duma.
At the party conference held in Finland in July 1907, eight of
the nine Bolshevik delegates led by Bogdanov voted to go

back to the policy of a boycott. Lenin voted with the Mensheviks, the Polish Social Democrats and the Bundists to defeat the boycott.

When elections were held under the new law in the autumn of 1907, the Social Democrats managed to win nineteen seats.

A section of the Bolsheviks formed themselves into a group known as Otzovists (Russian: *otzovisty* – recallists) after the 1907 party conference. In 1908 they gathered organizational strength and became a serious challenge to Lenin's position among the Bolsheviks. Contests were waged between Leninists and Otzovists for the allegiance of local organizations. Lenin retained control of the Moscow organization only by a very narrow margin. In May 1908, at a general city conference in Moscow, the Otzovists had 14 votes, while Lenin's supporters had 18.[2] The Regional Bureau of the Central Industrial Region was staunchly Otzovist.[3]

A less extreme form of opposition, called 'Ultimatism', prevailed in St Petersburg. Its adherents demanded that the Social Democratic Duma delegation should be served with an ultimatum demanding that it make its conduct more uncompromisingly radical. The Ultimatists remained in control of the St Petersburg Bolshevik organization until September 1909.[4]

Although the main issue dividing Lenin and the boycotters was whether Social Democrats should participate in the Duma elections and have representatives in the Duma, the latter also wanted to boycott the legal trade unions. If the trade unions registered with the police and conducted only legal activities, then the boycotters considered them to be of no value to the cause of revolution.[5]

The leaders of the Otzovists included some very prominent people. These were Bogdanov (Maximov), second-in-command of the Bolsheviks for a number of years; the top Bolshevik organizer, Krasin; the propagandists and authors Lunacharsky, Gorky and Bazarov; the historian M.N.Pokrovsky and the leader of the Bolshevik group in the Duma, Alexinsky. They accused Lenin of 'going over to the Menshevik point of view of parliamentarism at any price'.[6] At the all-Russian Conference of December 1908 the Menshevik Dan declared, 'Who does not know that the Bolsheviks are now accusing Lenin of betraying Bolshevism.'[7]

The collapse of the revolutionary movement created the conditions for the bacillus of ultra-leftism to multiply. The similarity between the psychology of the revolutionaries after 1905 and after the revolution of 1848 is almost uncanny. To quote Marx's words on Willich and Schapper, the Bogdanovs of his time :

> The violent suppression of a revolution leaves a powerful imprint upon the minds of those involved, especially if they are torn away from their homes and cast into exile. So that even people with steady personalities may lose their heads for a longer or shorter period. They can no longer keep pace with the march of events. They refuse to admit that history has changed direction. Hence that playing around with conspiracies and revolutions which compromises the cause they are serving no less than themselves; hence, too, the errors of Willich and Schapper.[8]

After the crushing of a revolution, what could be more psychologically satisfying than to pose as an immediate task the preparation for a new armed uprising, as Bogdanov did?

The terrible period of reaction caused many revolutionaries, especially those in exile, whose opportunities for concrete action were very few, to turn to abstract propaganda, whose verbal extremism was directly proportionate to its actual passivity. Devoid of practical revolutionary responsibility, this revolutionism was limited to self-glorification, and verbal intransigence became a façade for passive complacency.

When revolutionaries are isolated from any real support in the working class the conditions are ripe for ultra-leftism. The more isolated they are, the less they are open to correction from workers in struggle, and the greater the attraction of extreme slogans becomes. Since practically nobody is listening, why not use extreme revolutionary phrases? In a void, the pressure to adjust to a new situation is minimal.

The impatience of Bogdanov and his friends for quick results, whatever the objective obstacles, could have been corrected by the party – this is the democratic element in democratic centralism. Unfortunately, however, the party hardly existed, and could not correct its leaders' errors. Lenin accused them of rejecting 'petty work', especially the utilization of the parliamentary platform. In practice, their tactics amounted to waiting for 'great days'. They 'hinder the thing that is most important and most urgent, namely, to unite the workers in big and properly functioning organizations, capable of functioning well under *all* circumstances, permeated with the spirit of the class struggle, clearly realizing their aims, and trained in the true marxist world outlook'.[9]

New times demand new tactics, Lenin argued.

> During the revolution we learned to 'speak French' i.e. to introduce into the movement the greatest number of rousing slogans, to raise the energy of the direct struggle of the masses and extend its scope. Now, in this time of stagnation, reaction and disintegration, we must learn to 'speak German', i.e. to work slowly (there is nothing else for it), until things revive, systematically, steadily, advancing step by step, winning inch by inch. Whoever finds this work tedious, whoever does not understand the need for preserving and developing the revolutionary principles of Social Democratic tactics *in this phase too, on this bend of the road*, is taking the name of marxist in vain.[10]

The revolutionaries, he said,

> would do their duty even should it consist in an onerous, slow, humdrum daily grind, if history, after the issue of the struggle and after all opportunities for revolutionary action were exhausted, should condemn us to plod along the by-paths of an 'autocratic constitution' . . . In order to fulfil this obligation to the proletariat, it was necessary to take patiently in hand and re-educate those who had been attracted to Social Democracy by the days of liberty (there even appeared a type of 'Social Democrat of the days of liberty') who were attracted chiefly by the vehemence, revolutionary spirit and 'vividness' of our slogans, but, who, though militant enough to fight on revolutionary holidays, lacked the stamina for work-a-day struggle under the reign

of counter-revolution. Some of these elements were gradually drawn into proletarian activities and assimilated the marxist world outlook. The others only memorized a few slogans without grasping their meaning, could only repeat old phrases and were unable to adapt the old principles of revolutionary Social Democratic tactics to the changed conditions.[11]

There is no doubt that in the long period of reaction and the slow subsequent rise Bolshevism would have died if the ultra-left policies of Bogdanov and his allies had not been thrown overboard. In retrospect, many years later, Lenin could write in his book *Left Wing Communism: An Infantile Disorder* (1920),

> Bolshevism took shape, developed and became steeled in the long years of struggle against *petty-bourgeois revolutionism*, which smacks of anarchism or borrows something from the latter, and in all essential matters, does not measure up to the conditions and requirements of a consistently proletarian class struggle ... A petty bourgeois driven to frenzy by the horrors of capitalism is a social phenomenon which, like anarchism, is characteristic of all capitalist countries. The instability of such revolutionism, its barrenness, and its tendency to turn rapidly into submission, apathy, phantasms, and even a frenzied infatuation with one bourgeois fad or another – all this is common knowledge.[12]

He knew that to prepare for the great revolutionary battles to come, a revolutionary party must learn how to go through the period of reaction, *together with the masses*, in their front ranks, without dissolving into them, but also without detaching itself from them. This is also the period in which tough cadres can be trained and tempered. This training cannot, however, be done in a void, in isolation from the struggle, even if its scope and depth are very restricted indeed.

Bogdanov Expelled

Between 8 and 17 June 1909 Lenin convened a conference of the extended editorial board of the Bolshevik journal *Proletary* in his apartment in Paris. At his instigation, this conference set aside the old Bolshevik Centre, elected at the London Congress of 1907, and assumed the power to appoint, remove and legislate. It adopted a decision that 'Bolshevism, as a definite tendency in the RSDLP, has nothing in common with Otzovism or Ultimatism,' and expelled Bogdanov (Maximov), the guiding spirit of Otzovism, from the ranks of the Bolsheviks. Bogdanov vainly challenged the right of a new editorial conference to remove people appointed by the previous conference. His call for a new Bolshevik congress was ignored.

Lenin recognized the *formal* justice of Bogdanov's case. 'From the formal point of view the removal of Maximov was "irregular", say the removed ones, and "we do not recognize this removal", for Maximov was "elected by the Bolshevik section of the London Party Congress"!'[13] But, knowing that the Bolshevik faction was a mere shadow of its former self, and fearing that Bogdanov might well have won over the majority at a new conference, Lenin fought strenuously against the convening of a Bolshevik congress. He successfully moved a resolution that, as

calling special Bolshevik conferences and congresses would inevitably split the party from top to bottom and would deal an irreparable blow to the section which took the initiative in bringing about such a total split in the Russian Social Democratic Labour Party, the extended editorial board of *Proletary* resolves:

To warn all its supporters against agitating for a special Bolshevik Congress, as such agitation would lead objectively to a Party split and might radically impair the position which revolutionary Social Democracy has won in the party.[14]

The struggle against Bogdanov within the Bolshevik faction proved very difficult. Ultra-leftists are formalistic, sterile and divorced from reality – but how can one prove this without mass action? Lenin could not turn to active workers, to the living movement, to obtain support for his stand against Bogdanov, and thus was forced to use whatever alternative was to hand – in this case the artificial, unrepresentative meeting of an enlarged editorial board.

Among Lenin's supporters there were many who did not like the seemingly arbitrary measures taken against Bogdanov. Even Stalin, a most stalwart follower of Lenin at the time, rebuked him for this high-handed action and for splitting the Bolsheviks. While declaring his *political* solidarity with Lenin over the attitude to the Duma elections, he wrote, in an editorial of *Bakinsky Proletary* dated 27 August 1909,

> in view of the fact that, notwithstanding the above-mentioned disagreements, both sections of the editorial board agree on questions of major importance for the group (appraisal of the current situation, the role of the proletariat and of other classes in the revolution, etc.), the Baku Committee believes that the unity of the group, and hence cooperation between both sections of the editorial board are possible and necessary.
>
> In view of this, the Baku Committee disagrees with the organizational policy of the majority on the editorial board and protests against any 'ejection from our ranks' of supporters of the minority on the editorial board. The Baku Committee also protests against the conduct of Comrade Maximov who declared that he would not submit to the decisions of the editorial board, thus creating fresh grounds for new and greater friction.[15]

A Philosophical Stick Used against Bogdanov

One of the weapons which Lenin used against Bogdanov was philosophy. His connection with Bogdanov had been of long standing. The latter was a doctor of medicine, and a writer of considerable reputation on economics, sociology, natural sciences and philosophy. Lenin had known him by reputation since 1898, when a copy of Bogdanov's *Short Course in Economic Science* reached him in Siberia. He found the book so good that he rejected a proposal from a publisher to write a manual of political economy because 'it would be difficult to compete with Bogdanov'.[16]

When Bogdanov joined the Bolsheviks in 1904 he sent Lenin the first volume of his philosophical work *Empiriomonism* (the second volume was published in 1905 and the third in 1906). It was this work, strongly influenced by the philo-sophical writings of the neo-Kantians Ernst Mach and Rich-ard Avenarius, that became the main target of Lenin's philo-sophical attack in 1909.

Plekhanov, the main spokesman of orthodox marxist philosophy and now a Menshevik, taunted Lenin for his as-sociation with Bogdanov. Lenin replied at the third Congress of 1905,

> Plekhanov drags Mach and Avenarius by the ears. It is abso-lutely incomprehensible to me what these men, for whom I haven't the slightest sympathy, have to do with the social revolution. They write on individual and social organization of experience, or something of the sort, but really they have no ideas on the democratic dictatorship.[17]

Lenin did not agree with Bogdanov's philosophical views. In a letter to Gorky he wrote that he read Bogdanov's first volume immediately after receiving it, disagreed with it, and wrote a long letter of criticism to its author. When the third volume of *Empiromonism* appeared in 1906 Bogdanov sent Lenin a presentation copy and Lenin immediately wrote a further 'declaration of love, a little letter on philosophy which took up three notebooks'! But this did not stop Lenin from continuing to collaborate with Bogdanov politically, nor did he suggest that there was any need to break off the association on philosophical grounds, or that philosophy had any direct and necessary relation with political tactics.

In February 1908 he wrote:

> the editorial board of *Proletary*, as the ideological spokes-man of the Bolshevik trend, deems it necessary to state the following. Actually, this philosophical controversy is not a factional one and, in the opinion of the editorial board, should not be so; any attempt to represent these differences of opinion as factional is radically erroneous. Both factions contain adherents of the two philosophical trends.[18]

In a letter to Gorky of 25 February 1908, he wrote:

> In the summer and autumn of 1904, Bogdanov and I reached a complete agreement, as *Bolsheviks*, and formed a tacit bloc, which tacitly ruled out philosophy as a neutral field,

that existed all through the revolution and enabled us in that revolution to carry out together the tactics of revolutionary Social Democracy (= Bolshevism), which, I am profoundly convinced, were the only correct tactics.[19]

Proletary must remain absolutely neutral towards all our divergences in philosophy and not give the reader *the slightest grounds* for associating the Bolsheviks, as a trend, as a tactical line of the revolutionary wing of the Russian Social Democrats, with empirio-criticism or empirio-monism.[20]

On 16 April he wrote again to Gorky, 'Philosophy must be *separated* from party (factional) affairs: the decision of the Bolshevik Centre makes this obligatory.'[21]

However, when in 1908 it finally became clear that a revolutionary turn was not in the offing, the differences in tactics between Lenin and Bogdanov over such matters as the boycott, rather than receding, grew in importance. In the wake of the general ideological reaction philosophical differences also assumed greater significance. Bogdanov, Bazarov and Lunacharsky chose this moment to join with the Mensheviks Yuskevich and Valentin and other writers to publish a symposium on philosophy entitled *Outlines of the Philosophy of Marxism*.

It would be wrong to assume that Lenin's interest in philosophy was due solely to the fact that it provided a weapon in the faction fight against Bogdanov, although this element weighed heavily with him. Philosophy was inevitably coming to the forefront of marxist thinking at the time. Before the 1905 revolution the economic doctrine of Karl Marx was the most important subject for discussion among socialists. During the revolution its place was taken by marxist politics. In the period of reaction after the revolution marxist philosophy inevitably came to the fore. As Lenin put it,

Pessimism, non-resistance, appeals to the 'spirit' constitute an ideology inevitable in an epoch when the whole of the old order 'has been turned upside down', and when the masses, who have been brought up under this old order, who imbibed with their mothers' milk the principles, the habits, the traditions and beliefs of this order, do not and cannot see *what kind* of a new order is 'taking shape', *what* social forces are 'shaping' it and how, what social forces are *capable* of bringing release from the incalculable and exceptionally acute distress that is characteristic of epochs of 'upheaval'.[22]

With politics apparently failing to overcome the horrors of the Tsarist regime, escape into the realm of philosophical speculation became the fashion. And in the absence of any contact with a real mass movement, everything had to be proved from scratch – nothing in the traditions of the movement, none of its fundamentals, was immune from constant questioning.

The year 1904 was the centenary of the death of Immanuel Kant. In the next few years a number of marxists intensively discussed Kantian ethics and the 'neo-Kantian' theory of knowledge as it figured in modern scientific thought. In this discussion Bogdanov, Lunacharsky, Bazarov and others tried to combine marxism with the neo-Kantian theory of knowledge as put forward by Ernst Mach and Richard Avenarius. Lunacharsky went as far as to speak openly in favour of fideism.* Lunacharsky used religious metaphors, speaking about 'God-seeking' and 'God-building'. Gorky was influenced by Bogdanov and Lunacharsky and *The Confession*, a novel he wrote at the time, reaches its climax in the following passage:

> ... I called mankind to the new religion ... the people, they are the creators ... in them dwells God ... I saw here [the earth, T.C.] – my mother – in the space between the stars ... and I saw her master, the almighty and immortal people ... Then I began my prayer: 'Thou art my God, O sovereign people, and creator of all gods which thou hast formed from the beauties of thy spirit in the travail and torture of thy quest. And the world should have no other gods but thee, for thou art the only god that works miracles'.[24]

Lenin's reaction was very sharp indeed. He wrote to

---

* 'Fideism' is defined by Lenin as 'a doctrine which substitutes faith for knowledge, or which generally attaches significance to faith.[23]

Gorky, 'The Catholic priest corrupting young girls . . . is *much less* dangerous precisely to "democracy" than a priest without his robes, a priest without crude religion, an ideologically equipped and democratic priest preaching the creation and invention of a god.'[25]

He used the 'philosophical stick' against Bogdanov and his friends not only because of the factional differences between them regarding participation in the Duma elections, activity in the trade unions and so on, but also because he saw in neo-Kantian philosophical idealism a dangerous threat to the survival of marxism during the period of reaction. Socio-religious mysticism and political and social pessimism went hand in hand and threatened the remnants of the revolutionary movement.

Lenin's own work, *Materialism and Empirio-Criticism*, however, also suffered from the lack of real contact with a live movement. (One need only compare it with the magnificent, dialectically terse and lively *Philosophical Notebook*, Vol. 38 of Lenin's *Collected Works*.) It is significant that he never repeated its arguments in later pamphlets and articles, as he always did with his other writings. No special articles in the press elaborated the theses of this book. Nor is it referred to in any of Lenin's writings, including his vast correspondence, after 1909.

By 1909 the struggle with the religious, mystical, soul-searching anti-materialist moods of the period of reaction was practically over – the dawn of a new rise of the mass movement was not far off.

The Bogdanovists Fight On

After the split which Lenin forced in June 1909, Bogdanov and his supporters became an independent faction in the RSDLP. They proclaimed themselves the only 'true Bolsheviks'. In December they started their own journal, bearing the name of the first Bolshevik paper founded by Lenin and Bogdanov at the end of 1904 – *Vperyod* (Forward). For the next few years they were known as the Vperyodist Bolsheviks.

For a time they did reasonably well relative to the Leninists. Lenin wrote in December 1910, 'The Vperyodists . . . have consolidated themselves as a faction with its own transport, its own *agency*, and have grown *many times* stronger since the plenum of January 1910.'[26]

In order to promote their ideas, Bogdanov, Lunacharsky and Alexinsky, with the assistance of Maxim Gorky, organized a party school in Capri (Italy) in 1909, which continued for about four months. A second school was organized in Bologna at the end of 1910 and the beginning of 1911.

> The students at the Capri school invited Ilyich to come to Capri to lecture there. Ilyich categorically refused. He explained to them the factional character of the school and asked them to come to Paris. Within the Capri school, a factional struggle flared up. In the beginning of November, five students (there were twelve in all) including Vilonov, the organizer of the school, officially declared themselves to be staunch Leninists and were expelled from the school. This incident proved better than anything else how right Lenin was when he pointed to the factional character of the school. The expelled students came to Paris.
>
> Five other students of the Capri school arrived with Michael . . . Ilyich delivered a series of lectures to them and devoted a great deal of attention to their studies. Then they left for Russia, except Michael who had tuberculosis . . . At the end of December the studies at Capri came to a close and the rest of the students arrived in Paris. Ilyich delivered lectures to these also. He spoke to them on current topics, including 'The Peasant Movement and Our Tasks' and 'The Agrarian Policy of Stolypin'.[27]

These were days of very small deeds: a tiny party school abroad was an achievement. To all intents and purposes the party hardly existed. The split with Bogdanov and his associates seemed to be the last straw.

To the participants in the quarrels amongst the Bolsheviks, and also to the bystanders, it looked as if Lenin's party was finished. The number of members declined to a very low level, from over 40,000 in 1907 to a few hundred in 1910. They were broken up into small groups and were infiltrated very heavily by the secret police. The groups hardly had any contact with one another or with the leadership abroad. Lenin also lost all the best writers whom he had had with him until then – Bogdanov, Lunacharsky, Pokrovsky, Rozhkov and Gorky. The Mensheviks gloated over the intellectual poverty of the Bolsheviks. Thus, a few years after the expulsion of Bogdanov and the others, Martov felt he could practically write off the Bolshevik leadership :

> a handful of people literally without names or with names that had an unsavoury ring, a group which belonged rather to the intellectual *Lumpenproletariat* than to the intelligentsia. Having taken the baton into their hands, they turned corporals, carrying the name of one intellectual – Lenin – as their ideological banner.[28]

But this was a Menshevist illusion. The talent of party cadres for leadership could not be measured by the single yardstick of literary prowess. And Lenin kept hundreds of his cadres during the period of reaction, recruited a few more hundred and trained them – always preparing for the future.

17

The Final Split with Menshevism

The Mensheviks Swing to the Right

After the revolution, during which they had been very much to the left, the Mensheviks veered strongly to the right. At the Stockholm Unity Congress of 10-25 April 1906 the left wing, influenced by Trotsky and Parvus, was hardly discernable. As Lenin put it,

> a striking thing was the complete absence among the Men-

sheviks of the trend that was so clearly revealed in *Nachalo*, and which in the party we are accustomed to connect with the names of Comrades Parvus and Trotsky. True, it is quite possible that there were some 'Parvusites' and 'Trotskyites' among the Mensheviks – I was told that there were about eight of them.[1]

Lunacharsky explained the *volte face* of the Mensheviks thus:

> The Mensheviks are impressionists, people who yield to the mood of the moment. When the revolutionary tide rose and October-November 1905 arrived, *Nachalo* galloped off at breakneck speed, and went even more Bolshevik than the Bolsheviks. It galloped from democratic dictatorship to socialist dictatorship. But when the revolutionary tide turned, when enthusiasm ebbed and the Cadets rose to the top, the Mensheviks hastened to adjust themselves to this subdued mood. They now trot behind the Cadets, and disdainfully brush aside the October-November forms of struggle.[2]

During 1905 people like Plekhanov and Martov had been lone voices arguing that the Social Democrats should show 'tact' towards the liberals. Now, during the period of reaction, the major tactic of Menshevism was an alliance with the Cadets. One of the spokesmen of Menshevism, Rakhmetov, put the following argument for this coalition:

> It is much easier for the Cadets to twist and turn when they are surrounded by a solid wall of hostility than it would be if they were approached with an offer of a *political coalition* ... Much more can be achieved by the pressure of public opinion on the Cadets (by sending to the Duma resolutions, instruction, petitions and demands, organizing protest meetings, *negotiations between the Workers' Group and the Cadets*) than by senseless, and therefore useless, rowdyism, to put it strongly [our italics].[3]

In an article entitled 'Blocs with the Cadets', written in November 1906, Lenin reacted: 'The sanction of blocs with the Cadets is the finishing touch that definitely marks the Mensheviks as the opportunist wing of the workers' party.'[4]

The most constant, right-wing trend in Menshevism was that of Liquidationism, which influenced it in much the same way as Otzovism and Ultimatism influenced the Bolsheviks. Where Bogdanov made a fetish of illegality and abhorred every effort at legal work in the Duma or trade unions, the Liquidators tried to limit the movement to legal, open activities: Duma elections, parliamentary activity in the Duma, legal trade unions and legal newspapers, and supported the curtailment or liquidation of illegal political organization and activity. Thus A.N.Potresov, the editor of *Nasha Zarya*, and the new spokesman of the Liquidators, stated bluntly in February, 1910, 'the party as an integral and organized hierarchy of institutions does not exist'. Commenting on this view, another Liquidationist magazine, *Vozrozhdeniye*, in its issue of 30 March 1910, stated,

> There is nothing to wind up – and we [i.e. the editors of *Vozrozhdeniye*] would add on our part – the dream of re-establishing this hierarchy in its old underground form is simply a harmful reactionary utopia, which indicates the loss of political intuition by the representatives of a party which at one time was the most realistic of all.[5]

Similarly the Menshevik B.Bogdanov wrote, 'The striving to break with the old underground and embark upon really open and public and political activity – such is the new feature which also characterizes the latest phase of our labour movement.'[6]

Martov went some way towards Liquidationism with his call for *equality* of rights between the legal and illegal party organizations. In his thinking the illegal organization ought to serve mainly as a *support* for the legal party.

> a more or less defined and to a certain extent centralized conspiratorial organization now makes sense (and great sense) only in so far as it takes part in the *construction of a Social Democratic party*, which by necessity is less defined and has its main points of support in open workers' organizations.[7]

Lenin commented on this idea that it

> leads *in fact* to the *party being subordinated to the liqui-*

dators, for the legalist who sets himself against the illegal party, considering himself on a par with it, is nothing but a Liquidator. The 'equality' between an illegal Social Democrat who is persecuted by the police and the legalist who is safeguarded by his legality and his divorce from the party is in fact the 'equality' between the worker and the capitalist.[8]

it is the *illegal organizations* that must *judge* whether the legalists are *in actual fact pro-party*, i.e. [we] specifically reject the 'theory of equality'![9]

For Martov the underground was to be a mere skeleton apparatus, held in reserve for use in the event of a forced relapse into complete illegality. To Lenin, on the other hand, the legal activities were only a skeletal affair, whose purpose was to broaden the sphere of operations of the underground party. The political consequences of turning one's back on the underground were bound to be far-reaching. It was, of course, impossible to advocate the overthrow of Tsarism in publications that were meant to be passed by the censor. Therefore to confine the party to legal forms of action meant virtually to abandon the republican principle. This was the first step towards advocating the gradual transformation of the Tsarist regime into a constitutional monarchy, a desire cherished by the Cadets.

When fighting the ultra-leftists, Lenin was careful to emphasize the danger of falling into Liquidationism, of restricting the programme to the needs of legality :

it is the combination of illegal and legal work that especially demands from us that we combat every 'belittling of the role and significance' of the illegal party. It is just the need to defend the party position on minor matters, in more modest measures, in particular instances, in the legal framework, that especially requires us to see to it that these aims and slogans are not *curtailed*, that the changed form of the struggle does not destroy its content, does not make it less irreconcilable, does not distort the historical perspective and historical aim of the proletariat.[10]

In a report to the extended editorial board of *Proletary* (June 1909) he called for a battle on two fronts – against the ultra-leftists and against the right-wing Liquidationists. He advocated

> the combating of both varieties of *Liquidationism* – Liquidationism on the right and Liquidationism on the left. The Liquidators on the right say that no illegal RSDLP is needed, that Social Democratic activities should be centred exclusively or almost exclusively on legal opportunities. The Liquidators on the left go to the other extreme: legal avenues of party work do not exist for them, illegality at any price is their 'be all and end all'. Both, in approximately equal degree, are Liquidators of the RSDLP, for without methodical judicious *combination* of legal and illegal work in the present situation that history has imposed upon us, the preservation and consolidation of the RSDLP is inconceivable.[11]

While Lenin was ready to expel the Otzovists from the Bolshevik faction, Martov, being basically a conciliator, was incapable of a relentless fight against the Liquidators, even though he opposed them.

The Labour Congress

One way of liquidating the party was to replace it with a broad Labour Party and Labour Congress. Larin, the *enfant terrible* of Menshevism, advocated this in a pamphlet called *A Broad Labour Party and a Labour Congress* (Moscow, 1906). A broad labour party, as conceived by Larin, should embrace something like 900,000 of the 9,000,000-strong Russian proletariat. The 'signboard' had to come down – the party must not be Social Democratic. The Social Democrats and the Socialist Revolutionaries must merge. The new party must be a 'non-partisan party'. The Social Democrats and Socialist Revolutionaries must play the role of propaganda bodies within the broad party.[12]

In similar vein the *eminence grise* of Menshevism, P.B. Axelrod, said,

> The Labour Congress will complete the liquidatory process that has been going on during the past few years, the liquidation of the old party regime that grew up on the outdated historical basis of the feudal state and the hierarchical socio-

political regime and at the same time will mark the beginning of a completely new epoch in the historical life of Russian Social Democrats, the epoch of development on exactly the same lines as the Social Democratic parties in the West.[13]

Another Menshevik, N.Rozhkov, suggested the establishment of an open, peaceful, labour organization – 'a political association for the protection of the interests of the working class'.[14]

> There is no advocacy of any violence in this; there is not a word, not a thought about a violent revolution being necessary, because in reality, too, no such necessity may ever arise. If anyone, blinded by such reactionary frenzy, took it into his head to accuse the members of such an 'association' of striving for violent revolution, the whole burden of an absurd, unfounded and juridically flimsy accusation of this sort would fall upon the head of the accuser![15]

Lenin wrote voluminously and vehemently against the idea of a Labour Congress. Firstly, he argued that the *Realpolitik* of the Liquidators regarding the Labour Congress was unrealistic. Thus at the beginning of December 1911 he wrote,

> It is obvious that the 'powers that be' will never permit such association . . . It is obvious that they will never agree to let it be 'put into effect'. Only blind liberals can fail to see this. It is a useful thing to organize legally functioning trade unions, as long as we are aware that under present conditions they cannot become either broad, or 'political', or stable. But it is an empty and harmful occupation to preach liberal concepts of a political workers' association that *exclude* any idea of the use of force.[16]

In March 1912 he repeated the argument.

> Obviously, under the political conditions prevailing in Russia, where even the party of the liberals, the Cadets, has no legal status, the formation of an open Social Democratic working-class party can only remain wishful thinking. The Liquidators repudiated the illegal party, but did not fulfil their obligation to found a legal party.[17]

Some time later, he was asking: Where is the Congress?

> For more than a year we have been telling the Liquidators:

stop talking and start founding your 'legal political societies', such as the 'society for the defence of working-class interests', and so on. Stop phrase-mongering and get down to work!

But they cannot get down to work because it is impossible to realize a liberal utopia in present-day Russia.[18]

Against the idea of a legal Labour Congress Lenin put forward the supremacy of the illegal party.

1. The only correct type of organizational structure in the present period is an illegal party as the sum total of party nuclei surrounded by a network of legal and semi-legal workers' associations.

2. It is absolutely obligatory to adapt the organizational form of illegal building to local conditions. A variety of forms of cover for illegal nuclei and the greatest possible flexibility in adapting forms of work to local and general living conditions guarantee the vitality of the illegal organization.

3. The chief immediate task in the field of organizational work at the present time is to establish in all factories purely party illegal committees consisting of the most active elements among the workers. The tremendous upswing of the working-class movement creates conditions in which factory party committees can be restored and the existing ones strengthened in the vast majority of localities.

4. ... it has now become essential in every centre to form a single leading organization out of the disconnected local groups.[19]

Of course revolutionary socialists should fight for 'freedom of association', but this should be part and parcel of the struggle to overthrow Tsarism. Not to point out the direct connection between the partial reform and the revolutionary overthrow of Tsarism is to cheat the workers, to fall into liberalism.

It is highly important to point out that freedom of the press, association, assembly and strikes is absolutely indispensable to the workers, but that it is precisely in order to bring it about that we must realize the inseparable connection between it and the general foundations of political liberty, a radical change in the entire political system. Not the liberal utopia of freedom of association under the 3 June regime, but a struggle for freedom in general, and for freedom of association in particular, against this regime all along the line, against the foundations of this regime.[20]

The workers demand freedom of association in earnest and therefore they are fighting for freedom for the whole people, for the overthrow of the monarchy, for a republic.[21]

Conditions during the period of reaction made the idea of concentrating completely on legal work a very attractive one. Hundreds of intellectuals transferred all their activities into various legal organizations – cooperatives, trade unions, educational societies, advisory committees for the Duma group, and so on.

The Liquidators were in the forefront during the most desolate years. 'They suffered less from police persecution', writes Olminsky. 'They had many of the writers, a good part of the lecturers and on the whole most of the intellectuals. They were cocks of the walk and they crowed about it.' The attempts of the Bolshevik faction, whose ranks were thinning every hour to preserve its illegal machine were dashed at each turn against hostile circumstances. Bolshevism seemed definitely doomed. 'All of present-day development', wrote Martov, 'renders the formation of any kind of durable party-sect a pathetic reactionary utopia.'[22]

Lenin identified Liquidators as intellectuals who ran away from the underground.

The flight of some people from the underground could have been the result of their fatigue and dispiritedness. Such individuals may only be pitied; they should be helped because their dispiritedness will pass and there will again appear an urge to get away from philistinism, away from the liberals and the liberal-labour policy, to the working-class underground. But when the fatigued and dispirited use journalism as their platform and announce that their flight is not a manifestation of fatigue, or weakness, or intellectual woolliness, but that it is to their credit, and then put the blame on the 'ineffective', 'worthless', 'moribund' etc., underground, these runaways then become disgusting renegades, apostates. These runaways then become the worst advisers for the working-class movement and therefore its dangerous enemies.[23]

By no means all the Mensheviks were Liquidators. However on the whole the Mensheviks at least tolerated them. While Martov and Dan did not support them, they defended them from Bolshevist attack in their journal *Golos Sotsial-demokrata*, published in Paris. At the same time these two were actively collaborating in the legal press published by the Liquidators.

The Issue of 'Expropriations'

With the decline of the revolution, the question of where to get funds for the party became more and more pressing. Even during 1905 the Bolshevik apparatus was very modest. In her memoirs Krupskaya relates that because of the pressure of work another secretary, Mikhail Sergeyevich Weinstein, was engaged, and also an assistant secretary, Vera Rudolfovna Menzhinskaya.

> Mikhail Sergeyevich was engaged more on the military organization, and was always busy carrying out the instructions of Nikitin (L.B.Krassin). I was in charge of appointments and communication with committees and individuals. It would be difficult to picture now what a simplified technique the CC secretariat made shift with. I remember that we never attended CC meetings, no one was 'in charge' of us, no minutes were taken, ciphered addresses were kept in match-boxes, inside book-bindings, and in similar places.
>
> We had to trust to our memories. A whole heap of people besieged us, and we had to look after them in every way, supplying them with whatever they wanted; literature, passports, instructions, advice. It is now difficult to imagine how we ever managed to cope with it all, and how we kept things in order, being controlled by nobody, and living 'of our own free will'.[24]

And this three-person secretariat was serving a party which in 1907 had 46,143 members!

The party full-timers were paid a pittance. 'Those members of the party who gave their entire time to the party work got very small remuneration, sometimes as low as 3, 5, or 10 rubles, and never exceeding 30 rubles per month.'[25] By comparison the average wage in 1903-05 was 28 rubles.

However modest the party apparatus, and however low

the wages paid to full-time workers, money was always a problem. During the revolution this problem was largely solved by the donations of rich sympathizers. For instance, in the Moscow Bolshevik organization, which had about 1,000 members in the spring of 1905,

> The accounts of the Committee for June 1905 show that it had a total income of 9,891r. (£989): 1,013r. being brought forward . . . The income includes several very large sums, 4,000r. from a 'friend', and one of 3,000r. 'for arms'. It is known that there were many rich sympathizers with the Bolshevik cause, including A.M.Gorky and the son of a factory owner . . . The other individual subscriptions amounted only to 1,378r.[26]

In October the large contributions from rich sympathizers increased: there were two of 4,000 rubles and 8,400 rubles from 'friends'.[27]

Martov reported the same situation among the Mensheviks. During the revolutionary period,

> the budgets of the party organization had increased enormously . . . Membership subscriptions played only a very small part in this. The treasurer's report from the party committee in Baku shows for February 1905, from an intake of 1382.8 rubles, only 38.9 rubles or 3 per cent were subscriptions from workers. In a report from the Riga party branch for August only 143.4 rubles out of 558.7 or 22 per cent came from workers' subscriptions. In a report from the Sebastopol committee 14 per cent came from members' subscriptions; in the reports from the Mariupol branch 33 per cent etc. We find that the highest percentage from membership subscriptions came from the Russian Social Democratic branch of Ivanovo-Voznesensk, where membership subscriptions made up 53 per cent of the total intake.[28]

One of the most important 'angels' was A.M.Kalmykova (called Aunty), who gave the original funds necessary to launch *Iskra*. She was a rich bookseller and publisher, a leading distributor of cheap popular books and progressive literature, and a close friend of Krupskaya. Another was the big textile magnate, Morozov, who regularly donated 2,000 rubles a month to the Bolsheviks via the engineer Krasin.

(Morozov committed suicide after the defeat of the 1905 revolution.) His nephew, N.P.Schmidt, to whom we shall refer below, was also a major contributor.

With the assault of reaction, practically all the rich sympathizers deserted the party. Lenin's golden touch in raising funds failed more and more frequently. Krupskaya, who acted not only as secretary of the Bolsheviks but also as their national treasurer, again and again complained about the lack of money. For Lenin, *salus revolutionis suprema lex*. If need be revolutionaries must crawl, even through the mud, onwards towards their goal. He was not impressed by a fastidiousness in obtaining funds. The case of the Schmidt inheritance provides an example of his attitude.

Young Nikolai Pavlovich Schmidt, a nephew of the textile magnate Morozov and owner of a furniture factory in the Presnya district of Moscow, came over to the side of the workers in 1905 and joined the Bolsheviks. He provided the money to found *Novaya Zhizn* and also provided money for the purpose of procuring arms. He became intimate with the workers and was one of their best friends. The police called Schmidt's factory a 'devil's nest'. The factory played an important part during the Moscow uprising. Nikolai Pavlovich was arrested. In prison he was subjected to every kind of torture. The police took him to see what had been done to his factory; they took him to see the murdered workers and finally they murdered him in prison. Before he died, he succeeded in informing his friends outside that he was leaving his property to the Bolsheviks.

Elizaveta Pavlovna Schmidt, Nikolai Pavlovich's younger sister, inherited part of her brother's estate, and she, too, decided to give it to the Bolsheviks. But she was not yet of age and in order that she might dispose of her money as she wished, it was decided to arrange a fictitious marriage. Elizaveta Pavlovna went through a form of marriage with Comrade Ignatyev, a member of the fighting detachment who managed to retain his legality, and being his wife officially, she was able, with the consent of her husband, to do what she liked with her legacy. But the marriage was really a fictitious one. Elizaveta Pavlovna was actually the wife of another Bolshevik, Victor Taratuta. The official marriage enabled her to obtain the legacy immediately and the money was handed over to the Bolsheviks.[29]

Even so the finances of the Bolsheviks were still in great straits. Lenin decided to use 'expropriations' ('exes'), – armed robbery of banks and other institutions – to raise funds for the party. After a number of 'exes' the Mensheviks raised an outcry. Trotsky criticized Lenin sharply in the German Social Democratic press. Even many of the Bolsheviks did not like the enterprise. At the Stockholm Party Congress (1906) a majority of 64 votes to 4, with 20 abstentions, supported a Menshevik resolution forbidding 'exes'. This meant that Bolshevik delegates had voted with the Mensheviks.

In his extensive report on the Stockholm Congress, Lenin avoided any mention of the resolution concerning armed acts, on the grounds that he was not present during the discussion. 'Besides, it is, of course, not a question of principle.' It is hardly likely that Lenin's absence was accidental; he simply did not want to have his hands tied.

At the London Congress of May 1907, where Lenin had his own way on practically every other issue, an overwhelming vote was passed against 'exes'. A majority of the Bolsheviks voted with the Mensheviks, and when delegates shouted from the floor 'What does Lenin say? We want to hear Lenin', he took advantage of his place in the chair to avoid registering his vote – he only chuckled 'with a somewhat cryptic expression'.[30]

In his report on this Congress, to which he was a delegate, Stalin tried to explain away the resolution in the following lame terms:

> Of the Menshevik resolutions only the one on guerilla actions was carried, and that by sheer accident: on that point the Bolsheviks did not accept battle, or rather, they did not wish to fight the issue to a conclusion, purely out of the desire to 'give the Menshevik comrades at least one opportunity to rejoice'.

In actual fact, the Bolsheviks 'did not accept battle' only because on that question they had ranged against them not only the Mensheviks, but also the Poles and the Bund, as well as many members of the Bolshevik faction itself.

On 23 June, six weeks after the London Congress, and

in spite of its resolution, Lenin's agents carried out the most audacious expropriation ever – that of the Tiflis treasury. This raid yielded 341,000 rubles, which were duly transferred to the Bolshevik treasury abroad. However, as the proceeds consisted of banknotes of very large denominations, it was not easy to exchange them in foreign banks, which had been warned to expect the attempts to do so. Several important Bolsheviks, including the future Commissar of Foreign Affairs, Litvinov, were arrested in Western Europe when they tried to exchange the money.

Both Trotsky and Martov strongly denounced the Bolsheviks at the London Congress, and some time later went so far as to carry their denunciation into the columns of the Western European socialist press.

It is probable that Stalin's role as a careful but audacious organizer of 'exes', including the Tiflis one, was what brought him to Lenin's attention. Among the comrades involved in 'exes' were some of the finest Bolsheviks. One need but think of Kamo (Semyon Arshakovich Ter-Petrosian) who carried out the raids at Tiflis and a number of other places. He allowed himself and a member of his band exactly 50 kopeks a day for maintenance. Among his exploits were a number of 'exes', a daring escape from Tiflis prison, and the smuggling of guns to Russia. He feigned insanity so successfully in a German prison that despite tortures of various kinds he convinced his gaolers, and was transferred back to Tiflis. He escaped, got caught and was sentenced to death, but his sentence was commuted to life imprisonment.

Split, Split, Split

After the Unity Congress at Stockholm, the quarrel over the Duma elections came to a head in Petersburg. When the time came to nominate the deputies for Petersburg, the Leninists, in secure control of the city, got their candidates adopted. However, 31 Menshevik delegates, obeying the instructions of the Menshevik-controlled Central Committee, walked out of the city conference, and held a special provincial conference which decided on an alliance with the Cadets.

Lenin immediately issued a pamphlet accusing the seceders of complicity with the Cadets, 'for the purpose of selling the vote of the workers' and 'bargaining to get their men into the Duma in spite of the workers and with the aid of the Cadets'. This was not merely a charge against the seceders but also against the Central Committee of the party. It was really a case of open violation of party discipline on Lenin's part. He found himself before a party court, charged with 'conduct impermissible in a party member'. He was allowed to nominate three judges, while the Central Committee appointed another three, and the Lettish, Polish and Jewish Bund organizations one each.

The trial itself is not now of great interest, as it was interrupted by a party congress which overturned the Menshevik majority and put Lenin in control. But Lenin's behaviour at the trial is very interesting, because it shows the relentless way in which he conducted a faction fight against the right wing of the party.

As the trial opened Lenin calmly acknowledged that he used 'language impermissible in relations *between comrades in the same party*',[31] but he made absolutely no apology for doing so. Indeed, in fighting the Liquidationists and their allies in the movement, he never hesitated to use the sharpest weapons he could lay his hands on. Moderation is not a characteristic of Bolshevism.

Lenin Proposes a Rapprochement with Plekhanov

Although he was absolutely relentless, Lenin never bore grudges. The moment he saw a move by any of his political opponents towards rapprochement he would move to meet them. A case in point concerned Plekhanov.

In 1908-09 Lenin saw a chance of reconstructing the party by sacrificing the ultra-leftist and attracting the anti-Liquidationist elements among the Mensheviks, that is those who had not abandoned the idea of building up underground organizations. The leader of this group was Plekhanov.

In December 1908 Plekhanov left the editorial board of the Liquidationist newspaper *Golos Sotsialdemokrata*. At the same time he resigned from the editorial board of the five-volume work *The Social Movement in Russia*, now edited by Martov, Maslov and Potresov. He wrote angrily attacking this symposium in *Dnevnik* (No. 9, 1909), singling out for particular criticism an article by Potresov, who argued the case for the Liquidators thus:

> I ask the reader ... whether it is possible that there can exist, in this year of 1909, as something that is actually real and not a figment of a diseased imagination, a Liquidationist tendency, a tendency to liquidate what is already beyond liquidations and actually no longer exists as an organized whole.

Plekhanov retorted:

> There is no doubt however, that *a man for whom our party does not exist, does not himself exist for our party.* [Plekhanov's italics.] Now all the members of the party will have to say that Mr Potresov is no comrade of theirs, and some of them, will, perhaps, stop accusing me on the score that I have long since ceased to regard him as such.[32]

'Potresov lost the ability to look at social life through the eyes of a revolutionary.' Liquidationism, says Plekhanov, leads to the 'slough of the most disgraceful opportunism'. 'Among them [the Liquidators] new wine is converted into a very sour liquid suitable only for preparing petty-bourgeois vinegar.' Liquidationism 'facilitates the penetration of petty-bourgeois tendencies in a proletarian environment'. 'I have repeatedly tried to prove to influential Menshevik comrades that they are making a great mistake in displaying at times their readiness to go hand-in-hand with gentlemen who to a greater or lesser extent are redolent of opportunism.' 'Liquidationism leads straight to the muddy slough of opportunism and petty-bourgeois aspirations hostile to Social Democracy.'[33]

After this declaration Lenin proposed a reconciliation with Plekhanov. In November 1909 he called for

a *rapprochement of pro-party members* of all factions and

sections of the party, above all a *rapprochement* between the Bolsheviks and the pro-party Mensheviks, and with the Mensheviks of the type of the Vyborg comrades in St Petersburg and the Plekhanovites abroad . . . we issue a call to *all Mensheviks* capable of openly combating Liquidationism, of openly supporting Plekhanov, and, of course, to all Menshevik workers above all.[34]

In practice very little came of Lenin's effort to co-operate with Plekhanov; the basic differences between them were too radical. The fact that in 1905 Plekhanov was on the extreme right wing of the Mensheviks, that he had opposed the December uprising because it would frighten the liberals, and that he called for tactfulness towards the Cadets, limited too severely the scope of this experiment in co-operation.

Lenin Fights Against the Conciliators

Lenin fought to overcome ultra-leftism in the Bolshevik faction and carried on a struggle against the Menshevik Liquidators. But no sooner had he expelled the Vperyodist Bolsheviks than a new source of opposition arose within the Bolshevik faction: the Conciliators or, as they called themselves, the 'Party Bolsheviks'. The RSDLP was in tatters, and so exhausted that its members were calling for simple unity, a conciliation between Bolshevism and Menshevism, and an end to all factionalism.

Meanwhile Lenin was beginning to lose support within the faction, as many leading Bolsheviks supported the call for a united party. The Conciliators included several who had been elected as members or candidates of the Central Committee at the fifth Congress, notably A.I.Rykov, V.P.Nogin, I.F.Dubrovinsky, S.A.Lozovsky and G.Y.Sokolnikov.[35]

In these circumstances the Menshevik leaders were able to call together a Plenum of the CC in Paris at the beginning of January 1910. Lenin, who was opposed to the meeting, was on this occasion in a minority, not only in the party as a whole, but within his own faction. The only prominent

Bolshevik supporting him against conciliation was Zinoviev. (From that time on Zinoviev was Lenin's closest associate, completely trusted, until the events of 1917 put him to a severe test.)

For three long weeks Lenin was badly hammered. He was forced to agree to turn over the Schmidt money. He had to liquidate his faction paper, *Proletary*, and agree to a common paper with the Mensheviks – *Sotsial-Demokrat* – with two Bolsheviks, Lenin and Zinoviev, joining the Mensheviks Martov and Dan, and a representative of Polish Social Democracy, Varsky, on the editorial board. Trotsky's Vienna paper, *Pravda*, was declared an official party organ (Kamenev was dispatched to assist him in editing it) and the Central Committee was instructed to give it financial support. To add insult to injury, while the Plenum condemned the Liquidators in words, it at the same time invited them to participate in the life of the party, and to name three of their number for the underground Central Committee.

Trotsky went so far as to hail the results of the Paris Plenum as 'the greatest event in the history of Russian Social Democracy'.[36] Lenin's attitude is clear from a letter he wrote to Gorky on 11 April 1910.

> At the CC Plenum (the 'long plenum' – three weeks of agony, all nerves were on edge, the devil to pay!) . . . a mood of 'conciliation in general' (without any clear idea with whom, for what, and how); hatred of the Bolshevik Centre for its implacable ideological struggle; squabbling on the part of the Mensheviks, who were spoiling for a fight, and as a result – an infant covered with blisters.
> And so we have to suffer. Either – at best – we cut open the blisters, let out the pus, and cure and rear the infant.
> Or, at worst – the infant dies. Then we shall be childless for a while (that is, we shall re-establish the Bolshevik faction) and then give birth to a more healthy infant.[37]

However, the 'unity' never became operational, not so much because of Bolshevik intransigence, but because the Mensheviks were not ready to carry out their part of the bargain. The January 1910 Plenum committed the Bolsheviks to have no dealings with the boycottists and the Mensheviks to sever their connections with the Liquidators. Lenin was easily able to carry out his part of the instruction, as he had already expelled Bogdanov, Lunacharsky and the other boycottists from the Bolshevik camp. However, the Mensheviks found it impossible to fulfil their obligation. The Liquidators' attitude was far too prevalent in their ranks. If they had expelled the Liquidators they would have completely destroyed the Menshevik group and this would have helped the Bolsheviks towards victory in the movement. Martov made it clear a little later that he had not ever intended to carry out this commitment and that he had agreed to the 'unity' in the Plenum only because the Mensheviks were too weak to risk an immediate break.[38]

The final blow was dealt to the scheme when the three Liquidators invited to join the Central Committee flatly refused to have anything to do with the underground organization. When the Bolshevik 'Conciliators', who had a majority in Russia, proposed further negotiations with other Liquidator leaders, Lenin ignored them. When Martov and Dan tried to put their views to *Sotsial-Demokrat*, the paper they were supposed to be editing jointly with Lenin and Zinoviev, they were prevented from doing so. (Varsky voted with Lenin and Zinoviev on the editorial board.)

Trotsky's *Pravda* also failed to serve as the paper of a united party. When his attempt at reconciliation broke down because – as he himself stated – the Mensheviks refused to disband their faction and get rid of the Liquidators, Trotsky did not condemn them but 'suspended judgement'.[39] Kamenev could not persuade him to take a firmer attitude.

Another factor intervened against the unity of the RSDLP – the Tsarist secret police. Initially the main spokesman of the Conciliators was I.F.Dubrovinsky, but he was soon arrested and driven to suicide in Siberian exile.[40] His place as leading Conciliator on the Central Committee was taken by Aleksei Rykov. When Rykov went to Russia to organize the Bolsheviks against Lenin's splitting tactics, the police picked him up in the street immediately after his arrival, before he could reach any of the Bolsheviks in the underground. The *okhrana* knew very well, from their key man, Malinovsky, where everybody in the Bolshevik leadership stood politically, and how to set about finding them. 'The Russian police at that time had a particular interest in supporting the Bolsheviks who stood for disunity. In order to prevent a united and therefore more dangerous Social Democracy, *okhrana* instructions were to concentrate on the arrest of the Conciliators.'[41]

The Mensheviks were infuriated by the fact that Lenin's splitting policy coincided with that of the *okhrana*. The *okhrana* hoped that the split in Social Democracy would weaken the labour movement; Lenin reckoned that it would steel the workers' revolutionary leadership. History has given its verdict; the secret police plot did not bear the hoped-for fruit.*

Who was using whom? This question was to arise again when Field Marshal Ludendorff, in order to weaken Russia's war effort and to divide Germany's enemies, allowed Lenin to return to Russia through Germany in the 'sealed train' in 1917.

---

* Lenin had no idea that Malinovsky was an agent of the *okhrana*. Again and again he praised him very highly and was vehement in defending him against the 'slanders' of Martov.

'What did *Nasha Rabochaya Gazeta* do?
'It spread insidious rumours and insinuations to the effect that Malinovsky is an *agent provocateur*.
'But then these intellectual gossips are past masters of the art of scandal-mongering, of going to or from Martov (or other filthy slanderers like him) and encouraging insidious rumours, or picking up and passing on insinuations! Whoever has been but once in the company of these scandal-mongering intellectualist gossips will certainly (unless he is a gossip himself) retain for the rest of his life disgust for these despicable creatures.
'Not a shadow of belief in the "rumours" circulated by Martov and Dan; a firm determination to ignore them, to attach no importance to them.'[42]

Lenin's Victory Over the Conciliators

Lenin called a conference in Prague in January 1912, from which the Liquidators were forcibly excluded. The Polish and Latvian national parties, the Jewish Bund, *Vperyod*, Trotsky and Plekhanov all refused to participate. The 14 voting delegates (of whom 2 were police agents) represented 10 party committees in Russia. This conference elected a new Central Committee made up of 'hards', seven in all – Lenin, Zinoviev, Ordzhonikidze, Goloshekin, Spandarian, Schwartzman and Roman Malinovsky (the police agent). Shortly afterwards the Committee co-opted two further members, I.V. Dzhugashvili (Stalin) and I.S.Belostotsky. Five members were dispatched to work inside Russia, including three Caucasians: Ordzhonikidze, Spandarian and Stalin.

Trotsky had not abandoned his *idée fixe* of unity among all the Social Democratic groups, and in response to Lenin's Prague conference he persuaded the Mensheviks associated with the Organization Committee to convene a conference of all Social Democrats in Vienna in August 1912. He hoped that, as in 1905, the rise in the revolutionary mood in Russia would bring about appeasement between the different trends of Social Democracy. He wrote, 'it is ridiculous and absurd to affirm that there is an irreconcilable contradiction between the political tendencies of *Luch* and *Pravda*'. 'Our historic factions, Bolshevism and Menshevism, are purely intellectualist formations in origin.'*

However, he was disastrously wrong: the cleavage that

---

* How little Trotsky, prior to 1917, understood the role of the party in the revolution and the place of Bolshevism in history is clear above all from his book *1905*. In the whole of this book neither the Bolsheviks nor Lenin receive a single mention. This failure explains why Trotsky's epigones never published this very interesting work by the leader of the St Petersburg Soviet, although far less important writings of his have been published again and again. Hardly a reference to *1905* can be found in the epigones' press.

had crystallized over the years between Bolshevism and Menshevism was too deep to be overcome, and the new political awakening could only deepen it further. Lenin was now reaping the fruits of his long labours. His followers led the underground, while the Mensheviks were a collection of loose, divided grouplets. The Bolsheviks refused to participate in the Vienna conference. The Mensheviks, the ultra-left former Bolsheviks (Vperyodists), the Jewish Bund and Trotsky's group came together and founded a confederation known as the August Bloc. Trotsky was its chief spokesman, persistently attacking Lenin for 'splitting tactics'. This confederation began to fall apart almost as soon as it came together.

After the Prague conference, in February 1912, Lenin decided to launch a legal daily paper. To Trotsky's indignation he appropriated the title *Pravda*. The first issue of the Bolshevik *Pravda* appeared on 22 April, and it was published until the outbreak of the war, playing a central role in building the Bolshevik Party. Plekhanov was for a time a regular contributor. Bogdanov and the rest of the *Vperyod* group were also invited to contribute, but with the exception of Alexinsky they did not continue this connection long. The questions of 'Ultimatism', Otzovism and even Machism had by this time lost their immediate importance. Lenin was very happy to have Plekhanov and Alexinsky writing for *Pravda*.

He found that, even among the 'hards', he had to continue the battle against conciliation with the Mensheviks and the Liquidators. For three months the word 'Liquidator' was even expunged from *Pravda*'s vocabulary. 'That is why Vladimir Ilyich was so upset when *Pravda* at first deliberately struck out from his articles all his arguments in opposition to the Liquidators. He wrote angry letters to *Pravda* protesting against this.'[43] 'Sometimes, although rarely, Ilyich's articles would get lost. Sometimes his articles would be held up and printed only after some delay. This irritated Ilyich and he wrote angry letters to *Pravda*, but that did not improve matters.'[44]

In a letter to V.M.Molotov, the secretary of the *Pravda* editorial board, on 1 August 1912, Lenin wrote,

You write, and as secretary, evidently, on behalf of the editorial board; that 'the editorial board in principle considers my article fully acceptable *including the attitude to the Liquidators*'. If that is so, why then does *Pravda* stubbornly and systematically cut out any mention of the Liquidators, both in my articles and in the articles of other colleagues?[45]

On 25 January 1913 he wrote to the Bolshevik deputies in the Duma :

we have received a stupid and insolent letter from the editors. We are not replying. They should be kicked out . . . The absence of news about the plan for reorganizing the editorial board is causing us great concern . . . Reorganization, or better still the complete expulsion of all the old ones, is absolutely essential. Absurdly conducted. They lavish praise on the Bund and *Zeit* : it's simply disgusting. They can't take the right line against *Luch*. Disgraceful the way they handle articles . . . Simply exasperating . . . We are waiting impatiently for news about all this.[46]

But the editorial board continued to provide cause for concern. On 9 February Lenin wrote to Sverdlov,

The use made of *Pravda* for keeping the class-conscious workers informed and reporting their work (the Petersburg Committee particularly) is beneath all criticism. You must put an end to the so-called autonomy of these editorial failures. You must set about it before all else . . . Take the editorial board into your own hands . . . If this is well organized, there will also be a revival in the Petersburg Committee which is ridiculously inept, incapable of saying a word, lets every occasion for a statement go by. And it ought to be making a statement almost daily in legal form (in the name of influential workers, etc.) and at least once or twice a month illegally. Once again, the key to the *whole* situation is *Pravda*. Here it is possible to conquer, and then (only then) organize the local work as well. Otherwise everything will collapse.[47]

The Central Committee sent Sverdlov to Petersburg to reorganize the editorial board.[48] Lenin wrote to him on 9 February 1913, 'Today we learned about the beginning of reforms on *Pravda*. A thousand greetings, congratulations and wishes for success . . . You cannot imagine how tired we are of working with an utterly hostile editorial staff.'

Things were arranged more or less in the way Lenin wanted. A joint meeting of the Russian Bureau of the Central Committee and the *Pravda* editorial board arrived at a compromise solution : three members of the existing board were to remain as editors, and in addition Sverdlov, although not on the board, was to have the right to vote and to censor all articles in the paper. This compromise did not last long, as Sverdlov was arrested less than three weeks later.

The new board, apparently cured of its leanings towards the Liquidators, at first worked amicably enough with Lenin. However towards the end of May another row blew up, this time because *Pravda* was moving in the other direction – towards co-operation with the Otzovists. On 26 May it published a declaration by the Otzovist leader, Bogdanov, in which he tried to clarify his group's attitude to the Duma faction. When Lenin received a copy of *Pravda* he was furious, and wrote a letter to the editorial board.

> The action of the editors in respect of Mr Bogdanov's distortion of party history is so scandalous that, to tell the truth, one does not know whether it is possible after this to remain a contributor ...
> I demand categorically that the enclosed article be printed *in full.* I have always permitted the editors to make changes in a comradely manner, but after Mr Bogdanov's letter *I do not grant* any right to alter or do anything else of that kind with this article ...
> I insist on an immediate reply. I cannot continue to contribute articles in face of Mr Bogdanov's despicable line.

They sent the article back to him, finding it too strong, but he agreed to make only one change – to drop the word 'Mr' (*gospodin*) in front of Bogdanov's name. The editorial board refused to publish – and the article was suppressed until 1939.[49]

Lenin then wrote to Kamenev asking him to apply some pressure on *Pravda* and in January 1914 sent him into Russia to take over the editorship. Once again good relations were resumed – although the Bogdanov affair was not completely over, for as late as February 1914 Lenin was still receiving reports of dissatisfaction in the Russian party over his treatment of Bogdanov.[50] Under Kamenev's editorship, *Pravda* and Lenin remained on good terms until the paper was closed in July 1914. Its closure averted another crisis, as the war was to divide Lenin and Kamenev very sharply on the key question of the correct attitude to the war.

Conciliation also affected the Bolshevik group of Duma deputies. The six deputies in the fourth Duma, holding office for nearly a year, between December 1912 and September 1913, did not see eye to eye with Lenin. The first thing they did after their election was to make an agreement with the Menshevik deputies to contribute both to *Pravda* and to the Liquidators' *Luch*. In a special resolution published in *Pravda* the united faction acknowledged that 'the unity of Social Democracy is a pressing need', expressed itself in favour of merging *Pravda* with *Luch* and as a step in this direction recommended that all its members become contributors to both newspapers. On 18 December *Luch* triumphantly published the names of four of the Bolshevik deputies (two having declined) in its list of contributors. The names of the seven members of the Menshevik faction appeared simultaneously on the *Pravda* masthead.[51]

At a meeting in Cracow later in December, Lenin insisted that the Bolshevik deputies should withdraw from their agreement to contribute to *Luch*, and the deputies made an appropriate announcement when the Duma reconvened at the end of January. However, the Cracow meeting also insisted that they should demand parity with the Menshevik group, which outnumbered them by one and thus outvoted them in the Social Democratic faction. The Duma group was hesitant about the reorganization of *Pravda* aimed at ending its Conciliationist leanings. Six months later, in June 1913, Lenin wrote urging them once again to demand parity with the Mensheviks, and proposing that they split if this was refused.[52] No action was evidently taken by the deputies, and at the Poronin Conference in September the issue was again stated in more or less the same terms.[53] This was a joint conference of the Central Committee and party officials, including the Duma deputies. After this the deputies made the demand, they were defeated and the faction split. This finally ended the fraternal relations between Bolshevik and Menshevik Duma deputies.

Malinovsky played an important role – actually a dual role – in splitting the Bolsheviks from the Mensheviks. The gendarme General Spiridovich wrote, 'Malinovsky, carrying out the directives of Lenin and of the Police Department, achieved in October 1913 . . . the final quarrel between the "seven" and the "six".'[54]

The fact that it took Lenin nearly a year to persuade the Bolshevik deputies to break away from the Mensheviks gives a very different picture from the commonly accepted one of Bolshevism as a totalitarian organization under his dictatorship. In fact, Lenin had to fight again and again to convince his own members; one might even say, to colonize his own party.

18

The Rising Revolutionary Wave
Economic Prosperity

In 1909 an economic boom followed the slump. Almost every industry recovered from the severe crisis of 1907-08. The next few years saw a continuous growth of production, as illustrated in the table below, which gives the output of the main branches of industry (in million puds).[1]*

---

* A pud = 16.38 kilos.

Industry	1910	1913
Pig iron	186	283
Iron and steel	184	246
Roofing iron	22.9	25.3
Rails	29.5	35.9
Copper	1.4	2.0
Coal	1,522	2,214
Petroleum	588	561
Coke	168	271
Cotton consumption	22.1	35.9

The revolutionary movement also revived. Among the popular masses the first to stir were the students.

Student Unrest

In the autumn of 1910 student demonstrations took place in connection with the deaths of the former liberal president of the first Duma, Muromtsev, and of Leo Tolstoy. They also occurred in response to the brutal mistreatment of political prisoners in the Zerentui gaol in Trans-Baikal. Meetings were held in universities, resolutions of protest passed, and attempts made to organize demonstrations in the streets. A general strike of students broke out at the beginning of 1911 in protest against the repressive measures taken by the government, and spread throughout Russia. Lenin welcomed the student awakening enthusiastically. He criticized in no uncertain terms a letter from a group of Social Democratic students who tried to belittle the importance of the movement because it was not related to any *workers*' mass action. The students' letter said, 'We envisage student action only as one co-ordinated with general political action, and in no case apart from it. The elements capable of uniting the students are lacking. In view of this we are against academic action.'[2] Lenin commented sharply :

> Such an argument is radically wrong. The revolutionary slogan to work towards co-ordinated political action of the students and the proletariat, etc. – here ceases to be a live guidance for many-sided militant agitation on a broadening

basis and becomes a lifeless dogma, mechanically applied to different stages of different forms of the movement. It is not sufficient merely to proclaim political co-ordinated action, repeating the 'last words', in lessons of the revolution. One must *be able* to agitate for political action, *making use* of all possibilities, all conditions and, first and foremost, all mass conflicts between advanced elements, whatever they are, and the autocracy.

Conditions are possible when academic movement lowers the level of a political movement, or divides it, or distracts from it – and in that case Social Democratic students' groups would of course be bound to concentrate their agitation against such a movement. But anyone can see that the objective political conditions at the present time are different. The academic movement is expressing the *beginning* of a movement among the new 'generation' of students, who have more or less become accustomed to a narrow measure of autonomy; and this movement is beginning when other forms of mass struggle are lacking at the present time, when a lull has set in.[3]

The students were more easily stirred to action than the workers, who suffered so severely during the period of reaction. But the student revival was the manifestation of a much deeper and wider awakening of the popular masses.

Workers Awake

The year 1911 saw the workers gradually moving over to the offensive. In 1908 the number of strikers had been tiny – 60,000, and in 1910 it was even lower – 46,623; in 1911 it rose to 105,110. The conference of Bolsheviks in January 1912 stated,

> the onset of a political revival is to be noted among broad democratic circles, chiefly among the proletariat. The workers' strikes of 1910-11, the beginning of demonstrations and proletarian meetings, the start of a movement among urban bourgeois democrats (the student strikes) etc., all these are signs of the growing revolutionary feelings of the masses against the 3 June regime.[4]

The movement received a tremendous impetus from the terrible massacre of gold miners in Lena on 4 April 1912. 6,000 miners were on strike in the Lena goldfields, which were situated in a region of *taiga* forests almost 2,000 kilometres from the Siberian railway. An officer of the gendarmerie ordered the unarmed crowd to be fired on, and 500 people were either killed or wounded. The Social Democratic Duma group attacked the government over the shooting and received an insolent reply from the Tsar's minister of the interior, A.A.Makarov: 'So it was, and so it will be!'

It is interesting to note that the demonstrations following the Lena massacre raised the slogan of a democratic republic from the outset, reflecting a much higher level of consciousness among the masses than had existed at the beginning of the 1905 revolution, which started with a naïve petition to the Tsar. In April 1912 the Russian workers started where they had left off at the height of the revolution some seven years before.

News of the bloody drama in the Lena goldfields aroused the anger of the working class. Street demonstrations, meetings, and protests took place all over the country. As many as 300,000 workers took part in protest strikes. These merged with the May Day strike, in which 400,000 workers took part,[5] and other political strikes followed.

Before the delegates from the workers' curia of St Petersburg *gubernia* could hold their congress to elect electors to the fourth Duma in December 1912, the Tsarist government declared the election of 21 of them null and void. In reply to the government move, workers in a number of St Petersburg factories called a political strike. As many as 100,000 workers were involved.

On 11 November, workers in Riga organized a protest demonstration against the death sentence passed on a group of sailors on the battleship Ioann Zlatoust by a court martial in Sebastopol, and also against the torture of political prisoners in the Algachinsky and Kutomarsky prisons. Over 15,000 workers marched through the streets of Riga singing revolutionary songs. Next day a number of large factories in the city began a political strike. In Moscow too, workers in a number of factories went on strike on 8 November against the Sebastopol executions.

When in November 1913 six workers from the Obu-khov works in Petersburg were arrested for contravening the law banning strikes in 'socially necessary factories', protest meetings were held in every factory in Petersburg. 100,000 workers went on strike in solidarity with the accused and there was a violent demonstration in front of the court build-ing demanding the workers' *right to organize*. Under the pressure of these events the court gave the accused workers only light sentences. Even so, an appeal was lodged and on 20 May 1914, when the appeal was heard, there was yet an-other protest strike in the capital, in which over 100,000 workers took part.[6] Again on 15 November, the day the Duma opened, some 180,000 workers went on strike.

Lenin could justifiably write in his article 'The Develop-ment of Revolutionary Strikes and Street Demonstrations' (*Sotsial-Demokrat*, 12 January 1913),

> we are witnessing *revolutionary* mass strikes, the beginning of a *revolutionary upsurge* . . . In no country of the world would it be possible, unless there were a revolutionary social situation, to rouse hundreds of thousands of workers to political action for the most varied reasons several times a year . . . the *beginning* of the revolutionary upswing is *in-comparably higher* today than it was before the first revolu-tion. Consequently, the coming second revolution even now reveals a *much greater* store of revolutionary energy in the proletariat . . . The Russian workers' revolutionary strike in 1912 was national in the fullest sense of the term.[7]

The revolutionary political strikes continued up to the outbreak of the First World War. We can list a few of the high-water marks in St Petersburg. On 9 January 1913, the anniversary of 'Bloody Sunday', about 80,000 workers downed tools. On 4 April 1913 – the anniversary of the Lena massacre – a one-day strike took place in which over 85,000 participated. A few weeks later, on May Day, some 250,000 workers came out on strike. On 1-3 July, 62,000 struck in protest against the persecution of the working-class press, the continual confiscation of newspapers, etc. In the first half of 1914 the number of workers participating in strikes was 1,425,000, of which 1,059,000 were in political strikes. This almost reached the figure for the whole of 1905, when the number of workers participating in political strikes was 1,843,000. The movement was pushing towards revolution, but the outbreak of the war sharply interrupted the rising tide.

Bolsheviks Take Advantage of the Parliamentary Situation

During the years 1912-14 the Bolsheviks took maximum advantage of the Tsarist Duma. Against the Otzovists and Ultimatists, Lenin made it clear that the work of Bolsheviks in the Duma must be integrated with and subordinated to the work of revolutionaries outside the Tsarist institution. They must

> establish team-work in this field . . . so that every Social Democratic deputy may really feel that he has the party behind him, that the party is deeply concerned over his mistakes and tries to straighten out his path – so that every party worker may take part in the general Duma work of the party, learning from the practical marxist criticism of its steps, feeling it his duty to assist it, and striving to gear the special work of the group to the whole propaganda and agitation activity of the party.[8]

Again he said,

> We must and shall work hard and persistently to bring the party and the Duma group closer together, to improve the group itself.
>
> With us in Russia the party's struggle with the Duma group to correct the latter's errors is only just beginning. We have not yet had a single party conference telling the group firmly and clearly that it must correct its tactics in such-and-such definitely specified respects. We have not as yet a central organ appearing regularly, following every step of the group on behalf of the whole party and giving it direction. Our local organizations have done still very, very little in that field of work – agitation among the masses on the subject of every speech of a Social Democrat in the Duma, explaining every mistake in this or that speech.[9]

In order to fight 'parliamentary cretinism' and to make it clear that the Duma had to be used as a platform for propaganda in the outside world and for nothing else, Lenin formulated a very clear set of rules for the behaviour of Bolshevik Duma deputies.

For Bills introduced by the Social Democratic group in the Duma to fulfil their purpose, the following conditions are necessary.

1. Bills must set out in the clearest and most definite form the individual demands of the Social Democrats included in the minimum programme of our party or necessarily following from this programme;

2. Bills must never be burdened with an abundance of legal subtleties; they must give the *main grounds* for the proposed laws, but not elaborately worded texts of laws with all details;

3. Bills should not excessively isolate various spheres of social reform and democratic changes, as might appear essential from a narrowly legal administrative or 'purely parliamentary' standpoint. On the contrary, pursuing the aim of Social Democratic propaganda and agitation, Bills should give the working class the most definite idea possible of the *necessary connection* between factory (and social in general) reforms and the *democratic* political changes without which all 'reforms' of the Stolypin autocracy are inevitably destined to undergo a 'Zubatovist' distortion and be reduced to a dead letter. As a matter of course this indication of the connection between economic reforms and politics must be achieved not by including in all bills the demands of consistent democracy in their entirety, but by bringing to the fore the democratic and specially proletarian-democratic institutions corresponding to each individual reform, and the impossibility of realizing such institutions without radical political changes must be emphasized in the explanatory note to the bill.[10]

Lenin rejected the reformists' idea that the parliamentary group should have a controlling position in the party. He held that it had to be subordinated to the party as a whole, and had to play a role subsidiary to that of the masses fighting in the factories and the streets.

The parliamentary group is not a general staff (if I may be allowed to use a 'military' simile) . . . but rather a unit of trumpeters in one case, or a reconnaissance unit in another, or an organization of some other auxiliary 'arm'.[11]

the Bolsheviks regard direct struggle of the masses . . . as the highest form of the movement, and parliamentary activity without the direct action of the masses as the lowest form of the movement.[12]

It is impossible to recognize the revolutionary struggle of the masses and put up with the *purely* legal, *purely* reformist activity of socialists in parliaments . . . It is essential to say clearly and publicly that Social Democrats in parliaments must use their position *not only* to make parliamentary speeches, but also to give all-round *extra-parliamentary* assistance to the illegal organization and revolutionary struggle of the workers, and that the masses themselves must, through their illegal organization, *check up* on such activity by their leaders.[13]

The party's control over its Duma deputies was so strict that, even when the leadership of the Bolshevik group in the Duma fell into the hands of the police agent Roman Malinovsky, the party benefited from his activities in the Duma far more than the police. Lenin wrote many of the deputies' speeches. On receiving his text from Lenin, Malinovsky delivered it to the Director of the Police Department. The latter attempted at first to introduce changes into the text. But the party control of the deputies was so stringent that Malinovsky could not make the changes. Even when he skipped a paragraph or so, claiming this to be an accident due to confusion in the Duma, the original text written by Lenin was printed in full in the party daily, *Pravda*. Malinovsky proved himself an extremely useful Bolshevik agitator!

A.Y.Badaev, the Bolshevik Duma deputy from St Petersburg, formerly an engineer, testified to the extent to which the work of the Bolshevik group in the Duma was closely linked with the work of the editorial board of *Pravda*, and of the Bolsheviks in the factories.

Pravda and the fraction worked hand in hand and only with the aid of the paper was the fraction able to carry out the tasks assigned to it by the party and the revolutionary movement. We used the Duma rostrum to speak to the masses over the heads of the parliamentarians of various shades. But this was only rendered possible by the existence of our workers' press . . . Had there been no workers' Bolshevik paper, our speeches would not have been known outside the walls of the Taurida Palace.

This was not the only assistance which we received from *Pravda*. At the editorial offices we met delegates from the St Petersburg factories and works, discussed various questions and obtained information from them. In short, *Pravda* was a centre around which revolutionary workers could gather and which provided the support for the work of the fraction in the Duma.[14]

The Bolshevik Duma deputies were deeply involved in helping the workers' struggle. Thus between the end of October 1913 and 6 June 1914, they raised donations of 12,819 rubles (of which 12,063 rubles came from 1,295 workers' groups) for the relief of comrades in prison or in exile, for aid to strikers in various factories, and for other needs of the working-class movement.[15]

In the 1912 elections to the fourth Duma the Bolsheviks performed well, getting six deputies elected (the Mensheviks had seven). *All* the Bolshevik deputies were elected in the workers' curias, whereas most of the Mensheviks came from middle-class constituencies. In the seven *gubernias* which returned Menshevik deputies, there were altogether 136,000 industrial workers, while in the six which returned Bolshevik deputies there were 1,144,000. In other words, the Menshevik deputies could claim 11.8% of the workers' electors, and the Bolsheviks 88.2%.[16]

All the Bolshevik deputies came from the shop floor – four metal workers and two textile workers. Malinovsky, Badaev, Petrovsky and Muranov were the metal workers, Shagov and Samoylov the textile workers. They were elected from the biggest industrial areas: Badaev for St Petersburg, Malinovsky for Moscow, Petrovsky for Yekaternioslav, Muranov for Kharkov, Shagov for Kostroma *gubernia* and Samoylov for Vladimir *gubernia*.

Raising the Bolshevik Banner

The electoral procedure imposed by the Tsarist authorities facilitated prolonged active election work by the masses. In order to separate the workers from the peasants, the election law, as we have seen, provided for the establishment of workers' curias, i.e. for the separate election of workers' deputies. The campaign in a workers' curia proceeded through several stages: election of representatives in factories and workshops, election of electoral colleges, and finally the election of deputies.

When stating their reasons for participating in the elections, neither the candidates nor the delegates electing them concealed the revolutionary programme for which they stood. Thus, for instance, the electoral college of Petersburg in the October 1912 elections issued the following statement:

The demands of the Russian people advanced by the movement of 1905 remain unrealized.

Not only are the workers deprived of the right to strike – there is no guarantee that they will not be discharged for doing so; not only have they no right to organize unions and meetings – there is no guarantee that they will not be arrested for doing so; they have not even the right to elect to the Duma, for they will be 'disqualified' or exiled if they do, as the workers from the Putilov works and the Nevsky shipyards were 'disqualified' a few days ago.

All this is quite apart from the starving tens of millions of peasants, who are left at the mercy of the landlords and the rural police chiefs.

All this points to the necessity of realizing the demands of 1905. The state of economic life in Russia, the signs already appearing of the approaching industrial crisis and the growing pauperization of broad strata of the peasantry make the necessity of realizing the objects of 1905 more urgent than ever.

We think, therefore, that Russia is on the eve of mass movements, perhaps more profound than those of 1905. This is testified by the Lena events, by the strikes in protest against the 'disqualifications', etc.

As was the case in 1905, the Russian proletariat, the most advanced class of Russian society, will again act as the vanguard of the movement.

The only allies it can have are the long-suffering peasantry, who are vitally interested in the emancipation of Russia from feudalism.

A fight on two fronts – against a feudal order and the liberal bourgeoisie which is seeking a union with the old powers –

such is the form the next actions of the people must assume. The Duma tribune is, under the present conditions, one of the best means for enlightening and organizing the broad masses of the proletariat.

It is for this very purpose that we are sending our deputy into the Duma, and we charge him and the whole Social Democratic fraction of the fourth Duma to make widely known our demands from the Duma tribune, and not to play at legislation in the state Duma . . .

We want to hear the voices of the members of the Social Democratic fraction ring out loudly from the Duma tribune proclaiming the final goal of the proletariat, proclaiming the full and uncurtailed demands of 1905, proclaiming the Russian working class as the leader of the popular movement and denouncing the liberal bourgeoisie as the betrayer of the 'people's freedom'.

We call upon the Social Democratic fraction of the fourth Duma, in its work on the basis of the above slogans, to act in unity and with its ranks closed.

Let it gather its strength from constant contact with the broad masses.

Let it march shoulder to shoulder with the political organization of the working class of Russia.[17]

Mass Activity in the Elections

The election campaign was by no means a tame affair. On the contrary, strikes and mass demonstrations played a central role. Badaev describes the campaign in the following words,

The atmosphere in which the elections were held and the hasty 'disqualification' of the delegates from half of the factories and mills aroused the indignation of the St Petersburg workers. The government had gone too far. The workers answered with a powerful movement of protest.

Putilov factory was the first to act. On the day of the elections, October 5, instead of returning to their benches after dinner, the workers assembled in the workshops and declared a strike. The whole factory came out – nearly 14,000 workers. At 3 p.m. several thousand workers left the factory and marched towards the Narvsky gate singing revolutionary songs, but they were dispersed by the police. The movement spread to the Nevsky shipyards, where 6,500 organized a meeting and a political demonstration. They were joined by the workers of the Pale and Maxwell mills, the Alexeyev works, etc. On the following day the workers of the Erickson, Lessner, Heisler, Vulcan, Duflon, Phoenix, Cheshire, Lebedev, and other factories struck.

The strike quickly spread all over St Petersburg. The strike was not restricted to those factories at which the election of delegates had been annulled, but many others were also involved. Meetings and demonstrations were organized. Several factories linked their protests against the persecution of trade unions with those against the nullification of the elections. The strike was completely political; no economic demands whatever were formulated. Within ten days more than 70,000 were involved in the movement.

The strike movement continued to grow until the government was convinced that it could not deprive the workers of their right to vote and was forced to announce that new primary elections would be held in the works affected. Many factories and mills which had not participated before in the election of delegates were included in the new list. In consequence the elections of electors had to be annulled and new elections held after additional delegates had been elected. This was a great victory for the working class and particularly for the St Petersburg proletariat, which had shown such revolutionary class-consciousness.

The supplementary elections of delegates from more than twenty undertakings were fixed for Sunday 14 October. *Pravda* and our party organization carried on as strong a propaganda campaign as they had during the first elections. The movement of protest against the workers being deprived of their electoral rights continued while the elections were going on, and the meetings at the factories and mills revealed a growth of revolutionary sentiment and a heightened interest in the election campaign.

The speeches of Bolshevik deputies and their notices of motions were also accompanied time and again by mass action. Indeed this was the main aim of their speeches and interpellations.

The aim of our interpellations was to demonstrate and expose the real nature of the existing regime.

[The] demonstration arranged by the Social Democratic fraction inside the Black Hundred Duma was supported and strengthened by the action of the St Petersburg workers who declared a one-day strike on the same day. While we were speaking from the Duma rostrum about the latest example of Tsarist oppression, the workers deserted the factories and works and, at hastily summoned meetings, carried resolutions of protest . . .

The strike did not end on 14 December. The next morning other factories and works joined in, while those already out did not return. Factory after factory came out and in all the strike movement lasted for over a week. It is difficult to form a reliable estimate of the number of workers who participated, but it was certainly not fewer than 60,000, i.e. the number employed in the largest works in St Petersburg. In addition, however, a number of small undertakings were involved: printing shops, repair shops, etc. This formidable protest strike of the St Petersburg proletariat demonstrated the full solidarity of the masses with their deputies . . . The members of the Social Democratic fraction, the workers' deputies, were in the thick of the fight. We were in constant communication with the strikers, helped to formulate their demands, handed over the funds collected, negotiated with various governmental authorities, etc.[18]

The workers' struggle for improvement in their material conditions, against persecution of the workers' press by the police, against Tsarist war preparations – such issues in different combinations were central to the propaganda and organizational work of the Bolshevik Duma deputies.

In March 1914, a number of events took place in St Petersburg which called forth a remarkably strong outburst of the workers' movement. A number of political strikes broke out in St Petersburg early in that month. The workers protested by one-day strikes against the persecution of the workers' press, the systematic rejection of our fraction's interpellations by the Duma, the persecution and suppression of trade unions and educational associations, etc. The movement spread all over the city and many works were involved. The workers also protested against a secret conference arranged by Rodzyanko, the Duma president, for the purpose of increasing armaments . . . when we denounced this fresh expenditure of the people's money on armaments we were supported by a strike of 30,000 workers.

Throughout March the movement continued to grow and it received a fresh impetus on the anniversary of the shooting of the Lena workers . . . In view of the impending anniversary, we decided to introduce a new interpellation . . .

All party organizations were preparing for the anniversary demonstration and conducting propaganda at all factories and works. A proclamation was issued by the St Petersburg Committee calling upon the workers to demonstrate in the street in support of the interpellation, and workers from a number of factories decided to proceed in a body to the state Duma.

The demonstration was fixed for 13 March and the strike began in the Vyborg district. At the Novy Aivaz works the night shift left off at 3 a.m. and in the morning they were joined by the other workers. The strike quickly spread through the city and over 60,000 men participated in the movement, 40,000 of whom were metal-workers.[19]

The Bolshevik Duma fraction also acted as a natural co-ordinating centre for all party work, not excluding illegal work.

Workers would call on me to ask all sorts of questions, especially on pay-days when money in aid of strikers was brought. Each worker who came with a contribution asked many questions. I had to arrange to supply passports and secret hiding-places for those who became 'illegal', help to find work for those victimized during strikes, petition ministers on behalf of those arrested, organize aid for exiles, etc. Where there were signs that a strike was flagging, it was necessary to take steps to instil vigour into the strikers, to lend the aid required and to print and send leaflets. Moreover, I was constantly consulted on personal matters.[20]

Finally Badaev could say, 'There was not a single factory or workshop, down to the smallest, with which I was not connected in some way or other.'[21]

Bolsheviks Implant Themselves in the Trade Unions

The trade union movement in Tsarist Russia was very weak indeed. Embryo unions appeared in the 1890s in the form of 'labour committees' and 'strike committees', as well as a range of mutual aid groups. Strike committees (often called strike funds) were actually the main type of labour organization after the strikes of 1895-97. They were not only concerned with the occasional organization of a strike, and with helping the strikers, but also aimed at building a permanent organization within industry. Several attempts were made to create a central body so as to unite all existing workers' organizations in a given locality or industry, but this aim was not achieved until the revolutionary period of 1905.*

Even at the time of the 1905 revolution only a tiny proportion of all industrial workers in Russia – some 7 per cent, or 245,555 in absolute figures – belonged to trade unions.[23] The unions which existed were tiny. 349 out of a total of about 600 had less than 100 members each; 108 had a membership in the range 100-300; the number of trade unions with over 2,000 members was only 22.[24] During the period of reaction, 1908-09, they ceased to exist altogether. In later years they picked up, but only to a limited extent. Nationwide trade unions did not exist at all. The few local unions that there were had a total membership of scarcely more than 20,000-30,000 throughout the country.[25]

However limited the opportunities for trade union activities, the Bolsheviks did their best to use them, and on the whole, especially in St Petersburg, they exerted more influence in the unions than their rivals, the Mensheviks and S.R.s. On 21 April 1913, elections to the executive of the St Petersburg Metal Workers' Union took place. Ten of the fourteen members elected were from the *Pravda* list, that is, were Bolshevik supporters. On 22 August 1913, a re-election took place for the executive of the same union. The meeting at which the election was held was attended by about 3,000 metal-workers. The Bolshevik list was adopted by an overwhelming majority, only some 150 casting their votes for the list sponsored by the Mensheviks.

In June 1914 Lenin could report that of 18 trade unions in St Petersburg the Bolsheviks controlled 14, the Mensheviks

---

*In Russian Poland and Latvia attempts to build permanent organizations out of strike committees were much further advanced, and by 1900 some 20-40 per cent of the Jewish working population were unionized. The Bund, created in 1897, was largely supported by the strike committees and based its activities on them.[22]

3, and in one union both parties had an equal number of supporters. Of the thirteen unions in Moscow, ten were Pravdist and three indefinite, although they were close to the Pravdists. There was not a single Liquidationist or Narodnik union in Moscow.[26]

Social Insurance

A legal institution which, though limited in scope, played an unique role in the labour movement at the time was the health insurance organization. In fact it played a more important part in building up the network of workers supporting Bolshevism than the trade unions.

The purpose which the Tsarist authorities hoped would be served by the introduction of social insurance was very different from the actual consequences. To prevent the revolutionaries increasing their influence among the mass of the workers, the authorities decided to improve the workers' lot by labour legislation in the field of social insurance. 'The better the workers are safeguarded financially, the less will the mass of the working population be influenced by revolutionary propaganda', wrote S.P.Beletsky, the vice-president of the Department of the Police.[27] In a confidential circular, the minister of the interior, N.A.Maklakov, argued the point as follows:

> Labour legislation with us is quite a new phenomenon without historical precedent, and the working classes are very much under the influence of revolutionary parties who exploit them in their own interests. But the working classes have realized from previous experience that the main burden of strikes falls on their own shoulders, and have ceased to believe in revolutionary slogans. The present moment is therefore very opportune for withholding the working masses from revolutionary activity by introducing insurance legislation ... But on the other hand the Insurance Act will put large sums of money at the disposal of the insured . . . and it is therefore very important that at the outset practical work should be so organized that the influence of the revolutionary party will be paralysed.[28]

On 23 June 1912 the Duma passed two laws on insurance, providing for payment to workers in case of accident or illness. These acts were a step forward compared to the existing act of 1903, but were still very unsatisfactory. Their chief defect was that they applied only to limited numbers of workers. All those employed in home industry or in enterprises with less than 20 people, all agricultural and building workers, all workers in Siberia and Turkestan, invalids, the old and the unemployed, were excluded from benefit. Only about 20 per cent of all industrial workers were in fact covered by the acts. Workers were not allowed direct responsibility in running the affairs of the insurance fund, but were offered instead the privilege of nominating candidates.

The Bolsheviks made it their task to explain the exact terms of the legislation, so that workers could get the maximum benefit from it. They also aimed to develop activity to extend its application and increase the workers' representation on the insurance body. During 1912 medical funds began to be set up in St Petersburg factories to handle the distribution of benefits to the sick. These organizations were established in single factories employing not less than 200 workers. Smaller factories were grouped together round one medical fund. In practice each fund catered for between 700 and 1,000 people. They were financed by workers' contributions (1-3 per cent of the wage) and by a grant from the employer equal to two-thirds of the total workers' contribution. They were run by management boards, partly elected by the workers and partly appointed by the employers. For every five members elected, four were appointed. Thus the workers had a fair degree of autonomy, although the employers could influence the elected members with the threat of dismissal, upon which membership of the fund instantly ceased. *Pravda*, the Bolshevik daily, concentrated its attack and exposure on the restrictions present in the management of the funds and called for total control by the workers, an end to financial contributions by the workers, and the shifting of the whole cost on to the employers.

The Social Democratic Duma deputies took up the attack on the management of the funds in December 1912. To extend the campaign, the St Petersburg Committee of the Bolsheviks issued a leaflet calling for a one-day strike in support of the deputies. This was the strike movement described above, which began on 14 December and continued for a week, with about 60,000 workers participating.

The other field of Bolshevik agitation was by active participation in the fund, using it to conduct propaganda far beyond the narrow limits of the insurance question. As *Pravda* of 3 November 1912 declared: 'The factory insurance funds will after all become workers' cells. Their membership will embrace many thousands of workers. They must extend into a network throughout Russia.'[29]

After running a series of articles on the funds, *Pravda* devoted a regular section to insurance under the heading 'Workers' Insurance: Questions and Answers'. The Bolsheviks urged workers to call meetings to discuss questions relating to insurance, and to keep the Duma deputies informed of all developments inside factories. As interest in the insurance campaign spread, the Bolshevik demands became quite specific: a central town fund, administration of the funds entirely by the workers, and transference of medical aid to the funds.

At the January 1912 conference of the Bolsheviks Lenin proposed a resolution on the government bill, which made it clear what kind of Insurance Act the party wanted.

> (a) it should provide for the workers in *all* cases of incapacity (accidents, illness, old age, permanent disablement; extra provisions for working women during pregnancy and childbirth; benefits for widows and orphans upon the death of the bread-winner) or in the case of loss of earnings due to unemployment; (b) insurance must include *all* wage-earners and their families; (c) all insured persons should receive compensations equal to their *full* earnings, and *all* expenditure on insurance must be borne by the employers and the state; (d) all forms of insurance should be handled by *uniform* insurance organizations of the *territorial* type and based on the principle of *full* management by the insured persons themselves.[30]

He argued that the Bolsheviks should fight for an Insurance Act without for a moment forgetting that the final aim was the complete victory of the revolution:

> The conference most earnestly warns the workers against all attempts to curtail or completely distort Social Democratic agitation by confining it to what is legally permissible in the present period of the domination of the counter-revolution; on the other hand, the conference emphasizes that the main point of this agitation should be to explain to the proletarian masses that no real improvement in the workers' conditions is possible unless there is a new victorious revolution.[31]

The Bolsheviks should take advantage of every opportunity to campaign openly on the issue of social insurance.

> Should the Duma bill become law in spite of the protest of the class-conscious proletariat, the conference summons the comrades to make use of the new organizational forms which it provides (workers' sick benefit societies) to carry on energetic propaganda for Social Democratic ideas in these organizational units and thus turn the new law, devised as a means of putting new chains and a new yoke upon the proletariat, into a means of developing its class-consciousness, strengthening its organization and intensifying its struggle for full political liberty and for socialism.[32]

To support the insurance campaign, the Bolsheviks launched a weekly paper in October 1913, called *Voprosy Strakhovaniya* (Problems of Insurance), which reached a circulation of some 15,000. Lenin wrote quite often for this journal. Instead of Maklakov, the minister of the interior, being able to use the social insurance to stabilize the Tsarist regime, Lenin skilfully turned it into a means for mobilizing hundreds of thousands of workers *against* the régime. Strikes and demonstrations were organized on the issue. A network of supporters of Bolshevism was formed around the funds.

> In March 1914 elections were held in St Petersburg for representatives of the workers' sick insurance societies of the All-Russian Insurance Board and the Metropolitan Board. To the first body the workers elected 5 members and 10 deputy members; to the second 2 members and 4 deputy members. In both cases the list of candidates put forward by the Bol-

sheviks was elected in its entirety. In the latter elections the ballot figures announced by the chairman were: *Pravda* supporters [Bolsheviks] 37, Mensheviks 7, Narodniks 4, unspecified 5.[33]

Lenin's genius in immediately grasping the value of even the smallest issue, if it made it possible to arouse a large number of workers and unite them as an independent class, was shown very clearly in the work of the Bolsheviks on the funds. This became particularly evident after the outbreak of the war, when the Bolshevik Duma group was exiled to Siberia, the legal daily paper of the party was closed, and the insurance institutions became the only legal opening for the Bolsheviks. The story takes us beyond the scope of the present volume, but it is necessary in order to demonstrate the importance of Lenin's skill in this respect.

In its first issue, *Voprosy Strakhovaniya* explained the central theme of its policy as follows: 'The introduction of *sickness funds* opens a legal and even an obligatory field of activity.'[34] After the outbreak of war it published a statement which was practically in open defiance of the war.

> The high cost of living is well known to all; we all know about it, we have all heard about it. But we have not heard about any increase in pay for the workers, of any improvements in the working conditions which could lighten the burden of high prices.[35]

In May 1916 the paper published an article by Lenin called 'German and non-German Chauvinism', which while openly and very sharply attacking German chauvinism, ended by saying that there was no qualitative difference between Prussian and Russian chauvinism. 'Chauvinism remains true to itself, whatever its national brand.'[36]

Voprosy Strakhovaniya was a particularly useful weapon for the Bolsheviks during the campaign preceding the elections to the War Industry Committees set up in the middle of 1915. These committees were intended to involve workers in boosting production. As opponents of the war, the Bolsheviks called for a boycott of the committees, while the Mensheviks supported participation. *Voprosy Strakho-*

vaniya published what amounted to an open denunciation of the War Industry Committees:

> Only in an atmosphere of political and civil freedom, when the danger of arbitrary rule has disappeared, when the possibility of a free All-Russian union of the proletariat will exist – only then can the working class give its authoritative opinion on questions of the defence of the country.[37]

During the war the funds attracted a massive movement, surpassing even Lenin's wildest dreams. By February 1916, 2 million workers were members of the funds.[38] And the Bolsheviks' influence among these workers was immense. In the elections to the Insurance Board in January 1916, out of 70 representatives 39 voted for the *Voprosy Strakhovaniya* list, i.e. were supporting the Bolsheviks.[39]

The *okhrana* was very conscious of the situation, and a report of one of its agents in September 1916 declared, 'Old party members have begun to make up the membership of the management of the Sickness Funds – elected by the worker members – and therefore the funds have received a definite political colouring.'[40] Clearly Lenin, rather than Maklakov, was right about the role which these bodies were to play!

The Bolsheviks' treatment of social insurance sets an example for all revolutionaries, whose aspirations for the future emancipation of mankind must be accompanied by continuing attempts to participate in the smallest struggles, knowing that

> any movement of the proletariat, however small, however modest it may be at the start, however slight its occasion, inevitably threatens to outgrow its immediate aims and to develop into a force irreconcilable to the *entire* old order and destructive of it.
>
> The movement of the proletariat, by reason of the essential peculiarities of the position of this class under capitalism, has a marked tendency to develop into a desperate *all-out* struggle, a struggle for complete victory over all the dark forces of exploitation and oppression.[41]

19

Pravda

The Legal Newspaper

The Bolsheviks made use of every legal opportunity to publish their literature. The January 1912 Conference of the party, as we have mentioned, decided to publish a legal daily, *Pravda*. This was to replace the earlier *Zvezda*, a weekly paper, which had been published legally in St Petersburg since 16 December 1910. In January 1911 it began to appear twice a week, and from March three times a week. The authorities banned it repeatedly. They confiscated 30 and fined 8 out of a total of 63 issues. *Zvezda*, by organizing mass collections of money from workers' groups, prepared the ground for *Pravda*, the first issue of which came out on 22 April 1912.

Pravda also suffered from regular persecution, and had to change its name eight times, becoming in turn *Rabochaya Pravda* (*Worker's Truth*), *Severnaya Pravda* (*Northern Truth*), *Pravda Truda* (*Labour's Truth*), *Za Pravda* (*For Truth*), *Proletarskaya Pravda* (*Proletarian Truth*), *Put Pravdy* (*The Way of Truth*), *Rabochy* (*The Worker*), *Trudovaya Pravda* (*Labour's Truth*).

Again and again the *Pravda* premises were raided, issues confiscated, fines imposed, editors arrested, and the newsboys selling the paper harassed. But still the paper continued to appear. From 22 April 1912 to 8 July 1914, 645 issues were published. This was made possible by the ingenuity of the paper's staff in circumventing prosecution, the financial support of the readers, loopholes in the press law, and the inefficiency of the police.[1]

The use of Aesopian language enabled *Pravda* to discuss the issues of the day without risking automatic confiscation. Since it was forbidden to refer to the Russian Social Democratic Labour Party, it spoke of the 'underground', the 'whole', and the 'old'. The three-part Bolshevik programme of a democratic republic, the confiscation of the landed estates and the eight-hour day, were referred to as the 'uncurtailed demands of 1905', or the 'three pillars'. A Bolshevik was a 'consistent democrat' or a 'consistent marxist'. The advanced workers knew how to read and understand the paper.

The press regulations required that the first three copies of each issue be sent to the censor. The *Pravda* editors were determined to distribute the paper whether the censor liked it or not. So they tried to gain as much time as possible between the dispatch of the three copies and the all-too-frequent arrival of the police at the printshop, and solved the problem ingeniously. The law requiring the dispatch of the copies to the censor did not specify how long the journey should take. The daily task of delivering them was entrusted to a 70-year-old printshop workman, whose advanced years and slow gait guaranteed that it would take him something like two hours to reach the censor's office. After delivering the papers, the old man remained in the office, ostensibly to rest, but really in order to keep a close watch on the censor, who was examining other papers besides *Pravda*. If after reading *Pravda* the inspector turned to another newspaper, the old man returned at a leisurely pace to the printshop. But if the censor telephoned the Third Police District, which included *Pravda*'s printing works, the old man flew out of the room, hailed a cab and raced back. Lookouts would be stationed around the printshop watching for his return and when they saw him coming round the corner at full speed they knew immediately what had happened. The alarm was raised and everyone started working feverishly. The newspapers were removed and hidden, the distribution department closed, and the press stopped. By the time the police arrived, most of the papers were gone, only a few being left behind for the sake of 'protocol'.[2]

Nominal editors were appointed who would go to prison while the real editors remained free. There were approximately 40 of these 'editors', who were quite often illiterate. In the first year of *Pravda*'s existence they spent some 47½ months in prison. Of the 645 published issues, the police tried unsuccessfully to confiscate 155, and 36 issues incurred fines.

Of each issue half was sold in the streets by newsboys, and half in the factories. In big factories in St Petersburg, each department had one person in charge. He distributed the paper, collected funds, and kept in touch with the editors. Distribution outside St Petersburg was very difficult. It is true that *Pravda* had 6,000 postal subscriptions, but to distribute these was not as easy as it might appear. Copies had to be packed in calico for protection, and mailed from half-a-dozen different post offices which were changed daily to throw the police off the track. In addition bundles of *Pravda* were delivered to the provinces by a number of intricate routes. Thus party members or sympathizers working on the railways would throw out bundles at specially arranged spots along the route where other comrades would wait for them. In one town copies were sent directly to the post office, where a comrade among the postmen took charge of them when they arrived.

The circulation of *Pravda* was quite impressive, especially if one takes into account the illegal status of the party publishing it. It ranged between 40,000 and 60,000 a day, the higher figure being achieved on Saturdays. This was a giant step from the original four copies of leaflets which Lenin wrote by hand and then copied carefully in printed letters. It was also a great contrast with the first paper on which Lenin collaborated in 1897, the St Petersburg *Rabochy Listok* (St Petersburg Workers' Bulletin), organ of the St Petersburg League of Struggle for the Emancipation of the Working Class. This early journal had had two editions – one mimeographed in Russia, with 300-400 copies (January 1897), and the second printed in Geneva (September 1897). A circulation of 40,000-60,000 may seem modest by present Western standards, but under the repressive conditions of Tsarism, it was a grand achievement, and the paper's ideas found response among hundreds of thousands of workers.*

---

*Pravda's circulation was quite unstable : changing very much according to circumstances. Thus in April and May

However Lenin was far from satisfied with the circulation. He wrote in April 1914, in an article called 'Our Tasks',

> Put Pravdy must be circulated in three, four and five times as many copies as today. We must put out a trade union supplement, and have representatives of all trade unions and groups on the editorial board. Our paper must have regional (Moscow, Urals, Caucasian, Baltic, Ukrainian) supplements . . . the chronicle of the *organizational*, ideological and political life of the class-conscious workers should be expanded many times over.
>
> . . . Put Pravdy in its present shape is essential for the class-conscious worker and should be still further enlarged, but it is too dear, too difficult, too big for the worker in the street, for the rank-and-filer, for any of the millions not yet drawn into the movement.
>
> There is need to start a kopek *Vechernaya Pravda*,* with a circulation of 200,000 or 300,000 copies . . .
>
> We must secure a much greater degree of organization on the part of the readers of *Put Pravdy* than there is now, in their various factories, districts, etc., and more active participation in correspondence and running and circulating the paper. We must get the workers to take a regular part in editorial work.[3]

Lenin's aspirations for a mass-circulation paper were not to be achieved until after the revolution.

A Real Workers' Paper

Pravda was not a paper for workers; it was a workers' paper. It was very different from its namesake, the bi-monthly edited by Trotsky in Vienna (1908-12), which was practically entirely written by a tiny group of brilliant journalists (Leon Trotsky, Adolphe Ioffe, David Ryazanov and others). As Lenin wrote, 'Trotsky's workers' journal is Trotsky's journal for the workers, as there is not a trace in it of either workers' initiative, or any connection with working-class organizations.'[5] In contrast, in Lenin's *Pravda* over

---

1912 its circulation was 60,000, while in the summer it went down to 20,000.[4]

* *Pravda* cost 2 kopeks.

11,000 letters and items of correspondence from workers were published in a single year, or about 35 items per day.

A few months after it started publication, Lenin spelled out his concept of a workers' paper :

> As they look through the reports on workers' collections *in connection* with letters from factory and office workers in all parts of Russia, *Pravda* readers, most of whom are dispersed and separated from one another by the severe external conditions of Russian life, gain *some* idea how the proletarians of various trades and various localities are fighting, how they are awakening to the defence of working-class democracy.
>
> The chronicle of workers' life is only just *beginning* to develop into a permanent feature of *Pravda*. There can be no doubt that subsequently, in addition to letters about abuses in factories, about the awakening of a new section of the proletariat, about collections for one or another field of the workers' cause, the workers' newspaper will receive reports about the views and sentiments of the workers, election campaigns, the election of workers' delegates, what the workers read, the questions of particular interest to them, and so on.
>
> The workers' newspaper is a workers' forum. Before the whole of Russia the workers should raise here, one after another, the various questions of workers' life in general and of working-class democracy in particular.[6]

Lenin believed that the workers themselves must write about their lives

> Workers should, despite all the obstacles, again and again attempt to compile their own, workers' strike statistics. Two or three class-conscious workers could compile an accurate description of each strike, the time it begins and ends, the number of participants (with distribution according to sex and age wherever possible), the causes and the results of the strike. Such a description should be sent in one copy to the headquarters of the workers' association concerned (trade union or other body, or the office of the trade union newspaper); a second copy should be sent to the central workers' newspaper; lastly, a third copy should be sent to a working-class deputy of the state Duma for his information . . . Only by getting down to business themselves will the workers – in time, after stubborn work and persistent effort – be able to help towards a better understanding

of their own movement and thus ensure bigger successes for that movement.[7]

Lenin knew how to write very popular, short articles for *Pravda*. They were always factual, and every article centred on just one idea, which was argued out. He might repeat one theme again and again, but always using different angles, a different example, different stories. To give an impression of what his articles were like, two samples are reproduced here.

RUSSIANS AND NEGROES

What a strange comparison, the reader may think. How can a race be compared with a nation?

It is a permissible comparison. The Negroes were the last to be freed from slavery, and they still bear, more than anyone else, the cruel marks of slavery – even in advanced countries – for capitalism has no 'room' for other than legal emancipation, and even the latter it curtails in every possible way.

With regard to the Russians, history has it that they were 'almost' freed from *serf* bondage in 1861. It was about the same time, following the civil war against the American slave-owners, that North America's Negroes were freed from slavery.

The emancipation of the American slaves took place in a less 'reformative' manner than that of the Russian slaves.

That is why today, half a century later, the Russians still show *many more* traces of slavery than the Negroes. Indeed, it would be more accurate to speak of institutions and not merely of traces. But in this short article we shall limit ourselves to a little illustration of what we have said, namely, the question of literacy. It is known that illiteracy is one of the marks of slavery. In a country oppressed by pashas, Purishkeviches, and their like, the majority of the population cannot be literate.

In Russia there are 73 per cent *of illiterates*, exclusive of children under nine years of age.

Among the US Negroes, there were (in 1900) *44.5 per cent* of illiterates.

Such a scandalously high percentage of illiterates is a disgrace to a civilized, advanced country like the North American Republic. Furthermore, everyone knows that the position of the Negroes in America *in general* is one unworthy of a civilized country – capitalism *cannot* give either *complete* emancipation or even complete equality.

It is instructive that among the whites in America the proportion of illiterates is not more than 6 per cent. But if we divide America into what were formerly slave-holding areas (an American 'Russia') and non-slave-holding areas (an American non-Russia), we shall find 11-12 per cent of illiterates *among the whites* in the former and 4-6 per cent in the latter areas!

The proportion of illiterates *among the whites* is *twice as high* in the former slave-holding areas. It is not only the Negroes that show traces of slavery!

Shame on America for the plight of the Negroes.[8]

BIG LANDLORD AND SMALL PEASANT
LANDOWNERSHIP IN RUSSIA

In connection with the recent anniversary of 19 February 1861* a reminder of the present distribution of land in European Russia will not be out of place.

The last official statistics of land distribution in European Russia were published by the ministry of the interior and dated from 1905.

According to these statistics there were (in round numbers) about 30,000 big landlords owning over 500 *desiatins* each, their total land amounting to about 70,000,000 *desiatins.*

---

* The anniversary of the abolition of serfdom in Russia.

Some 10,000,000 poor peasant households owned the *same amount* of land.

It follows that on the average there are about 330 poor peasant families for each big landlord, each peasant family owning about 7 (*seven*) desiatins, while each big landlord owns about 2,300 (*two thousand three hundred*) desiatins.

To show this graphically, we have drawn the above diagram.

The large white rectangle in the middle stands for the estate of a big landlord. The small squares around it represent the small peasant holdings.

Altogether there are 324 squares, and the area of the white rectangle equals 320 squares.[9]

What a marvellously simple unfolding of a complicated marxist analysis, with no vulgarization, and full of interest.

It is far more difficult to write in marxist terms for the masses than it is to write for party cadres. For the latter, the argument can be developed analytically. For the former it has to be based on the workers' own experience, without using arguments that demand a knowledge of marxism. Lenin excelled in writing for both kinds of audience. His style was simple and direct. He was simply a man who wanted to convince. He was indifferent to literary form. His writing is plain, hardhitting and repetitive. It is this strictness and directness of style which demonstrates the sincerity and depth of his thought. His writing is without embellishment or ambiguity, evasion or reservation.

Lenin admired G.N.Chernyshevsky as the greatest of the Russian revolutionaries. The similarity between the two men, including their style, was striking. Chernyshevsky, at the beginning of his *What is to be Done?* addresses the reader as follows. 'I don't have the shadow of an artistic talent. I even use the language poorly. But that is not important: read on, kind public. You will read this with benefit. Truth is a great thing; it compensates for the deficiency of the writer who serves it.' This was also Lenin's attitude. He detested poseurs, phrase-mongers and elegant stylists who erected a barrier between their writing and the reality it was supposed to depict. One would look in vain in Lenin, as in Cherny-shevsky, for any touch of stylistic grace.

In justifying an inelegantly written draft programme which he wrote in 1919, Lenin had this to say:

> A programme made up of heterogeneous parts is inelegant (but that, of course, is not important), but any other programme would simply be incorrect. However unpleasant it may be, whatever it may lack in proportion, we shall be unable for a long time to escape this heterogeneity, this necessity of constructing from different materials.[10]

He would not tolerate flowery presentation at the cost of facing reality honestly. He explained very complicated problems simply. He did not talk down to his audience, but on the contrary showed great respect for them.

> The popular writer leads his reader towards profound thoughts, towards profound study, proceeding from simple and generally known facts; with the aid of simple arguments or striking examples he shows the main *conclusions* to be drawn from those facts and arouses in the mind of the thinking reader ever newer questions. The popular writer does not presuppose a reader that does not think, that cannot or does not wish to think; on the contrary, he assumes in the undeveloped reader a serious intention to use his head and *aids* him in his serious and difficult work, leads him, helps him over his first steps, and *teaches* him to go forward independently. The vulgar writer assumes that his reader does not think and is incapable of thinking; he does not lead him in his first steps towards serious knowledge, but in a distortedly simplified form, interlarded with jokes and facetiousness, hands out 'ready-made' *all* the conclusions of a known theory, so that the reader does not even have to chew but merely to swallow what he is given.[11]

Lenin was a great teacher. He did not descend to his pupils from Olympian heights but rose to new levels together with them. He led workers and they led him. Together with them he strove to find ways of overcoming difficulties, and his listeners must have felt that the leader was thinking out aloud for them and with them. His speeches usually ended not with rhetoric, but with very simple phrases. 'If we understand this, if we act thus, then we shall surely conquer.' Or

'One must strive for that not in words but in deeds.' Or even more simply, 'That is all that I wanted to say to you.'

Many people, meeting Lenin for the first time, were disappointed. They expected to see a man nine feet tall, and saw instead someone very small. But after listening to him they themselves felt nine feet tall.

Lenin's simple, unpretentious style shows at its best in his numerous articles in *Pravda*. They gave the worker reader confidence in his own ability to grasp issues, to understand the world and to change it. At the same time they did not blur the line separating the Bolsheviks from other groups, especially the Mensheviks. They gave a clear political direction. In this too Lenin's *Pravda* was completely different from Trotsky's paper of the same name. Trotsky 'intended to address himself to "plain workers" rather than to politically-minded party men, and to "serve not to lead" his readers.'[12]

Deutscher comments on this statement that Trotsky's

> *Pravda's* plain language and the fact that it preached the unity of the party secured to it a certain popularity but no lasting political influence. Those who state the case for a faction or group usually involve themselves in more or less complicated argument and address the upper and medium layers of their movement rather than the rank and file. Those who say, on the other hand, that, regardless of any differences, the party ought to close its ranks have, as Trotsky had, a simple case, easy to explain and sure of appeal. But more often than not this appeal is superficial. Their opponents who win the cadres of a party for their more involved argument are likely eventually to obtain the hearing of the rank and file as well; the cadres carry their argument, in simplified form, deeper down. Trotsky's calls for the solidarity of all socialists were for the moment applauded by many . . . But the same people who now applauded the call were eventually to disregard it, to follow the one or the other faction, and to leave the preacher of unity isolated. Apart from this there was in Trotsky's popular posture, in his emphasis on plain talk and his promise to 'serve not to lead', more than a touch of demagogy, for the politician, especially the revolutionary, best serves those who listen to him by leading them.[13]

Lenin's *Pravda* articles were directed not only to the rank and file, but also to the cadres.

> The teaching of the ABC, instruction in the rudiments of knowledge and in independent thinking, will never, under any circumstances, be neglected in this big school. But if anyone sought to invoke the need for teaching the ABC as a pretext for dismissing questions of higher learning, if anyone attempted to offset the impermanent, dubious, and 'narrow' results of this higher learning (accessible to a much smaller circle of people than those learning the ABC) to the durable, profound, extensive and solid results of the elementary school, he would betray incredible short-sightedness. He might even help to pervert the whole purpose of the big school, since by ignoring higher education he would simply be making it easier for charlatans, demagogues, and reactionaries to mislead the people who had only learned the ABC.[14]

Lenin practically ran *Pravda*. The main editorial line was decisively shaped by him. Every day he sent the paper articles, criticisms of others' articles, proposals, corrections, etc. In order to direct the paper better in June 1912 he moved from Paris to Cracow in Austria (Polish Galicia), which was only 24 hours by express train from St Petersburg.

As well as *Pravda*, Lenin used other journals to serve the cadres. For instance, there was *Prosveshcheniye* (Enlightenment), a socio-political and literary journal published in St Petersburg from December 1911 to June 1914. Lenin was its main contributor and its art and literary section was edited by Maxim Gorky. The circulation reached 5,000 copies.

The party also had another theoretical journal directed at the party cadres, *Sotsial-Demokrat*. This was illegal, and could deal more openly than the legal press with certain questions. 58 issues were published between February 1908 and January 1917, five with supplements. Over 80 articles and items written by Lenin were published in this journal. In 1912-13, *Sotsial-Demokrat* appeared only at long intervals with a total of only six issues in the two years. Lenin found it very difficult to get *Sotsial-Demokrat* into Russia. In a letter of 1913 he says, 'It is almost impossible to establish proper transport into Russia. The experience of 1910 and 1911 shows that literature that had been brought in lay around by the puds* in store houses and there are no addresses, no meeting places for their distribution.'[15] This was not surprising, as the person in charge of the distribution of literature brought into Russia until 1912 was Brendinsky, an *okhrana* agent.

However, the *okhrana* made the mistake of underestimating the significance of the Bolshevik press published abroad. A report by one of its agents in June 1914 stated:

> Despite the energy and resources expended on transporting it, it brought no positive results: stuffed entirely by émigré theoreticians and arriving in Russia after a considerable delay, this literature has lost all topical interest, is not intelligible to the semi-literate lower classes and has no significance in arousing social feelings.[16]

On the contrary, *Sotsial-Demokrat*, like *Proletary* before it, played a key role in directing the leading cadres in the Bolshevik party. The journals provided the main channel by which the ideas of Lenin and the handful of émigrés round him reached their close co-workers in Russia.

The Bolsheviks also had a publishing house, which published books and pamphlets. One of the most popular publications was a pocket calendar for 1914, *Sputnik Rabochego* (Workers' Handbook). It contained essential information on labour legislation in Russia, the Russian and international working-class movement, political parties, associations and unions, the press, etc. The *Workers' Handbook* was seized by the police, but the issue was in fact sold out in one day, before the police managed to get their hands on it. When Lenin received a copy, he wrote to Inessa Armand that 5,000 copies had already been sold.[17] A second edition was published in February 1914, with deletions and amendments made for censorship purposes; altogether 20,000 copies were sold.

Lenin insisted that all political publishing should be completely subordinated to party institutions:

---

* A pud = 16.38 kilos.

In contradistinction to bourgeois customs, to the profit-making, commercialized bourgeois press, to bourgeois literary careerism and individualism, 'aristocratic anarchism' and drive for profit, the socialist proletariat must put forward the principle of *party literature*, must develop this principle and put it into practice as fully and completely as possible.

What is this principle of party literature? It is not simply that, for the socialist proletariat, literature cannot be a means of enriching individuals or groups : it cannot, in fact, be an individual undertaking, independent of the common cause of the proletariat. Down with the non-partisan writers! Down with literary supermen! Literature must become *part* of the common cause of the proletariat, 'a cog and a screw' of one single great Social Democratic mechanism set in motion by the entire politically conscious vanguard of the entire working class. Literature must become a component of organized, planned and integrated Social Democratic Party work.

. . . Publishing and distributing centres, bookshops and reading-rooms, libraries and similar establishments – must all be under party control. We want to establish and we shall establish, a free press, free not simply from the police, but also from capital, from careerism, and what is more, free from bourgeois-anarchist individualism.[18]

About a year later Lenin added the following remarks, dealing with Social Democrats and the bourgeois press.

Is it permissible for a Social Democrat to contribute to bourgeois newspapers?

Certainly not.

Have we any right to depart from these rules here in Russia? Some might retort : there is an exception to every rule. That is quite true. It could be wrong to condemn a person in banishment for writing to any newspaper. It is *sometimes* hard to condemn a Social Democrat who is working in a minor department of a bourgeois newspaper to earn a living. One can justify the publication of an urgent and business-like refutation, etc. etc.[19]

Pravda as an Organizer

The paper acted as an organizer not only because thousands of workers read it, wrote for it and sold it, but also because it encouraged the formation of workers' groups to collect money for it. Both the Bolshevik daily and *Luch*, the Menshevik daily, published regular reports of collections and donations. In *Pravda* of 12 July 1912 Lenin wrote:

> From the point of view of the initiative and energy of the workers *themselves*, it is much more important to have 100 rubles collected by, say, 30 groups of workers than 1,000 rubles collected by some dozens of 'sympathizers'. A newspaper founded on the basis of *five-kopek pieces* collected by small factory circles of workers is a far more dependable, solid and *serious* undertaking (both financially and, *most important of all*, from the standpoint of the development of the workers' democratic movement) than a newspaper founded with tens and hundreds of rubles contributed by sympathizing intellectuals.[20]

A couple of days later he added:

> It should be made a custom for *every* worker to contribute *one kopek* to the workers' newspaper *every* pay-day. Let subscriptions to the paper be taken as usual, and let those who can contribute more do so, as they have done in the past. It is very important, besides, to establish and spread the custom of '*a kopek for the workers' newspaper*'.
> The significance of such collections will depend above all on their being regularly held every pay-day, without interruption, and on an ever greater number of workers taking part in these regular collections. Accounts could be published in a simple form: 'so-and-so many kopeks' would imply that so many workers at the given factory had contributed to the workers' paper, and if there were any larger contributions, they could be stated as follows: 'In addition, so-and-so many workers contributed so-and-so much.'[21]

In 1912 *Pravda* received money contributions from 620 workers' groups, while the Menshevik paper received donations from 89 groups. During 1913 *Pravda* received 2,181 money contributions from workers' groups and the Mensheviks 661. In 1914, up to 13 May, *Pravda* had the support of 2,873 workers' groups, and the Mensheviks of 671. Thus the Pravdists organized 77 per cent of the workers' groups in Russia in 1913 and 81 per cent in 1914.[22] The formation of groups to collect money for *Pravda* made up for the lack of a legal party. And Lenin quite correctly drew the conclusion,

'. . . four-fifths of the workers have accepted the Pravdist decisions *as their own*, have approved of Pravdism, and *actually* rallied around Pravdism.'[23]

The total number of workers' groups making donations to *Pravda* from April 1912 to 13 May 1914 was 5,674 (of course some groups made several collections, but separate data for these are not available, so that the actual number of groups round the paper was considerably smaller). The average donation from workers' groups in the period from 1 January to 13 May 1914 was 6.59 rubles, or about the average weekly wage of a St Petersburg worker.

Pravda was almost completely dependent on financial support from workers. Of the donations to the paper between 1 January and 13 May 1914, 87 per cent came from workers' collections and 13 per cent from non-workers (for the Menshevik paper 44 per cent came from workers and 56 per cent from non-workers).[24]

Lenin wrote in *Trudovaya Pravda* on 14 June 1914: '5,674 workers' groups united by the Pravdists in less than two-and-a-half years is a fairly large number, considering the harsh conditions obtaining in Russia. But this is only a beginning. We need, not thousands, but tens of thousands of workers' groups. We must intensify our activities tenfold.'[25] Unfortunately, the war broke out a few weeks later, and *Pravda* never managed to achieve Lenin's target.

20

The Bolshevik Party Becomes a Mass Party

The Social Democrats of Plekhanov's generation could have been counted in single figures and later in tens. The second generation, to which Lenin belonged (he was 14 years younger than Plekhanov), entered political activity at the beginning of the nineties, by which time there were hundreds. The third generation, composed of people some ten years younger than Lenin (Trotsky, Zinoviev, Kamenev, Stalin, etc.), who joined Social Democracy at about the turn of the century, was numbered in thousands.

In December 1903 there were only 360 members of the Russian Social Democratic Labour Party in St Petersburg (supporters of both Bolshevism and Menshevism). During the winter of 1904 the membership declined considerably,[1] and by the beginning of 1905 it was less than 300. However, the outbreak of the 1905 revolution gave an impetus to party growth. Thus, in its Report to the Third Congress of 1905, the St Petersburg Committee claimed a total Bolshevik membership of 737.[2] The Menshevik *Iskra* claimed in April 1905 that the Mensheviks had 1,200-1,300 members in St Petersburg.[3] So total party membership in St Petersburg in the middle of 1905 was some 2,000. By January 1907, the Bolsheviks had 2,105 members, and the Mensheviks 2,156 – a total of 4,261.[4] In Moscow the numbers attached to the Social Democratic Party rose from 300 in November 1904 to 8,000 in September 1905 – a 25-fold increase in less than a year.[5]

A similar growth in membership occurred all over the country. On the evidence of reports presented to the second Congress (1903), membership of the party could not have been more than a few thousand – excluding the Bund.[6] However, by the time of the fourth Congress in April 1906, it is estimated that membership had grown to 13,000 for the Bolsheviks and 18,000 for the Mensheviks.[7] By 1907 the total membership of the party had increased to 150,000: Bolsheviks 46,143; Mensheviks, 38,174; Bund, 25,468; the Polish party 25,654, and the Latvian party 13,000.[8]

The party had become a basically working-class party, with very few intellectuals indeed; 'Young Russian workers . . . now constitute nine-tenths of the organized marxists in Russia', wrote Lenin in May 1914.[9] Of the intellectuals he wrote, in 1912,

the bulk of the 'educated' and 'intellectuals' of so-called

society . . . nine-tenths or perhaps ninety-nine out of a hundred practise . . . renegacy with such furious success as to become millionaires, but nine-tenths, or perhaps ninety-nine out of a hundred, practise the very same renegacy, *beginning* as radical students and ending up holders of 'cushy jobs' in some office or other, in some swindle or other.[10]

At the end of March 1913 Lenin wrote to L.B.Kamenev, 'All the "intelligentsia" are with the Liquidators. The mass of the workers are with us, but the workers are producing their *own* intelligentsia with the greatest difficulty. Slowly and with difficulty.'[11] And on 20 December 1913, in a letter to V.S.Voitinsky, he wrote, 'the intelligentsia have cleared off (and good riddance to the whores) and the workers have found their own feet against the Liquidators'.[12]

Badaev, describing the work of the St Petersburg Party Committee, again and again referred to the lack of intellectuals in the party. 'Leaflets are of great importance and the committee devoted much effort to perfecting its machinery for their printing and distribution. The committee consists entirely of workers, and we write the leaflets ourselves and have difficulty in finding intellectuals to help in correcting them.'[13] S.V.Malyshev, secretary of *Pravda* in 1914 until he was arrested, stressed how difficult it was to

> know how to organize and manage a working-class newspaper. We had never been able to go to school. We were all semi-literate Bolsheviks – we all put off studying until we were imprisoned, as we nearly always were. There, day after day, we wrote out declensions, verbs, subordinate clauses and participles. When we were released from prison, we sat down at a secretary's or editor's desk on party orders.[14]

The class composition of the Bolshevik Party corresponded with its class programme. Outside the party, splits, combinations and further splits were the order of the day. But the Bolsheviks, with their roots deep in the masses, did not suffer any splits, or even any individual expulsions, in the years 1912-14. The mighty force of the masses welded the Bolshevik Party together.

Groups which have no mass roots are bound to vacillate

in practice. Lenin remarked :

> Instead of a firm, clear line which attracts the workers and is confirmed by living experience, *narrow circle diplomacy* reigns in such groups. The absence of contact with the masses, the absence of historical roots in the mass trends of Social Democracy in Russia . . . and the absence of a consistent, integral, clear and absolutely definite line tested by many years of experience, i.e. lack of answers to the questions of tactics, organization and programme – such is the soil on which narrow circle diplomacy thrives, and such are its symptoms.[15]

He made the same point elsewhere : 'in politics in general and in the working-class movement in particular only those trends which exercise mass influence can be taken seriously';[16] 'politics without the masses are adventurist politics'.[17]

Whereas the 1905 revolution greatly boosted the growth of the party, during the period of reaction it nearly disintegrated. There are no reliable figures for the period, but in 1910 the total membership was probably no larger than it had been before the 1905 revolution. However, as the period between the end of the first revolution and the rise of a new revolutionary struggle was a comparatively short one – a matter of four or five years – many workers who left the party during the period of reaction later rejoined.

The Bolsheviks now reaped the fruits of their labours in the underground. The few who had held out now recruited thousands. In fact, history proved that it was easier to move from a thousand to ten thousand members than from tens, as in the early 1890s, to a thousand. Lenin and his co-workers had the capacity to make inroads into the masses and to make use of the legal opportunities, without for one moment sacrificing their political intransigence and their uncompromising revolutionary principles.

The 'Instability' and Stability of Bolshevism

The history of Bolshevism provides evidence of instability and discontinuity – largely inevitable consequences of the illegal conditions under which the party operated.

A veteran Bolshevik activist estimated that, owing to police intervention, the average life of a Social Democratic group at the beginning of the century was only three months.[18] A report in 1903 from Tver, a small town on the railway line between Moscow and St Petersburg, and an important centre of Russian Social Democracy, claimed that there was a very rapid turnover of membership in workers' circles: 'a large number came regularly, others after attending once or twice left the circle'.[19] Similarly, Lenin wrote in November 1908, 'the average "life expectancy" of the revolutionaries during the first period of our revolution [1905 – T.C.] probably does not exceed a few months'.[20]

The higher bodies of the party were no more stable. Members of the Central Committee and its agents were, in fact, even more exposed to police persecution. Very few of them remained at liberty inside Russia for any length of time after returning from abroad. Of the Bolsheviks of the first rank, Dubrovinsky, Goldenberg, Tomsky, Breslav, Shvartsman, Serebryakov, Zalutsky, Stalin and Sverdlov were all arrested within three months of their return to Russia. Ordzhonikidze, Inessa Armand, Goloshchekin, Kamenev, Piatnitsky and Spandarian were arrested within a year. Only four escaped arrest altogether: Belostotsky, Zevin, Malinovsky, and Iskraiannistov, of whom the last two were police agents. Only fifteen remained at liberty inside Russia for a year or more: Rykov, Kostrov, Belostotsky, Zevin, Goloshchekin, Spandarian,* Lobova, Shvartsman, Rozmirovich and the six Duma deputies. This state of affairs is not surprising: as we have remarked, there was no conference of the Bolsheviks at which at least one police agent was not present![21]

Party committees were very unstable. Thus it took years for a Russian Bureau of the Central Committee to be set up – this was finally achieved early in 1912.[22] A St Petersburg Committee was not established until November 1912.[23] A committee had been established in Moscow in the summer of 1912 but had collapsed by the spring of 1913.[24] In the spring

---

* As his period at liberty was exactly a year, I have included him in both lists.

of 1914 Krupskaya was complaining of a virtual collapse of party organization.[25] In July 1914 three members of the St Petersburg Party Committee were police agents.[26] Between January and July 1914 the committee was reduced by arrests no less than five times. As we have seen, the party committees were not homogeneous; they frequently vacillated and were quite often in conflict with Lenin.

Major changes took place in the top leadership of the party. In the years 1896-1900 Lenin's allies were Martov and Potresov. Between 1900 and 1903 Plekhanov, Axelrod and Zasulich were in the leadership. During the split of 1903-04 Lenin remained on his own. In 1904 he was joined in the leadership by Bogdanov, Lunacharsky and Krasin. These three then broke with Lenin and eventually left the party (Krasin in 1907, and the others in 1909). The leadership was then made up of Lenin, Zinoviev and Kamenev. During the events of 1917 these two opposed the October insurrection and broke with Lenin.

Why was there this quick turnover among the leadership? The very process of selecting people to lead the party has dangers inherent in it. The people coming to the top are naturally inclined to shape their methods of work, their thinking and their behaviour to fit the specific, immediate needs of the time. The Russian revolutionary movement underwent many changes in course, as a result of changes in the class struggle. A leader who adapted himself to the immediate needs at one stage found himself out of step at the next turn. For instance, Bogdanov, Lunacharsky and Krasin fitted the period of the rising revolutionary storm of 1905. But they could not adapt themselves to the period of reaction and the slow advance afterwards. Zinoviev and Kamenev learned the hard way that it was a mistake to exaggerate the immediate revolutionary possibilities, that one had to undertake the slow, systematic work of organization and agitation during the period of reaction, and the following period of small deeds – Duma activity, the insurance campaign, and so on. When it came to the stormy events of 1917, Zinoviev and Kamenev were found wanting.

The committee-men did not have to take key policy decisions, whereas the top party leadership did. Hence the higher his place in the party, the more the leader was likely to adapt to immediate circumstances, and the more conservative he became. To repeat Herbert Spencer's observation: every organism is conservative in direct proportion to its perfection. This applies equally to political organizations. Thus virtue turns into vice. Lenin was unique among party leaders in his capacity to adapt, while relentlessly continuing to pursue the same aim – workers' power.

The fact that, despite all these factors encouraging instability, the party survived with all the vigour it did, was due to its deep roots in the class, to its being a real mass workers' party. Of course all magnitudes are relative. A 1922 Bolshevik Party census covering 22 *gubernias* and *oblasts* showed that 1,085 members had joined the party before 1905.[27] A rough estimate puts the number at about double for areas excluded from the census. Allowing for the fact that a large number of party members must have lost their lives during the revolution and the civil war, we see a considerable continuity of membership between 1905 and 1922. These were the cadres who gave the party its stability. For a party working under illegal conditions, in a country where the industrial proletariat numbered only some 2½ million, a cadre organization of several thousands surviving for many years is a remarkable achievement.

St Petersburg, the Vanguard

St Petersburg played a dominant role in the development of the Bolshevik Party and the proletariat in the years 1912-14 – providing a foretaste of the 1917 events.

However, it did not have this importance in 1905. During the 1905 revolution the Mensheviks were stronger than the Bolsheviks in St Petersburg, while the relative positions were reversed in Moscow. Even in the years immediately after the revolution the Bolsheviks did not do very well in St Petersburg. This was especially true in the district of Vyborg, in the north-west part of the city, the centre of the most modern engineering industry. In 1907 Lenin referred to the 'Vyborg district, the Menshevik stronghold'.[28] In the election to the St Petersburg Committee held on 25 March 1907, the Mensheviks obtained 267 votes in Vyborg while the Bolsheviks received only 155. In the Neva district, where the Putilov works were situated, the Mensheviks got 231 votes and the Bolsheviks 202. As against this, in Okruzhov the Bolsheviks got 300 votes and the Mensheviks 50.[29]

To add to the Bolsheviks' difficulties in St Petersburg, in the years 1905-07 they were challenged for influence among industrial workers by the Social Revolutionaries, heirs of the Narodniks. In the second Duma elections in 1907, 17 Social Democrats (plus one Social Democratic sympathizer) were elected in St Petersburg, as electors against 14 Social Revolutionaries. The Social Revolutionaries were most successful in the very large factories – 9 of their worker electors came from two giant factories (the *Semyanikovki zavod* and the *Obukhovski zavod*). Taking the four largest factories we get the following picture: the total number of electors elected was 14, of whom 11 were Socialist Revolutionaries and 3 Social Democrats. In the small factories 15 Social Democrats and 3 Socialist Revolutionaries were elected. The Social Democrats' main support was in the medium-sized factories, with 50-100 workers.

The reason why the Socialist Revolutionaries fared so well in the large factories was the immaturity of the working class in general and in particular that of the large factories, which had a high proportion of unskilled workers who had recently come from the villages.

During the years of reaction the cadres of the Socialist Revolutionary Party fell victim even more than the Mensheviks to the diseases of the intelligentsia – instability, pessimism, factionalism, Liquidationism – and the party almost ceased to exist in St Petersburg. The Mensheviks suffered a similar fate.

The St Petersburg workers meanwhile matured in the vicissitudes of the struggle. 'He who has been whipped is worth two who have not', goes a peasant proverb often quoted by Lenin. The years of revolution and reaction developed the consciousness of the advanced section of the Russian working class, whose spearhead was in St Petersburg. The St Petersburg strike record was well ahead of Moscow's, although there were only half as many industrial workers in St Petersburg as in Moscow. The number of strikers in St Petersburg in 1905 was 1,033,000, while in Moscow it was 540,000.[30] In St Petersburg wages were nearly twice as high as in Moscow. The leading district was Vyborg, a name which is destined to reappear many times.

The Bolsheviks, relentlessly pursuing their work in the underground during the years of reaction, gradually gained ascendancy in the working class. From 1912 onwards they were well ahead in the leadership of the workers of St Petersburg. In *Trudovaya Pravda* of 2 July 1914, Lenin could write,

> During the past few years St Petersburg has been at the head of the working-class movement. While the proletariat in some (now few) parts of the provinces cannot yet rouse themselves from the lethargy of 1907-11, and in other parts are only just taking the first steps to fall into line with the St Petersburg proletariat, the latter has reacted to all events of concern to the working-class movement. The St Petersburg proletariat is in the forefront.[31]

The growth of the class struggle was reflected and assisted by the rise of Bolshevism in St Petersburg.

The experience of the months of the 1905 revolution had left a deep impression in the hearts and minds of millions. This was particularly true of party members, even those who deserted the party during the period of reaction and were slow to rise again from their torpor. Thousands of ex-party members kept not only their memories, but also much of the literature, pamphlets and papers of the intoxicating days of the revolution. In the years 1912-14, with the new revolutionary struggle, they rejoined the party in thousands. And while in 1905 and 1906 the Mensheviks had the edge over the Bolsheviks, in 1907 there was a small shift in favour of the Bolsheviks, who gained the upper hand among the organized workers, especially in St Petersburg.

The figures which we quoted in the last chapter of the numbers of workers' groups making donations to *Pravda*, and the numbers of letters and reports sent to the paper, show clearly that in the years 1912-14 the Bolsheviks became a mass revolutionary party (in the context of the size of the industrial working class). In August 1913 Lenin estimated party membership as something between 30,000 and 50,000.[32] However, this was probably an exaggeration.

Nevertheless, Lenin could justifiably say, 'The party is *where* a majority of the class-conscious worker marxists who take an active part in political life are to be found.'[33] 'For the first time, a real, proletarian foundation for a real marxist party is being securely laid.'[34] 'The only source of strength of the working-class movement – and an invincible one at that – is the *class-consciousness* of the workers and the broad scope of their struggle, that is, the participation in it of the *masses* of the wage-workers.'[35]

The Director of the Police Department confirmed Lenin's evaluation of the strength of Bolshevism in 1913.

During the past ten years ... the most energetic, courageous elements, capable of tireless struggle, resistance and constant organization, have been ... the organizations and persons concentrating around Lenin ... The permanent organizational heart and soul of all party undertakings of any importance is Lenin ... The faction of Leninists is always better organized than the others, stronger in its singleness of purpose, more resourceful in propagating its ideas among the workers ... When during the last two years the labour movement began to grow stronger, Lenin and his followers came closer to the workers than others, and he was the first to proclaim purely revolutionary slogans ... The Bolshevik circles, nuclei and organizations are now scattered through all the cities. Permanent correspondence and contacts have been established with almost all at the factory centres. The Central Committee functions almost regularly and is entirely in the hands of Lenin ... In view of the aforesaid, there is nothing surprising in the fact that at the present time the assembling of the entire underground party is proceeding around the Bolshevik organizations and that indeed the latter really are the Russian Social Democratic Labour Party.[36]

While Lenin was expressing optimism and confidence in the mass roots of Bolshevism, Martov was complaining about the organizational weakness of Menshevism. Thus in September 1913, on receiving the news of a Bolshevik victory in the elections of the Union of Metal Workers, Martov wrote to Potresov:

> I am dejected by the story of the Union of Metal Workers which exposes our weakness even more than we are used to. It is altogether likely that in the course of this season, our positions in Petersburg will be squeezed even further. But that is not what is awful. What is worse is that from an organizational point of view, Menshevism . . . remains a weak little circle.[37]

More than half the copies of *Pravda* were sold in St Petersburg. In the collections for *Pravda* between 1 January and 13 May 1914, St Petersburg gave 13,943.24 rubles, collected by 2,024 workers' groups, out of a total of 18,934.10 rubles collected by 2,873 groups. Thus St Petersburg accounted for 70 per cent of the groups and 74 per cent of the money collected.[38] Of all the workers' groups that collected donations for workers' papers in St Petersburg, 86 per cent gave to *Pravda*, while only 14 per cent donated to the Menshevik paper. As against this, in the provinces 32 per cent of workers' groups supported the Mensheviks.[39]

The Bolshevik Party organization was impressively strong in St Petersburg in the years 1912-14. By December 1911 a letter in *Rabochaya Gazeta* (a popular paper edited by Lenin and published in Paris) stated that links between the various party cells had been established, and that a St Petersburg Committee had been formed. It had links with the following districts of the city: Narvsky, Vyborsky, Petersburgsky, Gorodskoy and Vasileostrovsky. Of these the organization in Vasileostrovsky was the best, as there were both borough and sub-borough committees operating.[40]

At the end of January 1913 a meeting of the executive of the Petersburg Committee was held, which adopted the following plan for the structure of the city organization: a wide democratic Petersburg Committee, elected where possible, with no more than a third of its membership co-opted, and a narrow conspiratorial executive of three members; the latter to be mainly co-opted, in the interests of safety and continuity of activity, the co-options to be ratified by the St Petersburg Committee. The committee acquired ever more influence. Workers' organizations of every kind considered it to be the only authoritative local organization of the RSDLP.[41]

By the end of 1913 the organization had become more firmly based. Every borough had a group and there were representatives on the committees from more and more boroughs. The Petersburg Committee now had regular meetings every two or three weeks, and its executive was very active. This was composed of three members and two candidates, of whom three were workers and two were intellectuals. It met twice a week and discussed the current situation and what the party's response should be. The executive also maintained contact with the Central Committee abroad and informed them of all activities in the city.

In September 1913 Badaev reported to the Poronino Bolshevik Conference on the Bolshevik organization in St Petersburg and the nature of the work it carried out. His report gives a clear description of the existing state of affairs, which was obviously regarded as very satisfactory.

> All activity in the St Petersburg District is now controlled by the St Petersburg Committee, which has been functioning since autumn last year. The committee has contacts at all works and factories and is informed of all developments there. The organization of the district is as follows: At the factory, party members form nuclei in the various workshops and delegates from the nuclei form a factory committee (at small factories, the members themselves constitute the committee). Every factory committee, or workshop nucleus in large factories, appoints a collector who on each pay-day collects the dues and other funds, books subscriptions for the newspapers, etc. A controller is also appointed to visit the institutions for which the funds were raised, to see that the correct amounts have been received there and collect the money. By this system, abuses in the handling of money are avoided.

Each district committee elects by secret voting an executive commission of three, care being taken that the committee as a whole should not know of whom the executive commission actually consists.

The district executive commissions send delegates to the St Petersburg Committee, again trying to ensure that the names should not be known by the whole district committee. The St Petersburg Committee also elects an executive commission of three. Sometimes, for reasons of secrecy, it was found inadvisable to elect the representatives from the district commission and they were co-opted at the direction of the St Petersburg Committee.

Owing to this system, it was difficult for the secret police to find out who are members of the St Petersburg Committee, which was thus enabled to carry on its work, to guide the activities of the organizations, declare political strikes, etc.[42]

The lynch-pin of the organizational structure of the St Petersburg party as well as the party at the national level was the group of Duma deputies. The fact that this group was headed by a police agent – Malinovsky – and that all its other members were arrested shortly after the outbreak of the war, shattered the structure. But this is part of the later story.

Outside St Petersburg the state of party organization was very poor indeed, even in 1914. Thus Krupskaya wrote to Elena Stasova on 21 February 1914,

The illegal organization is cut to ribbons. There are no solid regional centres. The local organizations are cut off from one another and in the majority of cases everywhere there are only workers in the organizations, the professionals [professional revolutionaries] have vanished long since. There are no secret addresses anywhere, nor any such conspiratorial practices.[43]

In organizational terms the Bolsheviks in St Petersburg were streets ahead of their comrades elsewhere. In many towns the Bolsheviks did not even separate organizationally from the Mensheviks until well after the February revolution of 1917.

In such workers' centres as Ekaterinburg, Perm, Tula, Nizhni-Novgorod, Sormovo, Kolomna, Yuzovka, the Bolsheviks separated from the Mensheviks at the end of May. In Odessa, Nikolaev, Elizavetgrad, Poltava and other points in the Ukraine, the Bolsheviks did not have independent organizations even in the middle of June. In Baku, Zlatoust, Bezhetsk, Kostroma, the Bolsheviks divided from the Mensheviks only towards the end of June.[44]

In fact, 351 party organizations remained joint Bolshevik-Menshevik organizations, in many cases until as late as September 1917.[45]

As we shall see, in 1917 the local organizations frequently reproached the Central Committee – not without justification – for concerning itself only with Petersburg.

Revolutionary High Tide on the Eve of War

We have already noted that the number of political strikes in the first half of 1914 approached that of 1905. The May Day demonstration of 1914 was far larger than those of previous years. In St Petersburg 250,000 workers went on strike and in Moscow about 50,000; strikes also took place in a number of provincial towns.

The arch-reactionary Duma deputy Puriskevich, speaking on 2 May, gave this impression: 'We are witnessing remarkable scenes; we are passing through a period strikingly similar to 1904. If we are not blind we must see that despite certain differences there is much in common between what is happening now and what took place in 1904. We must draw the necessary conclusions.'[46]

The St Petersburg Bolsheviks called for a strike and demonstration on 7 July in protest against the shooting of workers a few days earlier.

> On the morning of 7 July the city looked as it had done during 1905. With very few exceptions, factories and works were closed and about 130,000 workers were on strike. The workers poured into the street and the police patrols were totally unable to control them; they could only manage to prevent any demonstration on the Nevsky Prospect. In order to avoid any 'scandal' in the presence of the French president, huge police forces were concentrated there to

prevent workers reaching the centre of the city. The movement was not confined to mere demonstration. The normal traffic was interrupted; tramcars were stopped and passengers forced to alight, and the controls were removed. Workers filled the cars and prevented them from moving. Later in the day the men at one of the tramway depots joined the strikers ... workers had lost all fear of the police; they put up a vigorous fight against the police brutality, and many hand-to-hand fights took place.

The same evening the city governor and the minister of the interior had an urgent consultation on the events of the day and decided to take strong measures. The next morning the city governor issued a proclamation warning the population of the consequences of these disorders and reproducing, in effect, the famous order issued by Trepov in 1905 : 'Spare no cartridges.'

In spite of this there were no signs of slackening and the movement continued to grow during the following days until 12 July. The number of strikers increased to 150,000, and on 9 July barricades were seen in the streets of St Petersburg. Tramcars, barrels, poles, etc. served as material for the construction of barricades which were built mainly in the Vyborg district. All traffic was interrupted and in many areas the workers had complete control of the streets.[47]

Alas, the July movement of 1914 was interrupted by Russia's declaration of war on 1 August. The movement retreated, but later surged up again. The war eventually accelerated, strengthened and deepened the revolutionary movement.

Notes

Chapter 1
Lenin Becomes a Marxist

1. V.I.Lenin, *Collected Works*, translated from the fourth Russian edition (henceforth referred to as *Works*), Vol.5, p.48

2. I.Lalaiants, 'On My Meetings with V.I.Lenin in the Period 1893–1900', *Proletarskaia revoliutsiia*, No.1 (84), 1929, p.49

3. A.Elizarova, 'Memories of Alexander Ilyich Ulyanov', *Proletarskaia revoliutsiia*, Nos.2–3, 1927, p.287

4. P.P.Pospelov et al, *Vladimir Ilyich Lenin: Biografiia*, Moscow 1963, p.9

5. E.Foss, 'The First Prison of V.I.Lenin', *Ogonek*, No.11, 1926, p.5

6. V.Adoratsky, 'After 18 Years (meeting Vladimir Ilyich)', *Proletarskaia revoliutsiia*, 3 (26) 1924, p.94

7. Lenin, *Works*, Vol.5, pp.517-8

8. G.M.Krzhizhanovsky, *O Vladimire Ilyiche*, Moscow 1924, pp.13-14

9. N.Valentinov, *Vstrechi s Leninym*, New York 1953, p.106

10. L.Trotsky, *The Young Lenin*, New York 1972, p.192

11. *ibid*. p.131

12. Lenin, *Works*, Vol.42, p.443

13. *ibid*. p.453

14. I.Deutscher, *Lenin's Childhood*, London 1970, pp.52-3

15. F.Venturi, *Roots of Revolution*, London 1960, pp.34-5

16. *ibid*. p.129

17. *ibid*. p.136

18. *ibid*. p.159

19. *ibid*. p.505

20. *ibid*. p.503

21. G.V.Plekhanov, *Selected Philosophical Works*, Vol.1, Moscow 1961, p.182

22. B.A.Chagin, *Proniknovenie idei marksizma v Rossiiu*, Leningrad 1948, p.10

23. A.Walicki, *The Controversy over Capitalism*, London 1969, p.63

24. *Manifesto of the Communist Party*, in K.Marx and F.Engels, *Selected Works*, Vol.1, London 1950, pp.36-7

25. *Perepiska K. Marksa i F. Engelsa s russkimi politicheskimi deiateliami*, Moscow 1947, p.341

26. Walicki, *op.cit.* p.26

27. Quoted by Plekhanov, *Selected Philosophical Works*, *op.cit.* p.439

28. Trotsky, *The Young Lenin*, *op.cit.* pp.52-3

29. V.Korolenko, *Die Geschichte meines Zeitgenossen*, Berlin 1919, Vol.1, pp.47-8

30. N.K.Karataev, *Narodnicheskaia ekonomicheskaia literatura*, Moscow 1958, p.631

31. V.Ivanov-Razumnik, *Istoriia russkoi obshchestvennoi mysl*, St Petersburg 1908, Vol.2, p. 335

32. S.H.Baron, *Plekhanov*, London 1963, p.44

33. Venturi, *op.cit.* p.511

34. *ibid.* p.481

35. *ibid.* p.516

36. M.N.Pokrovsky, *Brief History of Russia*, Vol.1, London 1933, p.220

37. G.V.Plekhanov, *Sochineniia*, Vol.1, Moscow 1923, pp.67ff

38. Plekhanov, *Selected Philosophical Works*, *op.cit.* p.844

39. Plekhanov, 'Our Differences', *ibid.* p.384

40. Pokrovsky, *Brief History of Russia*, *op.cit.* p.230

41. Plekhanov, *Selected Philosophical Works*, *op.cit.* p.451

42. *ibid.* p.224

43. *ibid.* p.266

44. *ibid.* p.120

45. *ibid.* p.452

46. *ibid.* p.138

47. *ibid.* p.390

48. *ibid.* pp.391-2

49. *ibid.* p.392

50. *ibid.* pp.402-3

51. Trotsky, *The Young Lenin*, *op.cit.* pp.189-90

52. Baron, *op.cit.* p.126

53. L.Martov, *Razvitie krupnoi promyshlennosti i rabochee dvizhenie v Rossii*, Petersburg–Moscow 1923, p.19

54. M.Gordon, *Workers before and after Lenin*, New York 1941, p.16

55. Lenin, *Works*, Vol.18, p.297

56. See N.S.Krupskaya, *Memories of Lenin*, London 1970, pp.14-15

57. E.Lampert, *Sons against Father*, Oxford 1965, p.173

58. D.Geyer, *Lenin in der russischen Sozialdemokratie*, Cologne-Graz 1962, pp.7-8
59. Baron, *op.cit.* p.144
60. G.V.Plekhanov, *Izbrannie filosofskie proizvedeniia*, Vol.4, Moscow 1956, pp.113-4
61. *ibid.* Vol.1, p.392
62. *ibid.* Vol.4, p.86
63. A.Gramsci, *Prison Notebooks*, London 1971, p.387
64. See Plekhanov, *Selected Philosophical Works*, *op.cit.* p.789
65. Lenin, *Works*, Vol.1, p.338
66. *ibid.* p.394
67. *ibid.* p.499
68. *ibid.* pp.400-1
69. *ibid.* p.401
70. *Perepiska G.V.Plekhanova i P.B.Akselroda*, Vol.1, Moscow 1925, p.271
71. Plekhanov, *Selected Philosophical Works*, *op.cit.* pp.116-7
72. Lenin, *Works*, Vol.1, p.503
73. *ibid.* Vol.18, p.359
74. *ibid.* Vol.16, pp.119-20
75. *ibid.* Vol.4, p.246
76. *ibid.* Vol.5, pp.474-5

Chapter 2

From the Marxist Study Circle

1. G.V.Plekhanov, 'The Russian Worker in the Revolutionary Movement', *Sochineniia*, Vol.3, p.131
2. *ibid.* p.143
3. E. Mendelsohn, 'Worker Opposition in the Russian Jewish Socialist Movement: from the 1890s to 1903', *International Review of Social History*, 1965
4. A.K.Wildman, *The Making of a Workers' Revolution: Russian Social Democracy 1891–1903*, Chicago 1967, p.31
5. *Vladimir Akimov on the Dilemmas of Russian Marxism 1895–1903*, edited by J.Frankel, London 1969, pp.235-6
6. Quoted in Mendelsohn, *op.cit.*
7. S.I.Mitskevich, *Revoliutsionnaia Moskva*, Moscow 1940, p.144
8. Wildman, *op.cit.* p.34
9. *ibid.* p.32
10. *ibid.* p.37

11. L.Martov, *Zapiski sotsial-demokrata*, Berlin-Petersburg-Moscow, 1922, pp.224-5
12. *ibid.* p.227
13. G.V.Plekhanov, *O zadachi sotsialistov v borbe s golodom v Rossii*, Geneva 1892, p.58
14. *ibid.* p.79
15. S.N.Valk, 'Materials on the History of May Day in Russia', *Krasnaia letopis*, No.4, 1922, p.253
16. V.V.Sviatlovsky, *Istoriia professionalnogo dvizheniia v Rossii*, Leningrad 1925, p.301
17. D.Pospielovsky, *Russian Police Trade Unions*, London 1971, p.7
18. *Ob agitatsii*, Geneva 1896, p.1
19. *ibid.* p.9
20. *ibid.* p.16
21. *ibid.* p.17
22. *ibid.* pp.17-18
23. L.Martov, *Istoriia RSDRP*, Moscow 1922, p.28
24. Martov, *Zapiski sotsial-demokrata*, *op.cit.* pp.250-2
25. Akimov, *op.cit.* p.238
26. *ibid.* p.288
27. Martov, *Zapiski sotsial-demokrata*, *op.cit.* pp.227-32
28. Akimov, *op.cit.* p.214
29. Martov, *Zapiski sotsial-demokrata*, *op.cit.* pp.227-8
30. A.Voden, 'At the Dawn of Legal Marxism', *Letopis marksizma*, No.3, 1927, p.80
31. Wildman, *op.cit.* p.166
32. *ibid.* p.164
33. L.Deich, editor, *Gruppa 'Osvobozhdenie Truda'*, Moscow 1928, Vol.6, p.174
34. *Perepiska G.V.Plekhanova i P.B.Akselroda*, *op.cit.* Vol.1, p.166
35. *ibid.* p.32
36. Deich, *op.cit.* pp.204-5
37. *ibid.* pp.207-8
38. Lenin, *Works*, Vol.2, p.114
39. *ibid.* p.115
40. *ibid.* p.72
41. *ibid.* p.85
42. *Novy mir*, June 1963
43. Krupskaya, *op.cit.* p.19
44. *ibid.* p.20
45. Geyer, *op.cit.* p.49
46. Lenin, *Works*, Vol.5, p.491

47. Krupskaya, *op.cit.* p.21
48. *ibid.* p.26
49. *ibid.* p.25
50. R. Pipes, *Social Democracy and the St.Petersburg Labor Movement, 1885-1897*, Cambridge, Mass. 1963, pp.93-4
51. Pokrovsky, *op.cit.* Vol.2, p.37
52. Krupskaya, *op.cit.* p.29
53. T.Dan, *The Origins of Bolshevism*, New York 1964, pp.211-2
54. Pipes, *op.cit.* p.124
55. Lenin, *Works*, Vol.4, pp.173-4
56. Martov, *Zapiski sotsial-demokrata*, *op.cit.* p.410
57. Lenin, *Works*, Vol.4, p.367
58. *ibid.* pp.293-4
59. *ibid.* p.367
60. *ibid.*
61. Dan, *op.cit.* p.212
62. Krupskaya, *op.cit.* p.27
63. Lenin, *Works*, Vol.36, pp.51-2

Chapter 3
Towards the Building of the Party

1. *What is to be Done?* Lenin, *Works*, Vol.5, p.467
2. *Kommunisticheskaia partiia sovetskogo soiuza v rezoliutsiakh i resheniiakh sezdov, konferentsii i plenumov Tsk*, seventh edition, Moscow 1953, Vol.1, p.14
3. Krupskaya, *op.cit.* p.43
4. Lenin, *Works*, Vol.4, pp.215-6
5. *ibid.* p.216
6. *ibid.* pp.216-7
7. *ibid.* pp.218-9
8. *ibid.* pp.222-3
9. *ibid.* pp.333-4
10. *ibid.* p.334
11. *ibid.* p.335
12. *ibid.* p.334
13. *ibid.* p.338
14. *ibid.* p.340
15. *ibid.* pp.341-2
16. *ibid.* p.348
17. Krupskaya, *op.cit.* pp.54-5
18. L.Trotsky, *My Life*, New York 1960, p.150

19. A.V.Lunacharsky, *Revolutionary Silhouettes*, London 1967, p.39
20. M.Gorky, *Lenin*, Edinburgh 1967, p.42
21. Letter to Lenin's Mother, 1 October 1900. Lenin, *Works*, Vol.37, p.592
22. A.N.Potresov, *Posmertnyi sbornik proizvedenii*, Paris 1937, p.299
23. Trotsky, *My Life*, op.cit. p.152
24. Z.Krzhizhanovskaia, *Neskolko shtrikov iz zhizhni Lenina*, Moscow 1925, Vol.2, p.49
25. C.Zetkin, *Reminiscences of Lenin*, New York 1934, pp.50-1

Chapter 4
'What is to be Done'?

1. Lenin, *Works*, Vol.5, p.349
2. *ibid.* p.375
3. *ibid.* p.384
4. *ibid.* p.386
5. *ibid.* pp.384-5
6. *ibid.* p.422
7. Gramsci, *op.cit.* p.197
8. Lenin, *Works*, Vol.4, p.315
9. *ibid.* p.316
10. *ibid.*
11. Marx, Engels, Lenin, *Anarchism and Anarcho-Syndicalism*, Moscow 1972, p.57
12. Lenin, *Works*, Vol.5, p.402
13. *ibid.* p.412
14. *ibid.* p.425
15. *ibid.* Vol. 6, p.475
16. See Trotsky, *My Life*, *op.cit.* pp.106-7
17. Lenin, *Works*, Vol.5, p.423
18. *ibid.* pp. 441-2
19. *ibid.* p.442
20. *ibid.* p.443
21. *ibid.* p.467
22. *ibid.* p.464
23. *ibid.* pp.472-3
24. *ibid.* Vol. 1, p.298
25. *ibid.* Vol. 5, pp.22-3
26. *ibid.* pp.514-6

27. *ibid.* p.515
28. *ibid.* Vol.6, p.238
29. *ibid.*
30. *ibid.* pp.243-5
31. *ibid.* pp.248-9
32. *ibid.* p.252
33. *ibid.* p.251
34. *ibid.* pp. 476-8
35. *One Step Forward, Two Steps Back, ibid.* Vol. 7, p.244
36. *ibid.* p.246
37. Lunacharsky, *op.cit.* p.69
38. B.Lockhart, *Memoirs of a British Agent*, London 1932, pp.233-4
39. M.A.Silvin, 'To the Biography of V.I.Lenin,' *Proletarskaia revoliutsiia*, No.7, 1924, p.68
40. Gorky, *op.cit.* p.13
41. Lenin, *Works*, Vol.42, p.457
42. *ibid.* Vol.16, p.253
43. J.Martow, *Geschichte der russischen Sozialdemokratie*, Berlin 1926, pp.49-50
44. *ibid.* p.60
45. Lenin, *Works*, Vol.19, p.329
46. *ibid.* p.330
47. *ibid.* Vol.7, p.384

Chapter 5
The 1903 Congress – Bolshevism Is Born

1. Krupskaya, *op.cit.* p.56
2. *ibid.* p.69
3. Trotsky, *My Life, op.cit.* p.152
4. Krupskaya, *op.cit.* p.78
5. *Pisma P.V.Akselroda i Iu. O. Martova*, Berlin 1924, Vol.1, p.46
6. I.Getzler, *Martov*, London 1967, p.75
7. Lenin, *Works*, Vol.36, p.112
8. *ibid.* p.113
9. Wildman, *op.cit.* p.241
10. L.Trotsky, *Stalin*, London 1947, p.39
11. Krupskaya, *op.cit.* pp.100-1
12. O.Piatnitsky, *Memoirs of a Bolshevik*, London n.d., p.57
13. Krupskaya, *op.cit.* p.71

14. Geyer, *op.cit.* pp.319-20
15. J.P.Nettl, *Rosa Luxemburg*, London 1966, Vol.1, pp.263-6
16. Krupskaya, *op.cit.* p.83
17. *Vtoroi sezd RSDRP*, Moscow 1959, p.374
18. *Protokoly 2-go ocherednogo sezda zagranichnoi ligi russkoi revoliutsionnoi sots.-demokratii*, Geneva 1904, p.57
19. *Vtoroi sezd RSDRP*, *op.cit.* p.169
20. For the draft submitted see *Iskra*, No.21, 1 June 1902; for the programme adopted by the Congress, see *KPSS v Rezoliutsiakh* etc. *op.cit.* pp.37-47
21. Lenin, *Works*, Vol.6, pp.502-3
22. *Vtoroi sezd RSDRP*, *op.cit.* p.169
23. Marx, Engels, Lenin, *Anarchism and Anarcho-Syndicalism*, *op.cit.* p.103
24. Martow, *Geschichte der russischen Sozialdemokratie*, *op.cit.* p.81
25. Lenin, *Works*, Vol.7, p.363
26. *ibid.* p.286
27. *ibid* p.395
28. *ibid.* p.31
29. *ibid.* Vol.34, p.195
30. Krupskaya, *op.cit.* p.52
31. *ibid.* p.53
32. *ibid.* pp.92-3
33. *ibid.* p.217
34. Letter to P.A.Krasikov, 5 April 1905, Lenin, *Works*, Vol.36, p.145
35. *ibid.* Vol. 35, p.99
36. Krupskaya, *op.cit.* pp.229-30
37. *ibid.* p.76
38. Quoted in Trotsky, *Stalin*, *op.cit.* p.42
39. Piatnitsky, *op.cit.* pp.59-60
40. Trotsky, *Stalin*, *op.cit.* p.42
41. Lenin, *Works*, Vol.7, p.39
42. *ibid.* Vol.18, pp.181-2
43. *ibid.* Vol.34, pp.164-5
44. *ibid.* Vol.7, p.206
45. *ibid.* p.404
46. *ibid.* pp.346-7
47. *ibid.* pp.147-8
48. Krupskaya, *op.cit.* p.79
49. *ibid.* p.89
50. Lenin, *Works*, Vol.7, pp.356-7
51. *ibid.* pp.391-2

52. *ibid.* pp.324-5
53. L.Trotsky, *History of the Russian Revolution*, London 1934, p.1156
54. Lenin, *Works*, Vol.34, pp.200-1
55. *Leninskii sbornik*, Vol.15, pp.249-59, 351-3
56. Lenin, *Works*, Vol.7, p.571
57. *ibid.* p.574
58. *ibid.* Vol.8, pp.143-4
59. D.Lane, *The Roots of Russian Communism*, Assen 1969, p.71
60. Trotsky, *Stalin*, *op.cit.* p.43
61. Geyer, *op.cit.* p.410
62. Lenin, *Works*, Vol.34, p.245
63. *ibid.* Vol. 8, p.37
64. *ibid.* Vol.34, p.303
65. *Listovki Petersburgskikh bolshevikov 1902–1917 gg.* Vol.1, Leningrad 1939
66. Lane, *op.cit.* p.74
67. *ibid.* p.101
68. V.I.Nevsky, *Rabochee dvizhenie v ianvarskie dni 1905 goda*, Moscow 1930, p.85, S.M.Schwarz, *The Russian Revolution of 1905*, Chicago 1967, p.65
69. Nevsky, *op.cit.*
70. *ibid.* p.157. Schwarz, *op.cit.* p.67
71. *Tretii sezd RSDRP*, Moscow 1959, pp.544-5
72. Martow, *Geschichte der russischen Sozialdemokratie*, *op.cit.* p.88
73. Lane, *op.cit.* p.72
74. Lenin, *Works*, Vol.8, p.143
75. *ibid.* p.145
76. *ibid.* Vol.34, p.293
77. *ibid.* pp.314-5
78. *ibid.* p.315
79. *ibid.* p.324
80. *ibid.*
81. *ibid.*
82. *ibid.* Vol.36, p.78
83. *What is to be Done? ibid.* Vol.5, p.467
84. K.Marx and F.Engels, *Werke*, Berlin 1966, Vol.27, p.185
85. *ibid.* p.186
86. N.Trotsky, *Nashi politicheskie zadachi*, Geneva 1904, p.4

Chapter 6
Fighting the Liberals

1. Lenin, *Works*, Vol.11, p.385
2. D.J.Dallin, *The Rise of Russia in Asia*, London 1950, p.79
3. *ibid.* p.81
4. Quoted in B.Pares, *A History of Russia*, London 1937, p.428
5. Dan, *op.cit.* p.297
6. Lenin, *Works*, Vol.7, pp.501-2-7
7. *ibid.* pp.509-10
8. A.Martynov, *Dve Diktatury*, Geneva 1904, pp.57-8
9. Quoted by G.Zinoviev, *Istoriia Rossisskoi Kommunisticheskoi Partii (Bolshevikov)*, Moscow-Leningrad 1923, p.158
10. Plekhanov, *Selected Philosophical Works*, *op.cit.* p.116
11. Plekhanov, *Sochineniia*, Vol.15
12. Lenin, *Works*, Vol.7, p.507
13. *ibid.* p.511
14. *ibid.* p.512
15. *ibid.* Vol.8, p.258
16. *ibid.* pp.511-2
17. *ibid.* p.492
18. See the collection of articles on the land question *Agrarnii vopros*, Moscow 1905, editors P.D.Dolgorukov and I.I.Petrunkevich, and especially the article by M.Ia.Gertsenshtein *Land Nationalisation*.
19. Lenin, *Works*, Vol.12, p.191
20. *ibid.* p.532
21. *ibid.* p.191
22. *ibid.* p. 257
23. *ibid.* Vol.15, p.22
24. *ibid.* p.25
25. Pokrovsky, *op.cit.* Vol.2, p.148
26. *ibid.* p.181
27. *ibid.*
28. *ibid.* p.246
29. S.E.Sef, *Burzhuaziia v 1905 godu*, Moscow-Leningrad 1926, p.82
30. P.N.Miliukov, *God borbi. Publitsisticheskaia Khronika 1905-1906*, St Petersburg 1907, p.171
31. Quoted by Sef, *op.cit.* p.109
32. *ibid.* p.101
33. Krupskaya, *op.cit.* p.17

Chapter 7
The 1905 Revolution

1. S.S.Harcave, *First Blood: the Russian Revolution of 1905*, London 1965, p.23
2. Pokrovsky, *op.cit.* Vol.2, pp.52-3
3. Lenin, *Works*, Vol.15, p.276
4. *ibid.* Vol.8, p.118
5. Harcave, *op.cit.* p.97
6. L.Trotsky, *1905*, New York 1972, p.77
7. *ibid.* p.76
8. Lenin, *Works*, Vol.8, p.97
9. *ibid.* p.98
10. *ibid.* p.167
11. *Tretii sezd RSDRP, op.cit.* p.54
12. N.Doroshenko, 'The Role of the Social-Democratic Bolshevik Organisations in January 1905 Days', *Krasnaia letopis*, No.3, 1925, p.211. Quoted in Schwarz, *op.cit.* pp.68-9
13. Doroshenko, *op.cit.* p.212
14. *ibid.* pp.213-4
15. *ibid.* p.214
16. *ibid.* p.215. Schwarz, *op.cit.* pp.68-70
17. Lenin, *Works*, Vol.8, pp.90-1
18. *ibid.* p.114
19. Krupskaya, *op.cit.* p.104
20. Lenin, *Works*, Vol.8, p.106
21. *ibid.* p.416
22. Krupskaya, *op.cit.* pp.104-5
23. 'The Correspondence of N.Lenin and N.K.Krupskaya with S.I.Gusev', *Proletarskaia revoliutsiia*, No.2(37), 1925, pp.23-4. Schwarz, *op.cit.* p.66
24. *ibid.* p.36. Schwarz, *ibid.*
25. 'The Correspondence of N.Lenin and N.K.Krupskaya with the Odessa Organization', *Proletarskaia revoliutsiia*, December 1925, p.62. Quoted in Schwarz, *op.cit.* pp.157-8
26. Lenin, *Works*, Vol.34, p.359
27. *ibid.* Vol.10, pp.160-1
28. V.S.Voitinsky, *Gody pobed i porazhenii*, Moscow 1923. Quoted in J.L.H.Keep, *The Rise of Social Democracy in Russia*, London 1964, p.230
29. Voitinsky, *op.cit.* p.194. Keep, *op.cit.* p.231
30. B.I.Gorev, *Iz partiinogo proshlogo*, Leningrad 1924, pp.75-6. Schwarz, *op.cit.* p.180
31. Schwarz, *ibid.* pp.180-1

32. *Novaia zhizn*, No.5, November 1905. Lane, *op.cit.* p.88
33. P.Gorin, *Ocherki po istorii sovetov rabochikh deputatov v 1905 godu*, Moscow 1925, p.60. Schwarz, *op.cit.* p.181
34. V.I.Nevsky, 'Sovety v 1905 godu', pp.39-40, 70. Schwarz, *op.cit.* pp.183-4
35. In Sverchkov, *Na zare revoliutsii*, Moscow 1921, pp.6-7; Trotsky's letter serves as a foreword. Schwarz, *op.cit.* p.181
36. Lenin, *Works*, Vol.10, p.19
37. *ibid.* p.20
38. *ibid.* p.21
39. *ibid.*
40. *ibid.* pp.23-4
41. Trotsky, *1905*, *op.cit.* p.224
42. Lenin, *Works*, Vol.8, p.99
43. *ibid.* Vol.11, pp.124-5
44. Nettl, *op.cit.* Vol.1, p.340
45. Trotsky, *1905*, *op.cit.* pp.251, 253-4
46. L.Trotsky in *Nashe slovo*, 17 October 1915. Quoted in L.Trotsky, *The Permanent Revolution*, London 1962, p.254

Chapter 8
'Open the Gates of the Party'

1. J.V.Stalin, *Works*, Vol.1, p.80
2. Trotsky, *Stalin*, *op.cit.* p.64
3. Krupskaya, *op.cit.* pp.114-5
4. Lenin, *Works*, Vol.8, pp.145-6
5. *ibid.* Vol.34, p.307
6. *ibid.* Vol.8, pp.409-10
7. *Tretii sezd RSDRP*, *op.cit.* p.255. Schwarz, *op.cit.* p.217
8. *Tretii sezd RSDRP*, *op.cit.* p.267
9. *ibid.* p.265
10. *ibid.* p.334
11. *ibid.* p.275
12. *ibid.* p.335. Schwarz, *op.cit.* pp.218-9
13. Lenin, *Works*, Vol.8, p.408
14. *Tretii sezd RSDRP*, *op.cit.* p.362
15. Lenin, *Works*, Vol.8, pp.407-15
16. Martow, *Geschichte der russischen Sozialdemokratie*, *op.cit.* p.136
17. Lenin, *Works*, Vol.13, pp.107-8
18. *ibid.* Vol.10, p.32

19. *ibid*. Vol.16, pp.301-2
20. *ibid*. Vol.13, p.102
21. 'The Reorganization of the Party', *ibid*. Vol.10, p.32
22. *ibid*. p.31
23. *ibid*. p.23
24. *ibid*. Vol.9, p.238
25. *ibid*. Vol.8, p.408
26. *ibid*. Vol.10, p.36
27. *ibid*. Vol.11, p.359
28. Lane, *op.cit*. pp.12-13
29. *ibid*. p.37
30. *ibid*. p.36
31. *ibid*. p.35
32. Lenin, *Works*, Vol.11, pp.354-5
33. *ibid*. Vol.43, p.613
34. Lane, *op.cit*. pp.25-6
35. *ibid*.
36. *Tretii sezd RSDRP, op.cit*. pp.547-53
37. *Proletary*, No.22, October 1905. Lane, *op.cit*. p.116
38. Keep, *op.cit*. p.287
39. Lane, *op.cit*. p.37
40. *ibid*. p.38
41. *ibid*. p.39

Chapter 9
Lenin on Armed Insurrection

1. Lenin, *Works*, Vol.9, p.132
2. *ibid*. Vol.2, p.342
3. *ibid*. Vol. 5, pp.515-6
4. *ibid*. Vol. 8, pp.373-4
5. *ibid*. Vol.9, pp.18-19
6. *ibid*. p.132
7. *ibid*. p.369
8. *ibid*. Vol.11, p.177
9. *ibid*. pp.176-7
10. *ibid*. pp.174-5
11. *Leninskii Sbornik*, Vol.26, pp.355-65
12. Lenin, *Works*, Vol.9, p.344
13. *ibid*. pp.344-6
14. *ibid*. Vol.8, p.153
15. 8 October 1917, *ibid*. Vol.26, p.181

16. Pokrovsky, *op.cit.* Vol.2, pp.208-9
17. *ibid.* p.212
18. Lenin, *Works*, Vol.23, p.250
19. *ibid.* Vol.10, pp.113-4
20. *ibid.* Vol.11, p.173
21. *Iskra*, 2 March 1904. Dan, *op.cit.* p.203
22. Lenin, *Works*, Vol.8, p.174
23. *Piatyi sezd RSDRP*, Moscow 1934, p.62
24. Lenin, *Works*, Vol. 8, p.398
25. *ibid.* Vol.11, p.178

Chapter 10
For a Revolutionary Provisional Government

1. Dan, *op.cit.* p.332
2. Lenin, *Works*, Vol.8, p.286
3. *ibid.* Vol.9, p.56
4. *ibid.* p.94
5. *ibid.* pp.56-7
6. *ibid.* p.23
7. *ibid.* pp.28-9
8. *ibid.* p.112
9. *ibid.* p.27
10. *ibid.* Vol.21, p.33
11. *ibid.* Vol.13, p.328
12. Trotsky, *1905*, *op.cit.* p.35
13. 'Results and Prospects', in Trotsky, *The Permanent Revolution*, *op.cit.* pp.194-5
14. *ibid.* p.201
15. *ibid.* p.203
16. *ibid.* pp.204-5
17. *ibid.* pp.233-4
18. *ibid.* pp.236-7
19. Marx and Engels, *Selected Works*, *op.cit.* Vol.2, p.161
20. Trotsky, *1905*, *op.cit.* pp.316-7
21. Lenin, *Works*, Vol.13, p.111
22. *ibid.* Vol.8, p.27
23. *ibid.* Vol.9, p.314
24. *ibid.*
25. 'Results and Prospects', in Trotsky, *The Permanent Revolution*, *op.cit.* pp.163-4

Chapter 11
The Muzhik in Rebellion

1. G.T.Robinson, *Rural Russia under the Old Regime*, London 1932, pp.155-6
2. L.O.Owen, *The Russian Peasant Movement. 1906–1917*, London 1937, p.20
3. Trotsky, *1905*, *op.cit.* p.188
4. *ibid.* pp.189-90
5. Lenin, *Works*, Vol.13, p.227
6. *ibid.* p.256
7. *ibid.*
8. *ibid.*
9. *ibid.* Vol.4, pp.44-5
10. *ibid.* Vol.10, p.170
11. *ibid.* Vol.6, pp.127-8
12. *ibid.* p.132
13. *ibid.* p.133
14. *ibid.* p.134
15. *ibid.* p.140
16. Krupskaya, *op.cit.* p.110
17. *ibid.*
18. Lenin, *Works*, Vol.13, p.257
19. *ibid.* p.256
20. *ibid.* pp.256-7
21. *ibid.* Vol.10, p.177
22. *ibid.* p.88
23. *ibid.* pp.194-5
24. *ibid.* Vol.13, pp.291-2
25. *ibid.* Vol.15, p.309
26. *ibid.* p.310
27. *ibid.* p.311
28. *ibid.* p.313
29. *ibid.* pp.313-4
30. *ibid.* Vol.13, pp.398-9
31. *ibid.* Vol.15, p.311
32. *ibid.* Vol.13, p.398
33. Plekhanov, *Sochineniia*, *op.cit.* Vol.3, p.119
34. *ibid.* pp.382-3
35. Lenin, *Works*, Vol.12, p.189
36. *ibid.* p.203
37. *ibid.* Vol.13, p.458
38. *ibid.* Vol.10, pp.158-9
39. *ibid.* Vol.13, pp.243-4

40. *ibid.* pp.292-3
41. *ibid.* pp.319-20
42. *ibid.* Vol.15, p.138
43. *ibid.* Vol.13, p.323
44. *ibid.* pp.324-5
45. *ibid.* p.430
46. *ibid.* Vol.10, p.411
47. *ibid.* p.191
48. *ibid.* Vol.15, p.59
49. *ibid.* Vol.13, p.121
50. *ibid.* Vol.12, p.467
51. *ibid.* Vol.15, p.349
52. *ibid.* Vol.12, pp.181-2
53. *ibid.* Vol.9, p.315
54. *ibid.* Vol.13, p.349
55. *ibid.* Vol.10, p.280

Chapter 12
The Great Dress Rehearsal

1. Lenin, *Works*, Vol.15, p.268
2. *ibid.*
3. *ibid.* p.269
4. *ibid.* p.268
5. *ibid.* Vol.23, p.241
6. *ibid.* p.237
7. *ibid.* Vol.16, p.387
8. *ibid.* Vol.15, p.53
9. *ibid.* pp.208-9
10. *ibid.* p.274
11. *ibid.* Vol.10, pp.253-4
12. *ibid.* p.259
13. *ibid.* Vol.17, p.293
14. *ibid.* Vol.23, p.240
15. *ibid.* Vol.13, p.26
16. *ibid.* Vol.8, p.563
17. *ibid.* Vol.11, p.435
18. *ibid.* Vol.16, p.123
19. *ibid.* Vol.29, p.563
20. *ibid.* p.396
21. *ibid.* Vol.13, p.65

Chapter 13
Dark Reaction Victorious

1. Lenin, *Works*, Vol.10, p.135
2. *KPSS v Rezoliutsiiakh etc. op.cit.* Vol.1, pp.100-1
3. Lenin, *Works*, Vol.10, p.152
4. *ibid*. Vol.11, p.17
5. *ibid*. p.130
6. *ibid*. p.351
7. *ibid*. Vol.12, p.142
8. Trotsky, *My Life, op.cit.* p.223
9. Trotsky, *Stalin, op.cit.* pp.126-7
10. Lenin, *Works*, Vol.16, pp.395-6
11. *ibid*. p.395
12. *ibid*. p.406
13. Pokrovsky, *op.cit.* Vol.2, p.284
14. Lenin, *Works*, Vol.15, p.17
15. *ibid*. p.345
16. Krupskaya, *op.cit.* p.192
17. Stalin, *op.cit.* Vol.2, pp.150-1
18. Lane, *op.cit.* p.104
19. Martow, *Geschichte der russischen Sozialdemokratie, op.cit.* p.195
20. Trotsky, *Stalin, op.cit.* p.95
21. Lenin, *Works*, Vol.15, pp.17-18
22. *ibid*. pp.345-6
23. *ibid*. Vol.34, p.411
24. *ibid*. Vol.16, p.289
25. *ibid*. Vol.17, p.17
26. *ibid*. p.202
27. *ibid*. p.581
28. *ibid*. Vol.36, p.21
29. Zinoviev, *op.cit.* p.241
30. Krupskaya, *op.cit.* p.148
31. Lenin, *Works*, Vol.18, p.319
32. *ibid*. Vol.37, p.372
33. *ibid*. pp.396-7
34. *ibid*. p.451
35. *ibid*. p.56
36. *ibid*. Vol.34, p.421
37. Krupskaya, *op.cit.* pp.185-6
38. *ibid*. p.218
39. D.A.Longley, 'Central Party Control in the Bolshevik Party 1909–1917', mimeographed 1973.

40. Lenin, *Sochineniia*, 5th Russian edition, Vol.48, pp.54-5
41. *ibid.* Vol.47, p.223
42. *ibid.* Vol.48, p.267
43. *ibid.* p.58
44. Stalin, *op.cit.* Vol.2, p.159
45. Piatnitsky, *op.cit.* p.162
46. *Proletarskaia revoliutsiia*, No.2(14) 1923, p.452
47. *Istoriia KPSS*, Moscow 1966, p.369
48. Lenin, *Works*, Vol.31, p.28
49. *ibid.* Vol.9, p.182
50. *ibid.* Vol.12, pp.513-4
51. *ibid.* Vol.9, pp. 182-3
52. *ibid.* Vol.10, pp.423-4
53. *ibid.* Vol.11, pp.80-1
54. *ibid.* p.141
55. *ibid.* p.145
56. *ibid.* Vol.13, p.60
57. *ibid.* Vol.11, p.278
58. *ibid.* Vol.13, pp.39-40
59. *ibid.* p.42
60. *ibid.* Vol.25, pp.305-6

Chapter 14
Strategy and Tactics

1. Lenin, *Works*, Vol.24, p.43
2. *ibid.* Vol.30, p.356
3. *ibid.* Vol.35, p.131
4. *ibid.* Vol.9, p.86
5. *ibid.* Vol.7, p.65
6. *ibid.* Vol.27, p.48
7. *ibid.* Vol.26, p.135
8. *ibid.* p.56
9. *ibid.* Vol.9, p.103
10. *Molodaia gvardiia*, February-March 1924, p.248
11. Gramsci, *op.cit.* p.201
12. I.Deutscher, *Stalin*, London 1949, p.116
13. Lenin, *Works*, Vol.17, p.280
14. *ibid.* Vol.9, p.146
15. L.Trotsky, *Terrorism and Communism*, University of Michigan Press 1961, p.101
16. Lenin, *Works*, Vol.13, p.36

17.   Trotsky, *History of the Russian Revolution*, op.cit. p.138
18.   Lenin, *Works*, Vol.9, p.149
19.   *ibid*. Vol.12, p.22
20.   *ibid*. p.489
21.   *ibid*. Vol.9, p.262
22.   Trotsky, *History of the Russian Revolution*, op.cit. p.978
23.   Lenin, *Works*, Vol.5, p.502
24.   L.Trotsky, *On Lenin*, London 1971, pp.124-5
25.   *ibid*. pp.193-4
26.   *Can the Bolsheviks Retain State Power?* in Lenin, *Works*, Vol.26, p.120
27.   Krupskaya, *op.cit.* p.106
28.   L. Trotsky, *Diary in Exile*, London 1958, p.81
29.   T.Deutscher, editor, *Not by Politics Alone*, London 1973, p.71
30.   Lenin, *Works*, Vol.5, pp.509-10
31.   *ibid*. Vol.35, p.242
32.   *ibid*. Vol.33, p.227
33.   *ibid*. Vol.31, p.57
34.   *ibid*. Vol.26, p.58
35.   *ibid*. Vol.8, p.523
36.   *ibid*. Vol.10, pp.310-1
37.   *ibid*. Vol.13, p.159
38.   *ibid*. Vol.10, pp.442-3
39.   *ibid*. Vol.11, p.230
40.   *ibid*. p.321
41.   Carl von Clausewitz, *On War*, London 1971, pp.164-5
42.   *ibid*. p.91
43.   *ibid*. p.166
44.   *ibid*. p.241
45.   *ibid*. p.389
46.   *ibid*. p.266

Chapter 15
Semi-Unity with the Mensheviks

1.   Getzler, *op.cit.* p.110
2.   Trotsky, *My Life*, op.cit. p.182
3.   Lenin, *Works*, Vol.12, p.352
4.   *ibid*. Vol.16, p.104
5.   M.I.Vasilev-Iuzhin, *Moskovskii sovet rabochikh deputatov v 1905 g.*, Moscow 1925, p.85

6. M.N.Pokrovsky, editor, *1905*, Moscow-Leningrad 1926, pp.443-5
7. B.D.Wolfe, *Three who made a Revolution*, Boston 1948, p.340
8. Trotsky, *My Life*, op.cit. pp.182-3
9. Lenin, *Works*, Vol.10, p.37
10. Piatnitsky, *op.cit.* pp.90-1
11. Lenin, *Works*, Vol.10, pp.251-2
12. A.Lunacharsky, *Vospominaniia o Lenine*, Moscow 1933, p.21
13. Lenin, *Works*, Vol.11, p.321
14. *ibid.* p.325
15. *ibid.* p.321
16. *ibid.* p.322
17. *ibid.*
18. *ibid.* Vol.7, p.306
19. *ibid.* Vol.11, pp.441-2
20. *ibid.* p.323
21. *ibid.* p.434
22. *ibid.* p.435

Chapter 16
Lenin Expels the Ultra-Leftists

1. A. Levin, *The Second Duma*, Newhaven 1940, p.70
2. Lenin, *Works*, Vol.15, p.458
3. *ibid.* Vol.16, p.42
4. *ibid.* pp.68-74
5. T.Hammond, *Lenin on Trade Unions and Revolution 1893–1917*, New York 1957, pp.56-7
6. Lenin, *Works*, Vol.16, p.67
7. *ibid.* p.48
8. K.Marx, *The Cologne Communist Trial*, London 1971, p.131
9. Lenin, *Works*, Vol.16, p.349
10. *ibid.* Vol.15, pp.458-9
11. *ibid.* pp.457-8
12. *ibid.* Vol.31, p.32
13. *ibid.* Vol.16, p.52
14. *ibid.* Vol.15, p.449
15. Stalin, *Works*, op.cit. Vol.2, p.172
16. Letters to his Mother, 14 February and 29 May 1898, Lenin, *Works*, Vol.37, pp.155, 264

17. *ibid.* Vol.8, p.389
18. *ibid.* Vol.13, pp.448-9
19. *ibid.* p.449
20. *ibid.* pp.452-3
21. *ibid.* Vol.34, p.393
22. *ibid.* Vol.17, p.51
23. *ibid.* Vol.14, p.19
24. M.Gorky, *The Confession*, London 1910, pp.309, 319-20
25. Lenin, *Works*, Vol.35, p.122
26. *ibid.* Vol.16, p.366
27. Krupskaya, *op.cit.* pp.174-5
28. *Nasha Zariia*, No.3, 1914. Getzler, *op.cit.* p.137

Chapter 17
The Final Split with Menshevism

1. Lenin, *Works*, Vol.10, pp.323-4
2. *ibid.* p.369
3. *ibid.* Vol.11, pp.57-8
4. *ibid.* p.320
5. *ibid.* Vol.16, pp.242-3
6. *ibid.* Vol.17, p.164
7. L.Martov, 'On Liquidationism', *Golos sotsialdemokrata*, August-September 1909. Getzler, *op.cit.* p.125
8. Lenin, *Works*, Vol.16, p.158
9. *ibid.*
10. *ibid.* p.153
11. *ibid.* Vol.15, pp.432-3
12. *ibid.* Vol.12, p.390
13. *Zhivaia zhizn*, 25 July 1913, *ibid.* Vol.19, pp.414-5
14. N.R-kov, 'The Present Situation in Russia and the Main Tasks of the Working Class Movement at the Present Moment', *Nasha Zariia*, Nos.9-10, *ibid.* Vol.17, p.322
15. *ibid.* p.323
16. *ibid.* pp.357-8
17. *ibid.* p.540
18. *ibid.* Vol.18, p.395
19. *ibid.* pp.458-9
20. *ibid.* pp.417-8
21. *ibid.* p.243
22. Trotsky, *Stalin*, *op.cit.* p.111
23. Lenin, *Works*, Vol.19, p.398

24. Krupskaya, *op.cit.* pp.127-8
25. E. Yaroslavsky, *History of the Communist Party*, Moscow 1927, Vol.5, p.15
26. Lane, *op.cit.* p.108
27. *ibid.*
28. Martow, *Geschichte der russischen Sotzialdemokratie, op.cit.* p.133
29. Krupskaya, *op.cit.* pp.161-2
30. Trotsky, *My Life, op.cit.* p.218
31. Lenin, *Works*, Vol.12, pp.424-5
32. *ibid.* Vol.17, pp.493-4
33. *ibid.* Vol.16, pp.19-20
34. *ibid.* p.101
35. Zinoviev, *op.cit.* p.162
36. *Pravda*, Vienna, 12 February 1910. Getzler, *op.cit.* p.132
37. Lenin, *Works*, Vol.34, p.420
38. L.Martov, *Spasiteli ili uprazdniteli?*, Paris 1911, p.16
39. *Pravda*, Vienna, No.12, in I.Deutscher, *The Prophet Armed*, London 1954, p.195
40. Zinoviev, *op.cit.* pp.244-5
41. M.A.Tsialovsky, editor, *Bolsheviki, Dokumenty po istorii bolshevizma 1903 po 1916 god bivshago moskovskago okhrannago otdeleniia*, Moscow 1918, pp.48ff. in O.H.Gankin and H.H.Fisher, *The Bolsheviks and the World War*, Stamford University Press 1940, p.106
42. Lenin, *Works*, Vol.20, pp.475-6
43. Krupskaya, *op.cit.* p.209
44. *ibid.* p.226
45. Lenin, *Works*, Vol.35, p.47
46. *ibid.* Vol.43, p.335
47. *ibid.* Vol.35, p.79
48. A footnote in Volume 16 of Lenin's *Sochineniia*, 3rd edition, p.696, quoted in Trotsky, *Stalin, op.cit.* p.148
49. Lenin, *Works*, Vol.43, p.356
50. *ibid.* pp.385-7
51. Trotsky, *Stalin, op.cit.* p.144
52. Lenin, *Works*, Vol.35, pp.101-2
53. See *ibid.* Vol.19, pp.425-6
54. Trotsky, *Stalin, op.cit.* p.160

Chapter 18
The Rising Revolutionary Wave

1. P.I.Lyashchenko, *History of the National Economy of Russia*, New York 1949, p.688
2. Lenin, *Works*, Vol.15, pp.214-5
3. *ibid.* pp.215-6
4. *ibid.* Vol.17, p.467
5. *ibid.* Vol.18, p.105
6. T.Dan, in Martow, *Geschichte der russischen Sozialdemokratie, op.cit.* pp.268-9
7. Lenin, *Works*, Vol.18, pp.471-2
8. *ibid.* Vol.15, pp.352-3
9. *ibid.* pp.298-9
10. *ibid.* Vol.16, pp.111-2
11. *ibid.* Vol.15, p.294
12. *ibid.* Vol.16, p.32
13. *ibid.* Vol.36, p.384
14. A. Badaev, *The Bolsheviks in the Tsarist Duma*, London 1933, p.179
15. Lenin, *Works*, Vol.20, pp.541-2
16. *ibid.* Vol.19, p.462
17. Badaev, *op.cit.* pp.21-2
18. *ibid.* pp.53-6
19. *ibid.* pp.135-6
20. *ibid.* p.86
21. *ibid.*
22. S.P.Turin, *From Peter the Great to Lenin*, London 1935, p.53
23. V.Grinevich, *Professionalnoe dvizhenie rabochikh v Rossii*, St Petersburg 1908, p.285
24. *ibid.*
25. S.M.Schwarz, *Labor in the Soviet Union*, New York 1952, p.338
26. Lenin, *Works*, Vol.20, p.387
27. M.Korfut, 'The 1912 Insurance Act', *Krasnaia letopis*, No.1(25) 1928, p.139
28. *ibid.* p.163
29. S.Milligan, 'The Petrograd Bolsheviks and Social Insurance. 1914-17', *Soviet Studies*, January 1969
30. Lenin, *Works*, Vol.17, p.476
31. *ibid.* p.478
32. *ibid.* pp.478-9
33. *ibid.* Vol.20, p.234
34. *Voprosy strakhovaniia*, 26 October 1913. Milligan, *op.cit.*

35. *ibid.* 20 March 1913. *ibid.*
36. *ibid.* 31 May 1916. Lenin, *Works*, Vol.22, p.184
37. *ibid.* 31 August 1915. Milligan, *op.cit.*
38. *ibid.* 16 February 1916. *ibid.*
39. *ibid.*
40. M.G.Fleer, *Peterburgskii komitet bolshevikov v gody voiny 1914–1917*, Leningrad 1927, p.69
41. Lenin, *Works*, Vol.8, p.426

Chapter 19
Pravda

1. For a very interesting description see W.Bassow, 'The Pre-revolutionary Pravda and Tsarist Censorship', *The American Slavic and East European Review*, February 1954
2. *ibid.*
3. Lenin, *Works*, Vol.36, p.283
4. *ibid.* p.212
5. *ibid.* Vol.20, p.328
6. *ibid.* Vol.18, p.300
7. *ibid.* Vol.19, p.324
8. *ibid.* Vol.18, pp.543-4
9. *ibid.* pp.586-7
10. *ibid.* Vol.29, pp.166-7
11. *ibid.* Vol.5, pp.311-2
12. *Pravda*, Vienna, No.1. Deutscher, *The Prophet Armed*, *op.cit.* p.193
13. *ibid.* pp.193-4
14. Lenin, *Works*, Vol.8, pp.454-5
15. *Proletarskaia revoliutsiia*, No.2(14) 1923, p.45
16. *ibid.* p.455
17. Lenin, *Works*, Vol.35, p.132
18. *ibid.* Vol.10, pp.45-7
19. *ibid.* Vol.11, p.262
20. *ibid.* Vol.18, p.188
21. *ibid.* p.201
22. *ibid.* Vol.20, p.363
23. *ibid.* p.320
24. *ibid.* p.369
25. *ibid.* p.370

Chapter 20
The Bolshevik Party Becomes a Mass Party

1. Lane, *op.cit.* p.72
2. *Tretii sezd RSDRP, op.cit.* p.547
3. *Iskra*, No.97, April 1905. Lane, *op.cit.* p.74
4. Lenin, *Works*, Vol.12, p.400
5. Pokrovsky, *Brief History of Russia, op.cit.* p.155
6. *Vtoroi sezd RSDRP, op.cit.* pp.514-685
7. Lenin, *Works*, Vol.11, pp.264-5
8. M.Liadov, 'The London Congress of the RSDLP in Figures', *Itogi Londonskogo sezda*, St Petersburg 1907, p.84
9. Lenin, *Works*, Vol.20, p.329
10. *ibid.* Vol.18, p.274
11. *ibid.* Vol.35, p.93
12. *ibid.* Vol.43, p.368
13. Badaev, *op.cit.* p.110
14. S.V.Malyshev in *Molodaia gvardiia*, Nos.2-3, 1925, pp.138-9
15. Lenin, *Works*, Vol.20, pp.471-2
16. *ibid.* p.465
17. *ibid.* p.356
18. O.Piatnitsky, *Iskrovski period v Moskve*, Moscow-Leningrad 1928, p.60
19. N.Angarsky, editor, *Doklady sotsial-demokraticheskikh komitetov vtoromu sezdu RSDRP*, Moscow-Leningrad 1930, p.616
20. Lenin, *Works*, Vol.15, pp.289-90
21. Longley, *op.cit.*
22. *Istoriia KPSS*, Moscow 1966, Vol.2, p.338
23. *ibid.* pp.384-5
24. *Proletarskaia revoliutsiia*, No.2(14) 1923, p.452
25. *Istoricheskii arkhiv*, No.1, 1957, pp.26-7
26. A.Kiselev, 'In July 1914', *Proletarskaia revoliutsiia*, No.7(30) 1924
27. Lane, *op.cit.* p.12
28. Lenin, *Works*, Vol.12, p.20
29. *ibid.* p.400
30. *ibid.* Vol.16, p.399
31. *ibid.* Vol.20, p.553
32. *ibid.* Vol.19, p.406
33. *ibid.* p.444
34. *ibid.* Vol.20, p.279
35. *ibid.* p.363
36. Quoted in Trotsky, *Stalin, op.cit.* pp.162-3

37. Quoted in L.Harrison, 'The Problem of Social Stability in Urban Russia, 1905–1917', *Slavic Review*, December 1964
38. Lenin, *Works*, Vol.20, pp.364-5
39. *ibid.* p.366
40. *Partiia bolshevikov v gody novogo revoliutsionnogo podema 1910–1914 gg.*, Moscow 1959, pp.284-7
41. *ibid.* p.291
42. Badaev, *op.cit.* p.109
43. R.H.McNeal, *Bride of the Revolution*, London 1973, p.145
44. Trotsky, *History of the Russian Revolution*, *op.cit.* p.445
45. V.V.Anikeev, in *Voprosy Istorii KPSS*, Nos.2 and 3, 1958
46. Badaev, *op.cit.* p.153
47. *ibid.* pp.176-7

Index

Adoratsky,V.V., 5

Agitation, definition of, 45; Plekhanov and agitation, 46ff, 50-2; pioneering role of Jewish and Polish workers, 46-7; A.Kremer and Iu.Martov's pamphlet on, 47-8; lays foundation for 'economism', 48, 59-60; worker members of study circles – attitude to, 58-9; Lenin and, 52-8

Akimov,V.P., 105-6, 109

Alexinsky,G.A., 282-3, 313

Armand, Inessa, 160, 180, 255, 349, 356

'August Bloc', 313

Axelrod,P.B., and Emancipation of Labour Group, 30; and liberals, 37, 112, 141; and factory agitation, 50-2; and *Iskra*, 72-5,114; on Lenin's personality, 78; at second Party Congress, 105ff; and Liquidators, 297-8

Babushkin,I.V., 56, 65, 169

Badaev,A.Y., Bolsheviks in Duma and *Pravda*, 324-5; Bolsheviks in Duma and workers' struggle, 325, 328-30; Duma electoral campaigns, 326-8; on structure of Bolshevik organization in Petersburg,363-4

Balabanov,A., on Lenin, 94

Bernstein,E., 61-2

Blagoev,Dmitri, 30

Bogdanov,A.A., joins Bolsheviks, 131; and Soviet, 163; on wide recruitment to Party, 172-3; and Capri school, 245; and elections to Duma, 251-282; expelled from Bolshevik faction, 285-7; and philosophy, 287-91

Bolsheviks, 255, 257; origin of, 105ff, split with Mensheviks seems unjustified to participants, 118-21; split anticipating future differences, 124-5; history of organizational relations with Mensheviks, 127; Bolshevik leaders oppose split with Mensheviks, 127-9, 130-1; Lenin removed from leadership of Bolshevik faction, 129; Karl

Kautsky, Rosa Luxemburg and August Bebel and Bolsheviks, 131; membership, 132-4, 179, 181,239-41, 353, 355, 358, 359, 361; and Gapon movement, 133-4; on demonstration of 'Bloody Sunday', 156; attitude to trade unions, 159-60; attitude to Soviets, 160-3; attitude to wide recruitment to Party 171-5; and social composition of Party committees, 173-4; age composition, 179-80; social composition, 181-2; in the armed insurrection (December, 1905), 185, 191-3; on class nature of revolution, 205-6; and peasantry, 215, 221, 224-7; steeled by 1905 revolution, 233-4; *okhrana* agents infiltrated into, 240, 242; learn to retreat, 247-8; and Duma elections, 248-51, 324-30; and unity with Mensheviks, 205, 275-6; finances of, 301-4; and 'exes', 304-5; and strike movement, 327-30; and trade unions, 330-2; and social insurance, 332-7

Brusnev group, 54

Bund, 101, 110, 111, 130, 179, 276, 313, 353

Cadets, *see* Liberals

Chaikovsky,N.V., 21

Chaikovists, 21-23

Chernomazov, Myron, 242

Chernyi Peredel, 21

Chernyshevsky,G.N., founds politics of Narodism, 10-11; and peasant rebellion, 11; and village commune, 11; founds first Narodnik underground organization, 11; arrest and exile (1862-83), 11-12; and liberals, 148-9; and style (influence on Lenin), 345

Chervanin,N., 274

Clausewitz,K., main authority for Lenin on military matters, 188-9; on science and art in war, 270; on relation between strategy and tactics, 271-2; on 'seizing the key link', 273

Cluseret, Gustave Paul, 188-9

Lengnik,F.V., 101, 111

Lenin (Vladimir Ilyich Ulyanov), family background, 1-2; influence of brother Alexander, 2-3, 5, 7-8; personality, 77-9, 93-5; personal relations and politics, 75, 114-8; style, 345-7

Early activities:

expelled from Kazan University (Dec. 1887), 4; joins Narodnik Circle, 4; under influence of Narodism, 4-9; and individual terrorism, 5-6; Plekhanov's intellectual influence on, 29-30, 34; youthful theoretical works compared with Plekhanov's, 31ff; and Narodism, 32-5; and G.N.Chernyshevsky, 34, 148-9; and V.V., 32-3; and Struve, 36-7, 73; and 'legal marxism', 36-7; and liberals, 37; attitude to liberals compared with Plekhanov's and Axelrod's, 37; and revolutionary contents of Narodism, 38-40; and organizational traditions of Narodism, 39-41; and youth of Russian proletariat, 41; and factory agitation, 52ff; on economic agitation and political class consciousness, 52-3; and exclusion of Tsarism from agitation, 54; and labour legislation, 56; learning from workers, 56-7; his first leaflets, 57-9; and 'economism', 63-7; 'bending the stick', 67

1900-03:

on national paper as Party organizer, 69-71; personal relations with Plekhanov, 71-5, 116-7; trade union consciousness and political consciousness, 79-81; operational role of *What is to be Done?*, 82; and all forms of oppression, 82-3; and religious sects, 83-4; and professional revolutionaries, 86-7; and intelligentsia, 87; on structure of Party, 67-81, 89-91; on Party Rules, 92-3; preparing for second Party Congress, 98, 104; and role of *Iskra*, 100-1; and workers' letters, 102-3; at the second Congress, 105ff; and definition of membership, 108-10; and editorial board of *Iskra*, 111-2; on sentimentality in choosing Party leaders, 113-4; personal relations with Zasulich, 114-5; personal relations with Martov, 115-6; personal relations and Party split, 120; initial differences with Mensheviks, 121-2; on

role of intellectuals in Party split, 122-4; and Bolshevik leaders' reluctance to split, 127-9; and weakness of Bolshevik leadership in Russia, 124-6; and priority of organization question, 137-8; and liberals, 142-5, 148

1905 revolution:

attitude to Gapon, 156-9; on Zubatovism, 157; on attitude to trade unions, 160; on attitude to Soviets, 163-4; on potential role of Soviets, 163-6; on mass recruitment to Party, 171-9; on spontaneity and socialist consciousness, 175-7; on role of intellectuals in Party, 178; on youth of Party members, 180; on organizational structures, 182-3; on armed insurrection, 183ff; on winning the army to side of revolution, 187-8; on concrete measures for insurrection, 189-91; and Plekhanov regarding insurrection, 193-4; and Martov regarding insurrection, 194-5; and 'democratic dictatorship of workers and peasants', 197-8; and bourgeois nature of revolution, 199-201; on hegemony of proletariat in revolution, 205-6, 225-7; and peasantry, 211ff; his first agrarian draft programme, 212-3; attitude to land nationalization, 213; and Gapon on mood of peasantry, 214; revises agrarian programme and attitude to land nationalization, 214-6; and the monarchist peasants, 216-9; on proletarian leadership of peasantry, 221-2, 224-5; on land nationalization and capitalist development, 222-4; on peasantry's direct action, 226; on peasantry smashing old state machine, 226-7; on international nature of revolution, 227; on revolution as test of all classes and parties, 228-9; on potentialities of working people, 229, 231-2; on revolution as school for proletariat, 230; on relations between Party and class, 232-4

1906-10:

on revolutionary prospects 1906-07, 234-6; on inter-relation between economic slump and revolution, 237; and disintegration of labour movement, 239-41; on role of intellectuals during period of reaction, 240; life in second

exile, 242-6; on learning how to retreat, 247ff; and Duma elections, 248-52; in minority amongst Bolsheviks on Duma question, 250-1, 282-5; on strategy and tactics, 253ff; compared to Marx, 254; on relation between theory and practice, 254-8; on slogans, 257; and relation between marxism and fatalism, 259; on sober evaluation of situation and decisiveness in action, 260-1; 'bending the stick', 261-2; and revolutionary intuition, 263-4; and inner Party democracy, 268-9; and self-criticism, 269; and Clausewitz, 253, 270-3; on need to fuse with Mensheviks, 275-8; bending Party rules, 278-80, 286; and Bogdanov's philosophical stand, 287-91; and Liquidationism, 295-300; on relation between legal and illegal Party, 299; on intellectuals and Liquidationism, 300; on rapprochement with Plekhanov, 306-8
1911-14:
on Conciliators, 308ff; on Malinovsky, 311; on Martov's 'slander' of Malinovsky, 311; and Conciliators on editorial board of *Pravda*, 313-6; and Conciliators in Bolshevik Duma group, 316-17; and student movement, 318-19; on work of Bolsheviks in Duma, 322-4; on social insurance, 334-6; on nature of workers' paper, 341-3; as writer of popular articles, 343-6; as writer for Party cadres, 347-8; on *Pravda* as organizer, 350-2
Liberals, attitude to Russo-Japanese war, 139-40; and Zemstvo banquet campaign, 140; attitude to agrarian problem and peasantry, 144-5; support the 1905 revolution at start, 146; support anti-Tsarist workers' strikes, 146-7; turn against workers and revolution, 147; from republicanism to constitutional monarchism, 148; on 'irrationality' of masses in revolution, 231
Lockhart, Bruce,R.H., on Lenin's personality, 94
Lunacharsky,A.V., on Lenin's single-mindedness, 77; contrasts Lenin's and Trotsky's personalities, 93-4; on insignificance of differences between Bolsheviks and Mensheviks (1903), 118; joins Bol-

sheviks, 131; in Capri school, 245; and participation in Duma elections, 251, 282; and 'God-building', 290; on ideological instability of Mensheviks, 294
Luxemburg,R., on the 1880s, 18-19; and Party administration, 104; and Bolsheviks, 131; and Soviet, 167

Makarov,A.A., 320
Maklakov,N.A., 332, 335, 337
Malinovsky,R., 242, 324, 364; and split between Bolsheviks and Mensheviks, 311, 317
Martov,L., on alienation of workers in study circles from proletariat, 45; with A.Kremer writes *Ob Agitatsii*, 47-8; leading role in turn to factory agitation, 48-9; founding with Lenin the St Petersburg League of Struggle, 54-9; joins Lenin in fighting 'economism', 53; and *Iskra*, 69, 71-4, 99-101, 114; and rule-mongering, 92-3; at second Congress, 105ff; and dictatorship of the proletariat, 107; and Party rules of membership, 108, 110; and liberals, 112; Trotsky on his personality, 125, 275; on Gapon movement, 154-5; and preparations for armed uprising, 194-5; nerves during 1905 revolution, 274-5; on bankruptcy of Bolsheviks because of poverty of their intellectuals, 293; and Liquidators, 295, 300; on 'exes', 304-5; on organizational weakness of Mensheviks, 362
Martynov,A.S., and RSDLP programme, 105; nature of revolution, 141-2; attitude to liberals, 141-2; on Mensheviks' 'madness' in 1905, 274
Marx,K., and Tsarist censorship, 14, 35; admired by Narodniks, 14-15; teaching adapted by Narodniks, 17; on relation between sectional-economic and general-political struggles, 81-2; indifferent to Party existence, 137-8; on permanent revolution , 203-4; on land nationalization, 222-3; on unity of theory and practice, 254; compared to Lenin, 254; on verbal extremism in periods of reaction, 283
Mensheviks and Menshevism, born, 105ff; original differences with

PLUTO  **PRESS**

For a list of
books and pamphlets available
write to:

Unit 10 Spencer Court,
7 Chalcot Road, London NW1 8LH

Lenin's Last Struggle

Moshe Lewin

Lenin's Last Struggle tells the story of Lenin's final four months of political activity – how in spite of partial paralysis and ignoring doctor's orders, Lenin fought against the tide of bureaucracy and chauvinism that was engulfing the first workers' state. It tells how he grew to realise that Stalin was actively promoting reaction from his post as Secretary General of the Communist Party and would have to be removed.

It was too late. Stalinism as a system of government and totalitarian control was already too strong.

90p paperback

Pluto  Press

Unit 10 Spencer Court, 7 Chalcot Road

London NW1 8LH

The Bolsheviks and the October Revolution

Central Committee Minutes of the Russian Social-Democratic
Labour Party (bolsheviks) August 1917-February 1918

Translated from the Russian by Ann Bone

Revolution in Russia, October 1917, meant that posterity was to
inherit a new society. What remains is a scrapbook – the notes for
the Bolshevik Central Committee, hurriedly pencilled on torn-out
sheets of paper.

Captured in these notes is the deep division that lay between
revolutionaries and routinists on the central committee, between
men terrified to lose and men terrified to grasp the opportunity to
change the pace of history.

The minutes are extensively supplemented by documents, the
official notes of the Institute of Marxism-Leninism, Moscow,
together with additional notes and comments for this edition.

£2.70 paperback   £6.60 hardback

Pluto Press

Unit 10 Spencer Court, 7 Chalcot Road

London NW1 8LH

Bureaucracy and Revolution in Eastern Europe

Chris Harman

Chris Harman analyses the self-styled 'socialist' societies established in Eastern Europe after the second world war. He shows how the post-war division of the world into rival spheres of influence allowed local Communist Parties to set up monolithic political systems under Russian protection; how the Parties were forged into weapons of totalitarian domination by internal purges and by repressing every competing organisation, especially those rooted in the working class.

The workers resisted – in East Germany, in Poland, in Hungary, in Czechoslovakia. Chris Harman shows why and how they resisted in each case; how they rejected bureaucratic 'planning' and refused to bear the cost of the regimes' crises.

The book ends with an analysis of the economic reforms, and shows how they only intensify the contradictions of Eastern Europe's class societies. There is no reformist road to socialism in these countries – workers themselves need to take power and exercise it in their name.

£1.50 paperback   £4.30 hardback

Pluto  Press

Unit 10 Spencer Court, 7 Chalcot Road

London NW1 8LH

Workers against the Monolith:
The Communist Parties since 1943

Ian Birchall

Workers Against the Monolith argues that the Communist Parties have ceased to be classic Stalinist parties and have become left social-democratic organisations. To a new generation of revolutionaries it gives an account of how Stalinism damaged but could not destroy the revolutionary socialist tradition.

The book presents developments inside the 'Communist' countries as essential background to its main theme. It then concentrates on the histories of the Communist Parties in France, Italy and Britain as major examples of the course of events in the non-Communist world. It selects a few key examples of Communist policy and activity in the 'Third World'.

In Part I, Ian Birchall traces the rise of the western European Communist Parties as a result of their participation in the Resistance movements during the war, and their role in stifling the post-war upsurge of revolutionary struggle. In Part II he shows the effect 'destalinisation' in Russia has had in hastening the western Communist Parties' integration into the political mainstream of bourgeois democracy. In Part III, he follows the disintegration of the international movement as a result of the reawakening of the European working class, the hardening of the anti-imperialist struggle in the 'Third World' and the Sino-Soviet split. The book ends with a review of the prospects for the Communist Parties and of the growing opportunities for the revolutionary alternatives to them.

£1.50 paperback   £3.75 hardback

Pluto  Press

Unit 10 Spencer Court, 7 Chalcot Road

London NW1 8LH